# Jazz
# and
# Culture
# in a
# Global
# Age

ALSO BY STUART NICHOLSON

*Jazz: The Modern Resurgence* (reprinted in 1995 as
    *Jazz: The 1980s Resurgence*)
*Ella Fitzgerald*
*Billie Holiday*
*Jazz-Rock: A History*
*Reminiscing in Tempo: A Portrait of Duke Ellington*
*Is Jazz Dead? (Or Has It Moved to a New Address)*

With Max Harrison and Eric Thacker
*The Essential Jazz Records, Vol. 2*

With Will Friedwald, Ted Gioia, Peter Watrous,
    Ben Ratliff, and others
*The Future of Jazz, Yuval Taylor (ed.)*

# Jazz and Culture in a Global Age

## Stuart Nicholson

~ *Northeastern University Press*
*Boston*

Northeastern University Press

An imprint of University Press of New England

www.upne.com

© 2014 Stuart Nicholson

All rights reserved

Manufactured in the United States of America

Designed by Eric M. Brooks

Typeset in Whitman by Passumpsic Publishing

University Press of New England is a member of the
Green Press Initiative. The paper used in this book meets
their minimum requirement for recycled paper.

For permission to reproduce any of the material in this
book, contact Permissions, University Press of New England,
One Court Street, Suite 250, Lebanon NH 03766; or visit
www.upne.com

Library of Congress Cataloging-in-Publication Data

Nicholson, Stuart, 1948–, author.

Jazz and culture in a global age / Stuart Nicholson.

   pages  cm

ISBN 978-1-55553-727-2 (cloth: alk. paper)—

ISBN 978-1-55553-844-6 (pbk.: alk. paper)—

ISBN 978-1-55553-839-2 (ebook)

1. Jazz—History and criticism.  2. Music and globalization.

I. Title.

ML3506.N515    2014

781.65—dc23      2013044223

5  4  3  2  1

*In Memory of*
*Beatrice Margaret*
*Nicholson*

# Contents

# Preface

**J**azz is the only art form originated in the United States. It was given iconic status by the 100th Congress of the United States, which declared it "a rare and valuable national treasure" in a resolution passed by both the House of Representatives and the Senate in 1987 and reaffirmed by the 111th Congress in 2009.[1] This remarkable music, which originated in the United States at the hands of the Afro-American community around the turn of the twentieth century, has been so dominated by American excellence that there has been an understandable lack of curiosity inside the United States about jazz outside American borders—the global jazz scene. This may have to do with what Milan Kundera has called "the parochialism of large nations," meaning that they do not feel the need to go beyond their borders, since all their perceived needs can be met within them. As *Downbeat* magazine noted in 2006: "[In] many jazz circles here, Europeans with the gall to play America's music are often given short shrift, especially if they're breaking any blues-and-swing rules."[2]

Nevertheless, despite the weight of American jazz history and the presumption of American exceptionalism, a gradual awakening to jazz from other nations has become apparent, not only among American audiences but also among global jazz audiences. It is well documented how jazz became a global phenomenon during the 1920s, but the success of the jazz education business in conquering global markets almost a half-century later is often overlooked. The effects of this have been profound. At the end of the twentieth century and the early years of the twenty-first, its results were beginning to be felt in local jazz scenes around the world. For example, a 2009 editorial in the German jazz handbook *Wegweiser*

*Jazz* noted, "Jazz in Germany and elsewhere in Europe has established itself to such a degree that there is talk in the U.S.A. of a new European assertiveness in matters jazz. Promoters in Germany are increasingly recognising that concerts, even festivals, with national or European acts are drawing large audiences."[3] But it wasn't that American jazz was suddenly somehow "doing badly." Just as in the world of tennis, when 20 Americans made the draw in the 2007 U.S. Open compared with 128 in 1977, the reason was that other nations were catching up: in 2007, the final 16 players in the U.S. Open came from ten different countries.

Jazz has been America's great gift to the world and, as the 100th Congress's resolution presciently noted, it has been "adopted by musicians around the world as a music best able to express contemporary realities from a personal perspective."[4] This is not to say that jazz from global sources is somehow "better" than American jazz, but rather that today it both complements and contrasts it in a way that contributes to a more rich, diverse jazz scene that speaks of the music's continuing good health as we look beyond jazz's centennial. Over the past couple of decades I have become more and more convinced of the need for mobility in interpreting today's fast-moving global jazz scene. Listening to jazz recordings from cultures other than our own reveals only a partial picture, since context can contribute to meaning as well as alter and transform it. Travel, as they say, broadens the mind, and there is no doubt that leaving the comfort blanket of your own sociocultural norms and experiencing those of others provides a direct route to reaching a deeper and more nuanced understanding of jazz in the global context. Since countless jazz fans around the world have traveled to the United States, or harbor a desire to travel there in the hope of deepening their understanding of American jazz by hearing, seeing, and experiencing it in its sociocultural context, it follows that the reverse may be true. To gain a deeper understanding of jazz outside the United States, it helps to experience it in person.

I am fortunate and privileged to have been invited to jazz events in more than twenty countries around the world over the last couple of decades. The extent of these peripatetic endeavors was brought home to me when I was invited to participate in a panel discussion at the Blackheath Jazz Festival in London in November 2011. One of the students asked me how much jazz I had seen in the last ten years. I did a quick calculation. Normally I attend two festivals a month in various countries, sometimes more, sometimes—but not often—less, so two festivals a month would be a fair average. Each festival typically lasts three (sometimes four) days, and between about three in the afternoon and midnight I would typically see about eight bands. Over a three-day festival that's 24 bands, or around 48 concerts a month, which equates to 576 concerts a year, or 5,760 concerts over a ten-year period. That's not as many as some of my colleagues, to be sure, but probably more than a lot of people, and certainly far more than I would have imagined. Over the years, these concerts have provided a valuable window through which to witness the changes in jazz in the global jazz scene at first hand, and to speak to local musicians, jazz writers, animators, educators, and fans to learn about the dynamics of their local jazz scene in its local context. Also, during this same period I have been the recipient of literally thousands of CDs, typically between thirty and fifty every week. This too has provided valuable background from which to piece together my thoughts. These chapters have grown out of these combined experiences.

In today's complex and often discordant world, "culture" can be a loaded word. Yet the term surfaces and resurfaces throughout this book in a way that seems to suggest a distant but unifying theme in a way that was never intended at the outset. Maybe this is a reflection of the times we live in, since "culture" is a term that's brandished daily in the media—a typical broadsheet in the Western world might cite the term between one and ten times each day. Similarly, magazines and radio and television programs make frequent use of the term, yet none feel the need to break off abruptly midflight to define their terms. This suggests that there is a "common usage" understanding of what the term means, which is perhaps hardly surprising, since the notion of what culture means was first put into words in Ancient Greece in the 5th century BC by Herodotus, the "Father of History," who described what made the disparate communities of Ancient Greece band together in a common culture: common blood, common language, common shrines and rituals, and common customs. Today, this has been modified to incorporate a set of values, beliefs, and practices that distinguish one group of people from another, whether it's the language we speak, the kind of clothes we wear, the kind of leisure we pursue, the social norms we abide by, or the traditions and values we embrace.

Toward the end of the nineteenth century, the whole notion of a distinctive culture came under particular scrutiny in the United States as intellectuals, artists, writers, and poets began to grapple with the notion of "American-ness" in their creations, trying to find ways in which they could reflect an "American culture" that would not subsequently be regarded as a footnote to European culture. The debate continued after World War I, with writers experimenting with notions of "American-ness" in modern American literature with the aim of creating an "imagined community" that built on the work of people like Walt Whitman, Carlos Williams, Marianne Moore, and William Faulkner. As events turned out, it would be Hollywood that would give greatest shape to this "imagined community," or an imaginary America, with the global reach of the American film industry selling the idea of America, its values, and beliefs to the rest of the world. By 1996, American cultural products—primarily films and pop music—had become its biggest export, outstripping aerospace, defense, cars, and farming. Today American films dominate some 70 percent of the French market, 85 percent of the Italian market, 90 percent of the German market, and nearly all of the British market. These figures are not too dissimilar in most Latin American and Asian countries: even in India, where Bollywood dominates, American films nevertheless maintain a good share of the market. But what does this domination mean? Neal Gabler has suggested that Hollywood's influence has created an imaginary America that constitutes "a landscape of the mind, a constellation of values, attitudes and images, a history and mythology that is part of our [American] culture and consciousness."[5]

Hollywood has been an ideal vehicle for the global transmission of American cultural themes, codes, norms, and values from which most people beyond the borders of the United States have acquired the *idea* of America. For them, an Imaginary America is a cultural space that is more glamorous and adventurous than their own, bound up in discourses of youth, glamour, energy, and newness; an America less concerned with history than with a vision of the future that resonates with the here and now, a locus of pleasure and escapism that is "cool," contemporary, and up-to-date. This *idea* of America abroad acts as a powerful Americanizing influence and along with the dominance of American popular culture fills the global cultural spaces with messages made in America. As John O'Sullivan wrote in the pages of *National Review*, "One of the curiosities of travelling abroad is to be continually reminded of America . . . the modern world has a sharply American look and a sometimes deafening American sound."[6]

Today, the nature and extent of America's global cultural presence passes almost unnoticed; it is the way of the world and few of us would want to do without the benefits of American-style consumerism and entertainment. But seeing the nature and extent of exported American culture duplicated in country after country after country during the course of my travels, I began to wonder how this might influence the consumption of jazz—is it possible we can consume it as a thing-in-itself, devoid of the cultural influence of an Imaginary America, or do we, as Duncan Webster asks in his book *Looka Yonder! The Imaginary America of Popular Culture*, consume "not just an American product, but 'America' itself"?[7] No questions can be answered until they are asked, and this question provided the starting point for this book and is explored in chapter 3.

While jazz is indisputably a part of American culture, the Thelonious Monk Institute pointing out that it has "contributed to and has been a reflection of American culture,"[8] jazz has also been *shaped* by American culture, and continues to be shaped by it. In her 1961 essay "The Crisis in Culture," Hannah Arendt warned against "the displacement of culture by the dictates of entertainment,"[9] and this is the underlying theme of the first chapter, that the very culture that enabled jazz to grow and thrive in its Golden Years is pushing the music aside through the dictates of entertainment, leaving the music increasingly isolated, rather like St. Patrick's Church on Fifth Avenue. This in turn poses the question of how it maintains a viable audience share in the broader sweep of American life. In a world increasingly drowned out by popular culture, it is a problem not unique to America, and is something that I feel is worthy of exploration.

Chapter 2 arose during the course of my travels, when I became conscious that certain nuances of meaning in jazz performances in country A are not necessarily shared in country B—for example, *Kind of Blue* may be the best-selling jazz record of all time, but in Sweden, the best-selling jazz album of all time is *Jazz pår Svenska*, meaning *Jazz from Sweden*. Clearly different cultures attribute different meanings to music, but how does this play out in jazz?

Since my last book, *Is Jazz Dead? (Or Has It Moved to a New Address)*, was published, I have had countless requests from academics on both sides of the Atlantic to develop my ideas on globalization. This I have done in chapter 4, expanding and refining my original ideas and updating them to take account of contemporary developments including what Mary Kaldor has called "the current wave of nationalism [that] has to be understood as a response to globalization,"[10] which in turn has resonated in jazz. Since the notion of globalization as a means of explaining the effects of the transmission of jazz across national borders has been contested by a small number of academics in favor of diaspora/transnationalism theory, I felt this chapter presented an opportunity to compare and contrast work in this field with globalization theory, since it provides an opportunity to rehearse certain arguments that provide further background detail surrounding jazz globalization that might not otherwise have been advanced and that I believe contribute to a broader understanding of the subject. Since the diaspora/transnationalism theory is argued within the context of relativism, which is gaining increasing traction within academe, it seemed appropriate to question whether we should welcome such postmodernist/poststructuralist techniques into jazz discourse as means of interpreting jazz history, given how more and more history is now being revised or reinvented by people who do not want the real past but instead a past that suits their purpose.

The final chapter deals with modernism in jazz and questions why jazz modernism in Europe began with the emergence of pre-jazz forms such as the Cakewalk and Ragtime, yet does not begin in the United States until the beginnings of bebop in the 1940s. Yet as early as 1919, it was clear that as jazz spilled out into the world beyond the United States, its early reception in Europe was different from that in its homeland. For example, the American journal *Current Opinion* reported in 1919, "Good or bad, fad or institution, Jazz was born in Chicago, developed in New Orleans and glorified in Paris,"[11] where jazz was immediately embraced as an aspect of modernism, an art form in its own right that seemed to parallel several strands of modernism. This contrasts with the early reception of jazz in the United States, where, Jed Rasula has pointed out, "The greatest difference between the European and American responses to jazz . . . [was] that the avant-garde was a pervasive phenomenon across Europe when jazz appeared, whereas it had played almost no role in the United States."[12] I would argue that with the passage of time, what we understand to be jazz has gradually become narrowed by the need to define it, and when these contemporary definitions of jazz are applied retrospectively they can act in an exclusionary way. If that is the case, then referring to some areas of early jazz as "jazz modernism" does not conflict with, or challenge, the existing status quo, but instead offers a broader context in which to understand pre-bop jazz, and how jazz modernism was influenced by and influenced "the real jazz." I also go on to examine modernism's legacy and argue that jazz's cultural capital is enhanced when we consider all of it a modernist music.

Finally, my most grateful thanks to all who have helped me in this journey, for the encouragement and friendship I have enjoyed along the way and for those who have kindly looked at early drafts of these chapters and given me the benefit of their sage advice. Both inside and outside America, jazz continues to be a music that is energizing and inspiring, and when the best *does* find a way of being heard and you experience tomorrow's classics today, you know the future of the music is in safe hands. If this book contributes in some small way to the interpretation of some of these developments, and maybe to encouraging thinking about them and hearing them in a slightly different way, then my goal in writing it will have been more than fulfilled.

*Stuart Nicholson,*
*Woodlands St. Mary,*
*Berks, England*
*July 2013*

# Jazz
# and
# Culture
# in a
# Global
# Age

# Jazz and the Perfect Storm

**J**azz's flowering in the twentieth century seemed to mirror America's spectacular ascendancy from a settler society to Madeline Albright's "indispensable nation." Titanic figures such as King Oliver, Jelly Roll Morton, Louis Armstrong, Fletcher Henderson, Benny Goodman, Charlie Parker, Miles Davis, John Coltrane, Charles Mingus, and Ornette Coleman seemed to echo what America itself was doing in trade, commerce, and finance—setting the agenda. As jazz burst onto the world stage in the early 1920s, New York eclipsed London as the global financial center, the American dollar became the standard in global trade, and Hollywood began its dominance of the cinema. As the 1940s gave way to the 1950s, Americans were enjoying the highest standard of living in the world, sustained by conspicuous consumption and consumer choice, a model that was adopted by countless nation-states around the world. It was with good reason that the twentieth century was dubbed the "American Century," with hopes expressed that the new millennium would herald the "Second American Century." But those hopes were rocked by 9/11, unsuccessful military interventions in Iraq and Afghanistan, and the near collapse of the banking system that had underpinned America's growth and prosperity. The financial crisis that began on Wall Street in 2008 and subsequently engulfed the rest of the Western world presaged a global recession whose ramifications have been predicted to last a generation. As the American government grappled with the enormity of its domestic problems, the National Intelligence Council cast its gaze toward the horizon and came up with their global trends review, published every four years, this one entitled *A Transformed World*. It concluded that the United States was now becoming a less dominant power and that the global system was moving toward a multipolar world, representing a dramatic shift from the "unipolar moment" the United States had enjoyed following the fall of the Berlin Wall and the two decades of unchallenged American supremacy that followed.

The speed of this transformation had been astonishing. Whereas the elder George Bush had been concerned about the possible collapse of Russia, the younger George Bush had been concerned about excessive Russian power. Emerging markets, such as China, India, and Brazil, now accounted for 40 percent of the world's economy and were challenging American dominance in key areas such as industry, trade, and finance. Yet while America indisputably remained a great nation, it was no longer a nation at ease with itself. It had seen a decade when the news media frequently reported on the polarization of American politics, from the House of Representatives to the Senate in Washington, DC, and out into in the red and blue states, where the divide between conservatives and liberals on issues such as abortion, faith teaching, single-sex marriage, foreign policy, and the size of the state seemed irreconcilable. Even the once iconic symbols of America's greatness were being put in the shade. The tallest building in the world was no longer to be found on the Manhattan skyline but in Dubai, where the Burj Khalifa stood more than half a mile high. The largest casino was not in Las Vegas but in Macao, the biggest movie industry in the world was no longer Hollywood but Bollywood, and the world's biggest shopping mall was now in Beijing. Lists like this are, of course, arbitrary, but it is striking that in the 1990s America topped the list in all of these categories. But this was not about American decline so much as the rest of the world catching up. It was a scenario that was finding resonance in the broader arena of global realpolitik. In his influential study *The American Ascendancy: How the United States Gained and*

*Wielded Power*, Michael H. Hunt concluded, "The time for U.S. hegemony may have passed. As the relative U.S. advantage in economic might and cultural appeal slips . . . the core U.S. cultural model—a faith in unending corporate-driven growth and the unending delights of consumerism—may be fading at least in the developed world. Western Europe and Japan have drawn alongside the United States in their technological capacity, their income levels, their capital resources and the depth and integration of their home markets. They need no longer look to the United States in these areas."[1]

Equally, in the world of jazz, the time for American hegemony seemed to be passing, with countries no longer looking to the United States for inspiration, direction, or a model of correctness. Not that this troubled most American jazz musicians and audience members, for them it was business as usual. As ever there was great music to be heard, from established stars to dedicated young professionals trying to establish themselves in a highly competitive music arena. The center of American jazz activity remained New York City, which, as bassist, composer, and blogger Ronan Guilfoyle noted, "May well be the best place in the world for jazz music—at least in terms of there being more great musicians in one small concentrated area than anywhere else on the planet."[2] And although Guilfoyle pointed out that "[in] terms of seeing great creative music, NY is hard to beat," he sounded a note of caution, asking at what cost this was to musicians: "The money that can be earned there from playing creative music is risible, and outside NY it just gets worse and worse."[3] Very few musicians engaged in the Big Apple's jazz economy would argue with Guilfoyle's assertion, but if adequate remuneration had become one problem facing American jazz musicians, then falling audience numbers was another. Yet those who attempted to highlight issues such as these often found their words unwelcome, un-American even, and likely to be shouted down—"Jazz has had more than its share of hand-wringers," thundered the *New York Times* when concern was raised at the results of the 2009 National Endowment for the Arts survey on audience participation in the arts, which revealed that the audience for jazz, especially among younger fans, was in decline.[4]

Times were changing, and changing fast. In today's world of fast-evolving information technology, young people have an unprecedented range of entertainment choices available to them, and, given the portability and sophistication of smart phones and tablets, it is entirely possible to go an entire day without being deprived of commercial entertainment for a single second. The easy availability and desirability of popular culture for the majority represented a serious challenge for jazz. Space was fast shrinking in newspapers and magazines for jazz features and reviews, jazz radio was in steady decline, there was a gradual winding down of jazz activity by major recording companies, and empirical evidence suggested that jazz audiences appeared to be in decline. "Culture is never static," one American observer blogged, arguing, "Music is a cultural artifact, and the culture has moved on. Jazz has moved on as well, further and further from being 'popular music.'"[5] It simply served to highlight how times had changed since jazz's Golden Years in the 1950s and 1960s, when the music seemed to reflect the optimism and drive of America's military, industrial, financial, and cultural ascendancy. So if, as the National Intelligence Council suggested, the American nation was confronting a "Transformed World," how was American jazz responding to these challenges?

⌣⌣

It is no exaggeration to say that the United States has felt the impact of the 2008 banking crisis more than any other nation. In 2010, a Pew Research Center survey revealed that a majority of Americans had been affected by the subsequent recession, which "brought a mix of hardships, usually in combination: a spell of unemployment, missed mortgage or rent payments, shrinking paychecks and shattered household budgets."[6] Young adults, especially those trying to enter the job market, were especially hard hit according to the Brookings Institution, which predicted that the road to recovery would be long and could be "rocky for many Americans."[7] The economic climate inevitably impacted on the leisure dollar, as jazz pianist and author Ted Gioia cautioned in 2009: "That big elephant in the corner of the jazz club that no one is mentioning is our current economic recession. Even in the good times, the jazz world seemed to be on a shaky financial footing, but what will happen [now]?"[8]

As if in answer, some six months later the *New York Times* ran a feature headlined "Doomsayers May Be Playing Taps but Jazz Isn't Ready to Sing the Blues," reporting a "robust, lively and engaged" crowd at a jazz gig in Williamsburg, Brooklyn, that it considered representative of "almost any given night on the New York club scene."[9] On the face of this anecdotal evidence, jazz seemed to be weathering the financial storm well. But as Jared Pauley, adjunct professor of history and music history at Rutgers University by day, and an active pianist on the New York jazz scene by night, pointed out: when you cross the East River to Brooklyn and enter Williamsburg, "You experience the bitterest portion of the NYC musical market. Ask most musicians how much money they make playing in Williamsburg. Large majorities of people that reside in Williamsburg are notorious for not paying covers or giving support when the money bucket comes around. On the other hand, it's not uncommon to encounter people splurging on fifty-dollar bar tabs. Where do musicians fall in this wacky game of musical chairs?"[10] Stated simply, those outside the musician's community had little idea of how hard it had become to make a living from playing jazz music in the new millennium. Yes, the public and the journalists who wrote about the music were aware that jazz was a harsh taskmaster, but few knew—or even wanted to know—about the nitty-gritty details of the "business" of jazz, such as how much a musician took home after a night's work. After all, most people who patronized live jazz events did so in the expectation of an evening's entertainment. We've all had our share of problems, so who wants to hear jazz musicians' hard luck stories? Besides, the jazz world had experienced difficult times before, but the musicians always seemed to luck it out. So no wonder some commentators had become inured to "Chicken Little laments" about the future of the music.[11] But Bob Belden, saxophonist, arranger, composer, producer, and Grammy winner who graduated from the jazz program at North Texas State University before moving to New York in the 1970s, had observed the popularity of jazz ebb and flow in the Big Apple for almost forty years. "Looking at 'the scene' today, it's not what it used to be, as it should be," he observed. "All of a sudden there are too few professional choices for musicians and there are way too many musicians working for door money."[12]

The growth of gigs where artists play for a share of admittance money, or "door money," instead of an agreed fee—or even worse, where artists pay a club, a bar, or a restaurant to perform in their space—was making it increasingly difficult for musicians to generate an adequate income stream from playing jazz exclusively, making it necessary for many to supplement their income stream with other lines of work. This form of concealed subsidy effectively underpins the American jazz scene and some national scenes abroad, such as in the United Kingdom. But while this is something that is hardly unknown in other branches of the arts—for example, artists who earn the main proportion of their income as college art teachers or writers whose income comes from teaching literature or "creative writing" courses—it simply serves to underline the equivocal position of jazz in the music marketplace. Critically acclaimed composer and arranger Darcy James Argue, leader of Secret Society, a critically acclaimed big band that performs his original works around New York City, reflected on the citywide scene as he saw it: "Jazz musicians are accustomed to scrabbling, but dwindling freelance opportunities plus disappearing venues, scuttled ventures and changing music policies have all contributed to a scene where it's not uncommon to see world class musicians fiercely competing for the privilege of playing pass-the-hat gigs."[13] Even the TV and press coverage given to the closure of the Tonic in 2007, a small jazz club on New York's Upper East Side, made no mention of the fact that most artists who performed there had done so for a share of the door money.

Perhaps unsurprisingly, musicians are reluctant to talk about their finances, thus presenting recurring difficulties documenting the "business of jazz" in contemporary times, since an apparent discrepancy or lack of proportion has emerged between, on the one hand, the elevated, high-toned rhetoric of the creative act, and, on the other, a pragmatic accommodation to contemporary circumstances. However, as saxophonist Mark Turner has pointed out, "In New York competition for work is very high. Here it is very difficult to make a living, it's pretty hard. But when you reach a certain level you are able to find work in Europe, and I would say for me, most of my playing, about 75 percent, most of my income is from Europe. If I had to earn it in New York, forget it. I work in New York, of course I do, with my band, different bands as a sideman, we all do that, and some great music, yes, but most of my income comes from Europe."[14] It is a view echoed by pianist Craig Taborn, who says, "There are a lot of places to play and do the stuff we do, but over time it's a struggle because it's super expensive here. Nobody is really making their money gigging in New York, that's not really where they are making their money—they are making money doing music but a lot of people teach, or they do other things."[15]

New York resident Andrew Collier, in *West View News: The Voice of West Village*, was one of the few to comment on the unusual paradox whereby "New York [may be] home to the world's best and largest jazz scene, [which] caters to the world's audiences for jazz, [yet] in one of life's twists, many musicians earn a big chunk of their daily bread touring overseas."[16] The reason for this was simple, he explained: "Clubs pay musicians as little as $25 per performance and players often fight over non-paying gigs in small bars and clubs. Such vicious competition creates an inhospitable lifestyle for professionals."[17] This despite the fact that New York is home to a lively, year-round tourist trade: "Drop into the famed Village Vanguard Jazz Club on Seventh Avenue and you'll usually spot a group of Japanese tourists sound asleep in the corner," continued Collier.

> It's not due to the jazz—which is the best in the world—but the tremendous jet lag due to the 12 hour time difference between New York and Tokyo. Visit most of the great jazz clubs of New York and the Village such as Blue Note, Smalls, Iridium and Smoke, and you'll find at least one-quarter and sometimes as much as half of the audience consists of Japanese, French, Italian, Swedish and other overseas tourists . . . There's no doubt New York's global jazz fans are a boon to the club market in New York. In 2010, the city hosted 8.5 million foreign tourists. Meanwhile, 16 per cent of New York University students are from abroad, a total of 8,000 students, forming a core audience for the Greenwich Village jazz clubs like Blue Note, La Lanterna, and Le Poisson Rouge.[18]

So where do all these tourist dollars go? Not, it seems, to the jazz musicians who play the New York jazz clubs and venues. As Ronan Guilfoyle has pointed out, "There are just far too many musicians in New York for it to make any sense on an economic level . . . the abundance and availability of musicians and the lack of places to play drive the price musicians can charge for NY gigs down to below subsistence levels. It's a buyers market for the clubs and the musicians suffer."[19]

Yet historically, it has always been difficult for young musicians to establish themselves in jazz. Established players look back on their younger days with affection, as one of making financial sacrifices and struggling to find work before eventually establishing a reputation, a period euphemistically referred to in the jazz world as "paying dues." The internationally respected guitarist and ECM recording artist John Abercrombie has sustained a successful career in jazz since the 1960s, and in the new millennium years was on the faculty of the State University of New York at Purchase. It provided him with a unique vantage point to reflect on the days when he was establishing himself in the jazz business and on the challenges the young musicians he teaches face today:

> Well, there are so many players today, there are more players now than when I was coming up, but there're still no more gigs. It's terrifying. There're all these good musicians and there's no place to play, and a lot of my students wind up playing in these restaurants and they make $20

a night or something. I made $20 back in the 1960s. How can you live on that now? Back in the 1960s things were a lot cheaper—you could buy food—and if you made $100 a week, you were on top of the world. Now $100 a week will keep you in cigarettes. I don't know how they're going to make it, so I always tell them, "You really have to want to do this music because you love it. Sometimes I have a hard time working in this country, and if I have a hard time, you may be up against a wall." So I try and be realistic with them, and I think they find that out pretty soon when they get out and start working, they see that there's not much there.[20]

Yet the heartening thing was that young musicians continued to emerge who were committed to the music and despite college loans and escalating accommodation costs were prepared for financial sacrifice and supplementing their income with a wide range of work, often remote from their musical aspirations. But it was not easy, as a thoughtful piece by Patrick Jarenwattananon on National Public Radio's *A Blog Supreme* highlighted:

> Picture a jazz musician. Perhaps he's sharply dressed, standing in a corner of a restaurant, a small but appreciative audience looking on. He seems to be lost in the moment; wrapped-up in a passionate solo, his eyes closed in intense concentration. For over an hour, he is thinking of nothing more than emoting into his instrument with all the present force of his conscious being. You may pause to ask yourself: Is this really his job? You know, how did he pay for that nice suit and the $6,000 vintage saxophone? Does he have a family, a landlord, a mortgage? The $15 I paid to get in, multiplied by the 60 people in the room—can he really support himself with the small cut he takes when the pot is finally settled-up with the venue and the other musicians?[21]

Musicians who run their own ensemble often top-up their sideman's fees and travel expenses from their share of the gig money in order to keep the show on the road—the alternative being a cooperative arrangement whereby all band members share expenses equally and split what is left over among them. In today's brave new world, if musicians want to release a compact disc they usually have to bear the recording and manufacturing costs themselves. And with compact disc sales at an all-time low through downloading on the Internet, sales are accumulated incrementally mostly at gigs, half a dozen sales here, a dozen or so there, and on a good night, twenty or more at a time. Effectively, the compact disc has become an expensive business card, used to send to promoters, club owners, festival producers, and animators in the jazz business in the hope of generating work. And although many musicians use social networking sites to announce gigs, mini festivals, and album releases and to post videos on YouTube in the hope of broadening their audience base, it presents a lifestyle that might be sustainable for a single, dedicated young musician prepared to hustle and go without in the short term, but may be unattractive to some in the longer term.

Would these young musicians want to be hustling twenty-five- or thirty-dollar gigs when they had a partner and maybe family commitments? It was a quandary that confronted the brother of the late Lester Bowie, trombonist Joe Bowie, known to jazz fans for his band Defunkt. He pointed out that sacrifice and paying dues as a young man were accepted as a way of establishing a reputation, but this kind of lifestyle had become difficult and almost impossible to sustain with family responsibilities.

> As I approached fifty I realized I had two options, to succumb, because you just get tired, you gotta survive. Eventually I would have had to go punch a clock somewhere and be satisfied to do an occasional gig, do that, or place myself in an environment that will support me so my voice can ring out. I used to be able to make a living playing in New York, but it's impossible now for myself and lots of other musicians who are not "mainstream"—like the Wynton Marsalis clan. I think it is almost impossible to make a reasonable living—$50,000 a year, not a fortune—unless you're a mainstream artist, so you must sacrifice a certain level of your creativity. You should be able to lead a decent middle-class life, struggling, but own a home, own a car, and raise a couple of kids. With your wife doing another job, that should be enough. But most of my friends in New York have gone into university and become teachers to survive. Why should I teach every day if I'm a performer? I think the long-term consequences for jazz in America are devastating.

Bowie's answer was to move to Europe to pursue his calling. "What's happening in America now is clubs disappearing, alternative venues are disappearing, we're looking at a future of TV-dictated culture. It fails to acknowledge the great inspiration that jazz—and art—has on other fields. Doctors, mathematicians, scientists—other people who are not musicians—gain so much inspiration by having alternative culture to experience, and without that, where will America be?"[22]

Clearly there is a need for precise empirical data on how the American jazz economy functions, and in 2000 the National Endowment for the Arts commissioned the Research Center for Arts and Culture (RCAC) to undertake a study to examine the working lives of jazz musicians. The resulting report, "Changing the Beat," painted a picture of a highly flexible workforce that earned less than expected given their high levels of education, with only modest institutional support from state regional arts agencies and nonprofit foundations. In 2011, the "Money from Music Survey" presented a snapshot of nearly nine hundred performers' earnings in the first comprehensive assessment of jazz musicians' earnings in the United States since their "Changing the Beat" survey eleven years earlier. Among their findings were the following insights:[23]

~ Jazz musicians have more formal education than most musicians, play many different roles, and have simpler support teams than musicians in other genres.

~ The mean gross estimated music income for jazz musicians who took the "Money from Music" survey was $23,300 for a non-AFM member. On average, jazz musicians made less money than classical or other musicians who took the survey.

~ A higher percentage of jazz musicians surveyed have graduate degrees than was the case a decade ago.

~ Jazz musicians are getting less airplay on terrestrial radio than they did a decade ago.

~ Surveyed AFM members are making 15 percent less than they were a decade ago, while non-AFM musicians are making 15 percent more.

In conducting this survey, the RCAC acknowledged that acquiring information was difficult: although the jazz community was relatively small, it was difficult to reach comprehensively. "A lot of musicians just won't make time to tell us how they are doing financially," said Jean Cook in 2011, one of the managers of the Future of Music project. "They're too busy making a living."[24] Nevertheless, while a survey of almost a thousand jazz musicians may not be perfect, it does represent a reasonably representative sampling, the kind of numbers that might be used, for example, in a media telephone poll in a city or state. Even allowing for the margin of error inherent in such surveys, a typical annual salary in the range of $20,000 to $27,000 will come as little surprise to those engaged in the American jazz economy. Inasmuch as the survey revealed that jazz musicians enjoy "more formal education than most musicians," how long will jazz students continue to regard jazz as a viable career option when their peers, with degrees in vocational studies, put their qualifications to work in better remunerated areas of the economy such as accountancy, law, engineering, medicine, architecture, pharmacy, or financial services? In June 2008, the Norwegian saxophonist Frøy Aagre completed a five-date tour of the East Coast with a US rhythm section and expressed her surprise at the poor level of remuneration American jazz musicians received, even at relatively well known jazz venues: "I wonder how long [young jazz musicians] can survive on the kind of money they do and how long students with big ambitions will keep on spending a fortune on jazz education that probably will result in a full-time teaching job with badly paid gigs on the side?"[25]

If the financial reality of the "business" of jazz in New York City presented a picture that was causing some observers concern, the national jazz scene presented an equally mixed picture. As the *New York Times* pointed out: "Live jazz is hard to come by outside of a handful of major cities,"[26] reflecting the erosion of jazz's core audience in the United States. It was a point echoed by Ronan Guilfoyle: "The U.S. jazz scene, as a national scene, is almost non existent," he blogged. "Apart from NY there are some scenes of reasonable size in a few places—Boston, Chicago, San Francisco, and maybe a few others. But all these pale into insignificance beside the bloated New York scene. . . . What you have in the U.S. is one huge scene with far too many musicians and no money and a series of cities, often with over a million people in them, with virtually no scene at all."[27] Outside New York, dedicated jazz clubs were usually found in major centers, and then there were usually only one or two, blogged jazz educator Kurt Ellenberger: "This means that there are (if the club books groups seven nights a week) only 30–60 possible engagements available each month. The rest of the work is casuals (weddings and parties), which tend to be clustered on weekends and holidays. . . . With the thousands of qualified musicians in any major center, it's easy to see how an oversupply of labor combined with diminishing demand have worked to keep fees near where they were in nominal dollars thirty years ago."[28] In Philadelphia, for example, Mark Christman, executive director of the critically acclaimed Ars Nova Workshop, a not-for-profit organization that promotes an ambitious program of creative music at their weekly jazz and experimental music concerts, says that the desire for musicians to perform is as great as ever, but the opportunities for them to do so are getting harder: "Jazz clubs in this town are few and far between," he says. "Bars where you can have a drink and listen to live music come and go across the city and offer a place where people can play and, yes, those people are playing for the door. The state of the local musicians, in local cities outside of Chicago and New York, is one of near poverty."[29]

The one area of the jazz economy that does make real profits is jazz education, an industry that has quadrupled over the last twenty years. But even this buoyant sector of the American jazz economy was rocked when the International Association of Jazz Educators (IAJE) unexpectedly filed for bankruptcy a matter of weeks after its 2008 convention. The IAJE was a forty-year-old organization whose annual conventions brought jazz educators together from around the world, so news of its unexpected demise caused the kind of reverberations in the world of American jazz that the failure of Lehman Brothers would cause in the financial world just a matter of months later. However, within three months the Jazz Education Network was formed to fill the void, holding its first annual convention in 2010 on the campus of the University of Missouri at St. Louis, with 1,250 people attending performances, clinics, and panel sessions. Bob Sinicrope, a teacher at the Massachusetts Milton Academy prep school and a board member for the Jazz Education Network, claimed that their inaugural event was something of a miracle, "a testament to how badly the people who were working to mount this thing wanted it to happen."[30] Each succeeding year saw a growth in attendance, with the 2012 conference held in Louisville, Kentucky, drawing more than three thousand delegates. Yet even though an important event in the American jazz calendar was making a comeback, one troubling question would not go away—why had the huge expansion of the jazz education industry over the last two decades not seen a commensurate rise in jazz audiences? At the 2012 conference, the Jazz Education Network held multiple sessions that focused on *The Jazz Audience Initiative*. This was both a valuable and a comprehensive analysis of audience demographics of those attending jazz concerts at several major venues across the United States that was commissioned by the Jazz Arts Group in Columbus, Ohio, and funded by the Doris Duke Charitable Foundation. Among the findings from the Jazz Arts Group Multi Site Survey of Current and Prospective Jazz Ticket Buyers, June 2011, were these:[31]

~ Demographically, jazz ticket buyers across the 19 communities are middle-aged, predominantly male, and very well educated. On average, only 17 percent are under age 45, and 80 percent are white.

~ Younger buyers are significantly different than older buyers, suggesting generational shifts in participation patterns and music preferences.

~ Jazz buyers want to move [to the rhythm of the music], suggesting a strong kinetic association. When asked what kind of jazz they like, a third of all buyers indicated they like jazz that . . . "makes me want to tap my toes and dance," while 31 percent said they like jazz that . . . "makes me think or challenges me in some way." Women are very different from men in this respect, with women prioritizing jazz that makes them want to move, and men prioritizing jazz that makes them think. Older buyers 65-plus prioritize the sentimental aspects of jazz "that takes me back to another time or place."

~ By a wide margin, jazz buyers prefer informal settings for live jazz shows, especially clubs and lounges. Younger buyers have an especially strong affinity for informal settings.

~ Results illustrate the generational shift in technology use amongst younger music consumers. Three quarters of all buyers in the 18–35 cohort use social networking websites, and 68 percent stream audio from the Internet.

One key finding of the Jazz Arts Group survey served to re-emphasize was the fragmentation of the jazz audiences into what might be called different "taste markets" (see paragraphs two and three). To all intents and purposes, there seems to be an absence of a general jazz audience who will turn out for a jazz performance irrespective of genre. Yet, since jazz discourse (for example, in jazz magazines) largely tends to treat all taste markets equally (with the possible exception of smooth jazz), it might be expected that a greater degree of musical curiosity and willingness to cross over into other genres might result, producing a more robust market for the music. One concern might be that less patronized taste markets will succumb to the homogenizing effect of the marketplace, and since cultural consumption determines cultural production, they may become commercially unviable to promote. However, the main cause for concern revealed by the survey was that on average only 17 percent of ticket buyers were under the age of forty-five. This served to underline the findings of the National Endowment for the Arts (NEA) study on arts participation in the United States published in 2009. For anyone seriously interested in, or concerned about, the arts in America, the NEA survey results were troubling, especially in the realm of jazz music. Briefly, there were two areas of concern. The first was an analysis of the Median Age of Arts Attendees across a wide range of artistic activity that included jazz, classical music, opera, musicals, nonmusical plays, ballet, and art museums (this latter category representing both art galleries and museums). The survey covered the period from 1982 to 2008 and discovered that the audience for all types of activities studied in the survey were aging, but it was the change in the jazz audience that was striking. According to the survey, the average age of a jazz event attendee in 1982 was twenty-nine, but by 2008 it had increased to forty-six. Between 1982 and 2008, the average age of a jazz event attendee in the United States had increased by seventeen years, as compared with five years for opera, six years for musicals, and seven years for art museums (or galleries).

The survey also revealed that while older fans broadly continued to follow the music, the appeal of the music to American teenagers and twenty-somethings had declined between 1982 and 2008. This conclusion was bolstered by the NEA's findings for "Cultural Event Attendance for People between the Ages of 18–24." Except for art museums, all the aforementioned categories showed a decline, but it was the drop in jazz attendance that again caught the eye—a shrinkage of 58 percent between 1982 and 2008. Once again, even allowing a generous margin for statistical error, the conclusion remains indisputable. American jazz appeared to be losing its younger audience, prompting a feature in the *Wall Street Journal* headlined "Can Jazz Be Saved?" While it offered no solutions to the problem, it commented, "It's no longer possible for head in the sand types to pretend that the great American art form is economically healthy or its future looks anything other than bleak."[32]

So what was the answer? The traditional response to lack of audience support in a cognitively demanding music like jazz had been the cry "education," the argument being that teaching young people about jazz through grade school, junior high school, and into high school would help to build a sustainable audience for the future. The sustainability aspect of audience-building is important, since it means attracting people not just to replenish the ranks of the older generations of jazz fans but also to grow the audience base at the bottom, among younger people. Thus, the theory goes, by exposing students to jazz in the younger age range you will be creating an informed group of young people, some of whom will go on to support the music during and after college and so help grow that crucial audience base.

Since the late 1970s, when jazz education began to be rolled out across the United States, hundreds of millions of dollars have been spent on jazz education, in colleges, universities, summer camps, and high schools:[33]

~ More than 500,000 high school and college students were involved in jazz activities.
~ Over 500 colleges were offering jazz-related courses for credit.
~ More than 70 percent of America's 30,000 junior and senior high schools had at least one stage band or jazz ensemble.
~ There were approximately 300 summer camp programs that included jazz.
~ Approximately 250 school jazz festivals were being presented each year, some attracting as many as 200 school ensembles.

You might expect that with the subsequent growth of jazz education—by 2012 there were more than 120 American colleges and universities where students could major in jazz studies[34]—the problem of replenishing the jazz audience at the lower age scale would take care of itself. But that has not happened. As we have seen, the NEA's survey found the audience for jazz in America to have dropped by 58 percent between 1982 and 2008 among young people—the key sector that it is hoped would become audiences of the future. Even allowing a margin for statistical error beyond those customarily used in consumer surveys, the $50,000 question confronting jazz educators was: Why was there so little correlation between engaging with the music as students and going on to support the music when they got older?

What seems clear is that there is no Alexandrian solution to this particular Gordian knot. Yet while the *answer* to building a sustainable audience for jazz among younger people might be elusive, there is, perhaps, some value in exploring possible *reasons* for this, since it is an issue that might have commonalities with jazz scenes in a broader, global context. An interesting place to begin might be the political theorist Hannah Arendt's essay "The Crisis in Culture," in which she expressed her concerns that market forces would lead to the displacement of culture by the dictates of entertainment. She wrote: "To believe society becomes more 'cultured' as time goes on and education does its work is, I think, a fatal mistake. The point is that a consumer society cannot possibly know how to take care of a world and things which belong exclusively to the space of worldly appearances because its central attitude towards all objects, the attitude of consumption, spells ruin to everything it touches."[35] This argument, that the logic of the market eventually annexes all areas of cultural experience, has some force: by the new millennium, the entertainment principle had been so taken over by the corporate need to generate profit that, in Arendt's forward-looking words, "culture [was] being destroyed in order to yield entertainment."[36] The desire to be diverted, entertained, and provided with a form of escapism had, by the new millennium, changed out of all recognition from the cinema—the first true medium of genuine mass entertainment, which had been born in the early twentieth century. With the power and commercialization of the Internet, the commercially constructed "popular" tastes of the majority had never been easier to fulfill via lap-tops, tablets, and 4G smart phones with instant Internet access to "the popular"—pop music, pop videos, computer games, and social networking sites—with the result that popular entertainment now occupied the dominant cultural space in young people's imagination.

In a society where consumerism and the mass consumption of popular culture are the predominant leisure-time pursuits, popular culture studies have become *en vogue* with students in colleges and universities, where the faculty members argue that their classes enable students to "deconstruct" and think critically about mass entertainment. This embodies the employment of certain relativist values that have gained widespread influence in cultural circles today and that set the context in which culture is communicated, debated, and funded. These relativist values contend that conceptions of the truth and morality are not absolute but relative to the people holding them. However, critics of relativism argue that when the truth lies in the eye of the beholder, when there is not one truth but there are many, forming a consensus around what ought to constitute standards of excellence becomes impossible. If all perspectives have equal validity then a limitless plurality of values is indistinguishable from no values at all. Yet to argue this point invites the relativist response, "That is your view" or "That is your opinion," which denies the possibility of reasoned argument that attempts to claim some things in life may have greater aesthetic merit than others. Indeed, there is a growing belief in cultural studies that any suggestion of higher cultural values is a denigration of mass taste and the preferences of the man in the street by invoking elitist values. The ideology of consumer choice means that the only acceptable indication of value is consumer demand, so any attempt to give the public something that might be considered somehow "better" than what some have argued represents the lowest common denominator of taste is considered "elitist."

Elitism has become a highly pejorative charge, implying that something that is far too demanding to be popular (such as jazz) is therefore alien and aloof from people's lives, a line of argument that relativism's critics contend is permitting an uncritical embrace of the ordinary. Clearly then, relativism, and the arguments that flow from its ethos, are not without controversy. The authority that culture once commanded is now treated with skepticism, since the conventional distinction between high and low culture makes little sense if the truth is relegated to the status of one person's subjective opinion.

Alongside relativism in the congested court of popular opinion lurks the weasel word "instrumentalism," a practice many feel is eroding the value of arts in Western culture. When a government adopts an instrumentalist approach to art and culture, it means that they treat knowledge and culture as a way of realizing a wider practical purpose: thus universities and colleges are promoted as being vital for "economic progress." It is not knowledge in itself, or ideas, or art, that is valued, but their utility in helping to achieve economic growth. It is rare for politicians to be forthcoming about the role of instrumentalism in their government's policies lest the charge of philistinism be laid at their doorstep; however, one of the most unapologetic expressions in its favor came from Baroness Tessa Blackstone when she was minister of state for the arts in the United Kingdom. Her words bear repeating. When asked, "Can the arts be more than frivolous, trivial, irrelevant?" she responded they could, but only if they could be used for purposes other than aesthetic ones.[37]

As a result of instrumentalism being adopted by most Western governments, many have argued that the development of literary or artistic studies is no longer a priority for educators and that instrumentalist pressure on knowledge production has meant that art and culture are not valued by criteria internal to themselves but by their utility to serve wider practical purpose—such as contributing to a nation's gross domestic product. So while great art—such as jazz—is still produced, society finds it difficult to value it on its own terms. As Arendt has pointed out: "Culture is being threatened when all worldly objects and things, produced by the present and past, are treated as mere functions for the life process of society, as though they were only there to fulfil some need, and for this functionalization it is almost irrelevant whether the needs in question are of a high or low order."[38]

The inter-relationship between relativism and populism, whereby the former provides the rationale for the latter, has seen the media, cultural institutions, and educational bodies falling over themselves to appear relevant, accessible, and in touch with popular opinion and quietly desperate to avoid any charge of elitism being waved in their faces. There is a distinction to be made here between the popular and populism; the word "popular" in many languages denotes not only that which is successful but also that which belongs to the "people" as distinct from the elites. Thus American studies scholar Ray B. Browne argues: "In a democracy like the United States, [popular culture] is the voice of the people."[39] Thus the popular represents the generality of taste or opinion and derives from the people, for good or ill, while *populism* is giving the people what they seem to want or are deemed to want, believing it is good for them. This has seen "entertainment" in all its forms now promoted as culture, with the newspaper industry eager to serve the needs of populism, conscious of falling sales through the pressure of free news portals on the Internet. Since "relevance" and "accessibility" are usually communicated in the media via popular culture, generous coverage is afforded to pop, rock, and film—pop music is especially useful as a tool for appearing relevant, since it provides an entry point into the affections of the young. In contrast jazz is perceived as being too demanding to be popular and thus is alien and aloof from most people's lives and so elitist—and is becoming increasingly marginalized in the print media by the extensive exposure afforded popular culture.

It is interesting how the views of academics such as Krin Gabbard seem to reinforce the populist notion that jazz is elitist. In *The Jazz Canon and Its Consequences* he writes of how the music will be ultimately claimed by "the sequestered world of professionalism." This world, he claims, will "establish autonomy most effectively by creating a metalanguage and a series of methodologies that close out the amateur. Anyone can engage in evaluation and express an opinion about a book, a play or film. Only a professional can speak a language and brandish a paradigm understood only by a small coterie of specialists with mastery over the same language and paradigm."[40] As the distinguished critic Max Harrison observed after reading Gabbard's words: "It will be no use in the future, then, for us to complain we have not been warned."[41] Mass culture theorists would need little evidence beyond Gabbard's assertion about jazz being "understood only by a small coterie of specialists" to demonstrate that the music was remote from the majority of ordinary people's lives and thus elitist. Gabbard's aspiration to sweep jazz appreciation into the closed shop of university research—where, as Harrison notes, "the rest of us will be able to watch, albeit only from an ignominious distance"[42]—might simply confirm younger audiences worst fears about the music—that it is so remote from their daily lives it is marginally more enticing than a barium enema.

From time to time, jazz has been harnessed as a soundtrack for commercial TV advertising, which, according to Gabbard, testifies "to the music's rising cultural capital."[43] It is a response that might be argued by advocates of populism to be exclusionary and elitist, since Billie Holiday's "God Bless the Child" was not used simply to sell an automobile but to sell a luxury German production car; Dinah Washington's "Mad about the Boy" did not advertise a brand of jeans but a designer brand of jeans; Sarah Vaughan's "Make Yourself Comfortable" did not tempt you to buy ice cream but to indulge in an expensive brand of ice cream; and Ella Fitzgerald's "Someone to Watch Over Me" was the soundtrack of an advertisement designed to persuade you to buy a brand of private medical insurance. One striking early success of this technique was the use of Nina Simone's "My Baby Just Cares for Me," which was used for a perfume advertisement—not just any perfume, but Chanel No. 5. A similar argument might be leveled at a series of advertisements that appeared in the jazz press for expensively clunky wristwatches modeled by jazz musicians and jazz-influenced singers for the kind of people who think the roulette tables of Las Vegas are glamorous. In examples such as these, the populist might argue that the people to whom the sales messages were being directed were the mature executive class and higher wage earners that could afford the goods and services being promoted. Thus the populist might claim that these advertisements present jazz as appealing to a privileged coterie of monied liberal elites (the haves) at the expense of "the people" (the have nots), and as such were at odds with the current populist aspiration of inclusion. "Evidently," noted Harrison, "the Western world's ultimate 'validation' of culture arises from its adaptability to selling goods and services on television while intellectuals like Gabbard . . . stand on the sidelines, cheering."[44]

The institutionalization of populism and antielitism in the media, politics, public life, and institutions of government and commerce has prompted some critics to argue that we are losing alternatives to mass popular culture, such as jazz, because popular culture is imbibed consciously, unconsciously, and effortlessly through the TV, audio, and digital portals that surround us all. It is a climate in which author Andrew Ross felt able to claim in his book *No Respect: Intellectuals and Popular Culture* that "today a code of intellectual activism which is not grounded in the discourses and images of popular commercial culture is likely to be ineffective."[45]

The culture of the United States may be many things to many people, but most would agree that it is overwhelmingly that of a consumer culture, which is about the continuous creation and accessibility of goods and services that are presented as new, modish, faddish, or fashionable. It is a culture predicated on the pursuit of the "always new," since if a product or enterprise does not keep reinventing itself, it is swept aside by something newer, bigger, or better. As Arendt has noted in connection with the entertainment industry, "[It] is confronted with gargantuan appetites, and since its wares disappear in consumption, it must constantly offer new commodities."[46] Thus in the broader cultural context of the United States, the pursuit of the always new is in tune with the American people's consumerist aspirations, while, in contrast, jazz, which has shown no significant evolutionary change since the 1970s, is no longer considered reflective of the always new and is thus out of tune with America's consumerist aspirations, and has come to be regarded as a cultural artifact remote from the day to day. It has meant that the majority have come to regard jazz in the context of the broader realm of American culture and the arts, and, like opera, ballet, and classical music, it is something to be "appreciated" rather than "enjoyed," its essential verities remaining largely static, like those of classical music or fine art in a gallery.

Perhaps this is one of the unintended consequences of the "Jazz Wars" of the 1990s, when an attempt was made to place swing and blues at the heart of jazz's meaning. In the past there had been a sense that jazz was a work in progress, and that the act of defining the music had the effect of limiting it. Thus for many jazz music was simply music that was taken to be jazz, offering a degree of flexibility that underlined the fact that the music was both a cultural and historical creation but still subject to change and evolution; it had to do with how the music was framed, thought about, and used, rather some mysterious element the jazz possessed that other genres did not. Claiming that the essence of jazz lay in a swing and blues component, although well intentioned, would, over the course of time, have unforeseen consequences. Swing and blues were elements that were central to the ritualistic and social function jazz played in urban black communities, when jazz was a shared culture and an expression of black engagement with modern life that articulated the experience of collective identity based on implicit notions of musical roots, authenticity, and community. This reading of jazz places its core values in its Golden Years, ambiguously located between the turn of the twentieth century and the mid-1960s. A line of reasoning was adopted by some that if the music moved beyond the shadow cast by the tradition of jazz's founding fathers, for whom swing and blues were integral to their music, it surrendered its meaning as jazz music, becoming something else.

Thus in claiming jazz as an exclusively African-American form, it became a means of asserting both cultural identity and of placing a specifically African-American art form at the center of American cultural life. These were highly laudable ambitions. But attempting to create a set of cognitive principles to define jazz's master narrative and unite the jazz community around them had its idiomatic strengths and weaknesses. Ultimately, it was the weakness of these arguments that had the effect of undoing these rationalizations after the fact. The very act of drawing inspiration and identity from a sense of connectedness with jazz's Golden Years had the effect of narrow-casting the music and setting in train a perception that, among other things, jazz was a mirror held up to American society through which to contemplate their sociocultural past. As a result many casual followers of the music came to think of the more traditional sounds of jazz of the 1950s and the 1960s as "the real jazz," and they tended to reject more experimental forms of the music as not being jazz at all. This tension between the prescriptivist view of jazz by those who are loyal to history and the descriptivist view of jazz as an inclusive music whereby jazz remains current by adapting musical elements from beyond the music (as it had traditionally done throughout its history) surfaced in an Internet posting when the distinguished trumpeter Nicholas Payton blogged: "The very fact that so many people are holding on to this idea of what Jazz is supposed to be is exactly what makes it not cool. People are holding onto an idea that died long ago." He concluded: "I am Nicholas Payton and I don't play 'the j word.' I play BAM."[47]

Prompted by Payton's posts, the inaugural BAM (Black American Music) conference was held in New York's Birdland Jazz Club in January 2012, where Payton, with others, reaffirmed that they no longer played jazz but BAM. The panel theorized, according to The Philly Blog, "that black audiences have largely turned away from the genre because of the word [jazz] itself."[48] Among the panelists was Orrin Evans, a pianist and recipient of a Pew Fellowship for the Arts award, who explained, "It's the image, not the music. The name is limiting audiences."[49] In other words, what these artists appeared to be claiming was that they believed audiences had come to associate the term "jazz" with certain performance practices associated with the past that were prejudicing the acceptance of more experimental forms of the music in the present. The panel not only theorized that the j-word was an impediment to employment but also went further by concluding that the j-word now had racist connotations, prompting *The Philly Post Blog* to headline: "The Word 'Jazz' Will Now Be Racist."[50]

In an attempt to bring jazz closer to the mainstream of American life, trumpeter Christian Scott came up with the descriptivist term "Stretch Music," meaning he wanted to stretch the definition of jazz beyond the prescriptivist definitions of the music through inclusion, explaining that he and others were attempting to "encompass as many musical forms, languages, cultures as we can."[51] Pianist Robert Glasper also broke ranks with the true believers with his album *Black Radio*, steeped in R&B, funk, rap, electronic sounds, and guest artists such as Erykah Badu. In a telling interview with the *LA Times*, Glasper said, "The jazz community kind of kills the alive to praise the dead. You look in any jazz magazine, 90 per cent of it is old people, reissues or people who are gone already. The other 10 per cent are new people when it should be the opposite way. [In] jazz we're so stuck on the old days, and then we get mad when there is no new audience. Well, why do you think there's no new audience? You're still playing [stuff] from 1965, that's why."[52]

Jazz, it seems, has gradually become deposed in the eyes of the general public as an essentially forward-looking movement by more enticing distractions elsewhere in popular culture, which appear better suited to reflecting the desires, instincts, feelings, and aspirations of young audiences. As vocalist and educator Alison Crockett has pointed out, it has ceased to be a typical musical experience for most young people, since they are listening to what they and their peers believe is hip, cool, and of the moment: "Drake, Rhianna, and Beyonce. They're black. That's where they're going," she says. "This music is part of their lives on a daily basis. It's on their iPods. They listen to it on YouTube. It's on the Disney Channel. It's in Church and school. It's the music playing at the ice-skating rink and the music they dance to in their dance classes. Music outside of that is 'special.' Music that you are told about in school for an assembly; your parents take you out to see to enlarge your cultural perspectives."[53]

On his blog *Jazzwax*, Marc Myers, author of *Why Jazz Happened*, noted: "Jazz is increasingly considered passé by young American audiences . . . [The term] has finally become the kiss of death—code for 'you're going to hate this music.'"[54] These connotations are not lost on young jazz musicians. For example, in a review of the Paradigm Studios four-part television documentary *Icons among Us: Jazz in the Present Tense*, Will Layman noted: "Musicians talk a great deal why they don't much care for the word 'jazz,' they talk about why they won't be, why they can't be, entirely confined by the history of the music, and they assert with conviction that the truth and beauty of the music 'is now.'"[55] These musicians are striving for contemporary currency, conscious that in the eyes of a broader public, it is something the music has lost. Yet despite these young musicians' best efforts to portray the music as of the present, the perception of jazz is increasingly one of historical endeavor, an image that is becoming increasingly difficult to shake off. "When the word jazz is used in the media—as it was [recently] in a *New York Times* headline—the story once again was about an artist who 'overcame heroin and prison,'" blogged Myers. "[This] tired drugs-and-jail storyline, though dramatic, isn't helping."[56] And certainly through the years jazz has had to battle this stereotypical imagery, no doubt helped into mainstream consciousness by Hollywood films such as the 1955 motion picture *The Man with the Golden Arm*. Yet that image has much basis in fact. The bop years were also jazz's drug years; for example, on May 29, 1957, a *New York Post* headline screamed DRUG ROUND-UP NETS 131 IN 24 HOURS. Three paragraphs down, the page detailed the arrest of John (Jackie) McLean, twenty-five, of 284 E. Houston Street, for "felonious possession of an ounce of heroin."[57]

Alto saxophonist Jackie McLean was far from alone, however. James Lincoln Collier has noted: "It is probable that 50 to 75 percent of the bop players had some experience with hard drugs, that a quarter to a third were seriously addicted, and that perhaps as many as 20 percent were killed by it."[58] But that was then and this is now, and despite the fact that the overwhelming majority of young jazz musicians are straight-arrow professionals, the myth of jazz-musicians-who-do-drugs and the hipster culture they inhabited has proved hard to shake off. It has not been helped, argues educator Kurt Ellenberger, by jazz education, which, he claimed, was stubbornly adhering to a stodgy conservatism. This, he believed, was hopelessly mired in romantic notions of the Golden Age of jazz, circa 1950–60, a decade, he pointed out, that had been reified by many performers, critics, and academics for a variety of legitimate reasons. Nevertheless, he wrote: "Here we are, a half century later, and jazz musicians continue to foster the attitudes, behaviors, and sometimes even the hopelessly worn-out hipster lingo from that bygone era. While I'm sure this is emotionally comforting as subculture signifiers, to the outside world, this nostalgic indulgence must appear archaic, comical, and desperate. Jazz and its affectations certainly aren't 'cool' anymore, and haven't been for decades; these signifiers no longer identify the user as a slick, modern, and rebellious hipster."[59] This failure to acknowledge that jazz long ago lost its counterculture appeal as a means of symbolic resistance to bourgeois hegemony simply reinforces the impression that the music and its culture are more of the past than of the present. It suggests that there may be some advantage in jazz educators portraying the music in a more contemporary context at preschool, grade school, junior high school, and high school level, and with less emphasis on the history and connotations of the hipster lifestyle, which, however romantic, has long passed. After all, young students are more likely to identify with jazz's young stars of today, who are very much alive, rather than with photographs of jazz's deceased heroes—however exalted—staring back at them from the pages of a history book. Yet to suggest this prompts nonaesthetic anxieties and concerns, since educators feel obliged to invest the music with the reverence and seriousness it is due by treating it as a historical endeavor, and so reinforcing the very stereotypical image jazz is trying to shed beyond the hallowed halls of learning.

In 2002, *Billboard* magazine's annual *Year in Review* feature pointed out how vocalists had "exploded into the top 10 of the jazz charts, selling better-than-respectable numbers and infusing the jazz world with hope."[60] However, it also cautioned that this new-found hope had prompted "many to ponder the fate of the unsung heroes behind the vocalists, namely the instrumentalists. Even as jazz vocalists were moving to the foreground of the record buying public's consciousness, it seemed that instrumentalists were losing ground."[61] Five years later, again in its end-of-year review, *Billboard* reflected that "jazz is one of the great instrumental genres but, in 2007, albums recorded by singers or featuring impressive line-ups of guest vocalists, commanded the charts."[62] By now it had become plain to music industry watchers that the major recording companies were responding to falling sales in instrumental jazz by winding down their jazz department activity, since they believed that instrumental jazz "did not sell"—or at least sell in the kind of numbers that were attractive to them. "[Jazz is] not an easy listen, so instrumental jazz artists who are creating much of the most imaginative music suffer," *Billboard* noted.[63] This depressing finding suggested that the very essence of jazz, the instrumental solo, had become less attractive to majority taste.

This might have something to do with the well-documented fall in attention spans, especially among the young. "They are growing up in a world that offers them instant access to nearly the entirety of human knowledge," says Janna Quitney Anderson, coauthor of a Pew Internet

Project study in conjunction with Elon University, published in 2012. "While most of the survey participants see this as mostly positive, some said they are already witnessing deficiencies in young people's abilities to focus their attention, be patient and think deeply. Some experts expressed concerns that trends are leading to a future in which most people become shallow consumers of information."[64] Substance was giving way to the demand for short phrases or sentences intended to convey information in highly condensed summary form, or "quick-fix information nuggets."[65] Yet even by the mid-1980s, drummer Jack DeJohnette had noticed that audience attention spans were falling, and he fine-tuned his music to take account of this, commenting in 2006: "An audience's attention wasn't what it was when Coltrane was playing. By [1984's *Album Album*] we were back to shorter cuts—it makes you concentrate, consolidate yourself."[66] Back then our attention span was around twelve minutes, according to data published in *Assisted Living Today*. It has now fallen, the report revealed, to around five seconds.[67]

It is entirely possible that such developments may have translated into the listening habits of younger audiences. For example, many would argue that the popular trend of passively consuming music "on the go"—via iPods or smart phones when walking, jogging, cycling, roller-skating, commuting, shopping, and so forth—is in tune with reduced attention spans where concentration flicks between audio and visual stimuli as the consumer interacts with and negotiates reality. What characterizes listening to music in the twenty-first century is how it has been transformed by both the technological revolution and mass consumerism to the extent that we are living in a world saturated by music—on the Internet, on the radio at home or in the car, on television and in films, in shopping malls, hotel lobbies, in restaurants, in bars, on the telephone while waiting on hold, and so on—but few people actually *listen to* or *engage with* music disseminated in this way. It fulfills the function of what Erik Satie called "Furniture Music," providing an undemanding background ambience, a pleasant and comforting soundtrack to modern life, its ready availability bringing into question the level of attentiveness that young audiences are prepared to commit to a cognitively demanding music like jazz. Indeed, majority taste may now be at odds with music of inherent complexity (of any sort), amid the growing trend of passive music consumption. The combination of technology and mass consumption has created a cultural landscape quite unlike anything in the past, or even the near past, since the immediacy of the Internet has meant that the distinction between everyday experience and cultural experience has collapsed; the Internet is no longer a supplement to cultural activity but a replacement for it. The arts are being made redundant by technological progress and are being replaced by spectacle, celebrity, and consumerism. Indeed, John Storey argues that it is no longer credible to see culture as an ideological representation, since we are witnessing not only the collapse of the distinction between high culture and popular culture but also the collapse of the distinction between culture and economic activity.[68]

In the 1960s, psychologist Daniel Berlyne, then of the University of Toronto, began to investigate whether aesthetic judgment can be ascribed to measurable features of objects under scrutiny, and in particular their "information content." Although Berlyne's experiments were confined to visual perception, he discovered that too little content led to negative judgments and too much content turned people off, with the highest degree of preference being expressed for a moderate degree of complexity. In music, for example, this might correlate with a composition that used a simple melody line of a few notes, whereupon negative judgments may ensue because boredom might be considered a reasonable response to the music; a piece utilizing a high degree of melodic complexity might also induce a negative response in some listeners as the ear "maxes out."

The significance of Berlyne's ideas for music were investigated by the American psychologist Paul Vitz in 1966. His work concluded that the "complexity" of a piece of music is partly a subjective quantity that depends on whether we possess a mental system capable of making sense of it. Nevertheless, a bias toward lower complexity levels in music was discovered by Tuomas Eerola and Adrian North in their studies of songs by the Beatles. They examined 182 Beatles songs recorded between 1962 and 1970, assigning each tune a complexity measure that included pitch-step expectations of melodies, tonal hierarchy of notes, rhythmic complexity, and so on, and concluded that the songs became more complex over time. The reaction of the record-buying public over the same period was that the number of weeks a hit single spent in the charts fell as the songs grew more complex—and the same story was repeated with the group's albums, which also became progressively more complex.[69] These findings might, on the face of it, serve to confirm what every Beatles fan already knew, but nevertheless they suggest that lessons can be learned by jazz musicians, since a large section of the public might argue that many jazz solos today contain too much information for untrained ears to comprehend, and thus sound less attractive than other genres of music with a moderate degree of complexity. Even to trained ears, virtuosity for its own sake has the effect of diminishing meaning, so that a perfectly reasonable response to a long display of instrumental pyrotechnics might be, "What was that all about? What was the musician trying to say?"

It's worth remembering in this post-Coltrane era that the most influential saxophonist who preceded him, Charlie Parker, valued brevity. He seldom played more than three or four consecutive choruses of the blues, but he knew what he wanted to say and said it. In an interview on BBC Television in 2011, guitarist Carlos Santana spoke about the importance of making every note count and making a musical statement that reaches out and moves the audience in some way: "When you take a solo," he said, "you are required to know where you are going, what you are trying to say, and then get the hell out of there and give it to the next guy. So what is required for you to understand is where you go when you take a solo, you are going straight to people's hearts and what you are trying to say to them—you say you matter, you are significant and you can make a difference in the world. Now *that* is a solo."[70]

The question jazz musicians must surely ask themselves in the new millennium years is how to adapt to the ways in which music is now being consumed among potential audiences, especially in the face of findings by bodies such as the Pew Internet Study Group, which was finding a tendency among young people to display "an expectation of instant gratification [and] a lack of patience," and an inability to "undertake deep, critical analysis of issues and challenging information."[71] In the past, jazz musicians proved remarkably flexible in reacting to sociocultural change: for example, when jazz lost its functional role as a dance music, and thus the specific role it played within people's lives as music for social interaction, the move from dancehall into the nightclub saw the music's function change to fulfill the expectations of a seated, listening audience. In the late 1960s, jazz musicians adopted the rhythms and tone colors of rock music to enable their music to appear relevant to audience expectations of the time. Now, with profound sociocultural changes flowing from the Internet's rapidly evolving digital information networks, jazz composers and soloists surely needed to consider whether performance practices that have barely changed in half a century are relevant for today's audiences.

More than ever there is a need to be sensitive to the changing tastes and aspirations of audiences, who while being open to the challenge of a jazz solo also attend a jazz concert to enjoy themselves. This creates an aesthetic balancing act that many artists fail to negotiate, seemingly unaware that today's consumer society brings with it the immediacy of wish fulfillment. Audiences are more willing than ever before to migrate to the unprecedented number of alternative musical forms on offer if they are not moved or otherwise engaged by the music at hand. Attention spans are short: we are in an age of TV channel zapping with a vengeance, so soloists need to understand the material they are engaged with and construct their improvisation around the need of the composition rather than launching out on their own personal muses, which may or may not relate to the thematic material at hand and so lose the interest of the audience. One common fault among younger musicians is to undervalue the importance of melody and melodic development; after all, having graduated from music college there is a desire to show the world what they have learned—technical accomplishment—which can result in a degree of complexity in their creations that audiences are unable to relate to. This was a hard but valuable lesson saxophonist Branford Marsalis was confronted with during his early years as a bandleader, after being signed by Columbia Records in the early 1980s:

> I had a couple of great learning experiences [as a young musician]. One of the experiences was when we were playing at Royal Festival Hall [in London], and we were opening for Stan Getz. At that time we were playing this burn-out stuff, and I went to Stan before the concert and said to him, "I'm really looking forward to hearing you," and he said, "Great, because you could learn a few things." And that pissed me off, so we decided we would play our most complicated music and at the end of the third song as I went to announce something, someone from the audience yells, "I can't hear a note you guys are playing," and half the audience applauded. Now the most damning aspect of that was at the time it was clear to me the guy was right, but unfortunately at the time I only knew how to play one way, so all we could deliver to them was more of the same shit that we were doing. And then Stan comes in, he backs away from the mike and they play bossa [novas] all night and the audience loves them. So, it was clear, because Stan walks off the stage and he says to me, "And have we learned something tonight?" And I said, "Yes sir, we have." And he said, "Good," and he walked away. So I started playing more ballads, *the next gig* I started playing more ballads, and I was horrible at it, but I kind of understood that the only way to get better was to keep doing it, so it's all these little things these older jazz musicians—because I had the privilege of being

around them—kind of imported to me either through direct conversation or empirical observation. Some of the younger guys today, they're here to blast everybody, they're there to let you know they're geniuses and that they're innovative.[72]

Today, the ability to harness melody and melodic development is in danger of being replaced by mechanical techniques to negotiate harmonic progressions that are becoming ends in themselves: the use of pattern running, or sequencing as it is sometimes known, such as melodic sequencing that preserves the relationship of a group of notes, one to another, through each succeeding chord, or rhythmic sequencing, which is the repetition of a rhythmic figure in which the notes do not necessarily retain the melodic relationship one to another but preserve their rhythmic relationship, that—together with familiar licks learned from recordings or study aids to negotiate common harmonic progressions—have become a familiar feature of contemporary jazz improvisation. It is a trend that concerns virtuoso vibist and jazz educator Gary Burton:

> It's easier to play based on a lot of patterns and things that you have learned and practiced, it's easier to do that than develop the ability to play really well-developed themes and build thematic solos. If I look at my heroes in jazz, it's Bill Evans, it's Miles, it's Coltrane, it's Sonny Rollins, these are all players whose solos unfold like a story, and you hang on every word, so to speak, as they work their way through their solo and you feel like you've been on a journey with them. The opposite approach to playing is to play patterns, one after another, but they don't tell a story. They sound correct and they sound impressive, perhaps, but they are familiar phrases that are almost clichés in many cases, familiar jazz phrases, and the soloist sort of strings them together and makes up a solo that way. That's much less interesting to me and there is a tendency among younger players to settle for that. When I was first playing with Stan Getz, I was standing next to a guy who could tell stories that could bring tears to your eyes, and so I felt challenged to do this also, like, "Yeah, this is what I'm supposed to be doing." So that's been my goal throughout my playing career, to really learn how to thematically develop a solo and turn it into a storyline and get that continuity. Listening to good examples is part of it; there is also trying to figure out how to get there from where you are to over there. In my teaching I put a lot of emphasis on the mental processes we go through to make it a storyline, why practicing phrases and patterns over and

over again works against us instead of helping us, and trying to point people towards the kinds of playing experiences they will benefit from and away from the kind of practices that will steer them in the wrong direction, but I have to honestly say that most teachers of jazz and improvisation probably don't talk about that sort of thing much because they are not sure of it themselves.[73]

Mastery of technique tends to be a dominant topic in jazz education, while discussion on the implications of melody, meaning, or emotion within improvisation is too often ignored. In both live performance and on recordings, an increasing use of patterns by young (and not-so-young) musicians today, together with an emphasis (often peer driven) on executive fluency, has meant that speed of execution has become a thing-in-itself for many musicians, a benchmark applauded by those in the business but often baffling to those outside it, the all-important audience. This tendency toward self-indulgence, whereby soloists expect audiences to meet them on their own terms, simply serves to drive a wedge between potential fans and performers; as saxophonist Branford Marsalis points out, "People are not interested in doing homework to attend a jazz concert."[74] The importance of melodic expressivity and melodic development, and rediscovering the soloist's story-telling privilege, is something saxophonist Joe Lovano emphasizes at his master classes:

A lot of times, up at Berklee [College of Music], at NYU and other faculties, I do a lot of unaccompanied playing in my class and I get a lot of cats to try that, and even though you practice alone I find that most of the young players of whatever instrument have a hard time playing unaccompanied and playing a piece right through by themselves, whatever instrument—a bass player, a trumpet player, a saxophone player—piano players do that all the time, guitar players also. Just play and accompany themselves and just play alone. But a lot of horn players, the single note players, they're not sure how to do it. "Well man, what do you do when you practice?" A lot of times they'll be playing patterns or something out of a book or I don't know what. "Play through a song or play three or four chords from a tune you love to play," that's what I tell them. Half the time they stand there and they're wondering what to do. "Man, play a song you love, what do you love to play?" That question takes a lot because to answer that as a young player you have to dig deep. You have to stop and think about it, "Wow, what do I really love to play? I love to play page 36, exercise 14." [laughs] You know?[75]

Eschewing the art of melodic construction within a solo and ignoring precedents set by the great masters of lyrical improvisation, such as a Lester Young, a Dexter Gordon, a Stan Getz, a Miles Davis, or a Clark Terry, and favoring instead complexity and pattern running, serves to distance the performer from the audience by not giving audience members something they can relate to. Joe Lovano points out that these great instrumentalists were all masters of melodic expressivity, reaching out to the audience by shaping the contours of a song in their own personal style, an art he believes is slowly being lost in jazz. "Well, do you know why?" he asks.

> I think a lot of teachers at some of these universities are cats who have studied music and can play, but they have learned from playing patterns so that's what they teach. These days there are more and more situations for people like myself to have opportunities to share other approaches, give people confidence to play with interpretation—I mean Dexter Gordon could play the same song twenty times in a row and it'll be the same song but he would play it with interpretation. Same with Miles Davis. He could play the same song all day, let's say twenty, thirty times, and every time it will be the same melody, the same chords, but his imagination, his approach is what it's about. Develop your own approach—and that takes a lot of confidence. There are a lot of cats today who would play that same song and you wouldn't be able to tell whether it's the fifth time they played it or the twentieth, they'd play it the same way every time, as far as their rhythm and phrasing and so on.[76]

Respecting the primacy of melodic expressivity and development within jazz improvisation is a significant step toward conveying meaning that is so essential to communicating with an audience. As psychologist Daniel Berlyne pointed out earlier, too much information turns people off, so rather than seeing a solo as an opportunity to work through all the licks and patterns learned in practice, musicians should see the solo as a challenge to find a voice within the composition that sustains and enhances the emotional climate of the thematic material at hand—a study of Duke Ellington's soloists at work in his 1940–41 band can be informative in this respect. "It's the strength of melody that people are really in tune with," reflects bassist Christian McBride. "I think as you grow as a musician you start to understand this and are more willing to embrace the beauty and the simplicity of melody. I think that probably comes with time, and this is not to say young jazz musicians don't deal with melody, because some do, but I wish I could find some sort of balance with a lot of younger musicians really trying to seek out melody, or embracing melody, to an extent that people outside of their generation understand what's happening."[77]

Equally, composers need to come up with material that has the potential to move the listener in some way, not simply to regard the composition as a vehicle for collecting royalties or a means of establishing key, tempo, and harmonic structure. As the British pianist Dan Nicholls observes, jazz artists today need to negotiate and consider their relationship between artistic production and audience perception:

> It's very easy to become wrapped up in your own world—especially seeing as such personal and individual music as jazz runs the risk of being very egocentric and inward looking—and to forget that there is an audience who are giving you their time and energy and paying for the experience. Too many jazz concerts feature something that is either totally disconnected from the audience, gratuitously complex and alienating, or presented in an apologetic nature, none of which interests me or the majority of people. Since I started trying to see the music more objectively and listening to the views of less experienced audience members, I began to see it, as well as hear it, differently. I now feel strongly that my music is primarily for the audience and, whilst keeping my artistic integrity and being uncompromising with my material, I hope to be able to communicate my ideas and present my music in a way which invites people in.[78]

Today, the jazz composition has to be something more than "a vehicle for improvisation"; audiences want an experience, to be to made to feel happy, sad, elated, or excited—otherwise what is the point? It is a given today that the contemporary jazz musician must posses a high degree of technical and theoretical skills. So once a musician has acquired the necessary skill and experience to function with a high level of proficiency within the improvising environment, the question then becomes: how do you separate yourself from the countless other young musicians with similar skills and experience, who also function with a high level of proficiency within the improvising environment? Increasingly, many are coming to believe that the answer lies in being able to create an original and effective context within which to frame your improvisational skills. While jazz was once primarily a soloist's art, it is now context that is increasingly coming to define originality. This dichotomy between the concept of a solo as a thing-in-itself or coming embodied within a broader concept was seen early on during the rise of bebop. In bebop, the "head" served as a springboard for the soloist to take flight, to follow his or her creative muse (guided by the underlying harmonies and rhythm) for as long as he or she liked before the recapitulation of the theme. On the Capitol recordings of Miles Davis's *Birth of the Cool* nonet, the opposite was true. Each composition was richly orchestrated, and the soloists were charged with integrating their work into the greater whole in a way that related to the overall context of the piece; as a result, their work somehow assumed greater *meaning*. But the conceptual nature of creating a musical environment such as this demanded rehearsals and arrangements—an investment of time and money that was often not practical in the day-to-day life of a musician—then as now. Today pick-up bands are ubiquitous, with the *Real Book* providing a common language and the means by which ad hoc ensembles function; that in turn imposes a kind of uniformity, because there is usually no money for rehearsal time to explore alternative ways of approaching jazz. Thus the domination of the soloist is in part a function of business imperatives, which often have a tendency toward homogeneity. Today it is possible that the similarity in style, concept, and execution of pick-up groups might simply not interest young audiences. The implicit problem here is of creating a music that speaks to itself but fails to engage the broader public: writer Francis Davis has written of the "deadening sameness" of what he was hearing on record and in clubs, pointing out that boredom was a reasonable response to "a lineup of soloists running down the chords to no apparent purpose."[79]

This raises the question of the role jazz musicians themselves have played in falling audience numbers. Saxophonist Branford Marsalis is one of many top jazz musicians who believe they have played a role in this: "I definitely think it is mostly the musicians' fault," he says. "If you're playing music and everything is highly intellectualized and cerebral, and remote and distant, you're basically . . . I don't know what. You're basically playing for your colleagues, and for the media that supports it, and when you go to concerts now that's kinda what you see. Fellas come on stage, they get on the microphone and they whisper into the microphone, 'thankyouverymuchladiesandgentleman,' they have this very distant, far-off relationship with the audience, and the audience picks up on that, and the majority of the audience are not interested."[80]

Marsalis points to other important factors in the presentation of jazz where many young jazz musicians fall short, saying he gradually came to understand that what musicians wear and how they carry themselves on stage play into how the music is perceived and by whom.

> When people talk to me about my band they talk to me about how much they enjoy *watching* us, how much they enjoy watching how much we enjoy playing with each other, they never talk about the music—except when we play a ballad, and then they say this ballad made me cry or this ballad was really moving, or something like that—they talk about the energy and body language on stage, call it charisma if you will. I think the old guys understood that, which is why you see them in those pictures smiling, and wearing suits—even Charlie Parker smiling and wearing a suit in the press photo—and they "got" that you had to give them something to see. There has to be a lifeline.[81]

It is interesting to note that a survey conducted by Dr. Chia-Jung Tsay of the University College of London's (UCL) Management, Science and Innovation Department in 2013 discovered that respondents could reliably select the winners of classical music competitions based on silent video recordings of performances alone. The results lend considerable resonance to Marsalis's observations in that they highlight the uncomfortable finding that we rely more on visual information when judging live music than the sound of the music itself. Visual cues, such as the perception of a performer's "passion" or "involvement," were found to be good predictors of winning performances according to the study, published in the journal *Proceedings of the National Academy of Sciences*. "The results show that even when we want to be objective in evaluating the sound of music, when it comes to live performance, the visual experience can be the most influential aspect," confirmed Dr. Tsay.[82]

Equally, it is perfectly possible for a musician to do everything "correctly," executing everything the right way, playing within the conventions of a certain style in an idiomatically correct manner to a high level of proficiency—and yet the results can appear mechanical or fail to evoke an emotional response from the listener, so boredom becomes a possible response. Another reason might be that a particular style has been so extensively exploited over the years it is almost impossible to come up with a fresh, surprising, original, or even interesting statement within the idiom. For example, listening to the recordings of the great New Orleans jazz masters can be a moving and exhilarating experience, but since 1917 there have been so many recordings and bands playing within the conventions of its style that the idiom exists today more as a historical endeavor. The long road that began near Lulu White's Mahogany Hall now extends over a century, and at some point along this route proliferation within the art form has inevitably led to its devaluation—as it does in all the arts.

At the height of bebop in the 1940s and 1950s, when improvisers created something exceptional they were imitated by other members of the musical community, and quickly assimilated into the broader syntax of the music. Certain key phrases or licks, exercised within the parameters of the bebop style, had, even by the mid-1950s, become widely disseminated and imitated. Today, like an inverted triangle, hundreds of thousands of students and thousands of teachers study this narrow repository of stylistic inspiration (the pantheon of truly "great" bebop players in all of jazz is probably fewer than fifteen musicians), which has resulted in a similarity of concept and execution among many musicians. Once again, the proliferation of a style or genre has led to its devaluation, and boredom becomes a possible response. "How can you play music from the 1950s like Art Blakey and the Jazz Messengers when you live in New Jersey, your bass player lives in West Chester, and you have to fly in your drummer—he's teaching in Michigan?" asks composer, saxophonist, and Grammy winner Bob Belden. "They rehearse, they have music stands up there, they're playing something that's been recorded, so you have a reference point, and yet none of the guys have played gigs from hell, had any poverty, and nobody has said to them, 'You can't eat in here,' so it's just an intellectual exercise. Okay, some people, some critics, might say, 'Wow, that's interesting.' But stamp collecting is interesting, butterfly collecting is interesting, is that all it is, interesting? Shouldn't it be mind blowing or devastating or life changing?"[83]

A similar question might be asked of tribute bands that are regularly hired by clubs and festivals. While they may be "interesting" to behold, they are seldom able to offer the sound of surprise. These ensembles, where musician X plays the music of Ray Charles, musician Y plays the music of Jaco Pastorius or some other deceased great, or, more commonly, musician A and musician B play the music of Miles Davis, mark the point where history becomes nostalgia before it becomes myth. Often seen as crowd-pullers by concert and festival producers, tribute bands often fail to live up to expectation and appear to reinforce the impression that jazz is now more about the past than the present. "Beware of those blasts from the past," headlined the *Pittsburgh Tribune-Review*, which went on to comment: "It is a little frightening when jazz fans pay so much attention to the past rather than being more concerned with what is down the road."[84] It was a point underlined by the *Kansas City Star*, with a feature headlined "Too Many Jazz Tribute Shows Leave Little Room for Innovation." In a hard-hitting but fair appraisal, it noted:

> Concert and club presenters sometimes fret that jazz doesn't bring in the crowds like it used to. But is booking tribute shows the way to bring the crowds back or build a new audience for the future? Some tribute shows make a populist appeal . . . but chances of a tribute show improving on the originals aren't good. Often it's a pale imitation of the original or a half-hearted reinterpretation.
>
> The tribute show pretty much guarantees that we don't get the best performers have to give, because performers are doing someone else's thing instead of their own. In fact, these shows might have the opposite effect of what presenters want: they might be driving people away by sending the wrong message . . . that the innovations have all been made, the greatest performances already played. That jazz is over.[85]

Certainly, undertakings such as the tribute band serve to highlight the fact that audiences exist for jazz as a nostalgic endeavor, a curious paradox whereby they feel nostalgic for an art form that is still largely of the present. How, then, can you feel regret for something that has passed when it is still present? The answer is, of course, that it is possible to experience nostalgia for the past if it speaks to you more loudly than the present. Today, with over one hundred years of recorded jazz history, consumers are faced with the paradox of plenty. Instead of exploring the wealth of information available to us via information technology, we systematically opt for that which agrees with our own ideological disposition, or so social scientific research has revealed. We are not the free radicals we like to think we are, becoming ever more selective in choosing what to consume. Writing of feeling like H. G. Wells's time traveler, the critic Gary Giddins once wrote: "Wells's hero chased the future; I prefer the past. In the future you may encounter a Parker or Monk or just a bunch of Molochs. With the past you've got the sure thing."[86]

This is perhaps an understandable response to the diversity of today's jazz scene, where some either choose to give up, or are unable to keep abreast of, current events,[87] so that, to paraphrase Donald Rumsfeld, "the known knowns" become more attractive when exercising consumer choice than the "known unknowns," the things we know we don't know — music that extends beyond that with which we are familiar.

In many ways it might be argued that falling audience numbers in jazz have been a result of a perfect storm, whereby a chain of seemingly unrelated circumstances combine to create an exceptional event. What seems clear is that more than ever jazz needs to create its own space in a hostile media landscape. It's not impossible. The fact that Miles Davis's *Kind of Blue* has continued to accumulate four-figure sales each month well into the new millennium suggests that instrumental jazz can sell—and be relevant to twenty-first-century consumer expectations. If we look a little closer at *Kind of Blue* from a consumer perspective, we see that it is an album that fulfills the function of both passive and active listening. The passive listener might regard it as sophisticated background music that cleverly sustains an intimate mood through the choice of slow-medium tempos, so providing an ambiance that may be appropriate for a dinner party or as an accompaniment to making love. But it is also an album that encourages active listening, where it functions as emotionally and intellectually stimulating foreground music. It is music that is challenging but does not exclude the nonspecialist listener who feels free to engage with the music on his or her own terms. Even though it was recorded in 1959, it still remains relevant to today's culture, illustrated by a scene in the motion picture *Runaway Bride*, where the character played by actress Julia Roberts gives Richard Gere's character an original vinyl copy of the album as a token of her undying love.

Today, when people leave their homes for an evening's entertainment, they want to be certain they are going to enjoy themselves more than they do when they leave for their workplace. They are prepared to accept an element of challenge, but challenge in the context of relaxation. The cachet jazz has acquired in the current populist climate implies the challenge but not the relaxation, so this might suggest that jazz musicians have some soul searching to do. The time seems right for the music to respond to the social and cultural changes that are occurring in society around them by shaping their music in a way that finds a function in people's lives that is in tune with twenty-first-century consumerist lifestyles and metropolitan attitudes. "There's an important function that jazz musicians have which is to reconcile their vision of music with the current state of the universe," says guitarist Pat Metheny. "That responsibility is neglected sometimes, in the face of just the grammar. And the thing is the study of the grammar is so fun and so fascinating it's really easy for me to see how young guys can just immerse themselves in that."[88]

While jazz is never going to be popular, it does need to appear relevant to the lives and expectations of those who seek a route toward it. Jazz needs to provide bridges over the yawning chasm between itself and popular culture to let people in, just as "My Favourite Things," "Take Five," "Poinciana," and yes, even "Hello Dolly" did in the past. The importance of pieces like these was that they communicated jazz's essential core values in accessible form. You only have to look at the huge success of *Kind of Blue* to realize that great jazz need not be defined in terms of complex, tormented brain puzzles that are beyond the ken of everyone except a specialist audience. Yet this is where the popular perception of jazz has ended up, with the nation's cultural gatekeepers believing the music to be too complex to be popular and so remote from popular taste as to be elitist. The domination of our cultural spaces by popular music is increasingly banishing any interest in, or perceived need for, any other kind of music. This is the challenge jazz musicians have to confront: to accept that they have a very real role in addressing the problem of falling audience numbers. The path ahead for jazz may be complex and full of potential pitfalls, but it is a path that has to be followed, since jazz must find a way to continue to speak to the society that spawned it. If it fails do that, or when society does not want to hear what it is saying, the future for the music becomes bleak.

# Jazz May Be Universal, but Does It Have a Universal Meaning?

**W**ithout the phonograph record, whose popularity and availability owed much to the rise of consumerism, it is quite possible that jazz, like the two musical crazes that preceded it, the cakewalk and ragtime, might have flared briefly, only to be remembered today as one more chapter in the history of American popular music. Instead, it emerged with perfect historical timing to take advantage of a burgeoning phonograph record industry whose early growth was given considerable momentum by a mania for social dancing that swept America from around 1911. Despite depressed business conditions in the United States at the time, the Victor Talking Machine Company, one of the significant early players in the industry, was ideally placed to take advantage of the dance craze. Like most recording companies at the time, Victor had used light orchestral or military bands to provide their dance titles prior to World War I but were among the first to look to popular ensembles from within the entertainment milieu to provide recorded dance music. In January 1917, the Original Dixieland Jazz Band opened at Reisenweber's "400" Room in New York City, and their overnight success, virtually on Victor's doorstep, proved impossible to ignore. "Word spread quickly," wrote H. O. Brunn, the band's historian. "Newspapers, in their age-old tradition, carried exaggerated stories. Friends told friends [and] night-clubbers flocked to Reisenweber's."[1] Hoping to cash in on this success, Victor recorded the band the following month in their Camden, New Jersey, studio. "Livery Stable Blues" (coupled with "Original Dixieland One-Step"), rush-released in March of that year, went on to become one of their earliest Black Label million-sellers. But significantly, these sales were not confined to the United States; they were accumulated worldwide. This was made possible by a sophisticated production and distribution network for recorded music in the Western world, established in the years before World War I. It meant that almost from the beginnings of the music, recorded jazz was available to a worldwide audience and would quickly inspire emulation and imitation in the remotest parts of globe, as American journalist Burnet Hershey discovered in 1921–22. Traveling through Hawaii, Japan, China, Hong Kong, India, Manila, Siam (now Thailand), Ceylon (now Sri Lanka), Egypt, Palestine, Monaco, France, and London, he chronicled his experiences in the pages of the *New York Times Book Review and Magazine*: "I set out on a tour of the world with a wanderer's lure of adventure, strange lands and quaint customs. My trail led along curious rough byways, but all along the route, yawping after me, ululating along with me, blatantly greeting me, was the inevitable jazz. No sooner had I shaken off the dust of some city and slipped almost out of earshot of its jazz bands than zump-zump-zump, toodle-oodle-doo, right into another I went. Never was there a cessation of this universal potpourri of jazz."[2]

By 1955, the *New York Times* felt able to report that "American jazz has now become a universal language. It knows no national boundaries."[3] As if to underline this, on July 5, 1958, an international big band of young jazz musicians was assembled under the baton of Marshall Brown to play the Newport Jazz Festival. Among the youthful faces assembled for the occasion were trumpeters Dusko Gojkovic of Yugoslavia and Roger Guerin of France, trombonist Albert Mangelsdorff of Germany, tenor saxophonists Bernt Rosengren from Sweden and Jan Wroblewski from Poland, baritone saxophonist Ronnie Ross from England, pianist George Gruntz from Switzerland, and guitarist Gabor Szabo from Hungary. Unable to speak each other's languages, they communicated with one another, reported Leonard Feather, "through the international language of jazz." In 1963, another international big band, this time assembled under the aegis of drummer Kenny Clarke and pianist Francy Boland, called their debut album *Jazz Is Universal*. In the liner notes, Willis Conover wrote: "Today the jazz language has become a *lingua franca* bypassing a score of spoken tongues, not to mention sectional prejudices and national passions."[4]

Today the American Jazz Institute refers to jazz as a "universal language,"[5] and it is not unreasonable to claim that most countries around the world have some form of jazz activity and, to all intents and purposes, jazz is indeed universal. But as Titon and Slobin have argued, while "music is universal . . . its meaning is not."[6] Although meaning in music has yet to be precisely defined, the *Oxford Handbook of Music Psychology* does make the point that "the idea that music's meanings are inseparable from the social and cultural situations in which they arise has become widely accepted in musicological, sociological and ethnomusicological circles."[7] If that is the case, then depending on who we are and where we are in the world, it is entirely possible that we might extract different meanings from the same piece of music. For example, a poll conducted by the German Marshall Fund in 2003 revealed that there was agreement on both sides of the Atlantic that Americans and Europeans have different social and cultural values,[8] so it is entirely possible that an American jazz recording made by American jazz musicians might arouse different responses among European audiences than those aroused among their American counterparts. This is not to say an American jazz recording played inside the United States somehow sounds "different" when played outside America, but to non-American ears it might produce a different set of connotations and referential meanings from those experienced by American listeners. Equally, it is quite possible the reverse is true—that a European jazz recording might evoke quite different connotations and referential meanings among American audiences than those experienced by Europeans. So if this is the case, does it mean that even though jazz may be universal, its meaning is not?

⌐⌐

Today the Internet has made it possible to hear music from faraway lands sung and performed in different languages by people from different cultures, with World Music now enjoying a considerable worldwide following in terms of album sales and concert attendances. In 2004, the

Senegalese singer and percussionist Youssou n'Dour recorded the album *Egypt*, a celebration of Sufism that included several religious texts of profound religious, ritualistic, and social significance for its followers. The album went on to become a worldwide best-seller, and it is interesting to reflect that the prospect of Western audiences enjoying songs in languages they do not understand would hold little promise for them if the melodies, rhythms, and harmonies did not move or stimulate their emotions in some way. Yet as non-Wolof speakers, it is quite possible that Western audiences extract different meanings from the music than do the Senegalese followers of Sufism. Lyrics define the emotions a song is intended to convey, but in a language with which we are not familiar we cannot be sure what emotions we are supposed to feel. We may agree in general terms that a piece of music is happy or sad, humorous or tragic, superficial or profound, but detailed responses as to how and why the music moves us may vary considerably. Music seems to create its effect without any mediation or explanation. Most of us are unaware of any interpretation, or of any cognitive process, that contributes to our enjoyment. Most listeners' responses are governed subjectively, and, in addition, personal emotion not related to the music itself can also intervene, so that a given response may not be entirely a result of the music itself. So what constitutes meaning, and the means by which it is conveyed, remains a contested area of musical discourse.

Broadly speaking, opinion is divided into two schools of thought. The absolutists or formalists would account for music's appeal in terms of a series of discrete sounds and sound complexes whose meaning lies exclusively within the context of the music, arguing that a work of music has no meaning outside of itself. It is not an argument without some force. For example, if Beethoven had not written the programmatic sounds of the nightingale, quail, and cuckoo into the second movement of his *Pastoral Symphony* and had not given each of the five movements (the convention at the time was for four) titles such as "By the Brook Side" or "Merry Gathering of Country Folk," it might have been regarded as a piece of absolute music—meaning that the music is nonrepresentational and not about anything other than the music itself. Stravinsky famously asserted in his conversations with Robert Craft, "Music is powerless to express anything at all," claiming it did not express feelings but simply expressed itself.[9]

This may be true, but a contra argument might be that music helps us find our own feelings, a position advanced by the referentialists (sometimes called expressionists), who contend that music communicates extramusical connotations that produce referential meanings, and it is here, they argue, we should look for the source of meaning. Certainly it is difficult to imagine our relationship to music not being shaped in some way by our previous listening experiences, and for many the passion for a piece of music rests on association—for example, on its being "our song," or the memories of a specific time, place, or event in our lives when the music was first heard and so on. Equally, the formalist's position that we can never *fully* understand a piece of music without an understanding of the musical techniques at work in a piece has merit too, since even a fundamental understanding of music theory undoubtedly helps to heighten our enjoyment of music.

Yet perhaps these positions are too extreme, and rather than being an either/or situation, a choice of black or white, the answer is more nuanced and comes in shades of grey. If music is indeed powerless to express anything at all, as Stravinsky claimed, it is perhaps surprising that responses to his music share a high degree of consensus among listeners who share closely related musical reactions to it. In any event, there is no denying that most people appreciate and enjoy music quite well without a formal understanding of the theories at work in a musical performance. Indeed, when a piece of music becomes embedded in the memory and listeners "know what's coming next," or are sufficiently familiar with the music to hum or whistle along with the melody or sing the song's lyrics, they have already grasped something of its formal musical structure.

Referential meaning, then, by its very nature, tends to be general rather than specific. The American music theorist, composer, and philosopher Leonard B. Meyer has pointed out that even though music cannot specify or particularize referential or extramusical connotations, it nevertheless is able to "express what might be called the disembodied essence of myth, the essence of expression central and vital to the human condition."[10] Meyer studied with Aaron Copeland and corresponded with Schoenberg, and his 1956 work *Emotion and Meaning in Music* is probably the most influential and quoted theoretical framework in the study of emotional responses to music. Rather than taking as his starting point "Why does music produce emotions?" he posits the question "How does music produce emotions?" Drawing on philosopher John Dewey's Conflict Theory of Emotions from 1894 and the work of others, Meyer argues that the emotional effect of music is not produced by having our expectations met, but rather by having them met in ways we do not anticipate, which in turn creates varying degrees of tension and release. "Under certain conditions we expect change," he writes. "Under others continuity, and under still others repetition; until finally we expect the conclusion of the piece. Thus in a very general way expectation is always ahead of the music, creating a background of diffuse tension against which particular delays articulate the affective curve and create meaning."[11]

One of the examples he cites to illustrate the many and varied ways of postponing expectation in music is Beethoven's String Quartet in C-sharp minor, Op. 131, where the relationship between harmonic and rhythmic completeness is very clear. He turns to the fifth movement, drawing our attention to the way Beethoven arouses our expectations without fulfilling them by destroying the rhythmic, harmonic, and melodic patterns that have been established, until finally he recapitulates the figure that opens the movement and, in so doing, "raises our hopes and redirects our expectations of completion and return."[12] Meyer argues that the great composers were expert in employing devices such as this to heighten our expectation, so that when resolution does arrive it is all the more pleasing, since our expectations have been fulfilled. "The customary or expected progression of sounds can be considered as a norm," he writes. "[An] alteration in the expected progression can be considered as a deviation. Hence deviations can be regarded as emotional or affective stimuli."[13]

Meyer's study offers three main sources that might govern our sense of expectation. The first he calls *extra-opus knowledge*, or style knowledge, that relates to our understanding of a particular genre. For example, in classical music it might be baroque music or Italian opera or the Romantic tradition, while in jazz it might be knowledge of hard bop or big band jazz or free jazz. In either case, knowledge of a particular genre (which need not be a result of formal musical training, but internalized through passive exposure) influences our expectations in a given musical context. Meyer calls his second source *intra-opus knowledge*, which instead of referring to the understanding of a particular genre, refers to the understanding of a particular piece of music and the expectations that arise based on knowledge of its characteristics. The third source is derived from principles of Gestalt psychology, which concerns the ways we group perceptions together into objects and coherent shapes, which he relates to music (in the Preface, Meyer explicitly acknowledges his debt to Kurt Koffka, one of the main proponents of Gestalt psychology). Meyer's work opened a door through which an increasing body of empirical evidence has passed involving a wide variety of behavioral and neurocognitive measures, including brain-scanning technology to discover what areas of the brain "light up" in response to certain musical stimuli, strongly supporting the theory that the expectations produced by listening to music give rise to feelings of tension, resolution, and release.

Today, Swedish psychologists Patrik Juslin and Daniel Västfjäll are generally considered leaders in the study of music and emotion. They argue that music recruits the same emotions we experience in everyday life, and that we do not, as some have suggested, possess emotions that are music specific. While they point out that researchers may not agree on a precise definition of emotion, they largely agree on the characteristics and components of an *emotional response*, which they summarize thus:[14]

~ *Cognitive Appraisal*. Example: You appraise the situation as "dangerous."
~ *Subjective Feeling*. Example: You feel afraid.
~ *Psychological Arousal*. Example: Your heart beats faster.
~ *Expression*. Example: You scream.
~ *Action Tendency*. Example: You run away.
~ *Regulation*. Example: You try and calm yourself.

To demonstrate that music can evoke these "real" emotions, they argue that it is necessary to provide evidence that music is capable of producing reactions in all six of the above characteristics. In their paper "Emotional Responses to Music: The Need to Consider Underlying Mechanisms,"[15] they produced a new theoretical framework featuring six psychological mechanisms of emotion-causation—later increased to seven in a subsequent paper—that they believed explained most emotions that are aroused by music in everyday life: (1) brain stem reflexes, (2) rhythmic entrainment, (3) evaluative conditioning, (4) emotional contagion, (5) visual imagery, (6) episodic memory, and (7) musical expectancy. Looking at each mechanism in turn:

1 ~ *Brain Stem Reflexes:* This response has its roots in the primitive instincts implanted in us by evolutionary biology, whereby the brain is "hard-wired" to pick up danger signals in our immediate environment. An unexpected auditory event like a fearsome roar, for example, suggests the proximity of an animal, connoting "danger." Sudden sounds that are loud and of very low frequency, or of high frequency, are capable of triggering powerful brain stem reflexes. (We tend to associate low notes with size—for example, the low, repeated two-note ostinato in John Williams's

soundtrack for the motion picture *Jaws*, which suggests the presence of the Great White Shark. Similarly, we may see an animal in distress, but only when we hear its high-pitched scream of pain are we powerfully moved.) Juslin and Västfjäll explain the brain stem as "an ancient structure of the brain that subserves a number of sensory and motor functions including, but not limited to, auditory perception and the mediation and control of attention, emotional arousal, heart rate, breathing and movement."[16] Brain stem reflexes are quick and automatic, and kick in before they can be suppressed by slower cognitive reasoning. Thus they may accentuate our response to a musical event with extreme acoustic characteristics, such as the sudden loud chord in the Andante of Haydn's Symphony No. 94 in G major, referred to as the "Surprise Symphony."

2 ~ *Rhythmic Entrainment:* Here emotion is evoked by the powerful rhythmic characteristics of a given piece of music that eventually "lock on" to the internal bodily rhythm of the listener, such as heart rate, producing an increased level of arousal. One example might be Techno music's implicit rhythmic characteristics, which are relatively close to the natural heart or respiration rate of the listener. Although the entrainment mechanism has a slower induction process than a brain stem reflex, it might produce feelings of arousal, communion, and perhaps even trancelike altered states of consciousness, such as those experienced at a rave.[17]

3 ~ *Evaluative Conditioning:* Juslin and Västfjäll define this response as "a process whereby an emotion is induced by a piece of music because this stimulus has been paired with other positive or negative stimuli."[18] For example, we may meet friends at an agreeable location and experience happiness. Perhaps there is a piece of music playing in the background, and after a while the music becomes paired with this happy feeling, so that even if we are not in our friends' company, hearing this particular piece of music causes the emotion of happiness to be reproduced. Significantly, we do not have to be aware of this connection for it to work, so it is often deployed in advertising.

4 ~ *Emotional Contagion:* Here an emotion is induced because listeners unconsciously react to the music as if they were in the presence of someone expressing emotions in the voice; "the listener perceives the emotional expression of the music and then 'mimics' this expression internally, which by means of either peripheral feedback from muscles, or a more direct activation of the relevant emotional representations in the brain, leads to an induction of the same emotion."[19] According to Juslin's Super-Expressive Voice Theory,[20] what makes a particular performance on, say, the violin,

so expressive is "the fact it sounds a lot like the human voice, whereas at the same time it goes far beyond what the human voice can do in terms of speed, intensity and timbre. For example if human speech is perceived as 'angry' when it has a fast rate, loud intensity and harsh timbre, a musical instrument might sound *extremely* 'angry' by virtue of its even greater speed, louder intensity and harsher timbre. This should render music a particularly potent source of emotional contagion."[21]

5 ~ *Visual Imagery:* This is a process whereby the music appears to conjure up visual images in the mind of the listener, inducing an emotion. Juslin and Västfjäll note that "certain musical characteristics, such as repetition, predictability in melodic, harmonic and rhythmic elements and slow tempo are especially effective in stimulating visual imagery . . . A special feature of the imagery mechanism is that the listener is very much able to influence the emotions induced by the music."[22] It has been suggested that these images may be manipulated and dismissed at will, allowing adolescents, in particular, to conceive strong emotional images in which a temporary sense of self can cohere. The music then becomes a "fantasy ground" for exploring possible selves when resolving personal identity in late adolescence.

6 ~ *Episodic Memory:* Here emotion is aroused because the music evokes a specific event in the listener's past life. Episodic memories tend to be associated with social relationships, and by their very nature, such responses are highly subjective but often play a role of great importance in the listener's relationship with a piece of music: a recording played at a first date, a holiday romance, or a marriage proposal might subsequently invest that recording with considerable meaning for the people concerned. A piece of music associated with the breakup of an *affaire de coeur* might produce feelings of sadness and loss; in the motion picture *Casablanca*, for example, the world-weary nightclub owner Rick, played by Humphrey Bogart, would not allow the club's pianist to play "As Time Goes By" because he did not want such feelings to be awakened by a performance of the song, reflecting how closely music is linked with our emotional lives. However, episodic memory can apply to all kinds of events, such as vacations, childhood memories, the death of close relatives or friends, and so on. Juslin and Västfjäll report recent evidence citing episodic memory as one of the most frequent and subjectively important sources of emotion in music, many listeners even using music to remind them of valued past events, which indicates that music can serve an important nostalgic function in everyday life. Music memories from early adulthood have a special

emotional significance, perhaps because music has an important function with regard to identity; people recall more memories from age fifteen to twenty-five, a period known as the *reminiscence bump*, when many self-defining experiences tend to occur. Thus as the listener grows older these associations are recalled as nostalgia.[23]

7 ~ *Musical Expectancy:* As we have seen, Leonard B. Meyer's *Emotion and Meaning in Music* has extensively theorized the process by which emotion is induced when the music postpones anticipated resolution, or violates our expectation of such resolution. Juslin and Västfjäll point out that Meyer's theory of musical expectancy does not refer to any unexpected event in relation to music: "A simple form of unexpectedness (for example, the sudden onset of a loud tone) would instead be an example of the mechanism called the *brain stem reflex*" [see (1), above]. Similarly, more general surprising features of an event that involves music (for example, a concert that was better than expected) would instead be an example of the *cognitive appraisal* mechanism. Musical expectancy refers to those expectancies that involve *syntactical* relationships between parts of the musical structure. Thus it seems likely that some of our emotional reactions to music reflect the disruption of style-specific expectations."[24]

All these mechanisms are not mutually exclusive but complementary. For example, Juslin and Västfjäll suggest that the bitter-sweet feeling of both happiness and sadness after a piece of music has finished might be explained by a combination of mechanisms: "A piece of music could make a listener happy because of the happy expression of the piece (emotional contagion), but at the same time make the listener sad because the piece reminds him or her of a sad event in the past (episodic memory)."[25]

Emotions, what Meyer calls "affective behaviour," have the capacity to guide and energize our actions in certain ways and play a vital role in our responses to music, which we often express in emotional terms— that a piece of music evokes happiness, sadness, longing, excitement, melancholy, nostalgia, and so on. Emotions directly influence the type of music we listen to and how long we listen to it, mediate our responses to it, and can appear as the source of music's meaning. Meyer has suggested we naturally respond to music emotionally, noting: "The listener brings to the act of perception definite beliefs in the affective power of music. Even before the first sound is heard, these beliefs activate dispositions to respond in an emotional way."[26] This presumed effectiveness in inducing emotional responses within us has been acknowledged in a

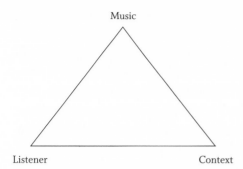

Music

Listener                    Context

*Meaning*
*in music*
*affected by*
*context.*

variety of contexts, such as the use of piped or "captive" music in social spaces, such as shopping malls to increase sales, or in the film industry as soundtrack music to heighten our emotional response to the on-screen action: the jarring dissonances of the shower scene in *Psycho*, for example, or the mood music that accompanies a love scene. "Music has a way of bypassing the human's normal, rational defence mechanisms," says Roy Prendergast. "Music can help build the drama in a scene to a far greater degree of intensity than any of the other cinematic arts. It is of little significance whether the scene involves an intimate love relationship or a violent fight; music evokes a gut reaction unobtainable in any other way."[27]

Perhaps one of the most important elements governing the depth of our emotional response to music is contingent on the context, or the circumstances, in which the music is consumed. For example, we might thoroughly enjoy a piece of music at a concert in the early evening, but our feelings toward that same piece of music blasting out of a neighbor's house at 4 a.m. might be quite different.

A broader view of how context can mediate our responses to music is offered by Meyer, who points out: "Meaning and communication cannot be separated from the cultural context in which they arise."[28] If we were to look for an example of this, we might turn to a report in the *Los Angeles Times* in 2009 that contrasted the lives of American baby-boomer retirees seeking low-cost, small-town values and solitude in Columbus, New Mexico, with their Mexican neighbors across the border in nearby Palomas, where the effects of economic depression have been exacerbated by their country's drug war.[29] In such circumstances, these two communities, even though they are separated by a short car journey, have been shaped by quite different cultural, social, linguistic, historical, economic, religious, and personal experiences, so it is entirely possible that their "beliefs and attitudes" toward a given piece of music in one community music might result in different connotative and referential responses in the other.[30] Juslin and Västfjäll point to the impact of "cultural impact/ learning" on a mechanism such as musical expectancy, which reflects certain learned criteria, and this learned criteria clearly might differ from one culture to another, making "listeners from different cultures react differently to the same piece of music."[31] In a paper that appeared in *Emotion Review* in 2012, Juslin developed this position, saying that "emotional reactions to music are strongly influenced by factors in the *listener*, the *music* and the *context*. Because all of these are likely to differ across cultures, what is surprising is not that there *are* cross cultural differences, but they are not even larger."[32] Every culture talks and every culture sings, and, as Meyer points out, "In most cultures there is a tendency to associate musical experience with extra-musical experience."[33] Such extramusical experiences acquire their force and immediacy from the culture and/ or the context from which they emerge, so that the association of a certain piece of music with a particular referential experience depends "on the beliefs and attitudes of the culture toward that experience."[34] For example, the melody of "God Save the Queen," the United Kingdom's national anthem, is likely to arouse quite different connotations and referential meanings than it is to those in the United States, where the same melody is used for "My Country, 'tis of Thee."

Depending on who and where we are in the world, there will always be cultural, social, linguistic, historical, economic, religious, and personal circumstances (what Meyer calls "the beliefs and attitudes" of the consuming culture) likely to influence meanings we attribute and extract from an artistic or musical experience. The point here is that music represents a specific form of communication, and, as Janet Wolff argues in her book *The Social Production of Art*, judgments and evaluations of works of art and music are socially enabled and socially constructed events.[35] But just as these unique circumstances can influence meaning for the consumer of art or music, they can equally influence the creator. In 1934, the English composer and conductor Constant Lambert argued that the creation of music should be set against its social background, rejecting the notion that musicians somehow remain splendidly autonomous from their personal circumstances, "as though they produced patterns of notes in a spiritual vacuum, uninfluenced by the landscape, social life and political situations surrounding them."[36] As Wolff points out, art and music are "repositories of cultural meaning,"[37] to which Joost Smiers has added, "Creators of art or music are hothouses of cultural meaning."[38] Thus the creation and consumption of art and music do not take place in a neutral field but are subject to unique socially and culturally constructed conventions at the point of creation *and* of consumption. Clotaire Rapille attributes these conventions to what he calls "Culture Codes," the unconscious reading we apply to any given thing as a result of the culture in which we are raised—be it food, relationships, consumer goods, art, or music. "It is obvious to everyone cultures are different from one another," he writes. "What most people don't realise is that these differences actually lead to our processing the same information in different ways."[39] Different national, ethnic, and racial audiences are likely to interpret the same materials differently, since media users selectively assimilate and interpret media texts, and this process of selection and interpretation is operated through their own specific cultural perceptions and experience. Responses to globally disseminated, mainly Anglo-Americanized culture, expression, aesthetic idioms, and stylistic elements might, or might not, be interpreted as the producers intended and may be highly differentiated, depending in part on levels of exposure at a national, regional, or global level, and in part on the social characteristics of specific publics. Studies have also revealed the existence of strong national and local cultural resistance to global or transnational media.[40]

Here it is useful to turn to aspects of the Reception Theory, which originated at the hands of Hans-Robert Jauss in the late 1960s to study the reader's reception to literary texts. Briefly, within this paradigm, audiences are understood to be active rather than passive, to be engaged in a process of making, rather than simply absorbing, meanings. In the 1970s the cultural theorist Stuart Hall at Birmingham University's Centre for Contemporary Cultural Studies in the United Kingdom developed the theory further in his influential essay "Encoding/Decoding." This densely theoretical account of how messages/meanings are produced and disseminated referred to television, but, inasmuch as it is a model that has been successfully adapted to literature, film, theater, and even landscapes, its broad application within jazz might help our understanding of how different audiences, social groups, and cultures might extract different meanings from jazz. Hall suggested that there are three possible ways of interpreting a text—the Dominant or Preferred Reading, the Negotiated Reading, and the Oppositional Reading. In the case of the Dominant or Preferred Reading, meaning comes embedded with "the everyday knowledge of social structures and 'how things work for all practical purposes in this culture,'"[41] a "hegemonic viewpoint" that appears "coterminous with what is 'natural,' 'inevitable' and 'taken for granted about the social order.'"[42]

However, while audiences from within the culture might accept a Dominant Reading, there is also scope for others to "negotiate" their own interpretation or take an "oppositional" stance to the Dominant Reading, so producing the Negotiated Code, which contains a mixture of adaptive and oppositional elements; this "accords the privileged position to the dominant . . . while reserving the right to make a more negotiated application to 'local conditions.'"[43] Finally, the Oppositional Code is when the text is "detotalised" in order to "retotalise" it within some alternative framework or reference[44]—for example, rejecting the text because it does not fit one's own life experiences and qualifying other aspects of the text. Consumers of the text are understood to be active rather than passive, engaged in processes of making, rather than simply absorbing, meanings based on their individual life experiences and cultural background. A basic acceptance of meaning of a specific text emerges when a group of consumers with a cultural background similar to that of the creator interpret the text in a similar way, while those consumers whose cultural heritage has less in common with the creator of the text will recognize less of the creator's intended meaning. For example, a translation of slang cannot be taken at face value by those outside the culture because of the nuances of meaning associated within it; we might guess at those nuances and think we have reached an accurate approximation of what they imply, but we can never be sure. Broadly speaking, then, the "Encoding/Decoding" model acknowledges the presence of a strong or preferred meaning, but Hall and his colleagues also saw texts as polysemic—that they are "open" to a number of possible meanings—and are affected by variable factors such as socioeconomic and cultural frameworks, past experiences, and context.

Within the realm of jazz, the polysemous nature of the music was suggested as early as 1927 by the British author R. W. S. Mendl in his book *The Appeal of Jazz*. "For the people of Europe," he wrote, "jazz music has meant something rather different from that which its original inventors intended or from that which it signified for the people of the United States of America."[45] For Americans, Mendl argued, jazz is "native to the soil," adding, "To the American citizen [jazz] is a home product expressing something of the life he has made his own,"[46] while to an Englishman, a music so suggestive of American modernity was "inapposite to his traditions, his ancient Gothic cathedrals and his old Elizabethan and Georgian houses."[47]

Although the analogy to Elizabethan and Georgian houses was of its time (1927) and could have been better made, the broader point here is that the cultural backdrop of English audiences is different from that of American audiences, so it is possible that they may extract different meanings from the music because they do not share the same sociocultural experiences (or the "beliefs and attitudes") of the culture instigating the music.

That such a possibility existed was observed some fourteen or fifteen years later by the writer, author, and social commentator Ralph Ellison when he noted the response of European jazz fans to the experimental forms of bebop being developed in the Harlem jazz club Minton's in the early 1940s. Recounting his observations in his 1959 essay "The Golden Age, Time Past," he wrote: "Minton's has more meaning for European jazz fans than for Americans, even for those who regularly went there. Certainly it has a *different* meaning."[48] He then goes on to describe how coming from a different culture may account for this: "For [the Europeans] it is associated with those continental cafés in which great changes, political and artistic, have been plotted; [Minton's] is to modern jazz what Café Voltaire in Zurich is to the Dadaist phase of modern literature and painting."[49] The analogy is well made: Café Voltaire, which opened in February 1916, featured the spoken word, dance, song, and music. Although it was the birthplace of the Dadaist movement, it featured artists from every sector of the avant-garde, many of whom went on to change the face of their artistic disciplines in just the same manner as the bebop artists went on to change the face of theirs. And "those continental cafés in which great changes, political and artistic, have been plotted" might also include the cafes on the West Bank (of the River Seine) in Paris such as the Café Procope, whose patrons in the eighteenth century included Enlightenment thinkers such as Voltaire himself, Rousseau, and Beaumarchais, who debated revolutionary ideas that would influence important thinkers of the French and American revolutions, as well as, later, Balzac, Verlaine, and Victor Hugo. As Ellison appositely concludes: "There is a context of meaning in which Minton's and the musical activities which took place there can be meaningfully placed."[50]

As Donald Sassoon has pointed out in *The Culture of the Europeans: From 1800 to the Present*, "The spread of jazz to Europe in the 1920s was the first great trend in music history to occur mainly through recording."[51] This meant that during the interwar period and immediate post–World War II years, the cultural context in which American jazz was consumed in Europe could hardly have been more different from the way it was consumed in the United States. The only access the majority of European fans had to American jazz was via shellac 78-rpm recordings with a playing time of around three minutes (nearer five minutes for a twelve-inch shellac recording), unless they lived in large urban centers such as London, Amsterdam, Stockholm, Copenhagen, or Paris, where they could see occasional live concerts by visiting American bands.[52] Thus their engagement with American jazz was largely through the disembodied sound of a jazz recording. In the early 1930s, jazz fans in London began to develop an institution known as the Rhythm Club, which celebrated jazz fandom as a culture of record collectors and scholars who, somewhat self-consciously, took the music *seriously*. As Francis Newton (the pen name of historian Eric Hobsbawm) notes in *The Jazz Scene*, these clubs multiplied rapidly, so that "by the end of 1935 ninety-eight had been formed" in London and the provinces.[53] They were, in effect, forums for weekly recorded music recitals, whereby fans would gather around a record player in a meeting room and a speaker would talk about an artist or style, illustrating his talk with recordings.

As the concept took off, some Rhythm Clubs also provided a forum for local musicians to perform and talk about their music. The concept quickly spread to several European countries, including France (most notably the Hot Club of France, formed in Paris in December 1932), Holland, Belgium, Denmark, Sweden, Norway, and, in 1934, Berlin (where one of the founding members was Francis Wolff, who escaped to New York in 1938 and together with Alfred Lion formed Blue Note Records). Each musical community practices critical choice in what it hears, and such responses can assume greater significance among those who share similar responses to the same music. It is from this approximation of objectivity that a consensus of values emerges, which might be at variance with the originating culture. As *Harper's Magazine* noted in 1947: "To understand the function of this sort of organization in the life of the European jazz fan, his utter dependence on the phonograph records will have to be remembered. Cut-off from a living music by time as well as space [they submit] to a peculiar shift of values."[54]

While context can help create meaning it can also alter and transform it, so the consumption of jazz in Rhythm Clubs of the 1930s and the immediate postwar period represents a unique socially and culturally constructed circumstance: audiences were completely dislocated from the inductive effect of the cultural and social ritual associated with the creation of jazz in American clubs, bars, and dance halls, where, as Kathy J.

Ogren has pointed out, "The rich exchange between performers and their audiences became a definitive feature of jazz entertainment."[55] In contrast, the disembodied sounds of American jazz on recordings were reinterpreted by Rhythm Club audiences in the context of an America of their imagination, an America they had never visited but whose landscape and urban space had been made mythic through the influence of Hollywood films and American media and literature. Consuming American jazz in this way allowed them to participate at one remove in an American musical culture they could not be part of but sought to re-create in their imagination.

In the United Kingdom, the Rhythm Club concept was transferred to a radio format on June 8, 1940, by the British Broadcasting Corporation (BBC) with the weekly program *Radio Rhythm Club*, presented by Charles Chilton with resident bands led by the likes of Harry Parry and featuring musicians such as George Shearing and later Buddy Featherstonehaugh. As Christina Baade notes, "first, the ongoing series signalled the BBC's recognition that the audience for jazz and swing deserved to be served in a sustained and specialized manner. Second, with its informative gramophone recitals, jam sessions, talks and guest appearances by professional musicians and critics, the program's format followed the model established in 1933 by Rhythm Clubs throughout the United Kingdom."[56] Key here, perhaps, is the way jazz was disseminated, first through the Rhythm Clubs and then on the radio, where a similar discursive format was maintained. Jazz was not regarded as mere "entertainment" aimed at a broad audience, but as a music that demanded careful, engaged listening that was framed by informative, analytical discussion on a par with classical music (the program was broadcast on the BBC's classical music network, the Third Program). It simply served to highlight the central role recordings played in European jazz culture, recordings that lagged behind developments in the American jazz scene. *Metronome* magazine noted: "They have heard scarcely of any of the great US jazz musicians who have come up in the last five or ten years."[57] This contrasted with the presentation of jazz by American broadcasters, where the emphasis was on live jazz of the moment, and talk was confined to introducing band members and repertoire, a word from the sponsor and a few wisecracks thrown in for good measure.

As the Rhythm Clubs gave way to jazz clubs in the late 1940s, the BBC moved with the times, renaming the program *Jazz Club* in 1947. Produced by Mark White, its intention was to reflect the trend away from Rhythm

Clubs to jazz clubs in the United Kingdom during this period. In its early years *Jazz Club* largely maintained the format of the *Radio Rhythm Club*, which included presenting features on historic American jazz recordings using British musicians playing the role of their American heroes. For example, trumpeter Humphrey Lyteltton's first appearance on the show was replicating Louis Armstrong's performance on "West End Blues" with clarinetist Sid Phillips as Johnny Dodds and trombonist Geoff Love as Kid Ory. "Before the idea that British jazz groups could write their own material and establish their own unique musical identities, *Jazz Club* would often feature British bands playing the music of famous American bands, imitating their style and sound," said British Library sound archivist Paul Wilson. "The closer the band sounded to the American model, the better they were considered to be."[58] This was a period when jazz fans and musicians outside the United States looked to America as a model of authenticity and modernity. For most European musicians during this period, the imperative was to sound "American" in order to sound "authentic." As the British saxophonist, bandleader, composer, and arranger Sir John Dankworth described: "There was a period, and I confess to being part of that period in the 1950s when I was a young musician, when to be told you sounded like an American musician, or your band had an American-style rhythm section, was the highest compliment you could ever receive."[59] And when that compliment came from a visiting American jazzman, it made news: for example, when the British band The Jazz Couriers, led by the then two top UK tenor saxophonists, Tubby Hayes and Ronnie Scott, opened for the Dave Brubeck Quartet at the Dominion Theatre, London, on February 16, 1958, there was wide coverage of Brubeck's comment that "they sound more like an American band than we do."[60]

In order to get closer to the source of jazz modernism, both Dankworth and tenor saxophonist Ronnie Scott took jobs as dance band musicians aboard Cunard transatlantic liners in 1947 in order to see Charlie Parker and his Quintet (with Miles Davis) and the Dizzy Gillespie Big Band on 52nd Street during the liner's three-day turn-around periods in Manhattan. These musicians, and others who had joined them in "Geraldo's Navy"[61]—including Tommy Pollard, Leon Calvert, and Laurie Morgan— were inspired to form the Club XI in London, Europe's first bebop club; a recording of Johnny Dankworth and his Club XI Quartet recorded live at London's St. George's Hall on April 9, 1949, reveals a conscious emulation of the broadcasts of the period from New York's Birdland Jazz Club, even down to a UK emcee imitating the unmistakable style of Symphony

Sid.[62] Dankworth subsequently formed the Dankworth Seven in 1950, which played in the style of Miles Davis's Birth of the Cool band, and in 1953 formed a big band that subsequently appeared at the Newport Jazz Festival in 1959.[63] Of the band *Downbeat* magazine reported: "This is top drawer big band playing, smooth swinging and powerful . . . and proved it is fit for consideration soon after such evidently unapproachable eminences as Basie and Ellington. To other American bands Dankworth takes no back seat."[64] Here, Dankworth and his musical colleagues were playing in the hegemonic style of American big band jazz; thus in terms of the Reception Theory, Dankworth's music during this period might be said to be performed in the Dominant model of jazz expressionism—a "preferred" reading for American and UK audiences and critics who shared these values, reflecting "how things work in the [American jazz] culture,"[65] and reflecting a "hegemonic viewpoint" of big band jazz.[66]

Dankworth's and Scott's experiences should be seen in the context of a Europe-wide trend in jazz during the 1950s where authenticity was perceived—both by musicians and by their audiences—in terms of "sounding American." Although there were brief appearances in Europe by visiting American jazz musicians—most notably by Charlie Parker, Miles Davis, and Dizzy Gillespie—key developments in American jazz continued to be experienced mainly through recordings. Attempts by local musicians at assimilation and emulation, to American ears at least, lacked the authenticity of their American counterparts. As the *Metronome Yearbook 1957* noted: "The word foreign has a specially poor connotation when it comes to jazz because the musicians of other lands . . . have nothing but records to work with."[67] For most European musicians and fans, then, a Dominant Reading of jazz prevailed where meaning was construed in terms of how closely they were able to sound like the American stars. "Local" trumpeters, trombonists, saxophone players, pianists, bassists, and drummers for the most part followed the lead of the American masters, whose latest recordings were eagerly transcribed and absorbed as soon as they crossed the Atlantic. "Local" vocalists even sang with American accents, including L2 speakers in Europe (to whom English/American is a second language), while "local" musicians, fans, and animators, both English and European L2 speakers, often somewhat self-consciously spoke in what was imagined to be the argot of American jazz musicians, possibly inspired by Hollywood films or through personal encounter. Thus musical instruments became "horns" or "axes," a musical phrase became "a lick," a repeated phrase "a riff," a drum set "traps," to practice was "to woodshed," and so on. Frequently, musicians, fans, and animators referred (and continue to refer) to their heroes by their first names or nicknames (as if they were personal friends, even though they may have never met, or never would meet in the case of the departed). It was an informality that suggests an "insider" status from which is derived a sense of identity,[68] to which might be added—to use Susan Marling's apposite term—"proxy membership" in an imagined American jazz culture.[69]

Despite the increasing sophistication of recording technology with the development of the vinyl long-playing record, both sides of which were capable of holding around thirty minutes of music, consumers abroad continued to remain remote from the social milieu in which the music was created. Fans and musicians attempted to compensate in other ways, often by creating their own readings of jazz in use. As early as 1952, the promoter Norman Granz noted how European audiences responded differently than American audiences when his Jazz at the Philharmonic Troupe made their first tour of Europe that year: "The reaction of the audience in Stockholm, and, as it turned out later, throughout Europe, was completely different from the reaction of a U.S. audience," he wrote in the pages of *Downbeat* magazine. "The European audiences . . . have a healthier respect for all art forms, whether it be dance, painting, or in this instance, jazz. As a result of their viewing it differently from us, they were inclined to ask different questions and to listen to different things from American jazz fans."[70]

By 1955, the *New York Times* was also commenting on the perceived difference of European audiences, who, they reported, "find in jazz a subject for serious study. Theirs is what most Americans would call a 'long-haired approach.' They like to contemplate it, take it apart and see what makes it what it is. They like to ponder the strength of its individuality and speculate on the qualities that differentiate it from the folk music of any other country."[71] In terms of the Reception Theory, this response broadly conforms to the Negotiated Code, whereby consumers of the text acknowledge the Dominant Reading but negotiate their own reading in use, influenced by their local sociocultural experiences.[72] Here jazz is submitted to analysis and enquiry and retotalized within the alternative framework of an imaginary jazz culture influenced by American media including films, literature, and magazines, mediated by variable factors such as the local socioeconomic and cultural environment in which the music was consumed. The result was that the music appeared to assume greater gravitas to European fans than was perhaps common inside the

United States, with American jazz musicians becoming cultural heroes abroad, a status that came as something of a surprise to most of them. Brubeck scholar Keith Hatschek reports that during Dave Brubeck's 1958 tour of Poland, the pianist's wife, Iola, became alarmed that they were being followed after their second tour stop in Gdansk. She had noticed that the same people that were lurking in the background on their first tour stop seemed to be on the train or bus with them once again. It turned out that a contingent of Poland's leading jazz musicians and fans were following the quartet from city to city.[73]

Brubeck's tour of Poland in 1958 was the first by a US jazz musician behind the Iron Curtain.[74] For Polish audiences and communist-dominated societies in central and eastern Europe after 1945, jazz was construed in largely ideological terms. In 1946, the Soviet government's daily newspaper, *Izvestia*, attacked jazz as an example of perverse Western vulgarity,[75] while in contrast, one Polish fan told Brubeck years later, "What you brought to Poland wasn't just jazz. It was the Grand Canyon. It was the Empire State Building. It was America."[76] For both the Russian apparatchiks and Polish jazz fans, jazz evoked quite specific metanarratives of extramusical connotations: on the one hand the apparatchiks saw jazz as a force that corrupted Soviet ideology, what S. Frederick Starr in *Red and Hot: Jazz in the Soviet Union* described as "a sinister plot by the American government to break down local cultural resistance to American imperial expansion,"[77] while on the other, Polish fans saw American jazz as a metaphor for freedom, disseminated and made real through short wave radio broadcasts such as Willis Conover's *Music USA* program on Voice of America. Here, meaning emerged from a subjective response to the music in which jazz is not simply a thing in itself, but part of something greater, an Imaginary America with its connotations of modernity, freedom, and democracy. It acquired its force from the culture and context in which it was consumed: totalitarian states where the denial of freedom—of expression and association—created a uniquely socially constructed circumstance at the point of consumption. Listening to jazz on radio (for long periods a subversive act in itself, since it was forbidden by the authorities), or on tape recordings of programs such as *Music USA* circulated in the underground, created an alternative reality in which to engage with a kind of "freedom" that was denied in the everyday.

In contrast, the reception of jazz in Western Europe could hardly have been more different from that of Eastern Europe, since it was quickly identified as an aspect of modernism that was sweeping through the arts at the time (examined in greater detail in Chapter 5). Thus, construing meaning in terms of jazz-as-an-aspect-of-modernism in the more affluent, democratic West, or in terms of freedom, an aspiration born of the denial of democracy in the Eastern European states, represents two fundamentally different perspectives from which to extract meaning from jazz. Yet whatever the connotations and referential meanings these audiences might attribute to a specific jazz performance, whether audiences in Western Europe or in the former communist-controlled states of Eastern Europe, they might be quite different again from those extracted by audiences in the originating culture, the United States. But as World Music has shown, even though music may not yield universal meanings, you do not have to be a part of the originating culture, or share their cultural values, to enjoy it. The problem comes when the values attributed to enjoying it—or indeed, producing a negative response—are assumed to be "universal" or the same as the originating culture. It is quite probable, for example, that American World Music fans who bought and enjoyed the best-selling album *Egypt* by Youssou n'Dour did not do so because they shared the Senegalese fans' response its Sufist lyrics in praise of Islam. In other words, American World Music fans may have enjoyed the music, but they did not share the originating culture's values of what the music meant to them. In jazz, some American fans and critics often claimed that European rhythm sections "did not swing," but many Europeans argued that they swung in a way that was right for them. As music psychologists Patrik Juslin and Daniel Västfjäll have suggested, cultural impact can make "listeners from different cultures react differently to the same piece of music,"[78] suggesting that while jazz may be universal, the connotative and referential meanings the music conveys are not.

# Jazz and American Cultural Power

**T**he twentieth century was undoubtedly—as Gertrude Stein claimed—the American Century, likely to be remembered less for the manifestation of American hard power, despite successful military interventions in World War I and Word War II and less successful adventures in Korea, Vietnam, Iraq, and Afghanistan, but rather for the extensive influence of its soft power. The terms "hard power" and "soft power" were coined by Joseph Nye, Jr.—while he was director of the Center for International Affairs at Harvard University—as aspects of a country's ability to achieve its purpose by "controlling the behaviour of others."[1] The difference between them is one of degree, since hard power is the ability to achieve a desired outcome through coercion, which stems from a country's military or economic might, while soft power, or what has sometimes been called "the second face of power," is the ability to shape the preferences of others through indirect means. A country's soft power resources stem from the attractiveness of its culture, its domestic policies, and the style and substance of its foreign policies, each of which can be effective in isolation or in combination. Unlike the realpolitik of hard power, soft power is at its most telling in securing broad ideological or philosophical goals. In the case of the United States, Nye points out that "American culture is a relatively inexpensive and useful soft power resource,"[2] that is routinely used as an instrument of foreign policy, since "a country that stands astride popular channels of communication has more opportunities to get its messages across and to affect the preferences of others."[3] America may be a superpower, but it is also a superculture that occupies a dominant cultural space in the world where mass popular culture is a form of power, a virtual empire of signs, myths, and signifiers. "The impact of this power," writes Derek Ellwood, associate professor in international history at the University of Bologna, "can be just as significant historically as the conventional military, political and economic forms of power, and can never be separated from them."[4]

For generations, the sounds, images, and subliminal messages of American popular culture have provided the soundtrack to the lives of Americans and countless millions of others around the globe. Wherever the dollar has gone, American popular culture and ideology have followed, the *New York Times* noting that "for Americans abroad, a troubling aspect of our popular culture is that there is so much of it."[5] Throughout the American Century, the increasing global footprint of American cultural themes, codes, norms, and values has represented a permanent advertisement for America's symbolic, iconic status in the world. As a result it has become easy and comfortable to think of imported American popular culture as if it were a natural part of the global cultural environment. But as Reinhold Wagnleitner has pointed out, "The sway of soft power has reached its highest degree of subtlety when an ideological and symbolic superiority is installed as quasi-natural."[6]

As the world's mightiest country in terms of soft power resources,[7] the United States has seen certain outcomes flow from them, not least the number of polls that reveal how popular its culture is among the citizenry of other nations. This in turn has had a powerful effect on consumer choice, since, as Maoz Azaryahu has pointed out, "In the popular mind worldwide, America is not only the 'land of the free,' but a consumer paradise. The notion of America as technologically advanced, economically prosperous and culturally vibrant makes it a model for the rest of the world."[8] Such powerful imagery exerts considerable allure for consumers of American popular culture, in the same way an expensive Paris fashion house attracts consumers—because of the added value it commands in the marketplace. This conflation of American cultural products with American cultural power presents a powerful—some have argued irresistible—form of cultural branding. For example, when the American fast food giant McDonald's went international it faced stiff competition from established local cuisine, but it was its very "American-ness" that made it attractive to consumers. As Victoria de Grazia of Columbia University points out, "The food at McDonald's was a matter of indifference. It was the *cultural associations* that made for its appeal."[9] As a 2003 report in the pages of the *New York Times* about the impact of American fast food in the Indian subcontinent noted, one Indian family described their experience of a McDonald's restaurant as stepping out for "a slice of America."[10]

This domination of the cultural spaces beyond American shores may owe much to America's economic and political strength, but as historian Eric Hobsbawm has pointed out, the real source of American cultural, or soft power, rests in "the attractions of the affluent consumer society enjoyed and propagated by the US, which pioneered it . . . and Hollywood's world conquest."[11] This chapter, then, briefly explores the influence of consumerism and Hollywood in their role as soft power resources, and then looks at ways in which the soft power potential of American jazz has been exploited by US governmental agencies. Since jazz historians in the past have tended to concentrate on the creators of the music rather than its receivers, this chapter asks if the soft power resources of consumerism and Hollywood and the messages of America they convey might somehow influence the reception and consumption of jazz beyond the shores of the United States. Or do audiences consume American jazz as a thing-in-itself, devoid of cultural and ideological meaning?

In 1941, the American magazine mogul Henry R. Luce, who believed passionately in the idea of an "American Century," declared, "American jazz, Hollywood movies, American slang, American machines and patented products are in fact the only things that every community in the world, from Zanzibar to Hamburg, recognizes in common."[12] Although it was probably only partly true then, it certainly seems true today following the emergence of the United States as the world's first (and only) superpower and superculture in the final half of the twentieth century. Ever since President Woodrow Wilson addressed the World's Salesmanship Congress in

Detroit on July 10, 1916, when he told those gathered that America's "democracy of business" had to take the lead in "the struggle for the peaceful conquest of world,"[13] Washington has well understood the importance of commerce in complementing its growing political, economic, and military influence. Before addressing the three thousand salesmen, managers, and executives gathered in the Arcadia Auditorium on the morning of the congress, President Wilson had met with Henry Ford. Just a couple of miles cross-town, in Highland Park, headquarters of the Ford Motor Company, Ford was revolutionizing mass production techniques to produce his Model-T motorcar. His moving assembly line was just one of many innovations that enabled American business to lead the world in marketing standardized, low-cost goods in volume. As America developed its big corporate producers, manufacturing know-how, and institutions of business, it was also establishing itself as the world's first mass consumer culture. Consumerism, as defined by the *American Heritage Dictionary*, means "the theory that a progressively greater consumption of goods is economically beneficial"; it embodies the allure of libertarian individualism, which promotes every individual's potential for fulfillment (the American Dream) through the pursuit of consumption (consumerism) with an implicit sense of modernity (the always new).

Consumerism has its roots in America's economic expansion in the 1880s, when, as William Leach points out, American business began to move toward a new commercial aesthetic of marketing goods in volume, which he describes as the core aesthetic of American capitalist culture.[14] As the production and distribution infrastructures of modern industry were set in place, the first stirrings of a mass market–led culture began to be felt, coming to fruition in the 1920s, which are usually portrayed as the first consumerist decade. The Jazz Age was celebrated by a young generation who had access to an unprecedented range of goods and services that were beyond the imagination of previous generations, creating a powerful link between consumption and modernism. Indeed, from the 1920s the world was modernized partly through consumption and the mechanization of daily life through a hitherto unimaginable range of consumer durables such as washing machines, vacuum cleaners, fridges, telephones, the box Brownie, and the automobile, which gave the decade its sense of momentum into the future. Consumerism's success was in its adeptness in recycling the American Dream into strategies of commercial persuasion, linking the world of self-fulfillment—a world where every dream comes true—to goods sold in the marketplace. This expanding frontier saw its mature development in huge shopping malls, discount chain stores, and a fast food culture that "dramatically transformed the nature of consumption."[15] If the meaning of life is to be found in the things we possess—or so the ideology of consumerism goes—then to consume is to be alive, and to remain alive we must consume. By 1968, consumerism had become such a feature of American life that playwright Arthur Miller was able to quip in his play *The Price*: "Today you're unhappy? Can't figure it out? What is the salvation? Go shopping."[16]

In 1945, the United States was seen as the apotheosis of modernity, the "always new," and happiness in its most updated form, consumerism. Although Europe had been willing consumers of exported American culture for several decades prior to 1945, the most forceful deployment of American soft power occurred in the years following World War II, when it became, as Geir Lundestad noted in *The United States and Western Europe since 1945*, "part of an American sphere of influence, even American 'empire.'"[17] Highly influential in maximizing this influence was $13 billion of Marshall Plan aid (also known as the European Recovery Program), carefully targeted by way of structural reform to rebuild Continental Europe. Setting the pace for economic revival were US diplomats promising European governments a rise in living standards if they adopted the model of American consumerism. Ultimately, the aims of the plan were to create a huge regional market for American goods, services, and media products and encourage an attractive, prosperous, consumerist lifestyle that would serve to discredit the ideology of the Soviet Union and its satellite states. One important element of the plan, as J. Bradford De Long and Barry Eichengreen point out, was that "as a condition for receiving Marshall Plan aid, each country was required to develop a program for removing quotas and other trade controls,"[18] in order to permit free trade and stimulate economic growth. It meant that once US governmental agencies had secured satisfactory agreements with client countries, a seemingly endless supply of American goods, services, and ideas flowed into everyday European life and consciousness. As Joseph S. Nye has pointed out, while "the dollars invested in the Marshall Plan were important in achieving American objectives in the reconstruction of Europe, [so too] were the ideas transmitted by popular culture."[19]

For a Europe still emerging from the horrors of World War II and the industrial, commercial, social, and cultural practices of the 1930s, modernity and all that it implied—Americanization through the spread of consumerism—represented profound changes that were widely perceived to be for the better, "America represented the coming 'consumer society' . . . and the new consumerism depended on different cultural values. Consumer society suggested a life orientated around acts of purchase and a materialistic philosophy. It valued the productive and the technical and was accompanied by the products of the new mass culture, from Hollywood films and comic strips to home appliances and fast food."[20]

Consumerism was a market about to take off in late 1940s Western Europe, since most households still did not possess a fridge, a television, or a motorcar.[21] All this was to change in a remarkably short space of time. As a fast-accelerating consumer boom took hold, one of its immediate benefits was a rapid rise in living standards. In the two decades after 1953, real wages almost tripled in Germany and the Benelux countries; in Italy they were higher still, and in the United Kingdom the purchasing power of the average citizen doubled.[22] In the face of growing economic prosperity, the specter of the "air conditioned nightmare" (as Henry Miller once labeled America) receded, and with it an increasing openness to American ideas and culture, especially among the young generation. No longer did Europe's youth look to the cultural mores of their parents and grandparents, but instead embraced a new order that seemed more glamorous, attractive, and modern. Consumerism represented a new realm of freedom and the basis of a new kind of resistance through the act of purchase. "American culture was attractive precisely because its pleasures were unauthorized," wrote Richard Pells: "From the 1940s on, youthful Europeans identified with those elements in American society that appeared marginal, alienated and definitely not middle class: juvenile delinquents (as long as they looked like Sal Mineo or James Dean), beat poets, black jazz musicians, rock stars . . . [because] they differed, culturally and stylistically, from complacent European bourgeoisie and could embody the adolescent spirit of disaffection and impudence."[23]

For a culture like the postwar United Kingdom, which had little to look forward to beyond the next Benjamin Britten opera, American-style consumerism seemed like a treasure trove of gleaming possibilities. For the first time teenagers represented a distinct target group of consumers with cash to spend. As Tony Judt wrote in *Postwar: A History of Europe since 1945*, "Young people were spending a lot of money on clothes, but even more—far more—on music."[24] In Europe, as in America, the first thing a liberated teenager did when the family budget permitted was to buy a record player and gramophone records. Transistor radios also had become ubiquitous by the 1960s, with many young fans tuning to Radio Free Europe and Voice of America (especially the long-running program *Music USA*) for the latest trends in popular music and jazz. A novel American device called the installment plan (or hire purchase in the United Kingdom) meant that for a small monthly repayment, expensive instruments like trumpets, saxophones, electric guitars, basses, and drum kits became available to most homes. These consumer items, such as Fender, Martin, or Gibson guitars; Rogers, Slingerland, or Gretsch drums; and Selmer or Conn saxophones; plus American long-playing records and singles made possible by the manufacture and distribution systems that served the consumer revolution, all acted as cultural signifiers and carriers of an American way of life that suggested to neophyte musicians and their fans that the real thing was happening elsewhere—in the America of their imaginations. "You just knew as a teenager there was something really going on over there [in the United States]," recalled guitarist Jimmy Page when he first heard Chuck Berry while growing up in England.[25] In his book *Revolt into Style*, George Melly observed: "Early or primitive pop [in the United Kingdom during the 1950s] looked exclusively towards America as its source and inspiration, and while it was true that this America was largely imaginary, it represented the present . . . the country of 'Now' where everyone is beautiful and nobody grows old."[26]

A compelling aspect of American-style consumerism was how it became associated with discourses of "freedom"—from the freedom to pursue abundance to the freedom of speech. "The epic of the frontier and America's mythical West had served as a symbol of freedom long before the consumer revolution," wrote Rob Kroes.[27] "Posters for shipping lines, emigration societies and land development agencies contributed to the continuing construction of America as the very site of freedom and space."[28] It is a theme that has continued into the present, and even though the Marlboro Man may be under siege at home, he is almost impossible to escape in Asia. Equally, the American Dream, the yang to the yin of American Freedom, was also appropriated by advertisers by linking the powerful imagery of the West to the sale of ordinary consumer goods. Consumerism, leisure-time, and freedom thus became inextricably woven together in the powerful world of advertising, where image is everything to the extent that today, the mere mention of the word "America" now "triggers an association with freedom."[29] The right, or "freedom," to pursue abundance might have been living the American Dream, but it also represented "prosperity and consumption as a way of life—the 'American way of life,'"[30] and despite the concerns voiced[31] at the perceived threat to

European cultural identity by an "American consumer-sustained cultural hegemony and the adaptation of the American lifestyle,"[32] consumerism's ideal of a normal life being abundant in the possession of goods that are advertised and merchandised to the masses became central to fostering common consumption practices around the globe. By 1992, Francis Fukuyama was able to write that the whole of humanity was linked through "the universal nexus of modern (American) consumerism . . . [and] while not every country is capable of becoming a consumer society in the near future, there is hardly a society in the world that does not embrace the goal itself."[33]

Ranking alongside consumerism as a powerful and compelling element of American soft power is the movie industry, with its power to Americanize the imagination through the seductive images of an affluent American consumer lifestyle. Hollywood entrenches the American Dream and reinforces the dynamics of American mythology. "Nowhere else is U.S. cultural hegemony as nearly all encompassing as in the area of the movies," writes Reinhold Wagnleitner,[34] pointing to Hollywood's world domination, where in the 1990s, between 85 and 90 percent of all movies screened in Western Europe were American. It is perhaps unsurprising, then, that U.S. governmental agencies have long regarded Hollywood as a key instrument of soft power whose ability to shape the behavior of others has long rested on the way cinematography projects an attractive vision of America's culture and ideology. "Pictures often convey values more powerfully than words, and Hollywood is the world's greatest promoter and exporter of visual images," writes John Fraim.[35] In all countries, art and entertainment act as carriers of social and political messages, but when it comes to the United States, Joost Smiers points out that "the difference lies in the rational and systematic ways in which the U.S. government and cultural enterprises have fine tuned economic interests, foreign policy concerns and cultural content . . . which [enhances] all manifestations of U.S. power."[36]

Historically, the US government's close cooperation with Hollywood dates back to 1915, when in response to a request for assistance, the US secretary of war, John Weeks, ordered the army to "provide every reasonable courtesy to D. W. Griffiths," who was then filming *Birth of a Nation*, resulting in more than one thousand cavalry troops and a military band appearing in the film. This collaboration became ongoing through the 1920s, with the Oscar-winning film *Wings* (1927) made with major support from the War Department. By 1941, Darryl F. Zanuck was able to argue convincingly before a congressional hearing that Hollywood produced "pictures so strong and powerful that they sold the American way of life, not only to America but the entire world."[37] In November 1944, shortly after President Franklin D. Roosevelt was returned to the presidency, the Office of War Information (OWI) produced a paper called "Draft Outline of a Directive on Projection of America" that attempted to confront the issue of "making other peoples favourably disposed toward us" after the cessation of hostilities in the European and the Far Eastern theaters of war.[38]

Along with the Hays Office and the Department of State, the OWI "worked to shape Hollywood products into effective propaganda tools, suggesting additions and deletions to films and denying licences to others."[39] This concern to ensure that America was projected in a favorable light reflected how the US government had become aware of the difficulty in sustaining American hegemony solely through military and economic means during the postwar years and the need to develop soft power resources to persuade others to buy into their values. These ends were pursued to such an extent that the Motion Picture Export Association of America had the reputation of being known as "the little State Department,"[40] and even moved to Washington, DC, to better coordinate its activities with government. One area where they successfully collaborated was in lobbying Capitol Hill to make it conditional for any country receiving Marshall Aid to open their markets to large quantities of American films. The political aim of this massive hearts-and-minds operation was "to present European audiences with a filmic counterweight to what the fascists and Nazis had shown them and to keep them away from communist and other leftist tendencies by seducing them with Hollywood films promoting the American way of life."[41]

And promote the American way of life they did, since there was no more powerful medium than the cinema to acquaint the world with American values, myths, and ideology. Hollywood gave everyone access to the same culture with set designs consciously constructed to popularize a lifestyle abundant in commodities that were advertised and merchandised to the masses. Films provided a diversion from life's daily grind that fueled a desire for entertainment and escapism. With unrestricted access to every film Hollywood could export, European audiences went in their millions to the cinema—in Italy three thousand new cinemas appeared, with 800 million seats sold in the year 1956, while in the first half of the 1950s, one thousand new picture houses opened in West Germany and about the same number in France.[42] As Brian Glasser has pointed out, "In France, the *cahiers du cinema* crowd loved the Hollywood product, seeing it in more depth, sophistication and subversion than the American public and infinitely preferring it to the stolid contemporary French fare of the period (dismissed as 'Le cinema du papa'). It would eventually lead to the French 'New Wave,' a very radical form of filmmaking (in certain aspects) that would in turn influence Hollywood. Equally, the post-war rise, or re-growth, of national cinemas, usually left leaning such as Italian neo-realism, meant that Hollywood was not the only player on the block in European cinema."[43] However, the sheer number of American films produced by the Hollywood studios far outstripped anything the European market was able to produce (whose main line of defense was to protect their domestic market share by making highly "national" films), nor were the Europeans able to compete with biblical blockbusters with casts of thousands, expensive chariot races, and special effects that showed the ten plagues of Egypt or the parting of the Red Sea.

Hollywood's appeal was rooted in the glamour and luster they brought to the gray surroundings in which they were viewed, so that "European teenagers identified the future with an America they hardly knew."[44] Cinema meant they were able to engage with an America of their imagination, a cultural space that offered something they did not have, but wanted. It may have been a cinematic, mediated version of reality, but it nevertheless represented a world of freedom without inhibitions or constraints for their escapist dreams. America was where the distinctions between myth and reality blurred, overlapped, and formed their own reality. As Rob Kroes observes, "Generation upon generation of Europeans, growing up after the war (1939–1945), can tell their own story of a mythical America as they constructed it, drawing on advertisements, songs, films, and so on . . . Mythical 'Americas' have become part and parcel of the collective memory of Europeans."[45]

During the 1950s, Hollywood responded to the perceived communist threat with a large number of films that participated in "the construction of a national consensus around national security policies and strategies,"[46] whereby a picture of everyday social idealism, self-discipline, respect for neighbors, civic life, and consumerism was threatened by alien forces at odds with the peaceful idealism of the United States. Of course, as Glasser points out, American cinema always had its dissenting voices, such as film noir in the 1940s and directors such as Douglas Sirk and Nicholas Ray in the 1950s, who often seemed to critique the Eisenhower Age even as they seemed to epitomize it.[47] But as Jean-Michel Valantin writes in *Hollywood, the Pentagon and Washington*, studio bosses, producers, and scriptwriters were well aware of

> the capacity for political interference following the redoubtable period of McCarthyism (1949–1953), with its black lists and denunciations on the pretext of Communist sympathies. Scriptwriters, who were receptive to the dominant trends of the national imagination and the pervading atmosphere of crisis, went along with and heightened the movement. They benefited at the same time from the more or less discreet support of organs of State liaison between Washington and Hollywood. The 1950s were thus not only a "propaganda plot," but an immense example of the realignment between State and society, notably through the cinema industry, national security ideology and a collective sense of threat.[48]

However, a schism in the cultural consensus began to develop in the 1960s with American society's growing opposition to the war in Vietnam. Despite the "hard-line propaganda" of a film like *The Green Berets*, this kind of uncompromising ideology became increasingly untenable in the face of a war whose objectives were unclear, a rising body count, and the certainty of victory appearing more and more remote. Hollywood, through financial necessity, saw little benefit in going against the rising tide of public opinion. Turning to small, independent producers, the landmark counterculture film *Easy Rider* (1969) reaped a box office take of $41 million and helped to trigger the "New Hollywood" phase that came to represent the counterculture generation's increasing disillusionment with its government and its actions on the domestic and world stages. Once a market for such films was established, Francis Ford Coppola's *Apocalypse Now* (1979) became the first large-scale war film since World War II "produced without the support of the American Army."[49] The film was regarded as a masterpiece of the New Hollywood Era, as "the Vietnamese experience split the 'military-cinema unit' into two opposing camps. A conservative one that spoke to the 'silent majority' defined by President Nixon and the liberal perspective that virulently denounced the conflict."[50]

This split continued until the presidency of Ronald Reagan, whose slogan "America Is Back" symbolized a new hawkishness toward the Soviet Union. Reagan, a former Hollywood actor, demanded a new consensus with Hollywood, which was established in the early 1980s. The Vietnam War had visited a profound shock to the American psyche, whose trauma left it unable either to assimilate or to mourn its losses. "While American identity has been constructed since the seventeenth century around the idea that American settlers are God's chosen people and that their manifest destiny is to illuminate and guide the world to its redemption and salvation," observed Valantin, "the Vietnamese trauma blurred American self perception; it threatened to deeply harm the collective identity by its character as an 'unjust war.'"[51] Against this national anguish, American cinema created a world of images, ideas, and ideology that countered this. The war was not over, but resumed in the alternative reality of the cinema with a wave of films that "put the finishing touches to history." The Pentagon and Hollywood were now united in their offensive against Reagan's "evil empire," and "the creation of a virtual threat which, while being rejected outside America, allowed a call-to-arms for its security and defence."[52]

This reconciliation between Hollywood and the Pentagon was realized with *Red Dawn* in 1984 and has continued to the present day. In many contemporary films,[53] billions of dollars of military hardware and manpower have been used to portray the us military in a positive light,[54] and, it might be added, America itself. As Jonathan Turley, Shapiro Professor of public interest law at the George Washington University Law School notes in *Operation Hollywood: How the Pentagon Shapes and Censors Movies*: "In comparison with other countries, the U.S. Military operates the most sophisticated and successful propaganda system in the world,"[55] where it "routinely reviews scripts and . . . the Pentagon compels changes to convey the government's message."[56] The alignment of American strategic interest with Hollywood's domination of the international cinema has proved to be a remarkably effective soft power resource, where, Valantin points out, "American strategic identity is established as one of the essential facets of national identity. The sense of being an elected people and conducting just wars are united in this national identity . . . because of the power of cinematic representation."[57]

However, the Pentagon was not the only arm of government concerned with using the cinema as a soft power resource for the positive dissemination of American values and identity. The *Guardian* newspaper pointed out in 2008 that "the cia's involvement in Hollywood is a tale of deception and subversion that would seem improbable if it was put on the screen."[58] Its shadowy role, the newspaper pointed out, has included decades "in which the cia maintained a deep-rooted but invisible influence of Hollywood . . . altering scripts, financing films [and] suppressing the truth."[59] In more recent times, for example, CBS secured official help when making its 2001 TV series *The Agency*, while the CIA has influenced the script of many films by putting forward former agents as "advisers." *The Hunt for Red October* and *The Sum of All Fears* were filmed with CIA input, while former agent Milt Beardon took on the advisory role in *The Good Shepherd* and *Charlie Wilson's War*, the latter a story of US covert efforts to supply Afghan rebels during the Soviet occupation of Afghanistan in the 1980s. However, in real life it was the Afghan rebels—or freedom fighters—who gave birth to al-Qaida, something the movie conveniently air-brushed out of the script. Even before the film came out, Beardon was on record as saying he would "put aside the notion that because we did that [supply arms to the freedom fighters] we had 9/11."[60] It was a remark that was revealing of the CIA's real reason for supplying consultants, which, the *Guardian* pointed out, was to "misdirect the filmmakers" where necessary,[61] in order to project American culture and values in a way that others might want to buy into.

An essential adjunct to cinema, and a highly marketable by-product of it, is the cult of celebrity, supported and fueled by the star system made in Hollywood. The lifestyles of the rich and famous and the public's desire to identify with them represent important elements in the internationalization of consumerist taste. Audience rapport with Hollywood's stars transcends their on-screen roles, and a major industry mushroomed around them to feed the public's insatiable desire for details of their love lives, lifestyles, and activities through fan magazines, gossip columnists, newspaper reports, and radio and television programs. Lifestyle magazines such as *Hello* and *People* dedicated to showbiz stars fill news stands around the world, which in turn generates a market for everything they wear and everything they surround themselves with. Celebrities sell the psychological desire and social need for their lifestyle and generate markets for goods and services they endorse. Product placement in key films has become big business, such as Julia Roberts's ringing endorsement of the BMW z3 sports car in her tile role in *Erin Brockovitch*. A celebrity encodes values and ideas, a function well recognized by commerce, since millions of people around the world measure their own success or failure by using celebrities as a yardstick in their own lives. As Neal Gabler argues in *Life: The Movie*, entertainment is the prime focus of American life: "The place where values are expressed, performed, endorsed, published, taught, broadcast, ratified and mythologized in diverting ways,"[62] and the main vehicle through which this is achieved is the film industry.

Hollywood and the cult of celebrity it spawned have been major tools in both colonizing the imagination and the way in which America represents itself to the world. From the time of the Hays Office to the present day, Hollywood has provided audiences at home and abroad with powerful mythic foci affirming and reaffirming America's national ideologies, nation-building, claiming the frontier and triumphing over adversity. As Sam Blumenfeld in *The New American* has pointed out, movies are "the conveyors of American ideas, values, stories, and personalities to the rest of the world. And today, American culture, through movies . . . is the dominant cultural influence in the world."[63]

This global dominance has been further aided, according to Zbigniew Brzezinski, by the rapid spread of the English language as a global lingua franca.[64] Thus, it could be argued that the dissemination of the English language in non-Anglophone countries actually facilitates US soft power. Today, the average citizen in most First and Second World countries—and many in Third World economies—knows more of America, its image of self and its belief that its history and myths are universal narratives, than of any other nation or people on earth. The American narrative has become a global narrative, and America's history a global history, prompting Reinhold Wagnleitner to suggest that "we are not only confronting a cultural process in the narrow sense, but also an economic, social and political [phenomenon]: the realms of symbolic hegemony, the power over cultural capital."[65] Even at a grass-roots level this hegemony is experienced uncritically as part of local cultural repertoire—in the way fast food outlets—McDonald's, Burger King, Pizza Hut, Kentucky Fried Chicken, and so on—have revolutionized the way we eat; in the casual clothes we wear—from jeans to T-shirts embossed with American cultural signifiers—or during leisure hours that may be filled by American entertainment (music, films, games). As Rob Kroes has noted: "In the course of this allegedly 'American Century,' America[n] . . . cultural products [such as movies] reach the far corners of the world, communicating American ways and views to people elsewhere . . . [while] American [consumer] products, from cars to movies, from clothing styles to kitchen apparel, all actively double as agents of American cultural diplomacy."[66]

While responses to American culture and the semiotics they embody are complex and varied, from accommodation, assimilation, emulation, and resistance, or combinations thereof, through to cultural appropriation and reinscription, some have argued that American cultural power is a benign power. If it is, then we have to ask ourselves why many nations around the world have acted to limit the importation of American popular culture to preserve their own indigenous culture, one being France, which during the Uruguay Round of International Trade Negotiations in the early 1990s introduced the "cultural exception" (*l'exception culturelle*) clause to protect its cultural industries—especially its movie industry—that included limiting the importation of American movies; why Canada introduced several measures to protect its cultural identity, including the Canadian Content regulations (CanCon), which require television and radio stations to play a specified percentage of domestic programming; why South Korea operates a screen quota system whereby Korean films must be played for seventy-three days per year and cable TV maintain a quota of 25 percent for domestic films; and why China's government sees control of the airwaves as one way of limiting foreign content as a means of preserving Chinese culture. Indeed, Rob Kroes has even argued that "American mass culture . . . may have affected the European sense of history."[67] So if the power of American mass culture can alter the way history is construed, it does not seem unreasonable to suggest that it might affect the way jazz is construed, especially since American jazz has been used "as a form of propaganda in support of American values."[68]

Deemed intrinsically American by a State Department website,[69] declared an "indigenous American music and art form" and "a rare and valuable national American treasure" in a 1987 congressional resolution,[70] jazz, as Lawrence W. Levine has suggested, is an integral part of American culture.[71] This made it a very attractive means through which US governmental agencies could project American values abroad, a practice that dates back to World War I and the very beginnings of the music. Although "soft power" was a term unknown in those times, propaganda was, and the nascent form of ragtime-into-jazz of James Reese Europe's Hellfighters was harnessed by the US military to stimulate and act as a focal point for black patriotism and recruitment at home, and for morale-boosting purposes abroad, by projecting a positive image of the United States.[72]

In 1916, William Hayward, a colonel from the Nebraska National Guard, was appointed to appeal to black patriotism by organizing the 15th Heavy Foot Infantry Regiment (Colored) of the New York National Guard. Hayward turned to James Reese Europe to organize a permanent regimental band whose initial role was as a recruiting device. On September 18 of that year, Europe, who had earned distinction as a dance-band leader that led to a recording contract with RCA Victor, "one of the first contracts ever given by a major record company to a black musician and the first ever to a black orchestra,"[73] answered the call to arms. Among those recruited by Europe for the regimental band were Noble Sissle as drum major and trumpeter (who began an advertising campaign for recruits in national black newspapers), drummer Buddy Gilmore (one of the first genuine jazz drummers), trumpeter Arthur Briggs, baritone saxophonist Raphael Hernandez, Ward "Trombone" Andrews, and clarinetist Elize Rijos. If not quite jazz as we know it today, this band, in energy and spirit, was certainly a harbinger of what was to come.

When the band arrived in Brest, France, on New Year's Day 1918, they were sequestered by General John Pershing, commander of the Allied Expeditionary Force, to entertain officers from the American, British, and French armies. Between February and March, the Hellfighters traveled two thousand miles, playing in twenty-five French cities in provincial France to boost morale among the French citizenry and to announce that Uncle Sam was now involved in the quest to defeat the Kaiser. With the Allies gearing up for a major offensive in September, Europe and his musicians remained in Paris, "to provide their morale-boosting service for the men in the city and in the camps and hospitals in the immediate environs."[74] The surviving 1918 newsreel shots of Europe's Hellfighters in France show them marching through a recaptured French village,[75] flag flying, preceded by a variety of orchestral instruments (saxophones, clarinets, trumpets, tubas, and so forth) followed by bugles and drums, and in a formal concert situation outdoors in Paris, revealing considerable detail. The audience is segregated,[76] black members of the audience to the left, with white French commissioned officers in the front row of the audience to the right of the band, and French civilians, including nuns, seated and standing behind. Clearly it is a sunny day, since there are several ladies' parasols in evidence. When the band completes its performance Europe turns to face his audience, smiling, with both hands held aloft to acknowledge what is clearly wild applause—even the French top brass are contributing enthusiastically. But what is especially interesting is a sudden surge from the civilian crowd, all caught on film, who burst onto the small space between the band and the French officers to demonstrate their enthusiasm for the music—some even improvising dance steps—despite the despairing efforts of a couple of troops to stop them. It is a remarkable moment, anticipating the crowd scenes at Benny Goodman's Paramount Theater opening in March 1937, when the music seemed to demand a physical response from the seated audience. Here was an early kind of "Beatlemania," and in Europe's instance it is captured on film, 1918's style.

As Europe's biographer Reid Badger has noted, "Europe took seriously the band's responsibility as an ambassador of good will to the French people,"[77] and by the time the band were welcomed home, along with other members of US forces, in a victory parade down New York's Fifth Avenue on February 2, 1919, the Hellfighters had accumulated 171 decorations for bravery—more than any other American regiment. Europe's band, wrote Emmet J. Scott in 1919's *Official History of the American Negro in the World War*, "wanted the French to be aware of its presence, so it blew some plain ordinary jazz . . . letting the countryside know that hope for defeat of the Kaiser's army was not dead."[78]

By the time of World War II, America's deployment of soft power, or propaganda, had become far more sophisticated. Perhaps the best known example of several armed forces bands formed during the conflict with a bias toward jazz was that of Major Glenn Miller's American Band of the Allied Expeditionary Force. Like James Reese Europe's experience, Miller's AEF band was initially used for recruiting and morale-boosting purposes—"Bringing a little of Uncle Sam to our fighting troops overseas," as Miller's wartime broadcasts claimed—but was later harnessed as an instrument of soft power. Miller, who in 1942 had enjoyed three years of remarkable popularity with his civilian dance band, volunteered as a musician in the armed forces at the age of thirty-eight. Entering the army on October 7, 1942, he secured a commission as captain and was posted to the AAF Technical Training Command in North Carolina as director of bands. In 1943, he received orders to set up a band for broadcasting to be stationed at the Technical Training School at Yale University at New Haven, Connecticut. It was there he took W. C. Handy's jazz standard "St. Louis Blues" and transformed it into a patriotic marching song by way of an arrangement by Jerry Gray, Perry Burgett, and Ray McKinley.

Formed with the pick of musicians enlisted for military service, Miller, according to London's *Sunday Times Magazine*, would "carry the formula for a jazz-tinged, but widely appealing, dance orchestra to its peak."[79] Known at this time as "The Army Air Forces Training Command Orchestra directed by Captain Glenn Miller," the band was engaged in broadcasting, recording V-Discs (it never made any commercial recordings, except for one session in Britain whose proceeds were intended for charitable purposes), and playing at savings rallies and recruitment drives. Between July 1943 and June 1944 they broadcast their weekly *I Sustain the Wings* program from New York's Vanderbilt Theater. The OWI, the civilian government's outlet for war news and propaganda, began using the entertainment industry, including jazz and dance bands, in programs designed to project the American way of life in support of its war aims. Miller, newly promoted to the rank of major, duly recorded a series of propaganda programs for the OWI, beginning on Friday, March 10. At the end of June 1944, the band embarked for London, where they arrived on June 29 and ten days later began broadcasting over the American Forces Network (AFN). Millions of civilians and members of other nations' armed forces would now either see the band, or hear its broadcasts courtesy of its heavy broadcasting schedule with the AFN, the American Broadcasting Station in Europe (ABSIE), the London office of the Canadian Broadcasting Corporation, and the BBC. "To be allowed, as a teenager, to stay up late for the American Expeditionary Forces programmes (signature tune: Charlie Barnet's 'Skyliner') was the high point of my week," wrote British music writer Derek Jewell: "In the latter half of 1944, [Miller's band and units drawn from it, *The Swing Shift*, *Strings with Wings*] could be heard on the BBC practically every day."[80]

After three months of almost nonstop broadcasts and concerts where they played almost every American base in England, the band, now known as the American Band of the Allied Expeditionary Force, was again engaged by the OWI for a series of broadcasts via ABSIE aimed at the German people, to project the American way of life, prepare them for liberation, and encourage support for the Allied cause. The band was introduced in German by Ilse Weinburger and Miller himself, the latter reading from a phonetic German script. Miller performed his usual repertoire, albeit with some songs sung in German, such as "Long Ago and Far Away," performed with immaculate phrasing, diction, and intonation by Sgt. Johnny Desmond. This was a classic use of American soft power in that the United States was attempting to achieve what Nye calls "[making] its power legitimate in the eyes of others," in order to "encounter less resistance to its wishes. If its culture and ideology are attractive, others will more willingly follow."[81] Postwar research revealed that despite German jamming, many of ABSIE's broadcasts got through to the German people. "Perhaps after all the Miller Band was really another Allied secret weapon," reflected Miller expert Geoffrey Butcher.[82]

Signs that jazz had acquired a significant international following were becoming more and more apparent during the postwar years, with a *Downbeat* cover from 1952 announcing: "U.S. Stars Invade Europe!"[83] Inside, a feature article by Leonard Feather declared: "Call it emigration or exportation; whichever way you look at it the big foreign push in the music business is on. Completely halted in the war years and heavily impeded for a while after armistice by currency and transportation difficulties, American bands, instrumentalists and singers are flocking across the Atlantic in unprecedented numbers."[84] By 1956, *Metronome* magazine was able to report, "Jazz is becoming a broad belt of understanding reaching out from the United States to all sections of the world. Its effect is only coming home to us in recent months because so many of our own jazz personalities are making trips abroad in the capacity of emissaries (both official and unofficial)."[85] This was the height of the Cold War, and the growing number of overseas tours by jazz artists and the enthusiastic response they engendered in foreign countries had begun to interest the State Department, especially after Louis Armstrong's African tour. Since President Dwight D. Eisenhower had decided to use cultural diplomacy as an additional prong of American foreign policy, a proposal from Congressman Adam Clayton Powell, Jr., in 1955 that jazz be adopted as a tool of cultural diplomacy was looked on with favor. The plan was to use jazz's potential as a soft power resource to promote us interests abroad by funding tours by jazz musicians. The success of what became known as the "Jazz Ambassadors" tours were widely celebrated in establishment and middle-brow circles of the United States as "the signature cultural export of the Cold War era."[86] Dubbed America's "Sonic Secret Weapon" by the *New York Times*, the first jazz group to be sent abroad as a cultural presentation was Dizzy Gillespie's big band, which toured Iran, Pakistan, Syria, Turkey, Greece, and Yugoslavia in 1956. According to *Metronome* magazine, the success of this tour "in terms of American propaganda, in addition to musical worth," was such that "several other tours [were] scheduled."[87]

By 1958, *Downbeat* magazine was able to claim that "jazz remains our best and most valuable export,"[88] citing the example of Benny Goodman's opening at the Brussels World Fair that year, which provided a dramatic diplomatic success for the United States on the cultural front. For the first month of the World Fair, Russian exhibits had been dominating the cultural phase of the event, with foot traffic at the us pavilion "static and [us] cultural prestige hurting."[89] Wide-screen showings of *South Pacific* and a style show were simply not cutting it with audiences, prompting columnist Art Buchwald to quip, "The main attraction has been our free washroom."[90] But when Goodman opened the American Performing Arts program on May 25, the *New York Times* noted that he brought "a well behaved first night audience to life whistling and shouting. And this was an audience not normally given to riotous behavior. It included diplomats, officials and other important persons to whom jazz is not the staff of life"[91]—the latter an allusion to a number of Russian officials who managed to obtain tickets and were among the enthusiastic first night crowd. Goodman would more famously tour the USSR in May/June 1962, including a conversation with Premier Khrushchev on Wednesday, May 30, on the lawns of Spaso House, the residence of the American ambassador. But although Goodman was featured on the cover of *Life* magazine on July 16, 1962, posing with his clarinet in front of St. Basil's Cathedral in Red Square, and his band was greeted enthusiastically by audiences in a country that a few years earlier had frowned on jazz, quite what American diplomats made of Goodman might make interesting reading, since his treatment of his band members has remained controversial. "Goodman Men Sound Off about Soviet Tour," headlined *Downbeat* magazine on the band's return to New York City,[92] and fifty years later details of Goodman's eccentric conduct were still emerging, recalled with erudition by Goodman's bassist for the tour, Bill Crow.[93]

The Dave Brubeck Quartet's twelve concerts in Poland in 1958 saw astonishing crowd scenes when he became the first of the State Department's "Jazz Ambassadors" to tour behind the Iron Curtain. The Brubeck tour of Poland was a major event in the history of jazz in that country, providing a source of inspiration for fans and musicians alike, including Polish jazz legend Tomaz Stanko. In 2001 he explained: "As a [Pole] living under a communist regime, jazz for me was freedom, it was Western culture, a different way of life that we all wanted but could not get."[94] Brubeck would go on to become his country's most effective Jazz Ambassador. Dana Gioia, chairman of the National Endowment for the Arts, wrote in 2008: "There is no American alive who has done more extensive and effective cultural diplomacy than Dave Brubeck. Dave is not only one of the greatest living American artists; he's also one of the greatest living diplomats."[95]

Jazz tours tended to be favored by US officials because they could claim the music as a uniquely American art form.[96] In so doing, the Eisenhower administration "reinforced and institutionalised the symbiotic relationship between American culture and American foreign policy."[97] Certainly, there was no doubt in governmental or musical circles as to the purpose of the jazz tours. *Downbeat* magazine reported in 1963: "The government's use of jazz as an adjunct to diplomacy, or, less politely, as a propaganda weapon—and nobody in Washington uses that phrase—is common knowledge."[98] Up to and including 1963, there were fourteen jazz tours sponsored by the State Department and US Information Agency: Louis Armstrong (Africa, 1960; Chile, 1962), Dave Brubeck (Poland, Near and Middle East, 1958), Charlie Byrd (Latin America, 1961), Cozy Cole (Africa, 1963), a second tour by Gillespie (South America, 1956), Benny Goodman (Asia, 1956–57; USSR, 1962), Woody Herman (Latin America, 1958), Herbie Mann (Africa, 1959–60), Ray McKinley (Poland, Yugoslavia, 1957), Red Nichols (Greece, Turkey, Cyprus, the Near and Middle East and Far East, 1958–59), Jack Teagarden (the Near, Middle, and Far East 1958–59), and Paul Winter (Latin America, 1962). These tours, wrote Penny Von Eschen, were designed "to make critics of U.S. policy identify with America or the idea of America."[99] Although these tours were sponsored for ideological reasons, the reception they received was generally in excess of what the artists concerned enjoyed at home. Phenomenal crowd scenes greeted Louis Armstrong in Africa: "His first performance on May 25, [1960,] drew a throng estimated at one hundred thousand, far more than would have turned out to see him in the United States, where he was ubiquitous and somewhat taken for granted," wrote his biographer, Laurence Bergreen.[100] Dizzy Gillespie's State Department tour of the Near and Middle East and South America was similarly successful: "The people were just remarkable. Just wouldn't stop the ovations. The ovations just kept coming and coming, and it was packed houses at all the concerts," said Marion "Boo" Frazier.[101] With successes like these, Cynthia P. Schneider noted in her paper "Culture Communicates: US Diplomacy That Works" that jazz proved to be "an extremely effective tool for diplomacy."[102]

But it was not just jazz artists who were sent abroad by the State Department and US Information Agency during this period. Described by the Washington Post as "emissaries of the American way,"[103] they included classical ensembles; theater groups, often performing plays by the likes of Eugene O'Neill, Thornton Wilder, and Tennessee Williams; and dance companies such as those of Martha Graham and Alvin Ailey. Another instrument of American soft power in the Cold War years was radio. Voice of America (VoA); Radio Free Europe (RFE); the army's Radio In the American Sector (RIAS), located since 1946 in West Berlin with broadcasts beamed primarily at East Germany; and Radio Liberty (RL) were among America's most successful Cold War weapons, and all featured jazz and American popular music extensively. RFE and RL were covertly funded by the CIA, while VoA received funding indirectly from the

CIA channeled through the Congress for Cultural Freedom and dummy foundations.[104] The VoA's broadcast activities came under the auspices of the United States Information Agency (USIA). Their most successful program, Willis Conover's *Music USA*, first broadcast on January 6, 1955, and subsequently heard eight times a week, attracted an estimated 100 million worldwide listeners at its peak.[105] It was so successful that following a trip to communist satellite countries in 1963, jazz promoter and pianist George Wein said, "Eastern Europe's entire concept of jazz comes from Willis Conover."[106] Even today, the impact of these broadcasts is remembered with considerable affection by members of former Russian satellite states.

American jazz struck a deep, responsive chord beyond the Iron Curtain, one Russian listener describing the experience thus: "Every night we would shut the doors and windows, turn on Willis Conover and have two hours of freedom."[107] Here, American jazz was sufficient to evoke connotations of America's symbiotic association with freedom. The paradox at this time was that projecting jazz abroad as emblematic of American freedom and democracy was contradicted by the realities of an apartheid regime in its Southern States at home. Among the aims of the Jazz Ambassadors' tours was combating the growing criticism of the United States as a racist nation by the promotion of both black and white artists. Keith Hatschek noted: "In large part, the government's use of jazz as a form of propaganda in support of American values was designed to help counter the troubling realities of America's segregation and racism then prevalent."[108] In this respect, the Jazz Ambassadors' tours could be considered a success, since, as Cynthia P. Schneider notes: "Visiting Americans exposed the cracks in the façade of the U.S., such as racism and McCarthyism, made the message of freedom all the more powerful."[109] For example, Dizzy Gillespie said that representing his country abroad did not mean for him apologizing for racism at home—one of the overt political aims of the tours.[110] Yet despite this troubling racial backdrop, the success of the Jazz Ambassadors' tours and Willis Conover's radio broadcasts must ultimately be measured in terms of the successful projection of image over reality, whereby American jazz ceased to be "a thing in itself," a neutral force devoid of any cultural, national, or ideological connotations, but instead came with the weight of American cultural power behind it, projecting the symbols and myths of American democracy and freedom to encourage other nations to be sympathetic to the ideology of the United States and to help bolster oppositional circles in Soviet satellite states.

Although the majority of jazz tours were sponsored by the US State Department, many were undertaken by the USIA. These included a veritable who's who of creative Americans, such as Toni Morrison, Edward Albee, Frank Capra, Joan Didion, Anne Sokolow, Alan Ginsburg, Frederick Weisman, Ishmael Reed, Alvin Ailey, Martha Graham, and jazz musicians Duke Ellington, Dizzy Gillespie (in 1989 to Egypt, Morocco, Senegal, Nigeria, and Zaire), and Dave Brubeck. An excellent latter-day example of Brubeck's role as a cultural ambassador is captured on the album *Moscow Nights*, recorded in Rossiya Concert Hall, Moscow, in March 1987 and subsequently presented to Secretary General Gorbachev at the historic Reagan-Gorbachev summit held in Moscow in 1988.[111] Charles Z. Wick, the USIA director from 1981 to 1989, was clear in his agency's objectives, stating: "I would hope American pop culture would penetrate into other societies acting as a parachute for the rest of American values."[112] In 1999 the USIA was effectively wound up, its broadcasting functions moved to the newly created Broadcasting Board of Governors and its artist exchange and nonbroadcasting information functions given to the newly created Under Secretary of State for Public Affairs and Public Diplomacy at the US Department of State. Today, jazz's value as a soft power resource continues to be recognized by the Department of State, albeit on a much smaller scale and a much reduced budget, in a collaboration with Jazz at Lincoln Center, which produces *Rhythm Road: American Music Abroad*. Unlike in the past, there are no big names; for example, the class of 2011 comprised ten bands that included roots music, gospel, and hip-hop, as well as jazz. As Margaret Ames, director of the State Department's Cultural Programs Division, told *Jazz Times*: "It's not only about reaching audiences in places that may not necessarily have access to Americans or American musicians," it was also about ensuring that "the *Rhythm Road* supports U.S. foreign policy interests."[113]

America's major foreign policy objective of victory in the Cold War owed much to its soft power resources. Long before the Berlin Wall fell in 1989, it had been breached by American popular culture. As Reinhold Wagnleitner noted: "However important the military power and political promise of the United States were for setting the foundation for the American success in Cold War Europe, it was the American economic and cultural attraction that really won over the hearts and minds of the majorities of young [Eastern bloc] people for Western democracy."[114] Here, American rock music proved to be the powerful ingredient of American soft power that contributed to eroding the Soviet system from within.

Vaclav Havel, the playwright and dissident who became the Czechoslovakian premier in 1989, went on record to say how impossible it is to overstate the importance of American rock music for the Czech resistance during the years of darkness between the Prague Spring and the collapse of communism in his country.[115] Interestingly, this forms a neat parallel to the influence of jazz during the years of Nazi occupation of Czechoslovakia during World War II, documented by Josef Skvorecky in his classic novel *The Bass Saxophone* (available in English translation).

Twenty-five or so years later, the suppression of the popular uprising known as the Prague Spring in 1968 gave rise to the formation of a band called The Plastic People, taking their name from a Frank Zappa song of the same name and inspiration from Lou Reed and Velvet Underground, the Fugs, and, of course, Zappa. Their subversive lyrics resulted in their arrest by the authorities in 1976, and their subsequent trial inspired the kind of resistance Havel and his colleagues had been hoping for. They responded with Charter 77, a document written with the deliberate intent that in signing it, Havel and his literary friends would acquire a similar kind of notoriety in the eyes of the authorities that their musician friends had suffered. During the years that followed, the pressure intensified on the revolutionaries, then eased once it became clear that the repression was failing to keep down what Havel called "The Power of the Powerless," the title of his greatest essay, written in 1978. "Everyone understands," he wrote, "that an attack on the Czech musical underground was an attack on the most elementary and important thing, something that bound everyone together . . . The freedom to play rock music was understood as a human freedom and thus as essentially the same as the freedom to engage in philosophical and political reflection, the freedom to write, to express and defend the social and political interests of society."[116]

By the winter of 1989 the regime was doomed and no longer able to turn to Mikhail Gorbachev's Moscow for aid, having collapsed in what became known as the Velvet Revolution (which took its name from the Velvet Underground—"Why," Havel would say later, "do you think we called it the Velvet Revolution?").[117] In December 1989 Havel was elected president of Czechoslovakia and invited Zappa to join the government. Zappa met Havel at Prague Castle, where they discussed Captain Beefheart's music, and Havel asked Zappa if, on a forthcoming state visit to the United States, he would help him meet those who had championed his cause in opposition, including Joan Baez. Zappa agreed and became a consultant to the Czech government on matters of culture, tourism, and trade.

In 2003, Andras Simonyi, then the Hungarian ambassador to the United States, delivered a speech in various venues across America, opening at the Rock and Roll Hall of Fame in Cleveland, entitled, "Rocking the Free World: How Rock Music Helped Bring Down the Iron Curtain."[118] As Nye has noted, "Soviet state-run propaganda and culture programs could not keep pace with America's commercial popular culture in flexibility or attraction."[119]

While the effect of soft power can never properly be measured, it is nevertheless widely acknowledged to be an extremely effective tool of public diplomacy—a euphemism for propaganda in government circles. For example, on the occasion of the North Korean dictator Kim Jong-il's death on December 17, 2011, and the succession by his son Kim Jong-un, the *Guardian* newspaper's headline was: "A Nation Hails Its New General as [Hillary] Clinton Puts Faith in Soft Power."[120] Nye argues that, in order to be an effective arm of cultural diplomacy, soft power relies on three dimensions: (1) daily communication—for example, every government has a press officer who feeds daily information to the media with the best possible spin, in the hope it may be consumed in a way favorable to the government's objectives; (2) strategic communication, in which a theme, or series of themes, are developed in a way similar to a commercial advertising campaign; and (3) the development of relationships with key individuals.[121] "Each of these three dimensions of public diplomacy plays an important role in helping to create an attractive image of a country and this can improve its prospects for selling desired outcomes," writes Nye.[122]

However, soft power is not a one-way street from America to the rest; it is a tool utilized by many governments today. Nye cites Norway as a good example of this: "It has only 5 million people, lacks an international language or trans-national culture, is not a central location or hub of organisations or multinational corporate brands, and is not a member of the European Union. Nonetheless it has developed a voice and presence out of proportion to its modest size and resources."[123] This is true not only in the geopolitical world but also in the world of jazz. By concentrating primarily on the third dimension of public diplomacy it has created international awareness of its world-class jazz scene through regular invitations to key individuals—jazz opinion formers such as journalists and concert animators—to attend Norwegian jazz festivals and events. These invitations, funded by government, have included both American and European journalists and animators who in turn have contributed to an increasing awareness of the Norwegian scene within both the United States and Europe. It has helped to create a perception of Norway as "upbeat, modern and cosmopolitan. . . . the sort of place in the global economy that would be attractive to inward investment, an agreeable environment to transact business and a vibrant and exciting place to live."[124]

Today, the exponential growth of information on the Internet has produced the paradox of plenty, which is leading to smaller attention spans. The more information there is, the less time there is to consume it. In these circumstances it might be expected that the impact of American soft power would become diffused, but the worldwide presence of American culture has, if anything, intensified, because of the ready availability of illegal, but nevertheless free, downloads of American music and motion pictures. In 2005, a BBC/ICM poll of global attitudes toward the United States conducted in twenty-one countries revealed that American "movies and music scored highly";[125] CNN World pointed out that, in "sixteen countries polled by Pew [Research Center's Global Attitude Survey] in both 2007 and 2012, a median of 65 percent embrace American music, movies and television [and] the appeal of American popular culture has increased even more in particular nations."[126]

The attraction of American popular culture (of which jazz is a part) in shaping a favorable impression of America has often been described as a halo effect, "whereby the perception of positive qualities in one thing or part gives rise to the perception of similar qualities in related things or in the whole."[127] The term was coined in a 1920 study published by psychologist Edward Thorndike to describe how global evaluations about a person (e.g., "She is likeable") bleed into further judgments about their specific traits (e.g., "She is isn't argumentative, she's spirited"). Subsequent studies have indicated that the halo effect can be applied to almost any situation or choice, and today its application is well known in the worlds of business, advertising, and politics. According to John Marconi's book *Reputation Marketing*, books published under the *Harvard Classics* imprimatur can command twice the price of the same book without it because of the halo effect associated with one of America's great institutions of learning. In marketing, the term is used to explain the bias shown by customers toward certain products because of a favorable experience with other products made by the same manufacturer. In this instance, the halo effect is driven by brand equity, one famous example being the enthusiasm for Apple's iPod transferring to its other products.[128] Here an analogy might be drawn with American popular culture, whereby, as Nye has pointed out, polls indicate that the perception of its positive qualities makes the United States seem to others "exciting, exotic, rich, powerful, trend setting—the cutting edge of modernity and innovation."[129] This was the principle that prompted US governmental agencies to sponsor foreign tours by famous American jazz artists in the 1950s and 1960s. Here the hope was that jazz's positive qualities (or halo effect) might give rise to a similar perception of brand America to the citizenry of places like the former USSR, Poland, Africa, South America, and the Near and Far East.

Today, jazz's halo effect is apparent in two main ways: one has to do with history, whereby the exceptionalism of jazz's great master musicians from its Golden Years—such as Louis Armstrong, Charlie Parker, John Coltrane, Charles Mingus, and Miles Davis—creates a brand loyalty to American jazz as a whole that extends to the current generation of American jazz musicians. The other has to do with how the halo effect of America as the home of modernity, futurity, and the always new often creates a "cultural cringe" factor in local contexts—that is, a feeling of inferiority causing people to dismiss their own (jazz) culture or aspects of their (jazz) culture as inferior to the American model. This has tended to shape how the music is presented, taught in jazz education, consumed, and debated in local jazz economies. In many countries, the history of the music is fetishized almost exclusively in American terms,[130] even though these communities may have a history of long engagement with the music and thus their own "history of jazz" and "local heroes" who may have "approached jazz performance in original ways, transcending the hegemonic influence of America's jazz titans."[131]

Often these "local heroes" have failed to receive due acclaim or sufficient work opportunities within local contexts that might be less about what their music was, more about the halo effect enjoyed by American jazz.[132] In 1963, for example, Johnny Dankworth had just completed recording *What the Dickens!* (an album inspired by English author Charles Dickens) and argued in the pages of *Melody Maker* that "[on] my new LP three or four of the guest players and one or two in my band would have had a couple of their own LPs out now if they were Americans. As it is, a couple of the guys were playing jazz in a recording studio for the first time."[133]

Interestingly, in 1977 the social psychologists Richard E. Nisbett and Timothy DeCamp Wilson demonstrated what little access we have to our subconscious thought processes that govern the halo effect.[134] In an experiment designed to examine ways in which student participants made judgments about certain lecturers, they demonstrated that although we might understand the halo effect intellectually, we often have no idea when our judgments succumb to it or how it influences the production of more complex social responses. Without realizing it we make judgments influenced by the halo effect, and even when these judgments are pointed out to us, *we may still deny its effect.* This is what makes it such a useful tool for marketers and politicians, and it poses a simple question: Are we really evaluating the traits of American jazz as a thing-in-itself, un-influenced by an imaginary America as a locus of pleasure, prosperity, modernity, and freedom? Or is that appealing and singular characteristic influencing our global view?

These complex and problematic issues suggest how difficult it is to separate American jazz from the nexus of powerful Americanizing influences consciously mediated to enhance all aspects of American Empire, whether consciously consumed or unconsciously absorbed. As Todd Gitlin has suggested, America has become most everyone's "second culture,"[135] making it almost impossible to untangle jazz from the kind of powerful connotative referents that are ultimately intended to imply American exceptionalism. For many, the reception of American jazz has not been simply as music-as-a-thing-in-itself, or an embodiment of its own romantic history, but a part of something bigger, America's enormous cultural power, whose influence on the perception and consumption of all forms of media, including jazz and popular music, is impossible to quantify yet impossible to ignore. In commercial advertising, where the perceptible, the imperceptible, and the symbolic are combined to create what is hoped will be a lasting impression on consumers and so drive their behavior in a certain direction, there is no dial or meter that is able to measure the effectiveness of a single advertisement. Equally, there is no way of calibrating the strength or effectiveness of American soft power, which equally relies on the perceptible, the imperceptible, and the symbolic for its effect. Ultimately both rely on positive perception, and the reception of American jazz abroad has undoubtedly benefited from this.

# The Globalization of Jazz

**T**oday it is hard to avoid the word "globalization." It crops up daily in newspapers, magazines, on the radio, television, and Internet, usually in connection with the globalized economy. Yet there is far more to globalization than global economics, although that is clearly its focal point and most evident feature, since global economic growth and the rise of liquidity—the ever-growing piles of money being shifted around the world's money markets that keep credit cheap and assets expensive—have been the big story of our times. At the same time a boom in low-wage economies has kept a lid on inflation in the Western sphere of influence, allowing central banks to maintain low interest rates for more than two decades. However, low interest rates and cheap credit led some in the financial world to act foolishly; bright young minds on Wall Street came up with new ways of repackaging mortgages so that the banks that originated the loans—which had hitherto required borrowers to demonstrate an ability to repay—no longer kept the mortgages on their books but sold them on to other institutions. It meant that the banks, which earned fees for selling the mortgages, now no longer had to worry about whether the loans could be repaid. They increased the limits of loan against income, lowered down payments, lowered the amount of repayment per month, and competed with each other by offering unsustainably low interest rates. The result of all this was a classic speculative bubble that burst in 2007 when those of us in the non-financial world woke up to the term "subprime mortgage." We learned how they had been repackaged and resold in complicated financial instruments such as collateralized debt obligations and credit default swaps, and how the volume of these deals—nobody knew the precise numbers—was making it difficult for banks to measure the size of their assets: analysts considered these instruments toxic, so forcing banks to significantly reduce their stated liquidity margins which made them, on paper at least, insolvent. The global credit crisis that followed may have had painful consequences, but massive quantities of new capital pumped into the global financial system from Sovereign Wealth Funds and powerful, emerging economies such as China, India, and Brazil gave the global economic system resilience to withstand the financial shockwaves that reverberated around the world in 2007–2008. As the dust began to settle following the dramatic fallout on Wall Street, the nature and extent of the free flow of capital between countries as a result of the interconnectedness of financial markets—financial globalization—became clear: it emerged that China had become the third-largest holder of US debt, underpinning the American economy to the tune of $1.2 trillion.[1]

The global nature of the 2007–2008 financial crisis serves as a potent example of the dynamics of globalization. Even Marshall McLuhan, the Canadian philosopher of communication theory who introduced the concept of the world as a "global village" in 1962, could never have imagined the impact of information technology on the international financial markets or how fast the global transmission of goods, services, information, and culture across national borders would become in the final years of the twentieth century and the mischievously dubbed "noughties," a moniker for the early millennium years. Nor could he have predicted the kind changes globalization would bring to modern society, improving, often quite dramatically, the living standards of billions of people around the world.

In today's world the very word "globalization" has itself "globalized," passing into common usage in almost every language in the world including German (*globalisierung*), Italian (*globalizzazione*), Chinese (*Quan Qiu Hua*), French (*mondialisation*), and Korean (*Gukje Hwa*). Researchers and students of the subject come from a variety of backgrounds including academe, journalism, politics, industry, and economics, and depending on who they are and where they are in the world, the term might variously mean: the pursuit of free market policies in the world economy ("economic liberalization"); the growing dominance of Western (mainly American) forms of political, economic, and cultural life ("Westernization" or "Americanization"); the global domination of American beliefs, values, and behavioral and cultural norms over weaker nations (cultural imperialism); or the means by which a single unified global community might be realized ("global integration"). Clearly, "globalization" means many things to many people, and the term is becoming so overused it is in danger of losing its original meaning. However, most researchers agree that simply understood, globalization means the ever-increasing fast flow of goods, services, finance, and ideas across international borders and the changes in institutional and policy regimes at the international and national levels that facilitate or promote such flows.[2]

It is beyond the scope of this chapter to deal with the full range of globalization processes, since they do not operate in the same way in every field of human activity, or to chart the history of globalization, since the global development of capitalism is hardly new: its harbingers date back in time to intercontinental voyage, trade, and conquest. However, the pace and magnitude of global change undoubtedly sped up in the final decade of the twentieth century and the new millennium years; following this premise, this discussion focuses on contemporary developments.

Like most nouns ending in "-ization," "globalization" implies some kind of change, and this chapter seeks to explore the kind of changes it has brought to the real world of jazz. Since culture is a constitutive element of globalization—John Tomlinson has argued that "globalization lies at the heart of modern culture; cultural practices lie at the heart of globalization"[3]—this chapter seeks to explore the implications of this inter-relationship within jazz. Obviously some background information has been introduced of necessity—albeit reduced to a minimum for reasons of space—in a study that seeks to draw commonalities between jazz and other forms of cultural globalization, such as popular culture, to better understand its effects on jazz.

I have used the term "real world of jazz" advisedly, since the extra material in and at the end of this chapter includes suggestions for further study, including seeking out jazz artists whose work reflects the effects of globalization on the various Internet audio platforms and portals. Students and the musically curious are encouraged to go beyond these examples and identify real-life examples of their own. Just as there is no precise definition of a beautiful melody, or of jazz itself, globalized jazz is best heard, understood, and internalized to reach a better understanding of the arguments at play in this text.

Perhaps the most unexpected side-effect of globalization in the real world has been the rise in nationalism at the end of the twentieth century and in the new millennium years, which has to be understood, as Mary Kaldor has noted, "as a response to globalization."[4] Since jazz history tells us that the music has always reflected sociopolitical changes in the milieu surrounding it,[5] this chapter briefly explores the global rise of nationalism in relation to the globalization of jazz. It also seemed appropriate to compare and contrast globalization theory with diasporism, or transnationalism, as an alternative method of studying the transmission of jazz across national borders, since some in academe offer it as an alternative to the current globalization studies. Since their arguments are couched in relativism, which is gaining increasing currency in academe, its premise is briefly outlined along with its potential impact on jazz historicity. In the event, by comparing and contrasting globalization theory and diasporism/transnational theory a broader context emerged to better understand the argument that globalization is the next major evolutionary stage of the music's continuing history. As Ted Gioia has argued, "The globalization of jazz is not just another engaging story, another sign of the music's growing acceptance . . . [It] is the main story, the overwhelming trend, the key evolutionary thread that is taking us to the music's future."[6]

With the fall of the Berlin Wall in 1989 and the end of the Cold War, the United States entered two decades of unchallenged supremacy during which it became obvious that no country in the world could stand apart from the global processes of economic change it was largely responsible for initiating. These had largely been achieved through the cooperation of institutional structures such as the International Monetary Fund, the World Bank, the United Nations, and GATT (General Agreement on Tariffs and Trade, succeeded in 1994 by the World Trade Organization, or WTO), since the US influence on these important organizations "was so over-whelming that, as a rule, it could determine the outcome of their deliberations on issues deemed of vital importance to the United States."[7] The United States could usually impose its own favored candidates on these forums, or remove those it regarded with displeasure, in its goal of achieving economic globalization by way of liberalizing all markets, sweeping aside all trade regulation, and privatizing everything in the public domain. "The most important aspect of economic globalization," says Tom Hanahoe, "is the concept of free trade—the right to move capital, goods, plants, profits and technology across national boundaries without hindrance from nation-states, thus opening up markets around the world to international competition."[8] The result has been a new world order driven by the trading interests of the world's largest (mainly American-owned) corporations. By 1999, for example, fifty-one of the world's one hundred largest economies were transnational corporations rather than sovereign countries, with the power to dominate the economies of small to medium-size nation states. According to the World Development Movement, "We are witnessing *Corporatisation* of the global economy where societies are rearranged to further the pursuit of profit."[9]

The enormous economic power concentrated in these transnational corporations has meant that the term "globalization" is seen by some as a corporate ideology intended to serve the interests of big business. This process has an empirical dimension—a process that can be observed—since the growing political, economic, social, and technological connectedness between nations has resulted in different cultures interacting with each other in different ways. Since this chapter is concerned with cultural globalization—as opposed to economic, political, or technological globalization—culture is taken to operate at three levels: "The lived culture of a particular time and place, only fully accessible to those living in that time and place . . . [a] recorded culture, of every kind, from art to the most everyday facts: the culture of a period . . . [and] as the factor connecting lived culture and period cultures, the culture of the selective tradition."[10]

In a broader sense, culture can also mean the characteristics of belonging somewhere and a particular way of life that expresses certain meanings and values. Jan Nederveen Pieterse has broken down cultural globalization into three main perspectives:[11]

1 ~ *Cultural Differentialism.* This argument contends there are lasting differences among cultures that are largely unaffected by globalization, and

that "cultural globalization is seen as a disruption as it involves ignoring borders and boundaries as well as outside cultural influences creating imbalances into any cultural system that receives it."[12] In this model, culture is a clearly bounded entity within a specific location. Thus global culture takes the form of a kind of mosaic of different cultures, with certain indigenous features separating one culture from another. Since culture is said to be long lasting and that change tends to occur slowly, then from this perspective cultures cannot easily mix without causing some form of disruption. Samuel Huntingdon argues in *Clash of Civilizations* that people's cultural and religious differences will be the primary source of post–Cold War conflict. While this paradigm acknowledges the effects of globalization on culture, it argues that the core of the culture remains unchanged because global processes tend to be strongly resisted or rejected for cultural unsuitability.

2 ~ *The Cultural Convergence Theory*. This thesis is essentially a center-periphery model—sometimes called "from the West to the rest"—whereby the global economic system is said to be dominated by advanced Western economies while the Third World remains at the periphery of the system with little control over its economic development. Some have argued that this model has become synonymous with the Americanization of the international order, since, as author and three times Pulitzer Prize winner Thomas L. Friedman has pointed out, "American based manufacturers and service providers, American brands and American moviemakers, American singers and American entertainers, American clothing designers and American fast food chains" appear to dominate the global marketplace.[13] It has prompted many cultural theorists to predict the onset of a "flat," homogenized, Westernized consumer culture, or global mass culture, threatening the diverse and distinctive indigenous cultures whose customs and practices date back centuries. This theory is sometimes known as "McWorld-ism," taken from the term "McWorld" to describe a concept developed by Benjamin Barber in 1995 to describe the increasingly homogenous and consumerist culture that is being produced by globalization, using fast food as a metaphor for the increasing influence of an American-led consumerist society advanced by multinational corporations that see everybody as a consumer.

3 ~ *Hybridization Theory*. This paradigm, sometimes known as the cultural flows model, emphasizes the idea of a "cultural mix" through the integration of local and global cultures resulting in a new and unique hybrid culture that transcends both. In his essay "Disjunction and Difference in

the Global Economy,"[14] Arjan Appadurai has argued that globalization is less likely to result in the onset of a homogeneous global culture, but rather a network characterized by enhanced connectivity producing a complex overlapping, unruly order "which cannot any longer be understood in terms of existing centre-periphery models . . . nor is susceptible to simple models of push and pull (in terms of migration theory) or of surpluses and deficits (as in traditional models of balance of trade) or of consumers and producers."[15] This increasing interaction between globally transmitted culture and local culture is in turn responsible for creating cultural hybridity.

Of Pieterse's three models of cultural globalization, we see that in the realm of popular culture, of which jazz is a part, the cultural convergence model has long coexisted alongside the hybridization theory. Contrary to many global theorists in the 1990s who were predicting cultural convergence, cultural globalization has turned out to be an uneven, nonlinear process with different outcomes in different locations, a process that has been described as "disorganised capitalism."[16] That it has involved both a degree of cultural convergence, or homogenization, *and* hybridization, or hetrogenization, seems undeniable. As Roland Robertson has argued: "It is not a question of *either* homogenisation or hetrogenisation, but rather of the ways which these two tendencies have become features of life."[17]

Expressed in terms of popular music, which is, of course, mass produced commercial culture, the cultural convergence thesis can be seen at work when local musicians adopt the dress codes of the globally promoted pop stars and perform in a similar style in a local context. In other words, "local" musicians try to replicate, in both content and style, the music of the originators, so homogenization ensues. In jazz, the cultural convergence model might be explained through local encounters with American jazz that result in loyalty, for a variety of reasons, to how jazz "sounds" when performed by American artists, an encounter that can be described as accommodation, assimilation, and emulation. Most local jazz scenarios have "local heroes" who have reached a high degree of proficiency performing in the manner and style of American jazz master musicians. Here, jazz represents something intrinsically American, whereby issues of "authenticity" are raised if the music is performed outside the "mother tongue" context of American styles.

There are many reasons for this. One possible explanation has to do with jazz history and loyalty to the influence of the Afro-American jazz greats in shaping the destiny of the music that has set in train a belief that "the real jazz" must follow their precedent. Another possible reason is the nature and extent to which American culture dominates a particular nation-state. For example, the strong American influence in the United Kingdom that has to do with history, a shared language, the particular affection the British political class have for America expressed in terms of a "special relationship," its openness to American trade, capital, and ideas and so on—or in Germany, where post-1945 American culture flooded into the country during the "de-Nazi-fication" program to provide an alternative ideology and bulwark to communist ideology. Another reason may have to do with the influence of soft-power American consumerist culture—Hollywood films, American TV programs, and popular culture (of which jazz is a part) that are bound up in discourses of America as a locus of pleasure, modernity, and the "always new"—whose influence to follow the "American Way" can be very persuasive.

Turning to the cultural hybridization model of globalization within popular culture, Arjan Appadurai has argued that cultural flows move in increasingly complex directions that have to do with certain disjunctures between economy, culture, and politics, so the result is less likely to be cultural convergence but more likely to be cultural hybridization, produced by the continuous interaction between global forces and local cultures.[18] An important aspect of cultural hybridization is that it produces different outcomes in different geographic areas—for example, the salsa tradition, whose practice varies in locations such as New York City, Cuba, Venezuela, the Dominican Republic, Puerto Rica, and Colombia. In this example, salsa breaks down into a series of "local" encounters resulting in hybridized—or localized—forms reflecting local culture and performance practices in what is essentially a popular form of Latin American dance music. Such global/local outcomes are not confined to popular music; they can occur in all forms of media, such as American TV soap operas that are adapted to local conditions because audiences generally find it easier to identify with local values, attitudes, and behaviors. Local outcomes can also occur in social, political, institutional, economic, cultural, artistic, and commercial activity.

Hybridization occurs from the interface between globalized culture and local cultural practice that results in the production of new meanings in local contexts and cultural settings. Here, globally transmitted culture is broken down into a series of individual encounters, each explained in terms of local, social, and cultural context and how it interacts with the global, a process often referred to as "glocalization." Through complex contacts of accommodation, assimilation, emulation, and resistance, global culture is reinterpreted, recast, or transformed as part of a local cultural repertoire and localized in a way that gives meaning and relevance to its local community through its adaptation of local cultural practices. Sometimes these cultural practices are a part of regular cultural repertoire, while at other times dormant cultural traditions can be revived and redefined, strengthening and reaffirming both national and local identity.

At this point some background information may be useful when considering the term "glocalization"—a conflation of the terms "globalization" and "localization"—since it first appeared in the late 1980s in articles by Japanese economists in the *Harvard Business Review*. The term was derived from the Japanese word *dochauka*, which means global localization, originally referring to the adaptation of certain farming techniques to local conditions. It was adopted by the business world to denote the importance of adapting a global product to local market conditions, and is now a common marketing perspective that involves the modification of goods and services to suit the lifestyle practices of "local" consumers—such as modifying left-hand-drive motorcars manufactured for the majority marketplace for the small number of nations that require right-hand-drive vehicles, or the McDonald's restaurant chain changing its international policy, after recording its first ever financial loss in 2003–2004, by downplaying its American-ness and "publicising its adoption of local and national culinary traditions."[19] Perhaps the most commonly cited example of glocalization in the business world followed Wal-Mart's expansion into the German market. Just as in the United States, customers entering German stores were initially met by "Wal-Mart greeters," whose welcome was intended to personalize their hypermarket shopping experience. However, the Wal-Mart brand struggled to make an impact until the social differences between the United States and Germany were taken into account and the "greeters," whom Germans found superficial and insincere, were removed.[20]

The popularization of the term "glocalization" within the realm of cultural globalization is usually attributed to the British sociologist Roland Robertson in the early 1990s, initially through his influential text *Globalization: Social Theory and Global Culture* (1992), in which he explored the glocalization process in relation to globalization, from which emerge certain elements that seem appropriate to this study:[21]

1 ~ Individuals and local groups have more power to adapt and innovate within glocalization, so avoiding the potentially homogenizing effect of globalized culture.

2 ~ Globalization provokes a variety of reactions that include the expression of local sociocultural values that help transform globalization into glocalization.

3 ~ Drivers of cultural change such as popular culture, the media, and technology are not seen as coercive, but as agencies that can aid glocalization through complex processes of assimilation, emulation, and resistance.

4 ~ Robertson's glocalization theories suggest that individuals and local communities can be key "creative agents."

5 ~ Glocalization can help reinforce local sociocultural values.

These elements provide a recurring theme and useful backdrop to understanding glocalization as a dynamic and selective process of interplay between global models and the local, which produces a local variation on a global theme; in the realm of rock music, for example, Luciana Ferreira Moura Mendonca has noted, "Rock has the capacity to strengthen feelings of local identity and autonomy. It is a form of participation in contemporary and global artistic expression and, at the same time, it is a means of renewing local, ethnic and national identities,"[22] while Russell White has illustrated the influence of the local on globally transmitted American rap music by turning to the scene in France:

> The desire to assert a sense of regional, local and national identity manifests itself in a number of ways. French rap artists deploy a range of visual and linguistic markers in an attempt to "represent" their locale (normally configured in hip-hop culture as the "hood"). Such markers can be found in the lyrics, videos, album art and even in some groups' names . . . perhaps the most interesting cultural marker and one of the most distinctive features of French hip-hop culture is the use of the *verlan*, a form of French slang that involves reversing letter orders and playing around with syllables. . . . Seen in a narrowly national context, French hip-hop artists have developed a youth culture that, while inspired by African-American tropes, is nevertheless independent and distinctively French.[23]

Here, local rap musicians have used an American cultural language and its associated cultural codes—and to this extent they have been

Americanized. However, while they have drawn on an American cultural repertoire, the influences of "local" cultural codes are also apparent, so Americanization is not an accurate description of what is now going on. As they negotiate, use, resist, reinscribe, and manipulate American cultural influences, they produce new meanings in use, enabling local musical communities to identify more closely with the music, since a greater range of musical reactions might be expected when hearing a performance that sounds in part or in whole familiar to them—such as local language and dialect.

In jazz, an early example of the glocalization process can be heard in the music of the Quintette of the Hot Club of France, which created a viable subgenre of the music called *jazz manouche*, or Gypsy Jazz, that expanded on existing Roma guitar techniques. Emerging from a "Hot Club" concert arranged by Pierre Nourry and Charles Delaunay at the Ecole Normale de Musique in Paris on December 2, 1934, the star of the Quintette, guitarist Django Reinhardt, showed what a short step the campfire extemporizations of a Manouche gypsy were from jazz improvisation. Reinhardt's and violinist Stéphane Grappelli's improvisations stood out because they were so quintessentially European at a time when everyone else sounded quintessentially American. More especially, their boulevardier brio convincingly suggested that American jazz could reflect a "local" cultural component without sacrificing the elements that made jazz so compelling and subversive.

It is important to stress that the globalization of jazz (the transmission of American jazz through the trade routes of the global cultural economy), and the glocalization of jazz, the interaction of globally transmitted American jazz with local culture, are not exclusionary processes; glocalized jazz *emerges from* a linear process of assimilation, appropriation and hybridity (see list below). Before meaningful glocalization can take place, local jazz musicians need to have absorbed and become fluent in American hegemonic jazz styles—in other words, have a thorough understanding of "the rules of the game"—before selectively borrowing from the local to produce a viable hybridized, or localized, product. It therefore follows that some jazz musicians perform in a global jazz style in one context and a localized, or glocalized, jazz style in other contexts. There are many reasons for this—jazz musicians typically are flexible, able to work in theater pit orchestras, Latin bands, society bands, function bands, rock bands, blues bands, and within a broad range of jazz genres in addition to their preferred style in order to preserve their income stream. Often,

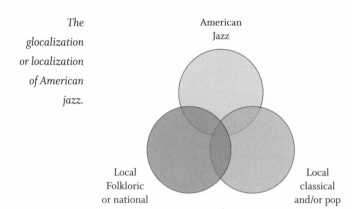

*The glocalization or localization of American jazz.*

American Jazz

Local Folkloric or national

Local classical and/or pop

moving between the local and global styles is necessary to achieve this. In any event, it is interesting to note that local musicians who do move between globally transmitted hegemonic jazz styles and localized styles often choose to define their *own* music, or aspects of their own music, in terms of the local. But it is important to note that playing in one style or the other is not an exclusionary process.

Thus it can be seen that glocal, or localized global, jazz styles do not somehow emerge in isolation from American jazz, but from the inter-face between the two, with the notion of "authenticity" increasingly being expressed in terms of local, rather global or American significance. A feature of glocalized culture is that "ownership" becomes increasingly irrelevant because "origin" becomes subsumed through local appropri-ation. This process of appropriation, involving hybridization, has become a particularly fruitful area for the growth and development of jazz in local contexts outside America, where the effects of globalization have meant that for many "local" musicians, jazz is no longer conceptualized in terms of hegemonic American styles but rather in terms of its extension into the local. This represents a major paradigm shift in how jazz is both perceived and performed outside the United States, and its effects are far reaching.

A useful means of illustrating the globalization and glocalization pro-cesses is through analogy with language. It is interesting to note that a Google search for the ubiquitous metaphor "the language of music" re-turns more than 1.5 million results, suggesting that it is an analogy that has frequently been turned to in the past. For example, Deryck Cooke's *The Language of Music* (1959) offered a semantic profile of Western music, while Leonard Bernstein presented a unified theory of music and lan-guage, embracing subjects such as Musical Phonology, Musical Syntax,

# Real-Life Encounters with Glocalization

"When I moved up north [in England] I really fell in love with the Yorkshire landscape and it became clear to me that if I was going to make honest music I would have to own up to all my influences, both musical and otherwise. I really love American jazz but I'm clearly not a product of urban New York, so I try and write music that reflects my life."

~ NIKKI ILES, PIANIST, UNITED KINGDOM[1]

"The people in Scandinavia—we are not born in Harlem, so we have different blues. We have folk music and the fjords and the mountains and snow and everything, so we are different to the guys in America."

~ JON CHRISTENSEN, DRUMMER, NORWAY[2]

"I am Italian, I play jazz but I am Italian, I think that something comes out, I have a very melodic sense, which is one of the characteristics of my country, melody. My instincts are of a person that grew up in Italy and is Italian, having Italian parents—that comes out in my music."

~ ENRICO RAVA, TRUMPETER, ITALY[3]

"It makes it much more interesting to involve your own culture in the playing or even take folk songs and the folk into your music, and not just try and go back to the tradition of jazz. [Jazz] doesn't really evolve that way, I think the best music is coming from Europe for now, for sure."

~ ALEXI TUOMARILA, PIANIST, FINLAND[4]

"I think there is a different flavour of jazz in different countries. . . . It is very interesting because there is difference, the differences are nice, because there are different flavours for the audience."

~ HENRI TEXIER, BASS, FRANCE[5]

"The so-called standards are not *my* standards. I don't feel a close attachment to that music, music that is made for the Broadway shows. They're great compositions, but I've never had the urge to use that music as a basis for my playing. . . . What I see as a major force of this music [is] we have players from any part of the world now doing their own, shall we say, native version. They find their own direction, influenced by their own culture, but still using very strong basic elements of jazz."

~ JAN GARBAREK, TENOR, SOPRANO SAXOPHONES, AND FLUTE, NORWAY[6]

"Things people associate the Dutch with is liberty, tolerance, a certain playfulness, not liking everything within set limits and following the rules and I think Dutch jazz is a very good example of illustrating this image. Whether it is the right image, or whether it is the wrong image there is something in it because many people say we are playful and Dutch design, for example, is playful and is much less rigid than say German design. And that goes for the music as well. The Willem Breuker Collectief, they've been working for decades and have built their reputation on this playful side, I'd say. These are things are not fixed, but since people say, 'What I think of Dutch jazz is whatever,' a general image does come up and they can't all be wrong, I would say."

~ FERDINAND DORSMAN, GENERAL DIRECTOR OF CULTURAL AFFAIRS, NETHERLANDS CULTURAL OFFICE, NEW YORK[7]

"When I meet people I tend to bow, I don't hug, I don't kiss, you know? I don't shake hands, I just bow, not because I'm trying to be Japanese, it is just in my culture, in my genes, so I'm sure even in music the culture is there, although I never try and put it in artificially, but it's there. I grew up in Japan and was born in Japan so . . ."

~ HIROMI, PIANIST, JAPAN[8]

"The Australian culture is generally less formal than a lot of other places, particularly the Continent [of Europe] and the United States, so that lack of formality in everyday life and how people interact is reflected in the music, and that informality is very interesting when you play it to jazz, which is a music that is supposed to be about 'freedom' and self-expression. It seems the Australian culture is very appropriate to play jazz in because of that, there are less restrictions to throw off when you want to be free with your music, if you've already come from a society that's a bit that way anyway. In one sense we're out of the scene and what's going on, so sometimes new trends and things that happen in music tend to pass us by—traditionally things have taken a lot longer to reach us here. But the upside of that is exactly that, it takes a long time for things to reach here so we're not influenced by them so we've tended to develop slightly differently here, so that we can make things sound more unique. Certainly players develop their own style because they haven't got everyone else around them to listen to or have bands coming through all the time from the United States or Europe—it's too far to come. They are few and far between so that has contributed to making the jazz scene here more unique."

~ JAMES MORRISON, MULTI-INSTRUMENTALIST, AUSTRALIA[9]

"I think it is important to say there are two ways to play jazz, people who play straight jazz and the people who try and import something of their own culture. Jazz is a music, music is a language, language has to change continually—you speak English in a different way to Shakespeare, there are different timbres, words, we talk Italian a completely different way to how Dante spoke it 800 years ago, this is normal. I have a very great respect for all those people who play bop all their life, they are very, very important. This is their history, but you have to consider that jazz for sure is a music that in its time included many different roots from the beginning, not only African, not only European, not only American but all those different cultures that found themselves in the States. This is the same story that happened a few centuries ago with classical Italian opera, and German symphonic music. In the beginning there was only Italian Opera, the opera was born in Italy, later on in Germany and Russia they start their own way to produce opera, they use local melody roots, and add them to the opera to try to tell their story. The same story happened with the German symphony. After it arrived in Russia, the Russian way was to include traditional melodies, and in jazz it is the same thing. Some are inspired to use the music and the colors from Mediterranean music, so what some musicians are doing today it is doing what is natural to do, what people did for many centuries. This is my opinion . . ."

~ GIUANLUIGI TROVESI, SAXOPHONE, FLUTES, COMPOSER, ITALY[10]

"When I studied at the beginning there is always this bebop thing with American musicians, and all that is very important when you are studying jazz. But I was pretty happy about the Hochschule der Kunste here in Berlin [where I studied] because they are very open to European music, so it wasn't necessary for us to play every Charlie Parker tune! For me, I grew up with classical music and pop music and a little bit of jazz, I'm a mixture of all that and there is not a lot in me of the American bebop style, I think because I didn't listen so much to it. I am a European person and that is important to me. You can't escape the culture you were brought up in and I wouldn't want to. For me, the classical music has a very strong German influence, and that's very important for me, Bach was very important for me."

~ JULIA HÜLSMANN, PIANO, GERMANY[11]

"I felt the right thing to do was to do your own thing and not copy the American style; it seems to me obvious that this music is not our music. I'm not American, and I'm not living in the Golden Age of Jazz. The fact that that music made me want to become a musician and led me in the direction of the saxophone and have a free, musically expressive life as an improviser, it's a wonderful legacy to have from that music, but it's no good pretending I'm a black New Yorker, because I'm not! Music is a way of finding your voice and your place in your time, and I knew that was the right thing for me to do before I fully realized why."

~ IAIN BALLAMY, SAXOPHONE, ENGLAND[12]

"It is true that you put your own surroundings in music. For me I realized, living three years in Manhattan, I realized that there was a lot of things I can put into my music from what I have experienced in Finland, and I had to go to New York to realize that! It was really important, living in a small country almost in the Arctic circle, I always looked up to New York, but then I made a decision to come back to Finland and live here. I realized I would like to form my own band that had the same musicians, that we wanted to develop together, that we want to have a tight group, we don't want to play standards since, after all, we have all the possibilities in the Finnish folk music, the Finnish tango, the Finnish humor, and the Finnish classical."

~ IILO RANTALA, PIANO, FINLAND[13]

"I should say now, there's American jazz that comes from the blues tradition, which I feel very close to, blues orientated playing, one's part of American culture, and in Europe now they like to take parts of the blues, American culture, and use it with their own roots, their own culture, their own tradition, and so in fact they mix it more so than in the States, that seems to be the tendency now, go back to your European roots, go back to your Asian roots, and put it into jazz."

~ GLENN FERRIS, TROMBONE, UNITED STATES,
   AND LONG-TIME PARIS RESIDENT[14]

"I think [the globalization of jazz] is a real interesting break in the mythology of jazz; it's harder and harder to support the myth of jazz as 'America's Classical music.' And in fact, to me, to try and support that myth is to kind of denigrate the incredible legacy of jazz. Jazz is now a vehicle for people everywhere to find themselves, what greater achievement for a form is that?"

~ PAT METHENY, GUITAR, UNITED STATES[15]

"The jazz [in Hawaii] is a very laid back style of music that is pretty notorious to Hawaii, but it made me think about how this jazz is pushing me and how this jazz is different than other kinds I've played. I started thinking about that in the greater context of the world and how it would be even more different. That was the springboard for my application [for a Watson Fellowship at Whitman College, Washington, W.A.] . . . Improvisation, whether articulated as bebop, cubop, or hundreds of more (dis)similar descriptors, is the essence of jazz, the language spoken by its practitioners. However, countries have created their own dialects of jazz by assimilating into it the indigenous music forms, rhythms, scales, and melodies of their own cultures. I will explore this cross-pollination of jazz and the indigenous music of various countries firsthand by integrating into their jazz communities and learning to listen, think, and speak in the local jazz vernacular."

~ ROSS EUSTIS, TRUMPET, UNITED STATES. 2011 RECIPIENT OF A
WATSON FELLOWSHIP, WHITMAN COLLEGE, WASHINGTON, W.A.[16]

## Notes

1 Nikki Iles, "In the Saxophonist's Chair," *Jazz* UK 90 (December/January 2009/2010).

2 Jon Christensen, interview with author, May 23, 1999.

3 Enrico Rava, interview with author, March 12, 2004.

4 Alexi Tuomarila, interview with author, December 3, 2007.

5 Henri Texier, interview with author, March 28, 2001.

6 Jan Garbarek, *Downbeat*, July 1986, 26–27.

7 Ferdinand Dorsman, interview with author, September 14, 2004.

8 Hiromi, interview with author, March 29, 2007.

9 James Morrison, interview with author, June 2012.

10 Giuanluigi Trovesi, interview with author, May 25, 2003.

11 Julia Hülsmann, interview with author, October 13, 2008.

12 Iain Ballamy, interview with author, December 8, 2003.

13 Iilo Rantala, interview with author, March 10, 2003.

14 Glenn Ferris, interview with author, March 28, 2001.

15 Pat Metheny, interview with author, October 21, 2004.

16 Ross Eustis, www.whitman.edu/content/news/RossEustisWatson.

and Musical Semantics, for the Norton Lectures at Harvard in 1973. Published as *The Unanswered Question*, he applied Chomsky's generative grammar to musical analysis. In more recent times, a common view among music theorists that most musical events are in principle describable by analogy to music emerged following Fred Lerdahl's and Ray Jackendoff's *A Generative Theory of Tonal Music*—now regarded as a classic in music theory since its publication in 1983.[24]

Today, the analogy between music and language is too persuasive, too rich in comparisons and images to do without; in fact, there is hardly a lecturer in music academe who does not reach for an analogy between language and music to describe certain musical processes—indeed, the analogy between jazz and language became enshrined in the famous congressional resolution of 1987 noting that the music had become "a true international language adopted by musicians around the world."[25] This, of course, is not to say that music, or jazz, is a language per se, or even a special language. Rather, analogy, often described as the core of cognition, can illuminate reasonable, plausible, and even compelling aspects of music by turning to linguistic experience. Of course, there will always be a point at which an analogy will "break down," but if used with care, analogy can provide a means of describing musical process and effect. In the latter context it is useful to turn to Professor Braj Kachru's work in examining ways in which the English language changes in the global context. His studies of World English provide a useful model that I have broadly adapted to explain the effects of globalization and glocalization on jazz. In his book *English in the World*, Kachru developed the concept of three concentric circles of English that have been widely adopted by linguists (see figure, p. 107).

Kachru's Inner Circle comprises traditional English-speaking territories, having English as their "mother tongue," which he calls the "Norm Providers." The total core of English speakers for whom English is their first language (L1 speakers) in the world is no more than about 380 million.

Beyond the frontline English-using territories in the Inner Circle lies the Outer Circle, nations whose second language is English: L2 speakers who are loyal, for a variety of reasons, to the "mother tongue" version of English. These nations account for some 150 to 300 million speakers.

Finally, the outermost ring, the Expanding Circle comprises countries that have a competent or approximate working knowledge of English but are not concerned with the notion of "mother tongue" English. A max-

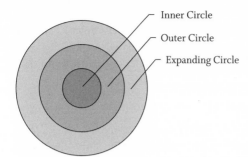

Inner Circle
Outer Circle
Expanding Circle

*Professor Braj Kachru's world English model from* English in the World.

imum figure for these language users, according to Kachru, is 1 billion. They have acquired a utilitarian knowledge of English, an adaptable "go anywhere" phraseology that is used as a tool to reach as wide and diverse a community as possible through a mixture of nonstandard English expressions and their own mother tongue.

According to Kachru, the Expanding Circle of his model is increasing at a rate of 3 to 1, in comparison to the Inner Circle. As the use of English around the world grows, so does the need for language to form locally distinct varieties—or dialects—that suit local needs. As the number of speakers in this Expanding Circle grows, so the type of English they speak becomes more and more disassociated from the norm providers, since they do not look to native, or "mother tongue," English speakers for a model of correctness. Some linguists predict that eventually these "lingua franca" types of English will divide off so far from inner-circle English as actually to form separate languages of their own; in fact, it is already happening. "Spanglish" in the United States is a mixture of Spanish and English that has its own vocabulary, grammar, etymology, morphology, and syntax and is already the majority language in several American cities; some experts predict it will become the majority spoken language in the United States, possibly as early as in thirty or forty years' time.

So, beyond the Norm Providers, the English language is changing as new versions of English are developing around the world; significantly, the Norm Providers, or mother tongue speakers, have no influence or control over the way these "new" Englishes develop. Kachru makes the point that "the global diffusion of English has taken an interesting turn: the native speakers of this language seem to have lost the exclusive prerogative to control its standardization."[26] The very fact that English is an international language means that no nation has custody over it.

Now, using Kachru's model for World English and applying it to the globalization of jazz, it is possible to illustrate the effects of globalization and glocalization and their relevance for the future of the music.

Turning again to Kachru's three concentric circles, the Inner Circle in my example has been changed so that the "Norm Providers" become the great American innovators of jazz's Golden Years.

The Outer Circle comprises musicians outside the United States who are loyal to playing jazz in the style of America's great innovators, or Norm Providers, and believe that for jazz to be jazz—for it to sound "authentic"—it must "sound" American.

Finally, the outermost, or Expanding Circle comprises jazz musicians who do not look to Norm Providers for a model of correctness and are willing to break the conventions of the Norm Providers in shaping their own "localized" versions of jazz. The Expanding Circle in jazz, like the Expanding Circle in language, represents styles of jazz that are becoming more and more disassociated from the Norm Providers, and this is a trend that is growing all over the world. The result is that the Expanding Circle, comprising musicians playing jazz in their own particular "glocal" or local style, is expanding faster than the Inner Circle; once again, we see that beyond the Norm Providers of both English and of jazz, hybridized or glocalized versions of language and of music are developing around the world to suit the needs of their "local" language and music communities.

In jazz, as in World English, the Norm Providers have no control over how these "new" versions of English or of glocalized jazz develop, because English and jazz become denationalized in the global context—it is no longer the property of the Norm Providers. Just as the use of the English language in the global context does not always mirror the vocabulary and rules of grammar and syntax and the way English is spoken in Britain or America, there are jazz styles that have evolved outside the United States that do not necessarily follow the way that jazz is played inside the United States. No language, not even the musical "language" of jazz, remains pure in the globalized world. Often, American jazz styles are invested with different meanings in different countries, or even "misinterpreted" in creative or idiosyncratic ways; one might argue that this was a feature of Russian avant-garde jazz prior to the collapse of the Berlin Wall in 1989, where performances in their nonconformist, subversive underground frequently employed parody, vaudeville, theater, and vocals to poke fun at authority: a jazz group playing with buckets on their heads, or in gasmasks, or incredible fancy dress in an almost Da Da–esque deconstruction of the freedom principle.

*Jazz and Culture in a Global Age*

It is perhaps inevitable that artists in their creations, performances, and crafts will reflect, to a lesser or greater degree, the social and cultural climate in which they spend their lives. All of us are shaped by our culture; for example, the American musicologist, educator, and jazz pianist Dr. Billy Taylor has written how American cultural practices determined "*how* jazz would be played" in the United States,[27] thus by extrapolation it is not unreasonable to suggest that the culture-specific practices of other nations may contribute to how jazz is played those contexts. Today, the powerful impact of electronic media makes it very difficult to remain immune from national cultural influences such as international sporting events that foreground national identity, including the four yearly Olympic Games, which in 2012 played to a global television audience of 4.8 billion (or about 47 percent of the global population). Football, or soccer in the United States, is the most global of all sports but paradoxically is the most national. For the global television audience of 3.2 billion who watched the 2010 Football World Cup, the eleven young men who composed each participating nation's team embodied the hopes and aspirations of "the nation" or "the state" in a way that presidents, monarchs, or generals could never do. The same is true of the competing teams in the annual Six Nations Rugby Football tournament in the Northern Hemisphere, an event that attracts a global television audience of about 70 million and was described by BBC TV as "sporting nationalism."[28] Other events that evoke the national spirit might include state ceremonies or occasions, events where the political elite seek to appeal to a spirit of national unity in times of political or economic turbulence, or the death of a famous national politician or celebrity. Today, nationalism is something we encounter in our daily lives through radio, television, features in newspapers, magazines, and the news portals of electronic media that shape our cultural, artistic, and aesthetic outlook.

## Globalization and Nationalism

The concept of the modern nation-state is a construct that emerged from a particular treaty signed in a particular place on a particular date—the Treaty of Westphalia of 1648. The organizational methodology of nation-building involved creating a unified national culture and identity, and, as John Tomlinson has noted, considerable cultural effort was exercised by nation-states in binding their populations into cultural-political orders of local identification.[29] Combining folkloric romanticism, political nationalism, and the traditions of sociocultural groups, certain referents of identity were enshrined in national mythology and folklore and passed down the generations as essences of national culture. Over the last three hundred years and more, industrial, economic, and cultural life and the relationship between cultural and national identity, or the characteristics of belonging, were gradually consolidated along national and territorial lines.

Today, the modern nation-state implies an entity within a specific geographical location with its own language, values, norms, myths, and symbols that make it possible to distinguish one culture from another. However, during the 1990s, the notion of the nation-state came under threat by globalization's seemingly irresistible progress toward economic convergence, causing many globalization theorists to predict that the interconnectedness of global capital flows and economic integration would ultimately undermine national autonomy. As one theorist observed, "Where states were once the masters of the markets, now it is the markets which . . . are masters over the state."[30] From this premise it seemed possible that cultural and even political convergence would follow, since the expansion of transnational flows, particularly in the economic realm, made it difficult for individual governments to pursue their domestic agendas, with the balance of power shifting away from the state in favor of capital markets, causing some theorists to question the effectiveness of the nation-state: "Is Westphalia's nation state a 'west-failure'? Has the inexorable marching juggernaut of economic globalization turned nation states into victims of the market economy?"[31]

Central to the organization of this new global capitalist order were the transnational corporations spanning every sector of the world economy and prevailing on national governments to reorder economic activity in ways that furthered their interests. It was widely believed in corporate circles that American English would become an international lingua franca and that differences between national cultures would recede in favor of a mass global culture. As a result it was thought that one of the challenges of the twenty-first century would be managing tolerable limits of convergence, or cultural homogenization. Instead, such assumptions proved only partially correct. Clearly convergence could be observed in technology, some aspects of architecture (the similarity of airports, shopping malls, office blocks, and sports stadia around the world, for example), and Anglo-American popular culture, but a mass global culture failed to materialize. Instead, by 2005, what Zbigniew Brzezinski called a "global political awakening" was being expressed through a rising trend of nationalism fueled by economic success, national pride, higher levels of education, greater information, and memories of the past.[32] What seemed to be happening was the emergence of cultural differentialism, albeit expressed very unevenly, suggesting that the nation-state was unexpectedly resilient to the effects of globalization, with politics and structures of governance remaining surprisingly remote from the effects of globalization. This was due largely to the effects of education, which has proved to be a stronger barrier against cultural homogenization than experts had imagined, since in tying national language and culture to the state it effectively acted as an engine of national identity by preserving national myths, culture, history, and customs. These enduring values seemed more attractive to the perceived ephemeral values of a so-called global mass culture, as Christian von Campe explained in his essay "Globalization and Its Effects on Nationalism": "The notion of a newly emerging universal culture more or less implies the loss of national culture . . . [and] fosters nationalist thinking, as humans tend to turn towards things they know and they understand. In opposition to a universal culture, national cultures have a common and coherent heritage . . . In a globalised world nationalists tend to be proud of the achievements their country had made. Globalisation in their opinion is a competition between nation-states and it is fairly obvious that this notion clearly accounts for a rise in nationalist thinking."[33]

This rise in nationalism is a surprising phenomenon and something few, if any, experts predicted, since the concept had come to be regarded as a backward ideology, certain to be erased by the onward march of progress and increasing prosperity brought about by economic globalization. In an examination of nationalism in a contemporary context, Liah Greenfield points out how the meaning of nationalism has changed over time but still can embody the best or the worst in society. "Nationalism was the form in which democracy appeared in the world," she wrote in *Nationalism: Five Roads to Modernity*. "The national principle was collectivistic."[34] At its best, nationalism can take on a positive form, tied to cultural and civic self-confidence, openness, and the public good, and where the universalist aspiration of imagining "the other" takes on an inclusive form— which collectively might be described as cultural nationalism. Negative nationalism, however, is dependent on ethnic loyalty, an active mythology of having been permanently wronged by "the other," and the pursuit of geopolitical and geoeconomic advantage—which might be called political nationalism.

Fortunately, in the world of jazz at least, we are less concerned with political nationalism, rather versions of cultural nationalism, which takes the form of national pride and civic confidence that can be readily apparent to the regular traveler. A visitor to the United States, for example, quickly becomes aware of America's national pride, expressed by the number of national flags flying on buildings of every description. A short stay in Paris is sufficient for the non-Frenchman to become aware of the enormous cultural and civic pride of Parisians. In countries where economic fortunes have risen, so too has national pride: Norway, for example, once had an economy built largely on a fishing industry, but since the discovery of oil in its territorial waters it has carefully managed its economy to produce an affluent society confident of its place in the world. However, we should be careful not to portray such examples of positive nationalistic sentiment in a hysterical fashion by confusing the political nationalism of the tiny number that exist in every democracy who express extreme right-wing views with cultural nationalism, such as this assertion by one New Jazz Studies advocate: "In the context of a wider European culture, national sentiment *is often used* to promote xenophobia and fear of 'otherness'" [my italics].[35] Nevertheless, since this unexpected rise in cultural nationalism in the "real world" is well documented, it seems prudent to attempt to contextualize its impact within jazz, since an interesting precedent exists in classical music.

## Jazz, Classical Music, and Nationalism

The notion that a rising tide of national sentiment could influence a kind of "jazz nationalism" was first articulated in the 1960s by Yui Shoichi, who saw a movement for national independence surging through nation-states becoming a motive power for what he dubbed jazz nationalism. He saw that, contrary to the cultural imperialism thesis (now usually referred to as cultural convergence), whereby American/Western culture threatened the vitality and existence of local culture, jazz nationalism actually provoked a means of rediscovering local traditions. It was a prescient and forward-looking observation that can now be seen as largely consistent with most leading contemporary globalization theorists, such as that of Roland Robertson,[36] who writes of how globalization provokes a variety of reactions including nationalism that can feed back and lead to glocalization. In fact, this trend was prefigured by a significant development in classical music in the mid-nineteenth century by the rise of nationalist composers who wanted to escape from the shadow of Austro/Germanic influence and composers from the Slavic nations, denied a voice under the Austro-Hungarian Empire, who wanted to indicate their desire for cultural self-determination through their music. In both instances a return to nationalist and folk cultures provided a way for these smaller nations to discover their "National Soul" and assert their national identity against the cultural dominance of larger nations.

Since the invention of the recording cylinder, the inflections, nuances, and character of folksongs and their singers could be recorded faithfully, and many composers found new inspiration in their native music. Often their melodies followed centuries-old folkloric tunes or the patterns of speech of native language, while rhythms matched the energy of traditional folkloric dances. One of the attractions of these folkloric melodies was that they often used modes that were neither major nor minor. This provided an attractive alternative to the theorists and critics who held that Schoenberg's twelve-tone system was now the way music should develop. Béla Bartók, who meticulously collected and studied Eastern European music, was excited by the qualities of the melodies he found, while Claude Debussy had expressed impatience with the tonal system after earlier making two extensive visits to Russia as a young man and noting the use of modes and scales; one of these scales, the "octatonic," was much exploited by Rimsky-Korsakov and became an important influence on his pupil Igor Stravinsky. Debussy's fascination with modes that were neither major nor minor and the music he heard at the World Exhibition in Paris in 1889 by Javanese and Vietnamese musicians—in particular the use of the pentatonic scale—was ultimately reconciled into a melodic conception of tonality typical of primitive folk music and medieval music that seemed somehow relevant to the twentieth century. However, none of these nationalist composers merely imitated folkloric sources, but used their resources to develop techniques that answered their own needs. Composers such as Stravinsky and Bartók, for example, refracted these influences through the creative prism of their imagination where they emerged creatively distorted, reshaped, and reimagined.

Today, like the nationalist composers before them, many local jazz musicians in local environments are similarly finding inspiration in the songs and rhythms of local folkloric music, incorporating these elements as a means of broadening jazz expressionism. What classical music offers is a powerful precedent whereby the assertion of national cultural characteristics resulted in music of enormous creativity. Thus by briefly examining a few selected nationalist composers creates a broader context in which to understand the glocalization of jazz emerges, especially since some jazz musicians have taken inspiration from the work of the nationalists in their own creations.

Bedrich Smetana's Czech nationalist convictions had taken him to the barricades in Prague in 1848, the Year of Revolution across Europe. His cycle *Má Vlast* was an expression of his nationalistic convictions, a way of separating himself from the Germanic culture of the Habsburg Empire, which had prevented him, as a young man, from speaking or writing in Czech. His overriding objective was to reveal a national characteristic in his music, writing to a friend in 1880: "[My] goal is to prove that we Czechs . . . [are] endowed with creative force—yes, *that we have our own and characteristic music*" [author's italics].[37] From the 1860s, Smetana wrote a series of operas and tone poems inspired by nationalistic themes derived from Moravian and Bohemian folk sources. It was unimportant whether these sources were portrayed accurately; what was important was that his music was taken up as a symbol of Czech national identity at a time when the Czech people were agitating for linguistic and political independence. To this day, the connection between Czech nationalism and Smetana's music is such that when a Czech Airlines jet prepares to descend into Prague airport, chances are it will play *Má Vlast* over its public address system. Should we be surprised if some Czech jazz musicians also aspire to expressing their own nationalistic feelings in their music?

Antonín Dvořák, in many ways Smetana's nationalist successor, wrote *Slavonic Dance*, Op. 72, No. 2, in E minor, in 1886, which as a hymn to Czech nationalism was rivaled only by *Má Vlast*. Credited with finding "the fullest recreation of a national idiom with that of the symphonic tradition, absorbing folk influences and finding effective ways of using them,"[38] his folkloric sources, like that of Smetana, were principally derived from the folk music of Moravia and Bohemia. In the third movement of his *6th Symphony*, in D Major, Op. 60, he wrote a *furiant*—a spirited Bohemian dance—to replace the traditional scherzo or intermezzo movement of the symphony, a musical gesture that defined his nationalism and set him apart from Germanic composers, including his friend Brahms. The *furiant* would recur in his work, such as the eighth dance in his *Slavonic Dances*, Op. 46, while it also appeared in Smetana's *Prodaná Nivesta* (*The Bartered Bride*). Taking the sound of middle-European music to America at the very beginning of the twentieth century, Dvořák encouraged American composers *to find their own national voice*,[39] pointing the way with his

*9th Symphony, From the New World* (E minor, Op. 95), written while he was director of the National Conservatory of Music of America in New York City. Its success stemmed from the fact that it was in part inspired by what was then called "Negro Spirituals" and Native American music—making it of America, for America, in America. It played directly into the then current debate of what constituted "American-ness" and the belief at that time that a nation with its own symphonic tradition was somehow a "proper" nation.

Certainly the ambition of Charles Ives, described as "an American original," was to prove that America could hold its head high and create something as worthy as the European composers who had come before him, by realizing an approach to the symphonic tradition that represented the voice of his people and his nation. Using the European symphony as his starting point, with movements that corresponded to the scale, proportion, and colors of the European model, Ives took as his source material American tunes—the folk, popular, and church music that surrounded him—that can be heard flowing through pieces such as his *Holidays Symphony* (or *A Symphony: New England Holidays*) or his *Symphony No. 2* (1909, but not performed until 1951 under the baton of Leonard Bernstein) with the rousing appearance of "Columbia, Gem of the Ocean" played by *treble forte* trombones in the final movement—what could be more inspiring and evocative of an American national mood than that? Certainly the "American-ness" of Aaron Copeland's most popular work within the United States, *Appalachian Spring* (1944), has something to do with this. Often referred to as a nationalistic work, it celebrated the American pioneers of the nineteenth century. Commissioned by Martha Graham, the ballet was set in a Pennsylvania farmhouse, with sections based on the Shaker theme "Simple Gifts."

The desire of Leos Janacek and Béla Bartók to break away from German domination was reflected by turning a modern ear to the "local" folkloric sources and the speech patterns of the peasants and farm workers that sang them, which they believed represented the true musical voice of a nation. Their enthusiasm for folk music showed how the use of nationalist elements in their compositions was anything but restrictive and indeed opened doors for their music in countries that valued cultural richness for its own sake. Bartók, realizing that the type of music produced by a particular culture is inseparable from the nature of that culture, took his recording machine deep into the Hungarian plains, capturing the irregular rhythms characteristic of Magyar dances and the sounds of a people whose ways of life and music would soon be swallowed up as industrialization forced them from their rural settings into an urban work environment. By taking folk music that was "neither major nor minor" and imbuing it with elements that might have been "modern" in character, mixing his source material with dense textures and richly layered harmonies, he produced something fresh that, despite its modernist disposition, reflected the purity of the songs he had recorded in the field. Janacek also drew on the rhythms of speech patterns in his native language and systematically recorded the melodic curves of speech and what he called "speech melodies," which remained central to his method of composition. Together with Bartók, he created music that resonated with a deep-rooted national consciousness of their own "local" musical communities and beyond.

Perhaps no composer from the nineteenth century, then or now, has evoked more controversy than Wilhelm Richard Wagner. Composers such as Tchaikovsky and Stravinsky treated the brouhaha surrounding him with disdain, but the most extreme response to Wagner's music came from France. After the humiliation of the Franco-Prussian War of 1870–71, most French composers saw it their nationalistic duty to turn away from Germanic influences—indeed, the Société Nationale de Musique was symbolically founded during the German bombardment of Paris with the express aim of working toward a French style that would carve out a non-German identity. Composers Camille Saint-Saëns and Cézar Franck, cofounders of the Société, acted as mentors to young French composers, such as Gabriel Fauré, whose music sounded as if it came from a different planet from Wagner's—as did that of Erik Satie, who steadfastly rejected Wagner's legacy. Here was something fresh in French music created in the spirit of national sentiment that would become dominated by Claude Debussy and Maurice Ravel and spill into the world's classical concert repertoire, even influencing modern jazz musicians such as pianist Bill Evans.

What these few selected examples of nationalism in the classical world convincingly tell us—and here it is important to stress that this hardly constitutes a "history" of nationalism within the Western classical/romantic tradition—is that national and cultural differences complement the otherwise inexhaustibly surprising differences between human beings and their artistic creations. By combining local elements within the prevailing hegemonic Germanic Romantic tradition, they accurately prefigured what some local jazz musicians sought to do almost a century later—combining elements of "the local" within the prevailing hegemonic American jazz tradition.

## Jazz and Relativism

Relativism has acquired an increasing influence over cultural life over recent decades; it is a perspective that contends that conceptions of the truth and moral values are not absolute but relative to the persons or groups holding them. In effect, the truth is in the eye of the beholder, an ethos that has had significant impact on educational and cultural institutions. As the historian Eric Hobsbawm has written: "The fashion for what (at least in Anglo-Saxon academic discourse) is known as 'postmodernism' [skeptical interpretations of culture, literature, art, and history associated with deconstruction and poststructuralism] . . . throws doubt on the distinction between fact and fiction, objective reality and conceptual discourse. It is profoundly relativist. If there is no clear distinction between what is true and what I feel to be true, then my construction of reality is as good as yours, or anybody else's."[40] Since relativism contends that there is no such thing as objective truth, that anything written has the same status as anything else, and no point of view is privileged, then it follows that different opinions represent different truths (frequently taking the form of "subjective insight"). This results in the authority and pursuit of "knowledge" for its own sake becoming compromised, since relativism contends that all "knowledges" become in principle equally valid, and "real knowledge" becomes a point of view of no special significance. Here is Dr. Tony Whyton on a presentation given by Dan Morgenstern, widely acknowledged as the greatest living authority on jazz: "I was amazed at the audience's low level of critical engagement with the subject matter and the general awe-inspired response to the material being presented. The silence and total obedience of the audience were disrupted only when Morgenstern uncovered one of the great untold secrets of jazz history. A gasp ensued as, wait for it, Morgenstern confessed to witnessing Billie Holiday . . . eating a chicken in a basket in a nightclub."[41]

The doctrine of cultural relativism has contributed to a flourishing of academic theories that encourage a cavalier attitude to "real knowledge," where historical fact is not regarded as absolute and where different opinions represent truths. This clearly asks questions of jazz scholarship today, since a relativist reading of jazz history means that "subjective insight" and historical fact, or real knowledge, become different perspectives that share equal validity, a methodology that may have particular value to, as Hobsbawm has noted, "those who see themselves as representing collectivities or [the] milieux marginalized."[42] But even so, he says, such methodology "is wrong."[43] Instead, he insists on the distinction between verifiable historical fact and fiction that is, he asserts, "one of the ways of exercising the historian's responsibility."[44]

In 2008, Krin Gabbard, professor of comparative literary and cultural studies at Stony Brook University, published *Hotter than That: The Trumpet, Jazz and American Culture*. Gabbard's work as been welcomed by many New Jazz Studies advocates, such as Dr. Tony Whyton, as demonstrating how "the study of jazz could be enriched by perspectives from outside formalist musicology."[45] No doubt perspectives from outside formalist musicology *can* enrich the study of jazz, but historian Randall Sandke doubts if Gabbard's book-length study, based on his 1995 essay "Signifyin(g) the Phallus: *Mo' Better Blues* and Representations of the Jazz Trumpet,"[46] succeeds in this ambition. Gabbard focuses on the trumpet as "a symbol of manhood," a "masculine signifier," and an emblem of "masculine display," prompting Sandke, who is also a highly respected trumpeter and composer on the New York jazz scene, to observe:

> An overriding flaw in this book is that . . . [Gabbard] constantly puts forth myths and spurious conventional wisdom as incontrovertible fact, or offers half-baked academic theories. For example, "One school of psychoanalysis has theorised that boys grow up wanting the father's phallus, the symbol of power. If they are right, then the primal fantasy came true at only one remove for young Louis Armstrong." These remarks are prompted simply because Armstrong was given Oliver's old cornet after his mentor acquired a new one. (The repetition of phallic imagery quickly grows tiresome. The author speaks of Armstrong's "ability to 'get it up' with high notes," and Dizzy Gillespie's horn, with its upward pointing bell, "suggests an erection." Even "advertisements for minstrel shows featuring a caricatured black man holding a banjo in front of his crotch" are overt references to male genitalia).[47]

In a sixteen-page study detailing inaccuracies, "[Gabbard's] book is riddled with factual errors";[48] with speculation passed as fact, "Gabbard owes it to his readers to draw a clear line between fact and supposition";[49] and a list of shortcomings too long to dwell on here, a relativist reading of jazz emerges where "myths and spurious conventional wisdom" are presented as "incontrovertible fact," since real knowledge is not valued above opinion or conjecture (or what the relativists call "subjective insight"). For example, Gabbard claims that "if nothing else [the Miles Davis album *Kind of Blue*] contained no altered chords. The musicians simply improvised around a set of scales. Modal jazz was born."[50] In just three short sentences a young student exploring jazz and American culture can be deeply misled in two important respects. First, as Sandke points out, "'Blue in Green,' the third title on the original LP, includes nine [altered chords] in the space of ten bars . . . [and] might rightfully be considered a *study* in altered chords. Other tracks on the album, such as 'All Blues' and 'Flamenco Sketches,' likewise contain altered chords."[51] Secondly, modal jazz was by no means "born" with *Kind of Blue*; George Russell was experimenting with modal ideas in the late 1940s, Shorty Rogers and Duane Tatro in the early 1950s, George Russell's Smalltet recording *Jazz Workshop* from 1956 included several modal pieces, while pianist Bill Evans had impressed the jazz world with his modal solo on *All about Rosie* (recorded with George Russell) in 1957. Davis himself had been dabbling with static harmony/modal concepts on *Ascenseur pour L'echafaud* (1957) and *Porgy and Bess* (1958) prior to the modal "Milestones" from his album of the same name, recorded a year before *Kind of Blue*.

Gabbard's text, of course, serves as a device to make an ideological point, and since relativist reasoning believes conceptions of the truth are not absolute but are relative to the persons holding them, frequently taking the form of "subjective insight," a relativist response to *Hotter than That* might take the form of: "Gabbard has a point because I consider the historical record may not be that accurate and precise, so we should not be limited by it since it is open to many readings." As Sandke concludes: "Gabbard should take a long hard look at the culture he comes from: one in which the arduous task of seeking informed and impartial conclusions has been supplanted by a glitzy pursuit of easy acclaim through a zombie-like adherence to fashionable ideologies. The aim of scholarship now seems too often bound up in formulating theory first and then selectively marshalling evidence to support it."[52]

## Jazz through the Relativist Prism of Diaspora/Transnationalism

Sandke's thoughts might be kept at the forefront of the mind when considering the application of Paul Gilroy's diaspora/transnational theories to jazz by New Jazz Studies advocates to explain the transmission and effect of jazz moving across international borders.[53] This involves placing to one side the settled belief (among others, Sassoon's, previously quoted) that the spread of jazz was the first great musical trend in music history to occur mainly through recordings and instead envisaging its spread through the prism of migratory movement. Gilroy was a professor at Kings College, London, a scholar of cultural studies and black Atlantic diasporic culture and the author of *The Black Atlantic: Modernity and Double Consciousness* (1993), among other works. Since his arguments about black Atlantic diasporic culture have proved to be influential in some circles of British social sciences, it is perhaps worth noting at this point that in British social studies the term "diaspora" is often used, while in the United States the term "transnationalism" is preferred. As Steven Vertovec has pointed out, "The term 'transnationalism' is fairly new and currently *en vogue*,"[54] and as a result "it is clear that much more conceptual and empirical work remains to be done with regard to sharpening the transnational approach to migration research and analysis."[55] Thus no one conceptual model is regarded as definitive. Nevertheless, with caveats expressed about diasporism/transnationalism theory needing "considerable conceptual tuning concerning modes, levels, extents and impacts,"[56] Gilroy's thesis, first promulgated in *The Black Atlantic* (1993), was embraced by the New Jazz Studies, despite concern that his study was dangerously abstracted from the material world and limited by its postnational stance.

Gilroy argues that the black African experience is central to the modern history of the West. He argues against essentialist versions of identity and nationalism in favor of a shared, heterogeneous culture that is not specifically African, American, Caribbean, or British, but all of these at once—a "Black Atlantic" culture that transcends ethnicity and nationality which should be treated as "one single, complex unit of analysis" to "produce an explicitly transnational and intercultural perspective."[57] As defined by Basch, Glick Schiller, and Szanton Blanc, transnationalism is "the processes by which immigrants forge and sustain multistranded social relations that link together their societies of origin and settlement. We call these processes transnationalism to emphasize that many immigrants today build social fields that cross geographic, cultural and political borders."[58] Thus diasporas emerge as the exemplary communities of a transnational movement, and much sociological discussion is centered around diaspora consciousness that is marked by dual or multiple identities—"home away from home," "here and there," and "British and something else"—whereby several identities link migrants to one or more nations. This involves a reconceptualization of what Gilroy calls "double consciousness," which builds on W. E. B. DuBois's oft-quoted concept as a means of negotiating being "both European and Black." Here Gilroy argues for a modernity broad enough in scope to include the marginal positions of slaves and places them at the heart of modernity itself: "A preoccupation with the striking doubleness that results from this unique position—in an expanded West but not completely of it—is a definitive characteristic of the intellectual history of the Black Atlantic."[59]

Looking to understand other forms of identity not encompassed by national boundaries, "the Black Atlantic" challenges national identity as being fixed to a specific geographical location with its own language, values, norms and symbols, and "links between place, location and consciousness."[60] Seeking to go beyond the nation and the binaries of America/non-America, Gilroy unpicks the concept of nationality and the nation-state, since his diaspora theory is formulated in direct opposition to the nation-state and "codes of modern citizenship."[61] Thus there can be no allegiance to the nation-state, since "by embracing diaspora . . . more highly than the coercive state of the nation, the concept becomes explicitly anti-national."[62] In fact, Gilroy sees the nation-state as a threat to diaspora/transnationalism: "The nation state has regularly been presented as the institutional means to terminate diaspora dispersal, as in the founding of the state of Israel."[63] While some have hailed his thinking as influential, others have cautioned against his "transfigurative, utopian vision."[64] Ien Ang, founding director of cultural studies at the Centre for Cultural Research at the University of Western Sydney, where she was professor and ARC professorial fellow and fellow of the Australian Academy of the Humanities, briefly summarizes Gilroy's position thus: "Simply put, the nation-state is cast as the limiting, homogenising, assimilating power structure, which is now, finally, being deconstructed from within by those groups who used to be marginalised within its borders but are now bursting out of them through their diasporic transnational connections. Global diaspora, in this context, signifies triumph over the shackles of the nation-state and national identity."[65]

Since the elaboration of relativism in jazz academe is never made explicit, it is worth reminding ourselves that when the New Jazz Studies describe jazz as a transnational music,[66] it is to align the music with Gilroy's thesis. At this point we can now see how closely the study "Europe and the New Jazz Studies" follows certain key features of Gilroy's thesis:[67]

*Jazz and Culture in a Global Age*

| PAUL GILROY | NEW JAZZ STUDIES |
|---|---|
| By embracing diaspora . . . the concept becomes explicitly antinational | We should avoid talk of national culture in jazz |
| Diaspora is . . . an alternative to nation and bounded culture coded into the body | The assumption that musical codes and conventions represent some kind of deep-rooted national consciousness is deeply flawed |
| There is a call [with the diaspora theory] to go beyond the nation and the binary of America/non-America* | Where simplistic [national] binaries remain intact . . . it becomes impossible to move beyond [them] |
| Europe is a "bleached continent" | [Discussion about] Nordic musicians inevitably contributes to the ideological and imperial bleaching of Europe |

Sources: Paul Gilroy, *The Black Atlantic: Modernity and Double Consciousness* (London and New York: Verso, 1993); Paul Gilroy, "Diaspora and the Detours of Identity," in *Identity and Difference*, ed. Kathryn Woodward (Milton Keynes: Open University, 1997); Tony Whyton, "Europe and the New Jazz Studies," in *Eurojazzland*, ed. Luca Cerchiari, Laurent Cugny, and Franz Kerschbaumer (Boston: Northeastern University Press, 2012).

*Neil Campbell, Jude Davies, and George McKay, eds., *Issues in Americanisation and Culture* (Edinburgh: Edinburgh University Press, 2004).

As we can see, the New Jazz Studies expressions of conformity to Gilroy's theory include the call to "*avoid* talk of national culture in jazz,"[68] since Gilroy argues that we should value "diaspora more highly than the coercive unanimity of the nation."[69] There is a reason for this, as Campbell, Davies, and McKay point out: "Critics such as Gilroy . . . are deeply suspicious about constructions of the nation for several reasons—nations enforce racial, ethnic and other hierarchies in the name of national unity and form the very boundaries diasporic thinking is designed to circumvent."[70] Since Gilroy explicitly rejects "distinctive cultures [and the] . . . fundamental power of territory to determine identity,"[71] globalization emerges as a threat because, as, Roland Robertson argues, its dialectical counterpart—glocalization—reinvigorates the power of territory to determine identity, ultimately creating "unique cultural constellations" reflective of the local: what Gilroy dismisses as parochial and the very thing diaspora is intended to subvert by disrupting the "links between place, location and consciousness . . . that express and reproduce absolutely distinctive cultures."[72]

However, as Ien Ang has written, "There is something deeply problematical about such celebrations of diaspora," pointing to diaspora's opposition to the nation-state and national culture.[73] However, events have moved on since *The Black Atlantic* was published in 1993, not least the rise in nationalism and the nation-state that few had predicted. As we have seen (page 111), the fear of cultural convergence and its implicit threat to national culture and way of life has prompted pride in the nation state and national values, something globalization theorists considered initially an aberration. They were wrong. The resilience of nationalist spirit in opposition to the onset of a global culture has been greatly facilitated by statewide public education that effectively tied national language and culture to the state, thus *reinforcing* notions of nationalism and the nation-state—precisely what Gilroy contends that diasporism/transnationalism is intended to overwhelm by calling for diaspora to be valued more highly than the "coercive unanimity of the nation," since the concept is "explicitly anti-national."[74] Turning to the music of the nationalists in classical music, we see it is specifically framed to *express* "distinctive cultures"—the very thing that Gilroy rejects[75]—whereby the frisson of binary opposition to the dominant Germanic culture or the Austro-Hungarian Empire (or in the case of Sibelius, the Russian Empire) became a creative spur. In fact, the work of the nationalist composers has to be understood *in terms of binary opposition* that produced music of enduring beauty and power—indeed, these days it is almost de rigueur at a classical music concert to include a piece by one or other of the nationalists, since their works are so popular within the classical oeuvre.[76] Equally, glocalized jazz seeks to express distinct local culture that often does not seek to move beyond the binary of America/non-America. The reason is that some local jazz musicians, as a matter of artistic or aesthetic choice, or political opposition to, say, American foreign policy (see the examples at the end of this chapter), or the realization that their creations subconsciously reflect their sociocultural background, or quite simply for nationalist reasons, do not want to sound "American" in their creations and want to reflect their own cultural identity in jazz (see quotations above). Thus for some, it might appear that a rote application of a sociological theory, however en vogue, raises the possibility of diminishing, rather than enhancing, our understanding of jazz in national and local settings, since dismissing glocalized jazz as a "simple inversion of the jazz-as-American/jazz-as-global binary"[77] would appear as questionable as dismissing Gabriel Fauré's *Pavane in F minor* as a "classical-music-as-Germanic/classical-music-as-French binary" inasmuch as in art it is not the means that are used to create an end but what the end achieves that matters.[78] At this point students of jazz (never mind the musically curious, researchers, writers, teachers, and some academics) may notice a curious asymmetry whereby the influence of national culture in classical music, rock, and hip-hop forms a standard area of musical discourse, while in contrast in jazz there is now a call to "*avoid* talk of national culture in jazz."[79]

In examining the congruence between Gilroy's diaspora/transnationalism theory and the "Europe and the New Jazz Studies" thesis, certain arguments, when explored in detail, provide a valuable context in which to rehearse subsidiary detail that might contribute toward a better understanding of jazz globalization. For example, when Gilroy specifically rejects "the fundamental power of territory to define identity,"[80] and thus the idea of "culture coded into the body,"[81] it is in turn echoed by the New Jazz Studies assertion that "the assumption that musical codes and conventions represent some kind of deep rooted national consciousness is deeply flawed."[82] However, examination of this claim opens up an exciting new dimension in which to consider the effects of jazz glocalization. If we leave aside how the *Independent on Sunday* dismissed this particular claim by Gilroy as "fundamentally wrong,"[83] and turn instead to early music, we see it had a well-defined social function that "validates ritual, accompanies dance and *encodes cultural meaning*,"[84] tropes that have continued to be part of music's function not only in the Western world but other civilizations as well. In the music of the baroque period, we see that certain musical devices were codified into a musical vocabulary that were used to portray emotions such as joy, rage, sadness, and elation that were well understood by audiences of the time—certain rising musical figures to imply the Ascension, the lowering of musical pitch to imply darkness and the inferno, and so on. This kind of culture-specific signification of specific codes is perhaps an inevitable outcome of a mature musical form, and musicologist Philip Tagg believes that they exist in modern popular music too. He dubs them "musemes," from biologist Richard Dawkins's idea of "memes" to describe ideas that propagate through culture.[85]

Since so much of the world's music is song, or derived from song, it follows that melodic construction is typically influenced by the meter and rhythm of language (language being both a code and a convention). In classical music, for example, it has long been acknowledged how language influences melodic construction. In their *History of Western Music*, Burkholder, Grout, and Plassica write how the English composer Edward Elgar (1857–1934) was not touched by the growing interest in folksong among European nationalist composers, suggesting that his "English-ness" was implicit in his melodic lines, which mirrored the intonations of English speech.[86] This symmetry between music and language becomes more apparent when, for example, we compare the melodic construction of a Verdi aria and a Schubert lieder. This is an exercise in which we can all participate, since it is not necessary to speak either German or Italian to hear how melodic contour follows the inherent rhythm of language. According to evidence produced by neuroscientist Aniruddh Patel and his coworkers, language patterns of rhythm and melody shaped the music of English and French composers from the late nineteenth and early twentieth centuries.[87] "Their focus on this period was intentional," writes musicologist Philip Ball, "both because it was a time when many composers strove to articulate a musical nationalism and because it would be hard to make a meaningful comparison with the imperfectly known language patterns of more distant periods."[88] Earlier, we saw how Janacek's "speech melodies" and Bartók's use of field recordings of peasant melodies and speech patterns represented "musical codes and conventions" that reflected a "deep rooted [Hungarian] national consciousness." As the composer, pianist, and conductor Antony Hopkins has pointed out, in classical music, "nationalist elements can be traced to the different accentuation of languages [since] rhythm tends to be closely associated with words, even in instrumentally conceived music. A tune by Bartók, Janacek, Dvořák, Borodin or Falla will be easily recognised as having national characteristics both rhythmically and melodically."[89]

It is interesting to note that despite the research that has been conducted on Mother Tongue language influence on melodic and rhythmic construction, it has received surprisingly little attention in the area of jazz studies. Yet the phonetics, phonologies, and syntax of a Mother Tongue language inhere in the very fabric of music; songwriters of all nations have always been very sensitive to matching the inflective contour of melody to the syllables and rhythm of speech patterns—which of course vary from language to language. We are all exposed to the relationship between our Mother Tongue and melody from a very young age, and the mnemonic power of music is such that most of us can remember the words of pop songs from our formative years more easily than the poetry or prose we were taught at school. How musical elements follow the rhythm and inflections of Mother Tongue language is hard-wired into our sub-conscious. Some classical music scholars have pointed out how language change over the centuries has influenced the evolution of musical genres, such as the interrelationship between language and melody, citing the example of the development of the Italian madrigal. As Danlee Mitchell and Jack Logan have pointed out, "The overall structure of music and the overall structure of language in Western culture are closely related. The overall syntax of language and the structural layering of musical events in a piece of music are strikingly similar. Both language and music mirror certain socio-psycho forces of our culture."[90]

Although the correlation between Mother Tongue language and me-lodic construction has surfaced infrequently in jazz, it is well enough known by some advanced European jazz musicians with a command of several languages. As the German pianist Michael Wollny has noted, "Your native language somehow has a lot to do with how you play your instrument because it . . . reflects national identity; people from Nor-way play differently from people from France, people from Germany will phrase in another way and I think that has a lot to do with native lan-guage."[91] Wollny's observation is echoed by Belgian jazz pianist Jef Neve, who studied in the Lemmensinstituut in Louvain, graduating with simul-taneous Master of Music degrees in classical music and jazz, and going on to postgraduate studies in chamber music, graduating cum laude (with honor) in 2001. Neve, who is fluent in six languages, observes: "This is the great richness of being here [in Europe], the languages. Each language has its own sound. I can almost tell when a person is a native English speaker when I hear them play. Or French, or Italian or German or Span-ish."[92] While Neve makes no claim to infallibility, he does however point out how language influences melodic construction when a European jazz musician improvises without recourse to certain rote performance habits such as pattern running or reciting certain "licks" acquired from record-ings or study: "My success rate [at guessing their nationality] is usually quite good." This suggests that a subtle form of localization, or glocaliza-tion, might be at work below an individual jazz musician's threshold of conscious perception, whereby Mother Tongue language (or codes and conventions) influence improvised melodic construction. That is some-thing the Swedish composer and arranger Nils Lindberg discovered quite by chance after the release in 1960 of his first album, *Sax Appeal*, now re-garded as one of the classics of Swedish jazz. "When my first LP came out in 1960—it was for four saxes and rhythm section with among others Lars

Gullin on baritone—it was a surprise to read my music had this Swedish touch," he recalled. "It was there from the beginning, I didn't realise it, it was only when people told me . . . I thought my arrangements were American jazz, West Coast style!"[93] Here, it is again interesting to refer to the responses of jazz musicians from several different countries (see above) to compare their perceptions of Mother Tongue influence on jazz.

Contemporary research has demonstrated how inherent structures in language shape our thoughts without our realizing it. "Patterns in language offer a window on a culture's disposition and priorities," said Lera Boroditsky, professor of psychology at Stamford University. "All this new research shows us that the languages we speak not only reflect or express our thoughts, but also shape the thoughts we want to express."[94] Thus the correlation between melody and language becomes ever closer, since language is more than just a means of communication. It is this "deep rooted consciousness," regrettably dismissed by the New Jazz Studies, that influences our culture and our thought processes, as Frances Simon has pointed out:

> Cultural identities can be created by the language that is used, and entire societies may define themselves based on the language and dialect they speak. [One example] is the country of Belgium. Most of its citizens speak either Belgian or French. The speakers of both languages feel that they are very different and better than those who speak the other language. Their identity is determined by the language they speak. One result of this is Belgium's recent inability to maintain a cohesive government. The effect of language on culture, of differentiating and uniting groups of people, is more profound than most people realize. Not only does the specific vocabulary reflect the culture, the language or dialect spoken can also both define and separate cultures.[95]

People make decisions and represent life through cultural codes learned and absorbed from early childhood, and reality is mediated by language, as can be demonstrated by turning to countries with gendered language systems—more than half the world—as Clotaire Rapaille points out:

> For example, "the sun" in French is *le soleil*, a masculine noun, and for the French, a word closely associated with the Sun King, Louis XIV. The French, who imprint this reference at a young age, perceive the sun as male, and by extension, see males as brilliant and shining. Women, on the other hand, are associated with the moon, *la lune*, a feminine word.

The moon, of course, does not shine by herself; she reflects the light of the sun . . . For Germans, these words have nearly opposite meanings. The sun, *die Sonne*, is feminine, and Germans believe that women are the ones who bring warmth to the world, make things grow, raise children. German men are night, the dark, the moon side, *Der Mond*, "the moon," a masculine term . . . [Thus] words like "sun" and "moon" can trigger completely opposite imprints among the French and Germans. Therefore, each culture has a different interpretation—a different Code—for these words. All of these different codes for all of the different imprints, when put together, create a reference system that people living in these cultures use without being aware of it. These reference systems guide cultures in very different ways.[96]

If we are allowed, for a moment, to invoke "such uncool notions as the existence of the real world,"[97] we see in the global jazz context countless musicians reflecting aspects of their cultural-specific codes in their music (see examples at the end of this chapter). However, it is not just jazz artists who are doing this in their cultural productions. It is something that extends across a wide range of artistic creation. When the American cultural anthropologist Margaret Mead claimed, "We are our culture,"[98] she put "are" in italics to emphasize how culture defines us. Whatever we may be, she argued, we could only be of our own culture, not that of somebody else, serving to underscore the uniqueness of individuals and of communities. For example, when the Iranian filmmaker Marjane Satrapi was interviewed for *Les Inrockuptibles* magazine to promote her film *Persepolis* (2007), she said, "Even if I have lived in France for twenty years, I didn't grow up here. There will always be a little Iranian core to my work. I love Rimbaud, of course, but Omar Khayyám will always speak to me more."[99] By turning away from cultural influence across a wide range of artistic creativity, the New Jazz Studies become less a response to engaging with a real and complex world, and more of adapting past texts in support of some metatheoretical analysis that deadens discussion that favors anything that is qualitatively different or dependent on new or changing circumstances. The demand/need for institutional affirmation or peer recognition is such that it seems it is less the quality of ideas that matter but more the claim to expertise through the application of a new theory. Some disquisitions speak less about the music, more about the application of a theory or practice adopted from other disciplines and couched in an obscurantist, jargon-filled language that is increasingly specialized and not framed within a vernacular that can be readily understood by the public; rather, it constitutes, "a metalanguage and series of methodologies that close out the amateur."[100] However, as Richard Dawkins has observed: "Suppose you are an intellectual impostor with nothing to say, but with strong ambitions to succeed in academic life, collect a coterie of reverent disciples and have students around the world anoint your pages with respectful yellow highlighter. What kind of literary style would you cultivate? Not a lucid one, surely, for clarity would expose your lack of content."[101]

For some, what is missing in the application of Gilroy's diaspora/transnationalism theory to jazz is its failure to address the music as a human expression with values that require human sympathy to interpret, treating the music instead as a vehicle to frame a fashionable sociological theory through the prism of relativism. Yet methodology such as this is depressingly en vogue: "Should it remain taboo for authors to challenge existing representations of jazz icons or to explore some of the more controversial or unsavoury aspects of their biographies?" demands one advocate of postmodernism techniques in the New Jazz Studies: "Indeed, interrogation of representation and the revision of interpretations of the past has formed the bedrock of critical and cultural theory and is an expected mode of criticism within the majority of academic contexts outside jazz; the now firmly established world of New Jazz Studies should be able to draw on such methods."[102]

This emphasis on "challenge," "controversial," "revisionism," "interrogation," and "criticism" often results in a curious asymmetry whereby the object of these "expected modes of criticism" is subjected to a more severe regime than those who employ such techniques. Rather than seeking a deeper understanding of a topic through engagement with the real world and depth of relevant research, real knowledge, and reflection, we are witness to, as Sandke observes, the "glitzy pursuit of easy acclaim through a zombie-like adherence to fashionable ideologies."[103] At this point we need to acknowledge the possibility that a measure of interpretive charity and wide responsiveness to the music may be being sacrificed in a search for meaning within a speciality using fashionable protocols at the expense of a more creative, informed, and interpretive approach to the music. As Randall Sandke has noted,[104] "Formulating theory first and then selectively marshalling evidence to support it" can result in problematical relativist conclusions that do not square with the objective truth, as can be seen when attempting to interpret "The Nordic Tone in Jazz" using Gilroy's diaspora thesis.

The Nordic Tone might be said to be the sound of some Scandinavian musicians (by no means all) defining their identity with an approach to jazz that has become associated with specific geographical location. But viewed through Gilroy's diaspora theory, this becomes a problematical construct since diaspora theory seeks to annihilate "the fundamental power of territory to define identity."[105] Thus it becomes necessary to downplay the Nordic Tone in the same way Gabbard downplayed Bix Beiderbecke's contributions to jazz in *Hotter than That*, since, as Sandke points out, "Beiderbecke is a perpetual thorn in the side of present-day believers [like Gabbard] in the 'jazz-as-black-music' paradigm,"[106] thus acknowledging the genius of the white cornet player "would compromise [his] central thesis."[107] Similarly, instead of attempting to reach the richest, most nuanced understanding of the Nordic Tone, it is dismissed as a construct intended for "the promotion of Norway as a cultural export,"[108] which "Scandinavian artists, promoters and policy makers have played a significant role in constructing."[109]

Such an assertion brings to mind Schopenhauer's characteristically sombre reminder that every man mistakes the limits of his own vision for the vision of the world, since there is a failure here to present the Nordic Tone within the broader context of Scandinavian music as a whole. What the New Jazz Studies seem to be attempting here is not to enlarge our view of life but instead to simplify it with a relativist reading of the music where real knowledge is portrayed as just one more opinion in competition with other equally valid perspectives. But if we were to turn to Nils Grinde's *History of Norwegian Music* and biographies of Edvard Grieg—such as Finn Benestad's and Dag Schejelderup's *Edvard Grieg: Chamber Music—Nationalism, Universality, Individuality*—we discover a very different tale of the Nordic Tone's origins. Grinde is most rewarding in his account of folk traditions, many of which are still extant. Herding songs, lullabies, mountain calls and rowing chants can still be sampled in the field and are music that is communal as well as practically communicative. In the eighteenth and nineteenth centuries, the music of the peasant Hardanger-fiddle tradition culminated in music that was simultaneously function, entertainment, and art. The *gangar, springar, halling,* and *pols* were dances—usually in triple time—that emerged at the hands of folk fiddlers who attained a high degree of virtuosity and were celebrated as much in towns as in rural villages.

These complementary strands came together in the music of Edvard Grieg in a way that differentiated his music from the Austro-German tradition of classical music. While Grieg's early piano and violin sonata, written when he was twenty-two, might not have displayed the craft and discipline of a Brahms, Benestad and Schjelderup-Ebbe point out how such values would have been inapposite in a work whose virtues lie in the feeling of spontaneity Grieg projects. His sweet-flowing lyricism with its folksy drones is devoid of Teutonic angst, and in the second movement Grieg often uses a motif of a descending second followed by a major or minor third that Benestad and Schjelderup-Ebbe call the "Grieg formula"—a device used by many folk-affiliated composers, notably Vaughan-Williams. Two years later, in 1867, Grieg called his Second Violin Sonata "my national sonata," in which we discover the "Grieg formula," peasant dance rhythms, *springar* triple time, and a coda that incorporates a Hardanger-style violin cadenza. Grieg's third violin and piano sonata has, in its Romanza, a fierce folk dance, while his String Quartet in G minor has an introduction based on the "Grieg formula" and whose extreme contrasts of tempo and mood culminate in fiery Hardanger fiddle rhythms.

Between 1867 and 1901 Grieg published ten volumes of *Lyric Pieces* that include vividly descriptive pieces such as "Wedding Day in Troldhaugen" or "Klokkeklang," evocative of his closeness to peasant culture and their customs he enjoyed as a boy. During this same period he wrote his Opus 66 and Opus 72, where he metamorphosed folksongs and Hardanger fiddle dances into piano pieces that rivaled Bartók's similar intensity in refashioning Magyar song and dance. This, as Benestad and Schjelderup-Ebbe remind us, was where Grieg's heart lay, in his national songs, *Lyric Pieces*, and folkloric song arrangements as much as his complex G-minor Quartet or his C-minor Violin Concerto. During his lifetime Grieg was celebrated as an international celebrity; his *Peer Gynt* suite, for example— the incidental music to the 1867 Henrik Ibsen play of the same name— remains a concert hall favorite to this day. Today, Grieg is revered as a national hero for putting Norway on the cultural map of Europe. Thus it is perhaps unsurprising that Scandinavian musicians have found it perfectly natural to draw on folkloric influences, like Grieg, within contemporary classical music, pop, rock (for example, the work of bands such as Sigur Ros or artists such as Bjork), and jazz—indeed, many Scandinavian jazz musicians have used Grieg as a direct inspiration in their own creations.[110]

It is worth reminding ourselves that the Nordic Tone in jazz existed for more than half a century *before* the Norwegian government took an active interest in promoting Norwegian jazz as an aspect of cultural diplomacy, as attested literature on the subject of the Nordic Tone in jazz—such as James W. Dickenson's valuable *From Grieg to Garbarek: Norwegian Jazz and National Identity* (2011)—makes clear. In other words, it existed well before the Norwegian government was the recipient of tax revenue from its native oil industry that allowed it to invest up to 1 percent of its gross domestic product on the arts, so making an investment in the subsidy of jazz possible. In fact, the Nordic Tone in jazz has its roots in Sweden in the 1920s and 1930s:

> Melodies associated with Swedish folk music or taken from the heritage of popular Swedish tunes cropped up in Swedish jazz as early as the 1920s and 1930s. Many of the Swedish musicians who ended up in jazz brought with them experiences from very different musical domains (old-time dancing, brass sextets and so on). In the '50s jazz musicians still earned their living playing in a wide variety of genres in dance bands, theatre orchestras and jazz groups, and audiences . . . expected to hear jazzed up Swedish melodies, preferably with a singer. Even the most skilled jazz improvisers could occasionally permit themselves a "national spree" in the midst of hero-worship of American idols. . . . In the Americanized, progressive Sweden of the '50s, "Swedish Tone" came to be synonymous with something utterly modern and serious.[111]

While the practice of incorporating Swedish folksongs into jazz was widespread in Sweden, the one question that troubled Swedish jazz musicians and critics was that of authenticity, whether incorporating Swedish elements into what was an Afro-American art form could be construed as the "real jazz." In 1951 Stan Getz toured Sweden with a Swedish pick-up band and on March 23 went into the recording studio. Among the pieces they recorded that day was a version of an old Swedish folksong called "Ack Värmeland Du Sköna." Back in the United States, these sessions were released on the Roost label which Getz passed to Miles Davis, who recorded "Ack Värmeland Du Sköna" as "Dear Old Stockholm" on May 9, 1952, in slightly modified form for Blue Note records. Davis recorded the piece again on June 5, 1956,[112] for his Columbia records debut album *Round about Midnight*. Because of Davis's commanding position in the jazz firmament, his recordings of what was in reality "Ack Värmeland Du Sköna" became influential in "sanctioning," or giving the green light to, the use of Swedish folkloric elements within Scandinavian jazz.

The Swedish baritone saxophonist Lars Gullin was one of the Swedish musicians accompanying Getz at the 1951 session that produced

"Ack Värmeland du Sköna," an experience that encouraged him to develop his own "Swedish" voice by incorporating folkloric elements into jazz. In 1952 he recorded a version of "Sov du lilla vida ung" (Sleep, Little Pussy-willow), and subsequent compositions such as "First Walk," "Merlin," "Danny's Dream," "Fedja," "Fine Together," "It's True," "Like Grass," and "Castle Waltz" were imbued with a pensive melancholy characteristic of his Swedish folk heritage and of Swedish composers such as Wilhelm Peterson-Berger and Hugo Alfvén.

Inspired by live performances and recordings of Gullin, the Norwegian critic Bjørn Kolstad, jazz critic for the Swedish daily *Bergens Tidende*, wrote in 1955 that: "Jazz has hitherto been practised by many gifted European musicians. But European jazz has not previously adapted itself to any national characteristic style, it has been a slavish copy of American ideals, and it has in fact been evaluated according to how closely it could copy American models . . . [But in the playing of Lars Gullin we have] . . . a mood we have never heard in jazz before . . . Gullin himself played so well that we felt we were on home ground, we felt that perhaps *we*, in our small corner of the world, could in such a way make jazz our own."[113]

This emergence of a localized form of jazz was followed by highly influential works such as *Old Folklore in Swedish Modern* by Bengt-Arne Wallin (1962) and *Jazz Pår Svenska* by Jan Johansson (1965), which influenced subsequent generations of Scandinavian jazz musicians in both Sweden and Norway. This was a result of the proximity of Norway to Sweden and their similar languages and culture (Norway was a part of Sweden until 1905). It was only years *after* Norwegian jazz stars such as Jan Garbarek, Terje Rypdal, Jon Christensen, and Arild Anderssen garnered international attention and acclaim as a result of their recordings for the Munich-based ECM label that their government began to see value in providing tour support for Norwegian jazz musicians as an aspect of cultural diplomacy. By then the "Nordic Tone"—originally "The Swedish Tone in Jazz"—was a pre-existing aspect of Scandinavian jazz that matches conventional notions of a musical culture with its own tradition and history, a body of real knowledge that is at odds with the relativist claims that the Nordic Tone was devised for the "promotion of Norway as a cultural export." The problem here is that selecting a theory, applying it to jazz, "and then selectively marshalling evidence to support it" means that other subsidiary arguments are also set in motion, also at variance with the objective truth, in order to maintain consistency with an off-the-shelf theory.

Thus we have the awkward problem of Scandinavian jazz musicians whose work is thought to conform to the stylistic parameters of the Nordic Tone. It then follows that their contributions have to be correspondingly diminished because they might compromise the central thesis of diaspora theory, thus these musicians are dismissed as having "developed musical concepts that feed into the romanticised depictions of the frozen north."[114] Here, the music of Bugge Wesseltoft and Nils Petter Molvaer was cited, but since there was no attempt to contact these artists to gain insight into their music *or* discuss the Nordic Tone in relation to their artistic outlook,[115] some might conclude that this application of "subjective insight" is opinion being passed as fact. Nevertheless, if we choose to agree with the conclusions of this particular application of the diaspora thesis, that "the Nordic Tone" is "not an expression of some collective Scandinavian consciousness,"[116] a certain amount of jazz history will have to be rewritten. By extrapolation, West Coast jazz was "not an expression of some collective Californian consciousness," New Orleans jazz is "not the expression of some collective New Orleans–ian consciousness," and so too Kansas City (1930s) and Chicago (1920s—where do we stop?) all are well-attested schools of jazz that, like the Nordic Tone, reveal a distinct, identifiable "localized" style that we associate with a specific geographic location.

Clearly then, to paraphrase Campbell, Davies, and McKay, we must be careful about the uses to which the work of postcolonial critics like Gilroy are put, since "the point of the *Black Atlantic* is that it is black."[117] So when Gilroy depicts Europe as a "bleached continent" the New Jazz Studies follow, claiming that Scandinavian jazz evokes "the synonymity of the terms 'white' and 'European,'"[118] which "inevitably contributes to the ideological and imperial bleaching of Europe."[119] Gilroy is attracted to the writing of LeRoi Jones, who once coined the phrase "the changing same," which, says Gilroy, "provides a valuable motif with which to supplement and expand the Diaspora idea."[120] The work of former SUNY, Stony Brook, professor Amri Baraka (back when he was LeRoi Jones), praised by Gabbard as "ambitious and provocative" in his book *Hotter than That*, caused controversy with his exclusionary claim that jazz was "Black music" following the publication in 1967 of *Blues People: Negro Music in White America*. It was a claim that was reawakened in the 1990s, the *New York Times Magazine* noting in 1997: "Over the past decade, in large part because of Wynton Marsalis's efforts, jazz has been widely celebrated as an essential element of the African-American cultural heritage, and white practitioners have been seen increasingly as interlopers."[121] Although in more recent times Marsalis has appeared to embrace a more ecumenical stance toward the music, this appears to be the philosophical starting point of *Hotter than That*, where, as Randall Sandke points out, "white musicians are given short shrift throughout this book."[122]

It reflects a fashionable view among some jazz academics in the United States, creating what Sandke calls a curious schizophrenia in jazz colleges: "On the one hand, universities happily take money from legions of young white musicians accepted into their jazz departments of their music schools. At the same time, professors in social and cultural studies loudly proclaim that jazz is black music."[123] It is a paradox that serves to undermine jazz as a truly democratic music. Clearly it is the product of Afro-American exceptionalism, but historically it was never an exclusionary music. Miles Davis had no qualms about hiring pianists Victor Feldman (formerly a member of Cannonball Adderley's quintet) or Bill Evans, guitarist John McLaughlin (at the time when he a member of Tony Williams' Lifetime), keyboardist Joe Zawinul (formerly Dinah Washington's accompanist and member of the Cannonball Adderley Quintet and subsequently coleader, with Wayne Shorter, of Weather Report, the most successful jazz band of the late 1970s and early 1980s); and he regarded arranger Gil Evans as his best friend. The notion that contemporary jazz — that is, jazz in today's globalized world—must somehow be rooted in the black experience of jazz's Golden Age and articulate a specific sociocultural identity fails to acknowledge that jazz is an art form, and like all art, it inevitably grows beyond its roots—Martha Graham's work was not dismissed because it did not conform to the *Ballets Russes*, any more than Wagner's *Tristan und Isolde* was dismissed because it did not conform to *Opera Seria*. Equally, jazz should be seen within this broader context of the arts. It is interesting to note that the move by some to claim "ownership" of the music is, *as Gilroy himself has said*, "an attempt to take out a copyright and say that, 'Actually, jazz is our property and no-one else's property.' Well, it breaks my heart to say this, but culture isn't property."[124]

Clearly, then, there is a need for flexibility in attempting to interpret the transmission of jazz across national borders, and it is quite possible that some may feel that the way in which the New Jazz Studies remain so ideologically tied to the coattails of Gilroy's diaspora/transnationalism theory, leaves little room for this kind of flexibility. As Laura Chrisman has suggested, it is "a decidedly mystical, idealist ideology, [that] constructs a transcendental category of blackness . . . [and] because his definition of this emancipatory black diasporism repudiates the potential resources of nationalism and socialism, and proceeds by way of positing absolute antinomies between these respective value systems, Gilroy's formulations become necessarily self-enclosed, hermetically sealed off, resistant to dialogism, dialectical transformation and cross-fertilization."[125]

For some, it seems, the sound of glocalized, or localized, jazz is too far removed from the tradition of jazz's great master musicians of its Golden Years—Armstrong, Ellington, Parker, Miles Davis, Coltrane, Mingus, and so on—and the specific environmental pressures they experienced for it to be jazz, so exiling it from a particular tradition of improvising jazz originality that maintains the idea that jazz must always sound rooted in the black experience. From this standpoint, jazz has a fixed identity, and those loyal to tradition and or history who are looking for signs of what jazz used to be when the towering greats of Afro-American exceptionalism hastened jazz's trajectory through the first three-quarters of the twentieth century will probably conclude that its greatest work is almost done: that the great Afro-American master narrative is approaching exhaustion, and all we are left with are distant echoes of the past. Yet the influence of these great masters of jazz's Golden Years is such that it has tended to fill the viewfinder, setting in train a belief that evolutionary change in jazz must naturally emanate from within the land of its origin. Looking at this proposition dispassionately there is no reason why this should be. Jazz went global as early as 1917—perhaps even before, with ragtime-into-jazz exponents performing in Europe before then—and in the course of a century of emulation and assimilation, greatly aided since the 1970s by a systematic form of jazz education imported from American conservatories and universities, other musicians in other countries have negotiated their own relationship with the music that has resulted in imaginative reconceptualizations of the music in local settings.

Today, with no single jazz musician dominating the 1980s, 1990s, and early millennium years, attention is moving from the American jazz scene to fresh approaches, recombinations of existing knowledge and hybridized versions of jazz to be found in the global arena. Of course, there is a temptation to see a hybridized, or localized version of jazz in isolation. But if we aggregate all forms of localized—or glocalized—jazz forms from around the world (see examples below), a significant trend emerges. This is not to say these versions of jazz are somehow "better" than American jazz, only to suggest that because of localization—or glocalization—they often contain properties that are not present in American jazz, and it is these differences that are attracting attention in a music that has not shown signs of significant evolution since the 1970s. Thomas Jefferson once famously said he liked the dreams of the future better than the history of the past, and if we were to look to where the future of jazz lies, it would be to the diversity of these individual contributors on the global stage. What began in the United States is now owned by the world, inspired by America's great Afro-American geniuses, yes, but no longer dominated by them as maybe, just maybe, those great icons would have wanted. After all, Charlie Parker expressed a desire to study classical music in Paris under Nadia Boulanger,[126] John Coltrane studied advanced theoretical concepts in classical music with Dennis Sandole and incorporated aspects of music from the subcontinent of India, while Louis Armstrong was not beyond quoting riffs from Italian Opera.

## Examples of Glocalization of Jazz
## as a Global Phenomenon

Just as the globalization of American jazz can be claimed a worldwide phenomenon, so too is the glocalization of jazz, which is "producing" unique outcomes in different geographic areas. In these instances, local jazz musicians seek to create original music that is both part of a universal language of jazz and a singular expression of identity (often cultural identity). Beyond the borders of the United States, the transformations brought about by glocalization occurred gradually, since initially most local musicians struggled to keep abreast of successive shocks announcing the new emanating from America following the decline of the big bands circa 1945: bebop was followed by hard bop and cool jazz, which was followed by free jazz and modal jazz, and so on. It was not until the 1960s that the most significant developments in glocalization occurred, given impetus in part by America's unpopular Vietnam campaign, which prompted widespread protest, including significant unrest within America itself. While Europeans had embraced American-style consumer culture and the improving lifestyle that accompanied it—the rise of the motorcar, the easy availability of white goods, the popularity of fast foods, easy access to movies, television culture, and the rest—as well as American social attitudes absorbed through film, theater, television programs, and literature, Vietnam prompted a lively debate about the extent and nature of the national soul, causing many to openly question American values, including many young jazz musicians. For example, in the United Kingdom the British Library website noted:

> By the early '60's, jazz was considered part of the mainstream American establishment, to the extent that it was being actively used by Washington to promote US interests and culture abroad. America's aggressive pursuit of an imperialistic and anti-communist agenda in both Vietnam and Cold War Europe increasingly alienated the anti-establishment subculture that was blooming in Britain in this period. Musicians such as SME (Spontaneous Music Ensemble) [which included drummer John Stevens and saxophonist Trevor Watts] and AMM [which included Keith Rowe on guitar, Lou Gare on saxophone, and Eddie Prévost on drums] began exploring ways to separate jazz from its American role model, taking inspiration instead from European influences, such as the avant-garde experiments of Stockhausen.[127]

Recalling these times in a 2002 interview, saxophonist Trevor Watts of the Spontaneous Music Ensemble recalled: "In the '60s we reacted against the jazz music scene here, and the fact that you were compelled to play jazz like an American or not at all. So the music of the Spontaneous Music Ensemble came about from the fact that we didn't want to dote on American jazz, but take the spirit of that music for ourselves, and move things along in the way we wanted. Quite a novel idea in 1964!"[128] The year before, on the tenth anniversary of his big band, the doyen of British jazz, bandleader, composer, arranger, and alto saxophonist Johnny Dankworth was interviewed by the British *Melody Maker* magazine. Under the headline "Our Jazz Is British!" he said: "I think there has not been a positive enough attempt by the [British] musicians to grit their teeth and say, 'We will have a British style,' and do something about it. One shouldn't say, 'I'm going to make this sound like an American.' It has been proved we can produce records that do sound American. To me it should be the exact opposite."[129]

For bandleader Mike Westbrook, who in 1969 topped the "Arranger" category in the *Talent Deserving of Wider Recognition* section of the 1969 *Downbeat* International Jazz Critics' Poll, the 1960s was a period when "the American influence remained strong," and "[one had] to be very strong in one's convictions to question the American orthodoxy and to work on developing an independent voice. I had a sextet and occasional big band to write for throughout the '60s and was lucky to have a platform at [Ronnie Scott's] 'Old Place.' I started to write extended compositions, including an anti-war piece, Marching Song."[130] Ambitious, critically acclaimed, and spread over two twelve-inch long-playing recordings, *Marching Song* was just one of several classics of British jazz Westbrook recorded during this period with his big band that also included *Celebration*, *Release*, *Metropolis*, and *Citadel/Room 315*, prompting trumpeter Ian Carr to write: "This body of work, probably more than anything else, was responsible for the emancipation of British jazz from American slavery."[131] Equally, for pianist Michael Garrick, whose own ensembles created several classics of British jazz during this period, such as *October Woman*, *Promises*, *Black Marigolds*, *The Heart Is a Lotus*, *Cold Mountain*, *Home Stretch Blues*, and *Troppo*, British jazz seemed to be undergoing a process of self-discovery: "The 1960s saw an upsurge of originality in British jazz," Garrick reflected in 2002. "All the wonders that the great American prototypes so gloriously exhibited were no longer enough. What began to surface and receive delighted attention were those doing something fresh and home-grown."[132] In 2010, Garrick published his autobiography, which he called *Dusk Fire: Jazz in English Hands*. Trevor Bannister, writing the book's introduction, said: "In the twentieth century British jazz was that played by British musicians putting the American ethos before everything else. By contrast English jazz emerged with the culture and historical heritage of England foremost in mind. Michael Garrick was arguably the first to give expression to it."[133]

Vocalist Norma Winstone was a member of Garrick's ensemble on such classics as *Troppo* and *Home Stretch Blues* before establishing herself as one of the great vocalists in jazz.

> Michael Garrick gave me some songs he had written and I learned them, and I sat in with his sextet and sang one or two of them, and I realised after I had sung these songs, which I had never heard anybody sing before, written by

an Englishman, that I didn't use an American accent. And when I sang standards again, when I came to one of the words—that either was "da-r-nce" or "da-e-nse"—I pulled up short and realised I had found out something about myself. The way I sang. I realised I felt uncomfortable singing in an American accent—even singing standards. I worked in the 1970s with—shall I say—a lot of original voices in jazz in England, they were trying to do their own thing that felt right to sound English and not be so influenced by the Americans. Of course, when it comes to language it's fairly obvious if you are putting on an American accent. I mean, Cleo Laine doesn't, she sings with an English accent, and I started to do it, and if that is one way I have retained an "Englishness," I don't know, but fine![134]

In Holland, up until the 1960s, as pianist Jasper van't Hof told the daily newspaper *Ahlener Zeitung*, "Most Dutch players were focussed on the USA. Real jazz in their ears had to come from there. Whatever happened in Germany, Belgium, France, Poland was largely ignored. What a pity."[135] The rising protest across Europe against the Vietnam War saw several Dutch free jazz musicians embracing political issues, participating in a series of concerts dubbed Musicians for Vietnam, while others sought to remove American influences completely from their music. One such was German bassist Peter Kowald, who called his music "Kaput-play." Jazz musicians in Sweden were also questioning their country's willing embrace of American values and influence following the Vietnamese conflict, which prompted lively debate around Swedish nationalism and the national soul.

Jan Johansson, one of Sweden's foremost jazz musicians, was saxophonist Stan Getz's pianist of choice when he lived in Sweden and then Denmark (1958–60). As a member of Getz's quartet, Johansson became the only European jazz musician to appear on Norman Granz's Jazz at the Philharmonic concert program. Playing in a blues influenced, hard-swinging style favored by the saxophonist, Johansson can be heard on albums such as *Stan Getz at Nalen* (November 1959) and *Stan Getz at Large featuring Jan Johansson* (January 1960), which reveal him performing in an accomplished, driving post-bop style. Equally on the album *Don Byas at Nalen* we hear signs of artistic growth in his mastery of what might be called a straight-ahead American style. It is especially interesting, therefore, to compare his often extrovert playing with Byas, recorded on February 5, 1962, to his playing on his own recording session a matter of days later, on February 28, 1962. This was one of three sessions that produced *Jazz på Svenska*, an album comprising jazz versions of Swedish folk tunes from Svenska Låtar, the huge collection of Swedish national folk tunes. Here Johansson is the model of restraint, and with just Georg Riedel on bass, he allows the melodies to speak for themselves with sparing embellishment and understated improvisations that are at one with the mood of the album: one Swedish journalist described it as "a rural symbol of security in a Sweden which in the '60s was marching towards anonymous, big-city wilder-nesses."[136] Described as a "visionary statement," *Jazz pår Svenska* was in tune with the national mood following the debate surrounding Swedish nationalism and remains the best-selling jazz album in Sweden to this day, a striking example of a *local* musician playing jazz that makes sense of his own *local* musical surroundings with immediate relevance to his own *local* musical community.

In South Africa, Township Jazz emerged as a recognizable glocal variation of American jazz that evolved out of *marabi*, the oral tradition of African songs adapted by South African jazz instrumentalists. This early musical confluence of the global (that had been copied from American jazz records) and the local was originally called *marabi*, but by the 1940s, brass instruments had the effect of mod-ernizing *marabi* as much as the influence of the bebop musicians in the 1950s. As guitarist General Duze recalled: "*Marabi* came from Natal," he said. "We enjoyed playing their stuff, but we changed it because of the orchestration thing. To them it was just a line of melody and improvisation thereafter. But it did add something to jazz, because many people had started with . . . [and] enjoyed *marabi*. So they could pick up the music from there, and then we played the instrumental version of the same thing."[137] Danceband Highlife music, often referred to as Highlife, emerged in Ghana and spread to Sierra Leone, Nigeria, and other West African countries including South Africa prior to World War II. Inspired by the American big band recordings and their question and answer riffs, Highlife was typically played over a rhythm similar to the clave in which electric guitars and local per-cussion played a vital rhythmic role. In an example of how cultural flows can move in different directions (as opposed to those who see globalization as a unitary process "from the West to the rest"), American jazz musicians that have recorded examples of Highlife music have included Pharaoh Sanders, Randy Weston, Sonny Sharock, Wayne Shorter, and Craig Harris, while the Highlife style was featured by the Danish band Pierre Dorge and his Jungle Orchestra.

In Brazil, Acácio de Camargo Piedade, professor of music at the State Uni-versity of Santa Catarina, points out that "Brazilian jazz [was] born within the instrumental world of bossa nova and involves from the outset . . . [a] friction of musicalities"—Brazilian and North American jazz musicalities.[138] Once again it is important to emphasize that glocal jazz does not emerge from some hermetically sealed forum, developed in isolation from American jazz, but from direct interface with it, a point emphasized by Piedade. He describes how Brazilian musicians see the bebop paradigm as "both valuable and fearsome," since it "demonstrates tech-nical know-how and mastery of the jazz language, which symbolically is a passport to global communicability, but at the same time it teleologically points to the need for dissolving bebop itself and expressing what distinguishes it from Brazil-ian jazz, that which is nearer to the root of Brazilian musicality."[139] In order to do that, Brazilian musicians found it necessary to deconstruct the bebop paradigm in a creative process that embodies the global and the local: "When a [local] soloist has free space for expression," writes Piedade, "there are moments when he gives himself frankly to bebop, seeking the weight of the jazz tradition that gives him legitimacy and confers on him the symbolic status of global improviser; but at the same time he tries to express something more Brazilian, making use of traits of other [local] Brazilian music genres, such as chorinho."[140] Piedade points out that the localization—or glocalization—process at work in Brazilian jazz comprises an amalgam of regional Brazilian "musicalities"—Northeastern, chorinho, samba, Afro-Bahian, free (urban atonalism, outside scales) that is bound up in [local] discourses regarding cultural imperialism, national identity, globalization and regionalism."[141] Once again, demonstrating that cultural flows can move in different directions, many American jazz musicians have adapted and performed Brazilian jazz, including most famously Stan Getz, whose "Desafinado," released in June 1962, reached 15 on the Billboard Hot 100, and "The Girl from Ipanema," released in April 1964, which reached 5 on the Billboard Hot 100.

It is important to emphasize that these examples are not intended to be a definitive listing of glocalized styles that have occurred around the globe; indeed, that would be a book-length task. But since, for example, Brazilian jazz or South African Township jazz is easily accessible on the Internet, it provides the opportunity to identify aurally certain characteristics that differentiate them from each other and from American hegemonic styles of jazz in which they are rooted. Students should seek to identify aurally the commonalities and the differences between American jazz and local characteristics. As the *New York Times* has noted, the French-Vietnamese guitarist Nguyen Le is "one of the most creative of the many jazz players exploring the marriage of 'America's classical music' with traditional music [and] Le focuses on his roots, in Vietnam,"[142] while Lionel Loueke, the acclaimed guitarist from Benin, West Africa, who rounded his jazz studies at Berklee and the Thelonious Monk Institute, extensively draws on his African heritage, even incorporating the Kalimba (African thumb piano) into his performances.

Joe Zawinul, the late Austrian pianist, moved from Vienna to New York in 1959, distinguishing himself as an accompanist to Dinah Washington, and as a member of Cannonball Adderley Quintet and Sextet, on key recordings with Miles Davis, as a coleader, together with Wayne Shorter, of the celebrated group Weather Report, and with his own ensemble, the Zawinul Syndicate. Throughout he revealed a nonpareil command of the American jazz idiom, but between winding up Weather Report and forming the Zawinul Syndicate, he performed solo concerts, often incorporating on electronic keyboards Austrian folk-songs and children's songs into his "American" jazz expressionism—for example, Austrian folksongs such as "Hairy Little Spider, Sitting in His Web." He said he learned a lot from the Volksmusik repertoire: "I come from the blues and I come from Volksmusik (folk music)—Slavic Volksmusik, Hungarian Volksmusik, Austrian Volksmusik."[143] There are no shortages of examples of compositions from his time with Weather Report and with the Zawinul Syndicate using the simple, singable yet profound melodies we associate with folk music,[144] played on synthesizer but patched to evoke, however distantly, an accordion. As the classical and jazz piano virtuoso Friedrich Gulda said of Zawinul, a lifelong friend, "He, just like myself, is ingrained in the ancient Austrian tradition. He is an archetypical Viennese musician through and through . . . [who] opened himself up to international music—not in order to deliver himself to it, but to master it and yet never forget what he owes to his own musical roots."[145]

Pianist and composer Toshiko Akiyoshi moved to the United States in January 1956 and worked in a variety of projects with her first husband, saxophonist Charlie Mariano, and her second husband, saxophonist Lew Tabackin, with whom she formed a big band in Los Angeles in 1973. Since moving to the United States, Akiyoshi has been inspired to musically explore her Japanese heritage, composing pieces with Japanese themes, Japanese harmonies, and even Japanese instruments (such as kotsuzumi, kakko, utai, tsugaru, and shamisen). Securing a recording contract with RCA she recorded *Kogun* in 1974, using traditional Japanese tsuzumi drums on the title track, reflecting a powerful and effective local influence within the conventions of big band jazz that Akiyoshi systematically broadened with a series of albums for the label that for many propelled her to the forefront of big band jazz in the 1970s and early 1980s. Today her RCA albums are seen as the finest of her career: *Long Yellow Road* (1975), with "Children in the Temple Ground" that draws in Japanese culture; *Tales of a Courtesan* (1975), with the title track again drawing on her Japanese culture; and *Insights* (1976), with the extended suite "Minamata" that on the "Consequence" section includes a traditional tsuzumi drummer. *Road Time* (1976) included a stirring live performance of "Kogun" (including kotsuzumi and ohtsuzumi drums performed live by native Japanese drummers—the album was recorded live in Japan).

At the age of twenty, South African trumpeter Hugh Masekela joined the Jazz Epistles, which included pianist Abdullah Ibrahim, and both musicians would escape the apartheid regime and carve out their own distinctive careers, which studiously reflected their South African heritage, a powerful glocal element that remained a constant feature of their music. Masekela's first album as a leader, *Trumpet Africaine* (1960), produced by Hugo Montenegro, was made in New York and signed with MGM records, which released *The Americanization of Ooga Booga* in April 1966. Masekela explained: "[It] was my way of saying I was combining the traditional music of South Africa with the sounds of America,"[146] as good a definition of glocalized jazz as you could wish. After MGM he formed an enduring relationship with producer Stewart Levine, forming the Chisa label that would result in eleven albums, including *The Promise of the Future* (1967) that produced the number one hit and 4 million–seller written by the Zambian composer Philemon Hou called "Grazin' in the Grass." Masekela has always believed his politics and his music were inextricably lined—be it hard bop, jazz ballads, or infectious Township beats. In the 1970s he embarked on a "pilgrimage of music," immersing himself in the traditional sounds of Guinea, Liberia, Zaire, and Ghana, where he performed as a guest with Fela Anikulapo Kuti and made several innovative highlife/Afro-beat albums with "Hedzoleh Soundz." In 1982 he settled for a time in Botswana, and in 1988 Masekela and his group formed the background of the commercially successful *Graceland* project with Paul Simon. He then embarked on a tour with his wife, vocalist Miriam Makeba, and his own Kalahari band, just as international attention turned to the hit musical *Sarafina!* for which he had cowritten the score with Mbongeni Ngema for both Broadway and film. In 1991, after thirty-one years of voluntary exile in protest against apartheid, Masekela returned home in support of the new political reality that had dawned at the hands of President Mandela.

Pianist and composer Abdullah Ibrahim began his odyssey in jazz as Dollar Brand in Capetown, South Africa. He learned piano from his mother, a pianist in the AME Church, and was soon aware that South Africa represented a unique confluence of three musical cultures: African, European, and American. During his formative years he adapted the popular music of the day to the sounds he heard around him from his own community. "Waltzes, quicksteps, fox trots, sambas . . . what we did was put that Capetown beat underneath," he said of what we now see as the glocalization process. He worked with South African jazz legends such as Kippie Moeketsi and Basil Coetzee, and these experiences would later be captured in his composition "Manenberg," one of the most memorable instrumental anthems on the joy and sorrow of South African life to have been written by any composer, in or out of jazz, and a powerful representation of glocalized jazz.

In 1962 Brand moved to Europe, beginning a thirty-year self-imposed exile in protest against apartheid. In 1963 he was working in an "exotic" coffee house in Zurich called The Club Africana with vocalist Sathima Bea Benjamin, whom he would later marry. On hearing that the Duke Ellington orchestra was due to perform in the city, Benjamin sought out Ellington and begged him to hear her boyfriend play the piano. Ellington agreed, and after the concert walked through the snowy Zurich streets to hear Ibrahim play at the Club Africana. The result was an invitation to record in Paris three days later, with Ellington producing the recording session. At the end of the year Reprise Records (Ellington's recording company at the time) released *Duke Ellington Presents the Dollar Brand Trio* that, in effect, launched the pianist's career in the United States. By 1965 he had played the Newport Jazz Festival; the following year he sat in with the Ellington orchestra and had toured with drummer Elvin Jones.

The man who considers himself "not a musician, but being played," acknowledges Ellington's influence as well as that of pianist Thelonious Monk on his play-ing. Of Monk he would say, "When I heard him I understood. Where I am trying to go, he is already there, so let me learn." These influences, imported directly from American jazz, woven together with his career shaping "local" influences in his formative environment in South Africa, in District Six, at the foot of Table Mountain, provided the key elements that shaped his musical conception. What emerged were folk images of Africa projected through the prism of the American jazz experience. The main characteristics of his style, hypnotic ostinatos, richly voiced chords, and powerful tremolos, became shuffled and reshuffled over the years to telling effect, underpinned with the spirit of *kwela*, South Africa's blend of jazz, choral music, and Highlife.

Brand's conversion to Islam in 1968 saw him adopt the name Abdullah Ibrahim, and the serenity of his spirit, his less-is-more ethic, and his essentially orchestral concept provided a unifying element that flows through his considerable discography. He is a master of producing profound statements from the most simple of materials, and there is no shortage of Ibrahim albums, with many including different versions of his compositions performed by his then current groups. At the outset of the 1980s he led an excellent group with Craig Harris on trombone, his frequent collaborator Carlos Ward on alto saxophone, plus Alonzo Garner on bass and Andre Strobert on drums. The leader's concern with the ordering of the dark, affecting tone colors at his disposal allowed Harris's and Ward's work to assume a majesty that was not so readily apparent in their work elsewhere.

During the mid-1980s, Ibrahim was featured in a documentary by Chris Austin called *A Brother with Perfect Timing*, which showed him rehearsing and performing with his group Ekaya, with whom he would make some of the finest albums of his career. "Ekaya means home," he explained, "not just in the ethnic sense but in the heart." Here the line-up was Ricky Ford on tenor sax, Carlos Ward on alto sax, Dick Griffin on trombone, Cecil McBee on bass, and Ben Riley on drums. It was a group well able to exploit the emotional depth of Ibraham's writing and essentially South African, or glocal, disposition of his music with powerful solos and empathetic ensemble work, as the album *Water from an Ancient Well* reveals, a re-examination of five compositions from the 1970s that was documented by Kaz Records on *The Mountain*.

Ibrahim returned to South Africa in 1992, performing at President Mandela's inauguration, after a lifetime of protest at the apartheid regime. A member of the ANC, he began an increasing involvement in music education for his country's youth, establishing a musical academy for deprived children he calls M7 that includes Quincy Jones among its trustees.

At this point, students should be further encouraged to identify examples of "glocalization" from around the globe in the contemporary jazz context—indeed, there is no shortage of examples—young Spanish jazz pianists in Barcelona using elements of Flamenco in their music; Hungarian jazz musicians using elements of Gypsy music and Transylvanian folkloric themes; Indian musicians from the Indian subcontinent using elements derived from ragas and Carnatic singing styles; Finnish jazz musicians taking inspiration from the poetry of the *Kalevala*, the Finnish national epic that has been a major source of national self-esteem in Finnish culture and art since it was first published in 1835, influencing classical music (such as Sibelius's *Kullervo*), jazz, and popular music;[147] Austrian jazz musicians introducing *Yodel* influences; Argentinean jazz musicians incorporating tango influences (tango is the national dance of Argentina); Portuguese jazz musicians incorporating *Fado* influences; Philippine jazz musicians incorporating Gamelan influences; Jewish jazz musicians inside and outside the United States introducing *klezmer* influences; jazz musicians from the former Yugoslavia incorporating Balkan folk themes with their complex rhythms, such as the pianist Bojan Zulfikarpasic; musicians from the Netherlands incorporating large swaths of Dutch humor (an acquired taste!); Greek jazz musicians inspired by composers such as Míkis Theodorakis's and Yannis Markopoulos's use of *Eneknho* (Greek orchestral music with elements of Greek folk music); pianist Danilio Perez reflecting the influence of his native Panama in albums such as the best-selling *PanaMonk*; and Azerbaijani musicians using Mugham—local folk tunes, such as pianist Shahin Novrasli.

This list is not intended to be definitive, rather a starting point for students, who are encouraged to seek out similar examples of glocalized jazz in the global jazz scene themselves.

## Real Life Examples of the Key Glocalizing Elements: Folkloric, Local Classical, and Local Pop

Taking each of the above three elements in turn, it is possible to cite brief examples of these processes at work in the new millennium years at a local level to gain a practical understanding through auditory experience of the glocalization process—and this is the key: "hearing" the ways in which glocalized jazz differentiates itself from American jazz, yet retains certain aspects in common with it. Thus the following are merely examples, *not a definitive list*, since this is worthy of a book-length study in itself, but is intended here to give students and readers alike an idea of how theory translates into real-life practice, and *to provide a starting point for the musically curious to begin their own enquiries into the glocalization processes at work.*

### Glocalization: Examples of Elements Derived from Classical Music

The phenomenon of jazz musicians turning to classical music is hardly new. In the late 1930s there was a craze for "swinging" the classics—Benny Goodman scored a hit with the Welsh composer/arranger Alec Templeton's "Bach Goes to Town," the John Kirby Sextet recorded several successful classical novelties by the likes of Chopin, Dvořák, Schubert, Lehar, and Donizetti, and Tommy Dorsey enjoyed huge success with Rimsky-Korsakov's "Song of India." Indeed, there is no shortage of examples dotted over the last eighty or so years of jazz history, not least Igor Stravinsky's "Ebony Concerto" written for the Woody Herman Orchestra in 1946, or Tchaikovsky's "Arab Dance" and Mussorgsky's "The Old Castle" brilliantly rearranged by Gil Evans for the Claude Thornhill Orchestra. (Evans would later successfully adapt Joaquin Rodrigo's "Concierto De Aranjuez" for Miles Davis in the 1950s.) During the 1950s a confluence of jazz and classical music emerged called Third Stream. The list that goes on through the decade to more contemporary times, such as tenor saxophonist Michael Brecker's *Cityscape* with Claus Ogerman, to Wynton Marsalis's *Swing Symphony*.

The Austrian pianist Friedrich Gulda (1930–2000) was one of the outstanding virtuoso concert pianists of the twentieth century, famous for his interpretations of Mozart and Beethoven, but he was also a musician with a deep understanding and love for jazz. He was no dilettante, as albums such as his first jazz recording, *Friedrich Gulda at Birdland* (1956), recorded at the Birdland jazz club in New York, and *As You Like It* (1970) through to collaborations in the 1980s with Chick Corea attest. The German TV documentary *The Three Faces of Friedrich Gulda* examined his work as a classical pianist, jazz pianist, and composer. In the latter context, his classical works often included provision for improvisation, such as his *Concerto for Cello and Wind Orchestra* (1980) in five movements, including jazz, a minuet, rock, polka, a march, and two improvised cadenzas for cello, while his compositions for the Eurojazz Orchestra included "Variations for Two Pianos," recorded with Joe Zawinul. As *Friedrich Gulda: Wanderer between Two Worlds* noted, "Gulda's intensive occupation with jazz enabled him to make particular congenial use of interpretational freedoms in 'classical' piano music by allowing ornaments, variations (modified recapitulations as it was known in his day), 'distinct' pieces and the old Rubato (the independence and ad hoc drifting apart of melody and accompaniment) to flow directly into his [music]."[148]

In the new millennium, the most striking use of classical music in jazz has emanated from the glocalization process rather than "Swinging the classics" or somewhat self-consciously appropriating classical devices and techniques and applying them in a jazz context, as happened in the past with Third Stream. Unlike most American universities and conservatories, where jazz departments and classical departments are often self-contained worlds where never the twain shall meet, most European jazz institutions insist that jazz students undertake parallel classical studies. "Most European jazz musicians have a thorough training in classical music," says Wouter Turkenburg, head of jazz studies at the Royal Conservatory in The Hague in the Netherlands. "Almost every jazz school in Europe puts an important emphasis on learning how to play classical music. Not only to improve the technique but also to know and understand another realm of music better. All of my students have one hour with a jazz teacher and half an hour with a classical teacher per week. If they fail the classical exams it's hard for them to continue their study."[149] This proximity of jazz to classical music in European jazz conservatories is now seeing more and more young musicians emerging who are un-self-consciously drawing on elements of both musical disciplines to shape an individual approach to jazz improvisation that is not rooted in the orthodox American bebop pedagogy. As a result of learning two "musical languages" simultaneously, elements of one seamlessly bleed into the other through a shared harmonic foundation; this is not so much "mix-and-matching" of two different musical disciplines or a kind of musical "code-switching," rather it evolves from an organic confluence of two idioms.

Another factor is that young European musicians are well aware that improvisation is hardly the exclusive province of jazz. A feature of Mozart's performances, for example, was his piano improvisations, such as his performance in Prague on January 19, 1787, where he conducted his D Major Symphony No. 38 (subsequently referred to as "The Prague") and followed it by not one but three piano improvisations. As the Belgian pianist Jef Neve notes, "When I started to play piano at the age of four Mozart was my hero, and what fascinated me was that Mozart was capable of improvising these little melodies and that was something I wanted to do as well," he explained in 2006. "So I actually improvised from the very beginning, even before I could read notes, so that's my starting point. It's quite normal that I should have this huge classical influence, it's my cultural heritage, something that's been there all my life."[150] While these young musicians can swing powerfully, they often do not choose to, preferring a rhythmic "elasticity" often associated with the Munich based ECM label and drummer Jon Christensen. There is also an emphasis on melodic, rather than pattern based improvisation and a move away from harmonic complexity to more open structures in the belief that the closed structure of the cyclical song form, sometimes with changes every two beats, forces the improviser to rely more on mechanical (or pattern based) improvisation at the expense of melodic improvisation. "With 'Giant Steps' or a complex harmonic structure," continues Neve, "there is always the danger you follow the mechanical process—chord, chord, chord, chord, chord—so a lot of jazz today is technique. Melody is lost. I say, 'Don't play 15 notes if you can tell it with three notes.'"[151] Students should seek out Neve's "Nothing but a Casablanca Turtle Sideshow Dinner" from his album *Nobody Is Illegal* (2006) to gain an aural impression of the "organic confluence" between jazz and classical by a musician who has achieved a high degree of excellence in both disciplines.

The breakthrough onto major jazz stages of Europe of Esbjörn Svensson with his trio e.s.t. represented one of the most important developments in European jazz between 1998 and the time of Svensson's untimely death in 2008. A graduate of Stockholm's prestigious Royal College of Music, where he studied classical piano, in 2004 he observed,

In the beginning I looked on jazz and classical as two different worlds, the classical world where you're supposed to play exactly what somebody has written
and the jazz world where you improvise and play more or less the way you
want to. But I guess those two worlds are coming closer and closer for me. I
realise more and more how all those great composers like Johann Sebastian
Bach and Chopin, Beethoven, Bartók must have all been great improvisers,
they must have been sitting improvising at the piano, that's how you compose,
that's one way, there are other ways as well. But I guess they improvised a
lot, and that thing is hitting me more and more. So I'm finding at the moment
much more inspiration in that kind of music. It inspires me and I just try to
compose. I compose from things that inspire me, so the music we play now
sounds more classical in a way.[152]

It was no coincidence that one of his albums, *Tuesday Wonderland* (2006), was inspired by Bach's *Well-Tempered Clavier*. As Neve points out, "I don't see any reason
why we can't use classical influences in jazz music. I think that's a typical European
attitude from European musicians—we actually don't mind that maybe some of
our music doesn't swing. That's not a rule here, we don't have that pressure that
maybe they might feel as Americans, so I think we are more free to adapt these
classical elements, like introducing *rubatos*, tempos that don't have to stay right
in line. Maybe if the music asks for it, why can't we do this or that? Use dynamics
more and so on?"[153]

The German pianist Michael Wollny, a graduate of the Hermann-Zilcher
Conservatory, studied classical music from the age of five and harnessed twentieth-century contemporary classical influences with jazz expressionism with
startlingly original results in a series of critically acclaimed albums for the ACT
label (2005–12). "For me the defining element of jazz always has been a search
for something new or innovative in the music," he said in 2010. "I think it is quite
dangerous for the music to take that away and stick with something that has
been done before. Tradition is very important in the music and is honoured by
everybody that plays progressive music; it's not necessarily the future of the music
to stick with the tradition alone."[154] As acclaimed German saxophonist Christof
Lauer has noted, "For me in Germany I am influenced by classical music. I think
this is the European way of jazz. I have an American friend, [saxophonist] Joe
Lovano, and he says that America is now looking to Europe, they are inspired by
the way we deal with music here, we have our own sound and they are interested
in this."[155]

## Glocalization: Examples of Elements Derived from Folkloric Sources
There is a reason folk music has been passed down the generations, and that
is that it often contains memorable, haunting, affecting, and beautiful melodies

that have stood the test of time; the very fact that they have been passed down the generations is a testament to their enduring qualities. The localization of folkloric influences in jazz was perhaps inevitable because local musicians are often steeped in the music; often many began their early music training playing simple local folkloric themes in school and family ensembles. The Scandinavian countries, with their strong folkloric traditions, pioneered the incorporation of folkloric sources into jazz, something that can be traced back to the 1930s, when dance band musicians played American dance band arrangements and took to "jazzing up" folk music themes for the dancers. As has been previously described, the practice took on a serious aesthetic following Stan Getz's tour of Sweden in 1951 and Miles Davis's recording of "Ack Värmeland Du Sköna" as "Dear Old Stockholm." In the liner notes of the Swedish trumpeter and arranger Bengt-Arne Wallin's pioneering big band album *Old Folklore in Swedish Modern* (re-released by the ACT label), Wallin argued that "folk music is a definite form, a living phenomenon, created by real people, inherited and brought to perfection through generations and is still full of life today."[156]

*Old Folklore in Swedish Modern* was something of an orchestral breakthrough in jazz through its masterful integration of folkloric influences. Reflecting on the album's influence today, contemporary Swedish trombonist Nils Landgren says, "It says a lot about European jazz, that we can take our own music and mix it with jazz; if we were to ask Bengt-Arne about it today, I feel sure he would say that back in 1962 when he did *Old Folklore in Swedish Modern* it gave him and all the other musicians in Europe a chance of finding their own identity, which was not the case before because everybody was trying to imitate as much as they could, and play as good as they could, the American way of playing jazz."[157]

As Landgren rightly highlights, identity is the key here. Many European musicians would say they love American jazz, but they were not born in New York, or Chicago, or New Orleans, so "sounding" American does not feel right for them. "It's culturally dishonest," said British pianist Dave Stapleton.[158] "In Europe we have a very personal jazz language, each country," says saxophonist Christof Lauer. "It's a kind of identity, from each country and it sounds totally different. I play a lot with French musicians, for example, and they have something different in their music, something that I have to say is 'French,' and this holds true with Italian musicians I often play with. On the album *Europeana* (ACT) orchestrated by Mike Gibbs, I played this song from Finland, 'Kylä Voutti Utta Kutta,' and it's a simple melody, but it sounds Finnish. It's a kind of tune you wouldn't find in Germany, for example."[159]

Yet incorporating folkloric or local influences into jazz expressionism is by no means confined to European musicians—and here students are encouraged to research examples for themselves. For example: how cultural influences from the Indian subcontinent play out in the music of American-Indian musicians such as

Vijay Iyer or Rudresh Mahanthappa; how the music of South Africa is a recurring theme in the music of Hugh Masekela; or how the South American tango colors the music of many Argentinean jazz musicians such as Ástor Piazzolla or Dino Saluzzi. The Panamanian pianist Danilio Perez became a member of Wayne Shorter's critically acclaimed quartet in 2000; he has allowed "local" folkloric influences to permeate his work with the saxophonist, but they became central to his work on albums such as *PanaMonk* (1996) or *Provedencia* (2010):

> For me in my role as a musician, as a player of my music, I have explored a lot the Spanish influences on [Panamanian] music, they have a lot of carnival festivities, they have a lot of music, I wouldn't call it ritual, it's not the same as the African music, but it has elements of that. I have used things from people singing on the street that are public domain, and I have worked with those, to create the essence of the community. I have taken a rhythm called Tamborito, very related to Panama, which means 'a little drum,' it goes back to the seventeenth century, influenced by Spaniards, and I have used that rhythm a lot—that's one aspect I have used in my music for some time. Another is the el Punto, the most elegant dance form we have in Panama, very traditional, which has its own forms. Also traditional conga dancing, three against two is used a lot, I use that, and the mejoiana, which is people singing with guitar, like a jam, the idea is to sing about any topic, but you have to have a rhyme, one person says something the other person has to answer him, and it develops and if you can't do it you're out of the game. I have used all that in my music.[160]

## Glocalization: Examples of Elements Derived from Popular Culture

Jazz was once itself an aspect of the popular culture in the teens, twenties, and thirties of the twentieth century and has a long history of dialogue with popular music—from Louis Armstrong appropriating the songs of Tin Pan Alley and popular Broadway musicals as a vehicle for jazz expressionism in the late 1920s to the interface with jazz and rock in the late 1960s. Subsequent interactions, such as Smooth Jazz, have been widely discredited as intended to fulfill a commercial function by crossing over into the pop market. However, in the late 1990s the term "Nu-Jazz" was coined to describe the work of Norwegian keyboard player Bugge Wesseltoft and trumpeter Nils Petter Molvaer and a number of other Scandinavian jazz ensembles who mixed jazz improvisation with the rhythms inspired by popular culture. In Wesseltoft's case it was Berlin Techno among other influences, and in Molvaer's case a more eclectic mix quite unlike the "chamber jazz" for which ECM records, his record label at the time, had become known. For a while Nu-Jazz captured the imagination of the young audiences in the European jazz underground. I well remember the long queues of young people stretching around the block waiting to see performers such as Wesseltoft, Wibuttee, and Molvaer at places like the New Morning Club in Paris, The Fabrik in Hamburg, and the club Bla in Oslo in the late 1990s—early millennium years. Something clearly was happening that was a European thing—naturally, Britain, cut off from Europe by two miles of English Channel and a thousand years of history, remained blissfully unaware of these developments, as did, for different reasons, the United States.

Albums such as *The New Conception of Jazz* by Wesseltoft and *Khmer* by Molvaer sold in their hundreds of thousands, with the result that they began headlining at European jazz festivals in slots normally reserved for the top American stars. Many musicians in European jazz saw this as a breakthrough, since Americans, as E. Taylor Atkins put it, "were virtually guaranteed to garner more exposure and recognition."[161] In the end Nu-Jazz was undone by its commercial success—everyone wanted to jump on a fast accelerating bandwagon and cash in on the craze, so that almost anything, including pop and rock, was suddenly being called Nu-Jazz. Wesseltoft gave up his "New Conception of Jazz" in 2004, but his popularity was a first step in the early millennium years of a growing realization among European musicians, audiences, and promoters that European jazz was coming of age and it need not be a pale imitation of American jazz, but a thing in itself in a way that European free jazz had, albeit failing to capture the public's imagination.

The late Esbjorn Svensson made use of the ad hoc song forms of contemporary popular music, conscious that younger audiences "needed to find their bearings in the music," and from his experience of performing pop music shortly after he left music conservatory was well aware of the importance of a good "hook." "The music we grew up with was rock n'roll, that was our music," he says. "Wanting to be a rock star, I was singing rock. The interest we have in the music comes to listening a lot to new music that is not jazz, more pop. Singer songwriters. Might be anything, just try and find new music, who is creating something, who is doing something new, we want to hear something that bites us, we try to find that music."[162] Equally, glocalization of jazz and popular culture can take place at a presentational level as well as a musical level. Svensson set great store in the presentation of his trio's music, aware that younger audiences were used to a strong visual imagery in popular culture, so he used a sound mixer and lighting engineer at his concerts, explaining in 2006,

> It's whether you have a vision or not, some people think its enough with the music, you just need a white light and you stand there playing. But I always thought it would be great to have something more than that. We have taken this further because [our lighting engineer] now works with a big light show plus he uses cameras where he's filming us and projecting it on the screen, where he can totally change everything, so you can see us playing through a computer, the important thing is that it has to support the music all the time. If it becomes too much it will take over because the visual things are so strong,

people are just watching instead of listening, and that's something very exciting to find the right balance. That's something we try to learn.[163]

In jazz singing, a new breed of singers are emerging who have paid their dues at karaoke machines and taken inspiration from TV talent shows such as *Pop Idol*, *Got Talent*, and *The X Factor* as much as Ella, Billie, Sarah, Carmen, and Betty. They certainly seem to be able to communicate with younger audiences in a way that more orthodox young jazz singers do not, and in an age when popularity is determined by the number of messages received on Twitter, who knows what the future holds.

This list is not intended to be definitive, rather a starting point for students, who are encouraged to seek out examples of folkloric, classical, and local pop influenced glocal jazz themselves.

# Jazz and Modernism

onsidering the wealth of modernist theories that have been published in recent years, especially from the perspective of literature and visual art, there have been relatively few attempts to
explore modernism's relationship with jazz. In fact, most jazz
history books contain few, if any, references to modernism, despite the fact that "jazz unquestionably informed modernism as intellectual challenge, sensory provocation, and social texture."[1] The emergence
of jazz very roughly paralleled the emergence of modernism in the United
States, both gathering momentum in the period immediately following
World War I. During the decade that followed—the first truly "modern"
decade—America set the pace on the global stage for social revolution
and change. A postwar economic boom, triggered in part by the return
of the troops from France in 1919, contributed to increasing wages and
leisure time, which created a climate in which a dance craze—helped in

part by the entrepreneurial audacity and artistic flair of the dancing duo Vernon and Irene Castle—swept the nation.

Today, the 1920s seem a romantic and irresponsible time when a generation that had lost its gods (to paraphrase F. Scott Fitzgerald in *This Side of Paradise*) embraced life and living in a decade-long party that was only stopped short by the stock market crash of 1929. It was an era when the new media came of age with newspapers, magazines, and newsreel shorts celebrating wild dance parties, fast cars, and jazz babes in short skirts. Young women known as flappers defined by the 1920 motion picture *The Flapper*, starring Olive Thomas, defied convention by insisting on enjoying life on the same terms as men. Encouraged by the mass media's celebration of the up-to-the-minute "New Woman," flappers and jazz babes became synonymous with exuberant dance styles such as the Charleston, the One Step, and a host of shimmies, toddles, and trots: "The music is sensuous, the female is only half dressed and the motions may not be described in a family newspaper," complained the *Catholic Telegraph*.[2]

Today, the decade's Art Deco stylishness tends to obscure the very real social debate about jazz in the early 1920s as the music made its way into the American people's consciousness. While some regarded the "jazz craze" as something that would quickly burn itself out, only to be replaced by the next musical fad, others saw it as a dangerous musical subversion and an incitement to licentiousness, its vernacular origins as troubling to polite black society as it was to white. It was a time when public bodies and institutions, governmental agencies, educational and religious leaders, periodicals, temperance organizations, Ivy League academics, and prominent individuals in public life all seemed united in voicing anti-jazz sentiments. "Poor jazz! It has been maligned in print and pulpit. All the sins of a wicked world have been traced directly and uncompromisingly to its door," reported *Metronome* in July 1922.[3]

The intensity of the debate surrounding the "Jazz Problem," as *The Etude* magazine called it,[4] meant that in the United States little correlation between the music and the emerging modernist movement was drawn, not least because modernism was by no means as well defined as it subsequently became. Although the 1913 exhibition of post-Impressionist and Cubist art, usually referred to as the Armory Show, mounted at New York's 69th Regiment Armory on Lexington Avenue between 25th and 26th streets, was the first major expose of modernism in America, for the most part it received a poor press, one startled critic calling it "unadulterated cheek," while the *New York Times* concluded that the exhibition was simply a way of "making insanity pay."[5] But modernism was not about to wither on the vine; the publication of two seminal modernist works in 1922, T. S. Eliot's *The Wasteland* and James Joyce's *Ulysses*,[6] may not have been recognized as the epochs of modern literature they subsequently became, or, as some have claimed, represent the beginning of modernity itself,[7] but the literary experimentation they embodied was nevertheless a harbinger of American modernism that would reverberate through American culture and around the world.

For the "Bright Young Things" who wanted to forget the past and ignore the future, jazz was more than a musical style, it was the style of times. The rapid rise of dancehalls to accommodate the demand for social dancing meant a young generation that was the most prosperous in history now had a focal point at which to meet members of the opposite sex socially who did not live on the same street or in the same neighborhood. Jazz musicians adapted to the changing times by expanding their ensembles, if only to be heard more clearly in these huge "dance palaces" (electric public address systems would not come until later in the 1920s), and by appealing to dancers by increasingly drawing on Tin Pan Alley for their repertoire. In such an environment, where success was measured by box office takings and hit recordings, the dichotomy of the so-called Jazz Age of the 1920s—and the Swing Era of the 1930s that followed—was that for some, the music's popularity and functionality as a "dance music" made any connection between jazz and the ethos of modernism appear equivocal. "However much the early genius of Armstrong and Ellington may have been apparent," wrote Mark S. Harvey, "they were not perceived as modern artists [in America]. And their music was emblematic of the modern mood for the very reason that it was not art, but rather popular."[8] In this reading, not uncommon, the beginning of American jazz modernism is deferred until the emergence of the bebop movement circa 1945, since "innovation occurred within the structural system of the music itself and clearly separated the jazz tradition from that of popular entertainment."[9]

It would take until relatively recently for a book like Alfred Appel's *Jazz Modernism: From Ellington and Armstrong to Matisse and Joyce* to attempt to "establish the place of classic jazz (1920–50)—especially Louis Armstrong, Duke Ellington, Fats Waller, Billie Holiday, Jack Teagarden and Charlie Parker—in the great modernist tradition in the arts."[10] Yet if we were to look more closely at the emergence of modernism in Europe, we would see that early jazz's "shocking" sounds and rhythms were considered part of broader changes occurring in the aftermath of World War I in literature, art, architecture, design, classical music, consumer goods, advertising, fashion, and popular culture. This chapter therefore attempts to explore the emergence of modernism on both sides of the Atlantic with specific reference to its interaction with jazz, and asks why modernism's influence—if we are to believe the jazz history books—appears so muted in jazz when it played such a vital role in the other arts.

The origins and ethos of modernism that swept through the arts at the end of the nineteenth and the early twentieth centuries might be said to have been a reaction against the conservative values of romanticism and realism, whose commonly held assumptions and institutional frames of reference had prevailed throughout much of the nineteenth century. These values, descended from Renaissance thinking, came under increasing interrogation as the pace of social, economic, and political change in broader society gathered pace. A growing number of aesthetes, poets, artists, writers, and musicians felt that "traditional" forms of realism in architecture, literature, and culture, as well as religious faith, social organization, and daily life were becoming outdated in the economic, social, and political conditions of the emerging industrialized world. They sought to move beyond traditions of Western culture, which they felt stifled rather than enhanced creative endeavor, by seeking to appear up-to-date, abreast of the times, and above all, modern.

Initially, modernism's reaction against romanticism and realism began, at least in part, by questioning the prevailing aesthetics of poetry and painting, which no longer seemed in tune with the times. As Clement Greenberg wrote in 1979: "What can be safely called Modernism emerged in the middle of the [nineteenth century] . . . in France, with Baudelaire in literature and Manet in painting, and maybe with Flaubert too, in prose fiction."[11] These events marked a conscious break with the hallowed traditions of romanticism, which insisted that the role of art and aesthetics was to teach, inform, celebrate, and glorify. Yet impressionism and symbolism would in turn be swept aside by the second great wave of modernism in the fin de siecle of the nineteenth century, which is where this chapter begins. Clearly this is not the place to rehearse the whole history of modernism, an endeavor that has filled countless weighty and erudite tomes to which the curious reader is directed, but instead to present a brief, necessarily selective, and personal overview of modernism and its interaction with jazz that might provide a context in which to probe more deeply why modernism in jazz begins around the period of World War I in Europe yet around the period of World War II in the United States. The chapter then concludes by briefly exploring the legacy of jazz modernism.

## European Modernism and Its Interaction with the Cakewalk, Ragtime, and Jazz

In the days before the twentieth-century media explosion, it was often said that the visual arts gave a premonition of cultural change; in the case of European modernism, the notion that traditions which had held good for centuries were about to come under pressure was reflected in the later work of the painter Paul Cézanne (1839–1906). Although he probably was not aware of it in his lifetime, his work laid the foundations of what would later become Cubism, a key aspect of modernism. Cézanne had exhibited at Paris's first Impressionist exhibition in 1874 and the third Impressionist exhibition in 1877, but later in his life he began to reduce what he saw into simpler forms and color planes, arguing that the viewer and the viewed are part of the same field, so that "This is what I see" becomes "Is this what I see?"

Meanwhile, Paul Gauguin had begun to enjoy a certain posthumous notoriety in avant-garde circles for his use of "primitive" techniques in his Tahitian paintings, following two powerful retrospective exhibitions at Paris's Salon d'Automne in 1903 and 1906. These works had a strong influence on Pablo Picasso, Henri Matisse, André Derain, and others in their circle. They, together with their dealers and leading critics of the era, were inspired to collect African sculpture, art, and tribal masks purely for their aesthetic value. While these artists had no anthropological interest in, or knowledge of, the meaning or function of these Western and Central African artifacts, they nevertheless recognized the spirituality they implied through the emotive distortions of the figure, simple outlines, absence of linear perspective, and use of repetitive ornamental patterns. Adapting the vitality these masks and carvings implied within their own work, they found a kind of freedom—the freedom to distort—and sought to move beyond naturalism, which had defined Western art since the Renaissance. Critics initially described this new school of painting as "exotic" or "primitive," which soon gave way to Primitivism.

Primitivism emerged at roughly the same time as the cakewalk emerged in Europe, among the first pieces of recorded evidence of its arrival being "A Cake Walk (At a Georgia Camp Meeting)," recorded on a phonograph cylinder at the Garden Society Restaurant in Göteborg in 1899 by the Kronoberg Regimental Band from Växjö in central Sweden.[12] The following year, to considerably more acclaim, John Philip Sousa appeared at the Paris International Exposition with his civilian band, and his performance included four cakewalks: "At a Georgia Camp Meeting," "Smoky Mokes," "Hunky Dory," and "Bunch o'Blackberries." They received a rapturous response from a delighted French audience, the *San Francisco Chronicle* reporting: "Paris Has Gone Rag Time Wild."[13] Within two years of Sousa's success, popular institutions in Paris were featuring the cakewalk, and in 1903 Sousa returned to the city, giving even greater momentum to the craze. The same year, Will Marion Cook's and Paul Laurence Dunbar's *In Dahomey*, featuring the cakewalking duo of Bert Williams and George Walker, opened in London following its Broadway success, playing for seven months and inspiring an international cakewalk craze. According to Edward Berlin, early cakewalk music was an unsyncopated form of march music that between the 1890s and early 1900s was supplanted by the rising popularity of ragtime, which became the general term for American syncopated dance music.[14] However, in Paris and London, for a while at least, it was the term "cakewalk" that had the greatest currency in the early 1900s, with cakewalk contests, in which any amateur dancer could participate, a feature of popular life.

These events could have hardly escaped Picasso and his circle, since cakewalk contests had become a Parisian craze, while ragtime had begun to be featured in the cabarets and music halls they frequented. Ragtime, whose essence is realized in syncopation, represented a kind of "distortion" of the regular metrics of European classical accentuation and presented an aural corollary to the visual "distortions" of "Primitivist" art. It reflected the growing influence of what become known as *l'art negre* in Paris during this period—Henri Matisse's use of bold color, for example, was inspired by African sources intended, as he noted in his treatise *Notes of a Painter*, "to stir the emotions," and helped define African art's relationship with modernism. Primitivism's emotional directness was reflected by two famous paintings by Matisse, "Music" and "The Dance" (1909/10), the former depicting the origins of music while the latter implies the shared rhythmic ecstasy of a circle of dancers. The influence of Primitivism was also felt in other artistic disciplines; Stravinsky's *The Rite of Spring* (1913), for example, is often cited as a "primitivist" work in that its programmatic subject is a pagan rite evoked through dissonance and loud, irregular rhythms intended to depict the abandonment of inhibition.

One of the central tenets of the emergent modernism was that art should be an expression of the times; with industrialization (that owed much to electricity and the internal combustion engine), science, and technology forcing the pace of change in society, the modernists found ready sources of inspiration for their creations. Since figurative art seemed in jeopardy from the machine, or more specifically, the camera—the Italian Futurist painter and sculptor Umberto Boccioni pointing out how representationalism had been taken over by mechanical means—painters sought to work *beyond* the camera's capabilities. They rejected conventional codes of representationalism—what the eye saw—in favor of deconstruction, fantasy, and abstraction, exemplified by Picasso's *Les Demoiselles d'Avignon* (1907), which heralded a new creative phase in the painter's career. No painting signaled change so profoundly in the history of art as this. Depicted were five nude women, all prostitutes; the faces of three figures were in a style that could be traced back to Spanish culture (Picasso was Spanish), but it was the facial masks of the two nudes on the right of the painting that caused a sensation—masks inspired by African carvings reflecting the growing influence of *l'art negre*. Some have even claimed that Picasso's exaggerated forms on this and *Blue Nude* "are as syncopated and *déhanchées* as those of the African-American music and dance of the cakewalk era."[15]

In fact, this was Cubism, where every shape is a report on multiple meaning, and for a while was central to the artistic endeavors of Picasso and his friend Georges Braque. Braque, in fact, once claimed that they were both "roped together like mountaineers" in their artistic endeavors —and together with Matisse and Gauguin were inspired to abandon the "homogenous space of linear perspective" that had dominated art since the fifteenth century by defying the traditional separation between the external reality of nature and the internal reality of art. They argued that our knowledge of an object comprises all possible views and sought to compress them into one moment that in its dissolution of perspective suggested a fourth dimension. Georges Braque's nail in *Still Life with Violin and Pitcher* (1909–10) shattered the principle—fundamental in Western art since the Renaissance—that the picture surface is a transparent surface offering an illusion of reality, while his *Guitar and Sheet Music* (1919) somehow suggests frozen music—and the music of the moment was jazz. When Picasso stuck everyday materials—initially a part of upholstery and a bar bill—onto his work, the intention was to strengthen the link between Cubism and the real world, or the everyday. By way of analogy, it might be said that Stravinsky cut up the sounds of Eastern European folk music and served it as a Cubist dish in his ballets *Firebird* and *Petrushka*. Stravinsky was himself the subject of the portrait *Igor Stravinsky* (1914) by the self-taught Cubist painter Albert Gleizes, whose early work was in the Impressionist tradition but who from 1910 had turned toward Cubism. After exhibiting at New York's Armory Show in 1913, he moved to New York in 1915 to escape the Great War, where he was introduced to the emergent new jazz that inspired *Le Jazz* (1915). This work attempted to reflect the excitement and animation of the music, which he considered more sensational than the music of Stravinsky himself.

In 1909 Futurism emerged at the hands of poet Filippo Tommaso Marinetti. Representing another aspect of modernism's desire to break with tradition, Marinetti wanted no part of the past, demanding the destruction of all museums and libraries. Calling himself the "Caffeine of Europe," he loved the cakewalk and was the first agent provocateur of modern art; his "Happening"—a montage in real-time of poems, painters, and ragtime influenced musicians on stage simultaneously—toured Europe with success. Issuing manifestos at regular intervals that glorified themes associated with the future, such as speed and technology, their manifesto of the machine sought to create a new class of visionary. For them the machine was power and represented freedom from historical restraint, while their love of technology prompted a conscious desire to parallel in their art the huge steps being made in science and industry. Futurist artists sought to replicate the machinery in ways that parodied sex and religion, realizing it provided them with limitless possibilities to give offense. They tried to capture movement by concentrating on rhythm and speed, seeking to depict how the machine changed people's idea of space—the airplane and the automobile making more of the world available in less time—with the automobile worshiped as a visible sign of the future and the phonograph hailed as the most radical extension of human memory since the printed book.

They also sought to depict noise on their canvasses, since Futurists loved any noise that was dissonant, loud, or made by a machine. Their love of what they called "sounds of life" meant they quickly made common cause with jazz, since, to their undisguised delight, it was roundly criticized by the establishment as a discordant noise. The irresistible combination of machine (the phonograph) and jazz recording (new media) meant that jazz quickly made headway in modernistic thinking. In their literature, the Futurists stripped language of what they considered unnecessary ornament, preferring short words and sentences without redundant adverbs, adjectives, or, if possible, verbs. Marinetti went even further, using what he called "words in freedom," or onomatopoeia, as in his poem "Zang Tumb Tuum" (1914). It was within this context that some credit Marinetti, or his Futurist followers, with coming up with the word "jazz," which they began using as an adjective to describe anything new from around 1909. They believed it the perfect modernist word, since it utilized the most modern letters in the Roman alphabet, "j" and "z."

This, of course, remains just one explanation among many of the word's etymology, since no one has quite nailed down the origins of the word satisfactorily. Perhaps the first use of the term in the English language was reported on April 2, 1912, in the pages of the *Los Angeles Times*, when a baseball pitcher, Ben Henderson, was quoted using the term in connection with what he called "a new curve" ball that he dubbed the "Jazz Ball."[16] Apparently Henderson's pitch was not a success, and other than a brief mention in the *Los Angeles Times* the following day there is little reference to the word in print for a while, indicating that Henderson was unlikely to have played a role in the popularization of the word. Nevertheless, it was enough to suggest the word was entering common usage in the United States by at least 1912. In March of the following year, E. T. "Scoop" Gleason began using the term in the *San Francisco Bulletin*, once again in connection with baseball,[17] and in April the term was taken up by Ernest J. Hopkins in the same paper under the headline, "In Praise of Jazz: A Futurist Word Which Has Just Joined the Language," so linking the term with the Futurists.[18]

Marcel Duchamp had experimented with Fauvism and Cubism until 1912/13 before deciding he had no desire to be influenced by either. An early exhibition of his work in 1909 in the Salon des Indépendants saw the modernist poet Guillaume Apollinaire—who later became a friend—criticize what he called "Duchamp's very ugly nudes." Like the Futurists, Duchamp was interested in change, movement, and distance and was intrigued with the concept of a fourth dimension. His first "machine" painting was *The Coffee Grinder* in 1911, but he became increasingly absorbed in challenging conventional thought about art. His painting *Nude Descending a Staircase No. 2* was one of the half-dozen or so of the most famous paintings of the twentieth century. When he exhibited it in America at the famous 1913 Armory Show, the press regarded it as a supreme joke. Nevertheless, the maxim that there is no such thing as bad publicity held good and the attention that was focused on him opened the way to his most influential piece, *The Large Glass*. By now he had become interested in Dadaism through the influence of fellow painter Francis Picabia, whom he first met in September 1911 at the Salon d'Automne in Paris, where they were both exhibiting.

Picabia considered the machine man's counterpart, which provided the underlying theme of his *portraits mécaniques*, seeking to find art's most vivid expression through machinery, mischievously claiming that pistons were steel Romeos inside cast-iron Juliets, and he saw jazz—which he loved—as the supreme expression of the machine age. For the modernists the increasing refinement of the machine and the modern production line were things of beauty that expressed the modern world; when Irving Berlin called jazz the music of the machine age he meant it as a compliment, that it was modern and of the moment. He was not alone. For a while it became fashionable in intellectual and artistic circles to link early jazz with machines. George Gershwin, for example, spoke of machine elements and rhythms in his music and the music of his American contemporaries, saying, "The Machine Age has influenced practically everything. I do not mean only music but everything from the arts to finance. The machine has not affected our age in form as much as in tempo, speed, and sound. It has affected us in sound whenever composers utilize new instruments to imitate its aspects."[19] For the modernists, the mechanical age was not so much a context, but a pretext—they wanted to explore its dynamism in their work, and the rhythmic intensity of jazz prompted a number of mechanical metaphors. Waldo Frank later suggested how it "expresses well a mass response to our world of piston rods, cylinders and mechanized laws."[20]

In 1922 composer George Antheil, whose *Jazz Symphony* was composed in 1925 on a commission from bandleader Paul Whiteman and premiered at Carnegie Hall in 1927, spent some time in Europe envisaging new types of music based on both jazz, such as his *Jazz Sonata* (1922), and machines. He produced a series of technology-based works including *The Airplane Sonata, Sonata Sauvage* (1922–23), *Death of Machines* (1923), *Mechanisms* (ca. 1923), and his best-known composition, *Ballet Mécanique* (1923/25). Painter Fernand Léger's machinist creation *The Disks* (1919) was a striking abstraction of jazz whose geometric forms and primary colors were made to conform to the machine age. And in 1922, Léger "permitted Antheil to illustrate his . . . article on 'Jazz' in *Der Querschmitt* with one of his machinist drawings of 1918."[21] Léger later designed the sets and costumes for the celebrated *Creation du Mond* in 1923, a ballet that used Darius Milhaud's jazz-influenced score.

One of modernism's most striking progeny, Dadaism, was launched in Zurich, Switzerland, on February 5, 1916, at the hands of a circle of friends surrounding actor, poet, and musician Hugo Ball including Emmy Hennings, Hans Arp, Tristan Tzara, and Marcel Janco, who had been meeting at the Holländische Meierei Café in the Spielgasse, the city's oldest district. As regular patrons, they succeeded in persuading owner Jan Ephraim to allow them to convert his *Stube* into a cabaret in the spirit of the Parisian and Berlin cabaret tradition that had prevailed before the outbreak of war in Europe in 1914. Renamed Cabaret Voltaire, its opening was preceded by a somewhat unexpected announcement in the Zurich press on February 2, 1916: "The Cabaret Voltaire. Under this name a group of young artists and writers has formed with the object of becoming a centre for artistic entertainment. In principle, the Cabaret will be run by artists, permanent guests, who, following their daily reunions, will give musical or literary performances. Young Zurich artists, of all tendencies, are invited to join us with suggestions and proposals."[22] During its relatively short lifetime, events at Cabaret Voltaire proved hugely influential within the rising tide of modernism. With Ball acting as emcee and the interior decorated by Macel Janco's primitivist art, a spirit of nihilism and mockery prevailed, each evening including a succession of sometimes bizarre spectacles that might include modern dance, modern songs, plays, a balalaika band, or music from the resident ragtime-influenced six-piece orchestra.

"The Cabaret Voltaire was a six piece band," wrote Dadaist chronicler Hans Richter, noting that its drummer, Richard Huelsenbeck, "was obsessed with Negro rhythms . . . his preference was for the big tom-tom."[23] For many Europeans, it would be drums that heralded the arrival of jazz, many believing "the jazz" to be drums—for example, in Germany drums were actually called "the jazz" for a while, and in England early drum kits were called "jazz-sets."[24] The Dadaists also developed an abstract art form that accorded primary importance to materials, to the detriment of representation. "We searched for an elementary art that we thought would save mankind from the madness of these times,"[25] recalled Ball, referring to the Great War being waged across the border in France. Driving the often fevered discussions of these young intellectuals "was a sense of disillusionment: destruction and death, corruption and deceit, had devoured their expectations and high hopes for a new century that had informed their childhoods. What good, then, were traditionally ordered systems of art, language and meaning—even social organisation—if all was ultimately chaos?"[26] Ball composed a phonetic poem, *Karawane*, which toyed with sounds and phonemes and was devoid of any meaning, seeking to denounce "language corrupted by journalism." During Cabaret Voltaire's short lifetime (it closed in early July 1916), it acquired a magical aura where all experiences were possible. What began as a "centre for artistic entertainment" laid the foundation for a movement of international proportions whose essential business was provocation—Dadaism's claim to modernity.

Although there is little agreement about what the term "Dadaism" actually meant (much like modernism itself), the movement was at least united in the belief that excessive rational thought and bourgeois values had precipitated the conflict of World War I. The emergence of jazz in Europe and its seeming iconoclasm appeared in line with the Dadaists' values; for a start, jazz had been roundly condemned by the establishment for its assault on musical values—which naturally delighted the Dadaists, who perceived in jazz anti-art qualities in line with their own. By 1920, Dadaist events usually involved jazz, which was fast becoming an aural signifier of modernism and proving to be a valuable ally in undermining traditional definitions of art. Events such as Festival Dada in Paris in May 1920 or the Grand Dada Ball held in Geneva in March 1920 embodied jazz elements, from an organist playing songs associated with Mitchell's Jazz Kings at the former to a "Jazz Band Dada" at the latter. Inevitably, jazz featured in the creations of Dada artists, most notably the Zurich Dadaist Marcel Janco's *Jazz 333* (1918), and in the work of the American photographer and Paris resident Man Ray. Disregarding the aesthetic quality of an object because he claimed the world was full of craftsmen, but no practical dreamers, Ray's famous black-and-white photographic self-portrait taken shortly after he arrived in Paris in 1921 consists of "found" objects imaginatively lit to resemble a drum kit (that in Europe had become synonymous with jazz). His cinematic creations included *Cinepoeme* (1926), inspired by jazz rhythms, and *Emak Bakia* (1926–27), intended to be shown to the accompaniment of jazz recordings, presenting a succession of breathless yet cleverly conceived Dadaist imagery that included goldfish in a bowl, a liberated "New Woman" driving a motorcar, and a banjoist alternating with images of a woman's legs dancing the Charleston.

There is no doubt that New York was aware of this burgeoning movement. Marjorie Perloff argues that something akin to Dadaism emerged in the aftermath of the Armory Show,[27] attributing it to what she calls the "Duchamp Factor"[28]—the arrival in New York of Marcel Duchamp and several European artists escaping the Great War, such as Francis Picabia, Mina Loy, and Baroness Elsa von Freitag-Loringhoven. Picabia had previously visited the United States in 1913, when he was the only Cubist to personally attend the Armory Show, at night seeking out ragtime entertainers on Manhattan's East Side and translating these experiences in *Chanson Négre I* and *Chanson Négre II* (both 1913), which reflected his love of the music and New York, which he regarded as a Cubist and Futurist city. As Perloff points out, not only was the so-called American avant-garde a European invention and intervention, "it would not have taken the particular form it did had Duchamp not settled in New York and quickly become the center of the Walter Arensberg salon where he met 'everyone.'"[29]

By 1917, Duchamp was a member of the board of New York's Society of Independent Artists, and when they mounted a public exhibition that year, their open admission policy meant that of all the twenty-five hundred artworks submitted, every piece was accepted—except one. Duchamp's famous Dadaist gesture in submitting a urinal called *Fountain* and signed "R. Mutt" predictably resulted in the society's rejecting it from the show. This caused uproar (and delight) among the Dadaists, culminating in Duchamp's resignation from the board. He would subsequently argue, through works of art called "Ready-mades," that the world was already full of interesting objects and that the artist need not add to them, but in selecting one, this ironic act of choice became the equivalent of artistic creation. This thinking was not designed to extend the potential of art, of works to be admired and contemplated, written about and objectified, but to declare their irrelevance in the modern age, such as his decision to paint a mustache on a picture postcard of the Mona Lisa, or declaring a bicycle wheel a "work of art."

It is just possible, maybe even probable, that a brilliantly talented young musician, who was born William Ernest Moenkhaus in Bloomington, Indiana, on June 30, 1902, became aware of, and even experienced, Dadaism vicariously during his schooling in Switzerland. His German father had insisted on a European education, but when war broke out in 1917 he was called home, entering Bloomington High School and continuing his studies on piano, cello, and composition with university faculty members. When he matriculated to Indiana University he seemed destined for a brilliant career. From his student writing in the October 1924 issue of *The Vagabond*, his poem called "Rhapsody in Mud" suggests that he was no stranger to the ethos of Dadaism. His leisure-time pursuits included playing bass horn with student jazz bands drawn from a circle that gathered around the perspicacious pianist Hoagy Carmichael who met at a local cafe called the Book Nook. Among their number was Howard Warren "Wad" Allen, who played C-melody saxophone, who had "read about the 1913 New York Armory Show and Marcel Duchamp's *Nude Descending a Staircase* and was hungry for more."[30] The intensity of discussions and Dadaist connections among the undergraduates, together with hot jazz recordings blasting in the background of the Book Nook, prompted Carmichael's biographer, Richard Sudhalter, to see this febrile atmosphere as a "middle-American adaptation of the Cabaret Voltaire spirit."[31]

Carmichael was also making himself felt in campus dance music circles, assembling groups to perform, play, and practice. "To watch him, pale and intense in a yellow slicker," wrote Sudhalter, "bobbing and jerking like a marionette at the keyboard, was to behold a man possessed by a purity of expression wholly consonant with the 'manifesto' of Cabaret Voltaire days. It takes no great leap of the imagination to see him as a Hugo Ball figure in Moenkhaus's mind, pounding away as the high-spirited japery of this Midwestern 'playground for crazy emotions' guggled and splashed around him."[32] Certainly by the early 1920s, reports of Dadaism had emerged in the American press, possibly prompting songwriters Edgar Dowell, Spencer Williams, Babe Thompson, and Bob Schafer to come up with the title "That Da Da Strain" in 1922. Although the lyrics are far from Dadaistic — it is simply a pop tune of the day — it was recorded by several jazz musicians including Mamie Smith (1922), Ross Gorman's Virginians (1922), Ethel Waters (1922), the Original Memphis Five (1923), the New Orleans Rhythm Kings (1923), the Louisiana Rhythm Kings (1929), Bobby Hackett (1938), Muggsy Spanier (1939 — perhaps the most enduring version), Bud Freeman (1940), Bob Crosby and his Bobcats (1942), and George Brunis (1943). Interestingly, some thirty years after Mamie Smith's first recording of the tune, Duchamp was asked to organize a Dada retrospective for the Sidney Janis Gallery in New York; he chose to exhibit a copy of her original 78 recording in a vitrine alongside other documents of the New York Dada period.[33]

Blaise Cendrars, or the "son of Homer" as John Dos Passos called him, the nom de plume of Frédéric Louis Sauser, was a poet and writer. Moving to Paris in 1912, he founded *Les Hommes Nouveaux*, a journal and a publishing house, with the anarchist writer Emil Szittya, publishing his poems "Les Pâques à New York" and "*Séquences.*" He was soon moving in a circle of Parisian artists and writers that included the painter Marc Chagall, painter and author Jean Hugo, and poet Guillaume Apollinaire, who in 1907 wrote an authoritative piece on the cakewalk entitled "La Danse est un Sport." Cendrars found a like mind in Apollinaire, and the two poets influenced each other's work; his poem "Les Pâques à New York" was a major influence on Apollinaire's poem "Zone," for example. In his play *Les Mamelles de Tirésias*, first performed in 1917, Apollinaire coined the word "surrealist," which was subsequently taken up by a new school of thought inspired by André Breton, who had trained in medicine and psychiatry, and the writer Jacques Vaché. They had begun experimenting with automatic writing—spontaneously writing without censoring their thoughts and giving reign to the subconscious—which led to the publication of Breton's *First Surrealist Manifesto* in 1924, which in turn attracted more artists and writers into their circle.

Their free association idealism inspired by Freud and rooted in Dada's disregard for tradition resulted in works that attempted to probe the artists' inner minds in bizarre, symbolic ways, and to respond to them through visual means. They believed that if ordinary and everyday objects and expressions were open to the full range of imagination, they could be juxtaposed to produce surprising, unexpected imagery. For them, jazz was seen as a sublime expression of surrealist art, since they imagined the jazz solo to be a direct expression of subconscious thought—the "free play of imagination"—which paralleled their own artistic ambitions. Later, in the 1950s, the surrealists would claim that Free Jazz exemplified this ethos. Marc Chagall was one of the early precursors of surrealist art, arriving in Paris when Cubism was the dominant form. Championed by Apollinaire, Chagall's animal/human hybrids and airborne phantoms would later, along with Julien Rousseau's depiction of jungle scenes, become regarded as early classics of surrealist art.

One of the founding members of their Paris surrealist circle, artist Max Ernst had initially come under the influence of the artist Giorgio de Chirico before going on to be a cofounder of the Cologne Dada group in 1919. By 1926, immersed in surrealist idealism, he produced the controversial 1926 painting *The Virgin Chastises the Infant Jesus before Three Witnesses: André Breton, Paul Éluard, and the Painter*. The series of works that followed—such as *Célébes*, *The Word*, and *L'Ange du Foyer*—often appeared to have no rational explanation. Escaping from the clutches of the Nazis in 1940, he settled in New York and, together with his friends Marcel Duchamp and Marc Chagall, helped to inspire the development of American abstract expressionism. Duchamp, in particular, was admired by the surrealists and considered an early precursor of their movement. In a television interview in the 1960s,[34] Ernst was asked about the origins of the often fantastic imagery he depicted in his paintings. He argued that since world history was not shaped by reasonable people but by madmen—he was thinking of Hitler, Stalin, and Mussolini—then if art was truly a mirror of the times, it too should appear mad.

Surrealist art frequently depicted ordinary objects in unusual contexts—exemplified by the work of one of its most popular exponents, Rene Magritte, who was also influenced Giorgio de Chirico. Magritte was an artist without whom modernist culture cannot be properly understood and whose work was characterized by a constant play of reality and allusion, a source of modernist disquiet that was exploited in works such as *Dangerous Liaisons*, *Homesickness*, *Hegel's Holiday*, *La Therapeute*, and *The Lovers*. His work would later be discovered by jazz musicians: *Golconda* (adapted by David Wilcox) appeared as cover art on the group Dreams' eponymously titled album (which included the Brecker brothers, John Abercrombie, and Billy Cobham) in the 1960s, while *The False Mirror* was used as the cover art for the group Sphere's album *Four in One* (with Charlie Rouse and Kenny Barron) in the 1980s.

The common thread of belief running through Cubism, Primitivism, Dadaism, Surrealism, and all the other modernist "isms" was that "the tradition" was responsible for stifling creativity, a belief shared by several European classical composers. To them the vitality and exuberance of ragtime and the emergence of jazz was a breath of fresh air that brought something new to the European arts, a view shared by a circle of Parisian composers who initially called themselves "Les Nouveaux Jeunes" but later became known as "Les Six"—Georges Auric, Louis Durey, Arthur Honegger, Darius Milhaud, Francis Poulenc, and Germaine Tailleferre. Together with their mischievous "grandfather" Erik Satie they shared a fascination for music-hall songs, ragtime, jazz, and the noise-making spirit of the Zurich Dadaists that had just arrived in Paris. These sources provided them with a source of inspiration in their own works, "Enough of clouds, waves, aquariums, water-sprites and nocturnal scents, what we need is a music of the earth, everyday music,"[35] exclaimed Satie, who wanted to create a new French art music based on popular sources. He was attracted to ragtime and jazz as music that "shouted its sorrows," and in 1917 he drew on ragtime's inspiration for his Cubist ballet *Parade* (one of his compositions for the production, "Steamship Ragtime," paraphrased Irving Berlin's "That Mysterious Rag").

Uniting a remarkable collection of modernist talent in the production —Pablo Picasso was responsible for the set and costume designs, Jean Cocteau wrote the libretto, Erik Satie wrote the music, Léonide Massine choreographed, and Guillaume Apollinaire wrote the program notes (throwing in the new word "surrealism" he had just coined in the process)—*Parade* was performed by Sergei Diaghilev's prestigious dance company, the *Ballets Russes*. Diaghilev had challenged Cocteau, *Parade's* de facto producer, to astonish him, and he duly obliged. The premier resulted in what has been described as a Parisian riot, but perhaps more accurately might be depicted as an eruption of controversy. A reaction against the complicated textures of romanticism and impressionism, *Parade* included the introduction of a typewriter, Morse apparatus, a rattle and a ship's siren, all part of the broader Dadaist trend of debunking of artistic conventions. Yet underlying all the Cubist fun and high jinks was a plot that has surprising relevance to jazz in the twenty-first century— how can an older art form, in this case it was classical music and ballet, still draw an audience in the face of the attractions of popular culture— then ragtime, Irving Berlin's Tin Pan Alley hits, the cinema, and the gramophone. Cocteau's tableaux portrays a traveling theater using music-hall performers—acrobats, a Chinese magician, a Little American Girl—to draw an audience for "high" culture within, but the music hall acts turn out to be so entertaining that no one wants to go inside for the main attraction. Low culture thus becomes the main attraction, supplanting high culture—a harbinger, perhaps, of how in the twenty-first century arts are being made redundant by technological progress and the Internet is increasingly becoming a replacement for cultural activity.

Cocteau was a bon vivant: witty, eclectic, and a brilliant talent in his own right—as a poet, novelist, dramatist, designer, playwright, and artist. An enthusiastic proselytizer on behalf of jazz, he wrote jazz criticism for *L'Intransigeant*, brought the Billy Arnold Jazz Band across from London (the first jazz ensemble to play a Paris concert hall),[36] and played drums. In December 1920 his "Parisian Jazz Band" performed a set of Dada-esque jazz to mark the opening of an exhibition of Picabia's work at Jaques Povolozky's Galerie La Cible. Featuring his elaborate drum setup, he was joined by composers George Auric and Francis Poulenc on piano and violin plus various noise-making efforts from others. Widely credited with introducing the Parisian fad for American cocktails, Cocteau was an energetic promoter of the talents of others, including Les Six.

The composer and member of Les Six, Darius Milhaud almost certainly heard Louis Mitchell's Jazz Kings perform at the Casino de Paris in 1918, which he partly appeared to acknowledge in a lecture he gave at the Sorbonne in 1924. His enthusiasm for what he called "negro music" prompted him to accept an engagement in New York, where he was able to indulge his interest in jazz by touring late-night Harlem jazz clubs. "The music I heard there was quite different to anything I had known before and was a complete revelation to me," he wrote later.[37] When he returned to France he took with him several recordings on the Black Swan label, including "I Wish I Could Shimmy Like My Sister Kate" and "The Wicked Five Blues." Later, in his autobiography, Milhaud would recall that he "never wearied of playing over and over, on a little portable phonograph shaped like a camera, Black Swan records I had purchased in a little shop in Harlem. More than ever I was resolved to use jazz for chamber work."[38] The fact that he regarded jazz as an art form and not a mere entertainment astonished American reporters accustomed to the indifference American composers displayed toward the music,[39] prompting headlines such as "Jazz, Says Darius Milhaud, Is the Most Significant Thing in Music Today" in the *Musical Observer*.[40]

Milhaud's love of jazz echoed the purview of Blaise Cendrars, inspiring their collaboration *La Création du Monde*. With Milhaud providing the music, Cendrars the libretto, and painter Fernand Léger designing the costumes and sets, this ambitious undertaking premiered in October 1923. An unprecedented level of ethnographic research had gone into the production, which drew on African folklore, dance, and design as source material. The libretto explored the genesis of life from an African perspective, with pantheism assumed to be central to African beliefs, so that the Creation takes place in the presence of totemlike deities who preside over an ever-changing landscape. Milhaud's music used elements suggestive of New Orleans jazz's collective polyphonic improvisation, introduced a jazz fugue, and "explored rhythmical combinations unknown in jazz of the 1920s."[41] The instrumentation included trumpets, trombones, saxophone, piano, and percussion: "[It] gave me at last a chance to use the elements of jazz that I had studied carefully," he wrote later. "My orchestra, like those of Harlem, was made up of seventeen soloists and I used the jazz style without reserve, blending it with classical feeling."[42] Although this elegant fusion of Bach and jazz predated George Gershwin's

*Rhapsody in Blue* by three months, it shared remarkable similarities of sound, especially in the blues-inflected sections.[43] "Despite this 'grafting' of ideas about Africa onto a European performance," writes art historian Petrine Archer-Shaw, "the finished product successfully created a modern genre: a balance between 'classical' and primitivized forms. Milhaud's score accompanying the narrative was majestic and hauntingly sonorous. Drawing on his Harlem experiences, Milhaud created a symphony that combined the swing mood with classical French style."[44]

Milhaud's idea of combing elements of jazz and Bach would resurface in the 1950s in the works of John Lewis, Bud Powell, Dave Brubeck, and Jacques Loussier, the latter building lifetime's a career on it. Jazz's influence also permeates Milhaud's instrumentation for *Caramel mou*, intended as an "orchestre de jazz," and the creations of fellow Les Six composers including Georges Auric, who suggests "blue notes" in *Huit Poémes*. In describing Auric's *Adieu New York* in 1924, Milhaud wrote: "Here is a case where the symphony orchestra discourses ragtime and foxtrot,"[45] while Poulenc's *Rhapsodie Négre* (1917), comprising five movements and owing something to Dadaism with its "Interméde Vocal," was debuted at a jazz night held by the Comte de Beaumont at his Parisian town house in August 1918. Although the essences of jazz seem distant, the point often missed, not just in Poulenc's case but all the composers within his circle, was that jazz's *inspiration*, rather than jazz elements per se, were harnessed as a means of broadening European classical expressionism. But it was not just members of Les Six who were excited by ragtime and jazz. As Milhaud pointed out in 1924: "In the *Piano Rag Music* of Igor Stravinsky we have a piano piece which employs the rhythmic elements of ragtime in a concert piece."[46] Stravinsky had originally been attracted to ragtime—*The Soldier's Tale*, *Three Pieces for Clarinet*, and *Ragtime for Eleven Instruments*—later saying:

> I must go back a little to mention a work I composed directly after finishing the score of *Soldat* [*l'Historie du Soldat*, or "Soldier's Tale"]. Its dimensions are modest but it is indicative of the passion I felt at that time for jazz, which burst into my life so suddenly when the [Great] war ended. At my request a whole pile of this music was sent to me, enchanting me with its popular appeal, its freshness and novel rhythm which so distinctively recalled its Negro origin. These impressions suggested the idea of creating a composite portrait of the new dance music, giving the creation the importance of a concert piece, as, in the

past, composers of their periods had done for the minuet, the waltz, the mazurka etc. So I composed *Ragtime* for eleven instruments, wind, string, percussion and a Hungarian cimbalom.[47]

As Andre Hodier has pointed out: "Stravinsky's writing shows a distinctly more developed sense of jazz [than that of other European composers at this time]. In places the formulas used by the Russian master attain a rhythmic flexibility that makes them resemble the riffs of jazzmen."[48] Other jazz-influenced works by Stravinsky included *Preludium for Jazz Band* (1936/37); *Tango* (1940), orchestrated for brass, saxophones, woodwinds, strings, piano, guitar, and percussion; *Scherzo á la Russe*, composed for the Paul Whiteman Orchestra and broadcast on the Mutual Broadcasting System in 1944; and *Ebony Concerto*, written for Woody Herman and His Orchestra (augmented by a French horn and harp) and premiered in Carnegie Hall on March 25, 1946.

During this period, the degrees of integration of jazz elements into what was considered "art music" varied in direct proportion to each composer's knowledge of jazz. In February 1922, the Chicago-based composer John Alden Carpenter premiered *Krazy Kat: A Jazz Pantomime* in New York's Town Hall, representing the first time a concert composer used the word "jazz" in a title. A ballet suite comprising jazz elements, his work contained the influence of his friends Prokofiev, Ravel, and Les Six, and was wildly applauded on its debut but met with a lukewarm reception from the critics. Other examples of classical composers of the period taking inspiration in varying degrees from pre-jazz and jazz elements include Claude Debussy's ragtime-influenced *Golliwog's Cakewalk* (1906–1908) and *Minstrels* (1910); Louis Gruenberg's *The Daniel Jazz, Jazz Suite*, and *The Emperor Jones*; and Arthur Honegger's *Clarinet Sonatina*. Prague composer Erwin Schulhoff moved from the influence of Dadaism in *Sonata Erotica* (1919) to the influence of jazz in solo piano works like *Esquisses de Jazz* (1927). Perhaps the most perceptive use of jazz devices in the context of European composition can be heard in Czechoslovakian composer Bohuslav Martinu's ballet *Kuchynská Revue* (1927) in the "Charleston" episode, *Trios Esquisses* (1927), *Jazz Suite* (1928), and *Sextet* (1928). That several European composers had taken inspiration from, and had even gone out of their way to laud, jazz did not go unnoticed among American composers. As Jed Rasula points out: "The American musical establishment, being Eurocentric in outlook, began to take note of the fact that serious composers like Milhaud, Stravinsky, Hindemith and Ravel were keen on jazz."[49] Aaron Copland, having experienced at first hand the Parisian enthusiasm for jazz while studying there, reflected a distinct jazz influence in *Ballet Grohg*, *Dance Symphony*, *Music for Theatre* (1925), and *Piano Concerto* (1927), while in *Piano Variations* (1930) "he starts from skeletonic fragments: the ambiguous thirds, sixths and sevenths of Negro blues, and the declamatory leaps of Jewish synagogue music."[50]

In the escapist freneticism of postwar Paris, leading members of the artistic community had begun to gather at Milhaud's home for dinner before decamping for a night on the town. As the numbers grew they moved to the more congenial Bar Gaya, a little restaurant on Rue Duphot, where the concert pianist Jean Wiener had been engaged to provide music from seven in the evening until two in the morning, a job he took because of straitened financial circumstance. His knowledge of jazz and ragtime had been gleaned from American troops, and he had begun to develop a reputation for his jazz interpretations, an influence that crept into his classical compositions including *Franco American Concerto* and *Sonatine Syncopée*, "a chamber music piece which owes its origin to various elements of jazz, although it retains the sonata form."[51] Paris intellectuals such as painters Picasso, Picabia, Derian, and Duchamp; writers such as Radiguet, Cocteau, Max Jacob, and André Breton; and fellow composers of Les Six, such as Poulenc and Auric and their colleagues Ravel and Satie gathered there most nights of the week, making Bar Gaya the unofficial headquarters of the Paris avant-garde. Here Wiener's reputation as a jazz pianist grew: "I had an American Negro called Vance Lowry, who played banjo and saxophone marvelously,"[52] Wiener recalled. "There was also a drum set Stravinsky had lent me. And from time to time, Cocteau used to come along and hit a beat or two on the snare drum."[53] On one occasion the Prince of Wales (himself an enthusiastic amateur drummer), Arthur Rubinstein, and Princess Murat sat listening to Cocteau playing the drums, while a crowd outside clamored to be let in. "In 1920–21, it was enough to hear Jean Wiener at the piano and Vance Lowry on saxophone and banjo, to become acquainted with jazz in an absolutely complete, pure and intact way," wrote Milhaud.[54]

With the Bar Gaya's increasing popularity, its owner Louis Moyses saw the advantages of moving to a larger and more central location, and on December 21, 1921, he opened Le Boeuf sur le Toit (named after Milhaud's fantasy on Brazilian motifs and rhythms) at 28 Rue Boissy d'Anglais. Francis Picabia's mural *L'Oeil Cacdylate* (1921) dominated the bar, with graffiti famously and enthusiastically added by the likes of Milhaud,

Auric, Poulenc, Tristan Tzara, Jean Hugo, and more. Here, Wiener was joined in duo by the Belgian pianist Clement Doucet (who added to his reputation by reading detective stories while playing); as jazz historian Robert Goffin notes, they became "such a great piano sensation that Jean Cocteau, Picabia, Radiguet and other poets took turns sitting-in on drums."[55] For the artists, poets, and authors who frequented Le Boeuf sur le Toit, jazz was more than mere background music; it was tailor-made to fit their philosophical outlook—for example, composer Maurice Ravel was impressed by the playing of the talented young French jazz trombone virtuoso Léo Vauchant (b. 1904), whom he heard perform there. "In that place, there were four other men besides Ravel who met regularly in 1924," recalled Vauchant, "Honegger, aged thirty-two, Darius Milhaud, same age, Poulenc, twenty-five, Auric, twenty-five, Ravel was forty-nine then, and I was twenty. I'm not taking an ad on myself now, I'm just telling you things the way they were. I know that those four guys were intrigued by what I was doing with the trombone. We were playing a jazz that was saccharine-coated by Wiener and Doucet. And the one who caught on best was Ravel, who was forty-nine—the others were thirty-two and twenty-five—and he caught on better than any of them."[56]

Ravel engineered a unique two-way exchange whereby he gave Vauchant composition lessons in exchange for lessons on jazz improvisation, an arrangement that lasted until 1928, culminating in Vauchant's providing "advice on the notation of trombone solos in two of Ravel's works."[57] This suggests that Ravel's engagement with jazz was not merely superficial, reflected in his famous *Bolero*, written while having "lessons" from Vauchant in 1928. As Nicolas Slonimsky has written, *Bolero* is "a veritable tour de force of modernity."[58] The famous ostinato ¾ rhythmic pattern that underpins the piece is wholly in context with modernism's desire to replicate the rhythms of the machine age—indeed, Ravel himself insisted it reflected his fascination with machines, his father being a Swiss engineer who had helped pioneer the automobile—while its use of two saxophones in the ensemble represented, perhaps, a nod of approbation toward 1920s jazz modernity. The composition is in C major except for a brief deviation into E major during the raucous coda, complete with trombone and saxophone glissandi. It would be wrong to attribute these effects to Vauchant's jazz influence, however, since Ravel had used them before, in *Rhapsodie Espagnole* (1908), which owed its influence to John Philip Sousa's virtuoso trombonist Arthur Pryor, who featured glissandi in numbers such as "Coon Band Contest" and "Trombone Sneeze" during

Sousa's Paris visits in 1900 and 1903. *Bolero* comprises two eighteen-bar themes (effectively nine bars A plus nine bars A1, alternating with nine bars B plus nine bars B1) that are repeated eight times; then nine bars A are alternated with nine bars B, which precedes an unexpected and dramatic modulation into E major before returning to the home key. The interest is sustained by Ravel's imaginative voicings of the repeated themes, such as the remarkable effect he achieves at around 6 mins. 50 secs., using French horn, two piccolos, and a celesta, and the slowly increasing crescendo that climaxes with the modulation into E in a resounding treble forte. From a jazz perspective the B melody is most interesting, spanning two octaves making use of syncopated figures and flattened tones suggestive of the Phrygian mode. It is very freely interpreted by trombone at 8 mins. 10 secs., Vauchant recalling an interesting incident as Ravel was completing the score: "I played the piece before anybody else did. I had him change the key from D to C. I told him, 'The trombone and the bassoon are not going to make those E flats above top C, eleven of which are consecutive.' So he said, 'How about a tone lower?' So he put it down a tone . . . And I said, 'If I were you, I would let the other guys interpret it the way they feel it. Don't write the slurs and so on—let them phrase it.' So now everybody's playing it the way he wrote it with no expression marks at all!"[59]

Ravel also betrayed his fascination with jazz, albeit seen through his own creative prism; his *Piano Concerto in G*, has melodic lines in which the blue note plays a role,[60] his *Violin Sonata* has a blues movement, the melodic theme that develops in *Concerto Pour la Main Gauche* borrows elements from the blues,[61] while three mildly jazzy compositions, including the *Five O'Clock Foxtrot* (1925), are revealing of his love of the music. But perhaps Ravel's enduring legacy in jazz is less with his own works per se but in his approach, like that of Debussy, to harmony. Both liked unresolved seventh and ninths, which would surface in the playing of musicians such as Bill Evans in the 1950s. By June 1928, Vauchant had joined Europe's most successful—and Paul Whiteman–inspired—jazz orchestra led by Jack Hylton in London, where he played cello and was featured, along with Lew Davis, on trombone as well as arranging "hot" numbers for Hylton such as "Mississippi Melody" and "Tiger Rag."

Ultimately, the essence of modernism was never simply an intellectual movement, an arts movement, a political movement (according to Franco Moretti, modernism's "unbelievable range of political choices can be explained only by its political indifference"),[62] a period in literature, or a form of cultural nationalism. It was a major cultural shift that was felt to a greater or lesser degree throughout Western civilization. Although modernism had no clearly defined objectives, its central thrust was less one of ideology, more one of "attitude and orientation."[63] Perhaps unsurprisingly, the cataclysmic upheaval of World War I was a pivotal event in its evolution. The ultimate dislocation with history—the Great War's mass-produced, industrialized death and destruction that left millions fighting to the death over scraps of land—was impossible for artists to absorb and represent through the traditional techniques of realism. As Paul Johnson has argued: "It needed the desperate convulsions of the great struggle, and the crashing of regimes it precipitated, to give modernism the radical political dimension it had hitherto lacked, and the sense of a ruined world on which it would construct a new one."[64]

The past had been torn away, leaving only the present, exaggerating and accelerating dramatic changes in society and allowing modernism to assume unexpected relevance as it entered popular culture via the Jazz Age of the 1920s, a pivotal decade in which a new consumer society revolutionized culture. Through a mixture of Fordist mass production and Keynesian economics, the 1920s was the decade in which America emerged as a modernist nation, in part through consumerism. Since consumer culture is dominated by the idea that everyday life could and should be modern, it created a powerful link between consumption and modernism. Even the burgeoning advertising industry focused not just on selling consumer goods but also on selling consumerism as the pathway to modernity. Using techniques that would be followed by subsequent generations of their profession, the public were incited to modernize their homes, themselves, and their means of transport. Goods were promoted that aided the mechanization of daily life, from washing machines to lawn mowers to the automobile, which gave a sense of momentum into a modern future. Through economies of scale made possible by mass production, leisure pursuits such as the reproduction of music through mechanical means (the Victrola) became possible in the homes of millions of Americans. Modern appliances, made by modern methods and placed in modern homes meant that modernity was being consumed by the population in general rather than existing in the abstracted modernist creations of the avant-gardists.

## The Impact of Jazz in "Jazz Age" Europe

Louis Mitchell's obituary in *Variety* called him a "forgotten jazz great," but it was not until the publication of *The New Grove Dictionary of Jazz* in 1988 that he appeared in any jazz reference book. Born in Philadelphia in 1885, he tried for a theatrical career but finally settled for a set of drums, traveling with minstrel shows until 1912, when he ceased touring in New York and formed the Southern Symphony Quintet, opening in the Taverne Louis in the Flatiron Building. When they moved to the Beaux Arts at 40th Street and Sixth Avenue, they were hailed as "the best Negro band extant, who besides playing ragtime present an extensive program of high class music."[65] The personnel of the band at the time were P. Jones (piano), Vance Lowry (banjo; Lowry would later settle in Paris), J. Hope (bandoline), W. Riley (cello), and Mitchell on drums, and they were reported to have played Reisenweber's Restaurant to acclaim in 1914, three years before the Original Dixieland Jazzband. Encouraged by Irving Berlin to take his band to Europe, he introduced his nascent form of ragtime-into-jazz to London in 1914, playing a brief residency in the Piccadilly Restaurant that summer, enabling him to declare in 1956, "I was not one of the first to bring jazz to Europe, I was the first!"[66]

This statement reflects, perhaps, an element of hyperbole, since an ensemble called the Versatile Four was playing in London as early as 1910, recording such items as "Down Home Rag" in 1916. Earlier still, the Black Diamond Band recorded "Wild Cherries Rag" in 1912. There are examples of banjo players recording rags that date back earlier, but suffice to say that while Mitchell may not have been the first to bring jazz to Europe, he was certainly the most popular. With the outbreak of war in 1914, Mitchell returned to Harlem and toured with the Clef Club, a band of seventy-five members directed by James Reese Europe. He was back in Britain in 1915, drumming at Ciro's Club off Leicester Square, and in August he played in a duo called Jordan and Mitchell at the Ardwick Empire and at the London Hippodrome in a show called *Joyland*. In a theater packed with troops on leave from the Western Front, Mitchell's specialty, "Oh, You Drummer," earned him regular curtain calls. In January 1917, Mitchell formed the Syncopating Septette and opened at the Alhambra in Glasgow, Scotland, apparently romping through "Ja Da" and "Down Home Rag," with the press hailing him as "a genius of agility and noise."[67] In the summer of 1917 he formed the Seven Spades, playing venues such as the Music Hall in Liverpool and the London Palladium and traveling to

France the following year to give free concerts for the Allied troops. Here he broke up the band and returned to New York, staying long enough to form a new group that included Cricket Smith (trumpet),[68] Frank Withers (trombone), Sidney Bechet (clarinet), and Walter Kildare (piano), possibly Vance Lowry (banjo), and an unknown bassist, comprising a seven-piece with Mitchell (drums).[69]

At the end of the war Paris was a wide open city, and Mitchell established himself as a star at the Casino de Paris, a music hall on the Rue de Clichy, where he remained for five years, earning, according to the European jazz historian Robert Goffin, "ten times the salary of a cabinet minister."[70] There he worked with many famed personalities of the age and performed for the Prince of Wales, Rudolph Valentino, Al Jolson, and the Dolly Sisters, among others, while Vernon and Irene Castle, the famed dancing team, apparently wrote to him for his advice on the latest rags. "He recorded some sides for Pathé, the first jazz recordings made in Europe, records which remain completely unknown in the USA," wrote Goffin. "It is unlikely that any copies are still in existence, but if found they would make an important and highly interesting addition to our store of recorded jazz."[71] Mitchell again recorded for Pathé in 1922–23, but with the exception of "Wabash Blues" among the small number of sides that have been reissued (of some fifty issued and unissued titles cut at this time), they are not helpful in substantiating the glowing first-hand-witness reports of the band. For example, when Goffin saw Mitchell's band perform at the Alhambra in Brussels, Belgium, in 1919, he recalled: "They left an extraordinary impression. That night something new was born for me and took its place alongside the poems of Guillaume Apollinaire and Blaise Cendrars and the paintings of Douanier Rosseau and Chagall."[72]

Goffin, like many European intellectuals of the period, saw no incongruity in situating jazz within the broader movement of modernism that was sweeping though European artistic life. Jazz's bawdy vitality seamlessly fitted into the European modernist continuum, making common cause with the Dadaists' experimentation with noise; the Futurists' love of the machine (echoed by jazz's insistent rhythms); the Simultanists' ("Simultanism" was a term invented by the French painter Robert Delaunay to describe his and his wife's abstract painting in 1910 — Apollinaire later chose to dub it Orphism) network of polyvisual images echoed by early jazz's polyphony and the surrealist's interpretation of jazz improvisation as a direct route to the subconscious untainted by ideological manifestos;

indeed, Goffin argued that "jazz was the first form of Surrealism."[73] As if underlining the perception of jazz as an aural expression of modernism, Goffin's response to hearing Sidney Bechet in 1920 was expressed by way of poetry, published as *Jazz Band* with a foreword by Jules Romains, a poet, author of a cycle of novels called *Les Hommes de bonne volonté* (The Men of Good Will), and the founder of *Unanimisme*, a modernist literary movement. The book was illustrated with five fashionably modernist Cubist woodcut plates and a woodcut head piece by Gaston De Beer, and was the first of Goffin's books to declare his passion for jazz: "Possessed immediately by a sort of frenzied lyricism I wrote *Jazz Band*, a collection of poems in praise of the new music, about this time," he recalled. "A great cubist artist contributed four [sic] woodcuts representing musicians to illustrate it."[74]

Louis Mitchell may have sowed the seeds of the jazz craze that would sweep Britain in the postwar euphoria that followed the end of the Great War. Eight weeks after the Armistice treaty was signed ending World War I, a report in the London *Times* described how the orchestra at the London Coliseum was attempting to "convert itself into a jazz band," adding that such a mission was "one of many American peculiarities that threaten to make life a nightmare."[75] On April 1, 1919, the liner *Adriatic* berthed at Liverpool, and among the passengers to disembark were the members of the Original Dixieland Jazz Band, who are now credited with making the first jazz recording ever, on February 26, 1917. They had just completed a sensational residency at Reisenweber's Restaurant in New York, and after a shaky UK debut they became fixtures on the British music scene for fifteen months, giving local musicians the opportunity to listen and learn at first hand to live American jazz. The ODJB became so popular they were even received at Buckingham Palace. But while the ODJB were receiving all the plaudits, Will Marion Cook's Southern Syncopators provided British musicians with a glimpse of a true jazz great in Sidney Bechet, who would later leave Cook's band to work in Britain and France, contributing significantly to the understanding of jazz there. Like the ODJB, the Southern Syncopators appeared at Buckingham Palace, and when King George V conducted the band, it effectively bestowed a nod of approbation upon jazz by polite society. By 1921 the *New York Times* was able to report that in trend-setting European capitals like London and Paris, "the American jazz fraternity are lords paramount."[76]

The lifting of wartime restrictions in London, including replacing the Defence of the Realm Act with the Licensing Act of 1921, resulted in the opening of hundreds of nightclubs from the luxurious Ciro's with its glass dance floor, the massive Kit Kat Club in the Haymarket, to more bohemian haunts such as Soho's Cave of Harmony or the 55 Club. The dance craze of the 1920s—the first British dance championship was held in London in 1923—saw dance floors crowded, more so with the arrival of the Charleston in 1925, which seemed to symbolize American modernism itself. A combination of mass production and mass media transmission was helping to make America appear synonymous with speed and a fast-accelerating world—what mass production did for mass consumption, the media did for speed of perception. What was distinctly American was celebrated as the essence of Western Culture—such as Coca-Cola, consumerism, Hollywood, streamlined cars, cocktails, bobbed hair, the Charleston, and jazz. For many, consuming American culture embodied the sense of consuming modernism—becoming modern—an intoxicating ideal, since no one wants to be seen as "old fashioned." Jazz music in particular seemed to embody the modernistic spirit, its consumption not so much "meeting, importing and reproducing an African-American genre," as Johan Fornäs has pointed out, as "encountering and trying to cope symbolically with *modernity*, of which jazz appeared to be the ultimate expression."[77]

In an "age of mechanical reproduction," as Walter Benjamin described the 1920s, the impact of jazz on intellectual opinion abroad owed much to phonograph recordings, and especially those by the great jazz masters— some of whom were yet to perform in Europe, such as Louis Armstrong and Duke Ellington, and others who would never cross the Atlantic, such as Joe "King" Oliver, Jelly Roll Morton, and Bix Beiderbecke. Not only did recordings present a confluence of new media and new music that was in tune with modernism, they were also a means of divorcing the music from its functional role for dance, allowing detailed study, discussion, and analysis remote from its social context. As Francis Newton (the nom de plume of historian Eric Hobsbawm) noted, this kind of discourse fitted "smoothly into the ordinary pattern of avant-garde intellectualism, among the dadaists and surrealists, the big city romantics, the idealisers of the machine age, the expressionists and the like."[78] It was from among these intellectuals that the first significant literature on jazz emerged:[79]

*Jazz und Shimmy, Brevier der neuesten Tänze* by F. W. Koebner (1921)
*Die Revolution des Gesellschaftstanzes* by Heinz Pollack (1922)
*Das Neue Jazzbuch* by Alfred Baresel (1925)

*Le Jazz: La Musique Moderne* by André Coeuroy and André Schaeffner
   (1926)
*Jazz Band and the Modern Music*, Semion Ginzburg, editor (1926)
*Stichwort: Jazz* by Meyers Lexikon (1927)
*Jazz, Eine Musikalische Zitfrage* by Paul Bernhard (1927)
*Das Jazz—Fremdwörterbuch* by Bernhard Egg (1927)
*The Appeal of Jazz* by R. W. S. Mendl (1927)
*Jazz* by Emil František Burian (1928)
*Jazz Band* by A. G. Bragaglia (1929)
*Die Moderne Musik* by Hans Mersmann in *Handbuch der
   Musikwissenschaften*, ed. Ernst Bücken (1929)
*Schule für Jazz—Schlagzeug* by Mátyás Seiber (1929)
*Jazz—Tidens Toner, Tidens Rytmer* by C. E. Hansen (1929)
*Salon und Jazzmusik* by Marek Weber in *Musikblätter des Anbruch*
   (1929)
*Aux Frontiéres du Jazz* by Robert Goffin (1930).

Many of these authors had direct links with modernism—such as André Coeuroy and André Schaeffner in Paris and Paul Bernhard and Alfred Baresel in Germany, who were connected to the "new music" of Milhaud, Stravinsky, and Hindemith. Emil Burian was strongly influenced by Dadaism, Futurism, and Poetism (an important movement in the Czech avant-garde of the 1920s that embraced all new art) and had performed with a jazz band in a Prague cabaret. He was the composer of *Cocktails* (1926) for voice and jazz band, *Bubu of Montparnasse* (1928), a jazz opera, and *Jazz-Requiem* (1928), before going on to become one of Prague's leading theater directors, opening his own theater, named perhaps unsurprisingly Da-Da, with Jiří Frejka in 1927. A. G. Bragaglia was a pioneer of Futurist photography, while Robert Goffin was an acknowledged expert on the modernist poetry of Guillaume Apollinaire. In addition to the nonfiction publications noted above, *Jazz* by Hans Janowitz was quite probably the first jazz novel. It was published in Berlin in 1927, and about it Janowitz asserted: "A jazz-novel has the right to fade softly in the middle of a motif's repetition and simply come to an end. To safeguard this inalienable right in the first jazz-novel having unfolded according to the laws of jazz music—well, this should naturally be granted to me."[80] Janowitz had studied in Prague, where he had known author and composer Max Brod, the author Franz Kafka, and writer, playwright, and poet Karl Kraus before going on to script *The Cabinet of Dr. Caligari*.

Three of the most important figures in early European jazz research were Robert Goffin, Hugues Panassie, and Charles Delaunay. "Their pioneering works not only raised the level of appreciation for jazz in Europe but began filtering back to the United States in the mid-1930s," wrote Ted Gioia. "The appearance of Panassie's *Hot Jazz* in America in 1936 remains one of the major turning points in the history of jazz criticism; the book, despite its flaws, went a long way to establishing jazz as a subject worthy of serious study in its land of origin."[81] While Panassie and Goffin were involved in research, study, and critique, Charles Delaunay was a pioneer of the discographer's art. The son of the celebrated modernist painter Robert Delaunay and the artist/designer Sonia Delaunay-Terk, the young Delaunay was thrust into a hotbed of modernist thinking from birth. The modernist poet Guillaume Apollinaire was one of Robert Delaunay's closest friends and moved in with the family for a short while in 1911, when he was suspected of the theft of the *Mona Lisa*, remaining until police charges were eventually dropped. While Delaunay had previously called his and his wife's work Simultanism in 1910, Apollinaire coined the term "Orphism" in 1913 to describe their version of Cubism, which used striking and contrasting colors to create movement; Sonia Delaunay's epic painting of dancing couples evincing this, *Le Bal Bullier* (1913), is now housed at the Centre Georges Pompidou in Paris. Her son Charles's first study, *Hot Discography*, appeared in France in 1936 and together with its many revised and updated editions became the standard reference work for recorded jazz at the time. As Ted Gioia points out, Charles Delaunay, Hugues Panassie, and Robert Goffin could well be viewed as the cofounders of jazz studies: "Just as American jazz crossed the Atlantic to take root in Europe, with jazz criticism Europe returned the favour. By the time jazz studies began in earnest in the United States, the discipline was already established by these role models from overseas."[82]

Almost as soon as the first pioneering attempts at jazz literature were appearing in Europe they were followed by jazz magazines, aiding with the dissemination of the music and catering to the perceived need of jazz fans to keep abreast of the latest news and opinion. One striking feature of their journalism, and something that has persisted to some extent to this day, was that European writers, as Ron Welburn has noted, "operated without the vested interest in the cultural issues jazz raised for Americans."[83] Among the first to be published of the thirty or so European jazz magazines that appeared during the interwar years were:

| MAGAZINE | YEAR | COUNTRY |
|---|---|---|
| Music—Le Magazine du Jazz | 1924 | France |
| Melody Maker | 1926 | United Kingdom |
| La Revue de Jazz | 1929 | France |
| Estrad | 1929 | Sweden |
| Jazz Tango | 1930 | France |
| De Jazz Wereld | 1932 | Netherlands |
| Prehled Rozhlasu | 1932 | Czechoslovakia |
| Jazz | 1932 | Switzerland |
| Orkester Journalen* | 1933 | Sweden |

Source: Graham Langley, British Institute of Jazz Studies

*Still in print

Ultimately, when considering the dissemination of jazz beyond the borders of the United States in general, and in Europe in particular, we are still left with a major question: How did American jazz music possess the capacity to conquer the Western world in the way it did? It is a question that ultimately must remain open, but Eric Hobsbawm has contributed to this debate with his suggestion that American jazz music quite simply benefited from being American: "It was received not merely as the exotic, the primitive, the non-bourgeois, but as the modern. Jazz bands came from the same country as Henry Ford. The intellectuals and artists who took up jazz immediately after the First World War on the European continent almost invariably include modernism among its attractions."[84]

## The Impact of Modernism in "Jazz Age" America

The emergence of American modernism took time to be felt following the Armory Show in 1913, intended to give the American public their first opportunity to experience European modernism. Featuring some 1,250 works of painting and sculpture by the likes of Picasso, Matisse, Cézanne, Gauguin, Duchamp, and Kandinsky alongside the works of American modernists such as George Bellows, Marsden Hartley, Walt Kuhn, Joseph Stella, Anne Goldthwaite, Patrick Henry Bruce, and Stuart Davis, its impact was perhaps not quite what was intended—some have called it a disaster—since a section of the press and public came to mock. Matisse and Picasso were pilloried, while Duchamp's "Nude Descending a Stair-case" prompted a cartoon in the *Evening Sun* on March 20, 1913, headed "Seeing New York with a Cubist," with the caption: "Rude Descending a Staircase (Rush Hour at the Subway)." The exhibition's failure to cap-ture the public's imagination may have been resistance to the "new ideas" from Europe that went far beyond the conventions of art of the time. The exhibition was later presented in Chicago and Boston, and in Chicago; students of the *Law and Order* league burned effigies of some of the artists, including Matisse.

In any event, most of the forward-looking American artists of the early twentieth century remained wedded to representational languages of painting—the Ash Can School of John Sloan, Robert Henri, Everett Shinn, and George Bellows and others from which Edward Hopper's evoc-ative canvases depicting the inner turmoil of lonely individuals emerged. For the public at large, Norman Rockwell's popular depiction of an ide-alized America for *The Saturday Evening Post*, Grant Wood's "American Gothic"—a lament for a lost nineteenth century—or the geometrical pre-cision of Charles Sheeler were more in tune with the times. Even Joseph Stella's "Voice of the City" did not cut its ties with realism. But there were dissenting voices, such as Arshile Gorky, who could not understand why America, such an exciting new country, had failed to embrace modern-ism. His murals for Newark Airport for the Federal Art Project in 1936, of which two remain, embrace Surrealism, Cubism, and machine-age mod-ernism and are examples of his work that would later have a seminal in-fluence on American abstract expressionism. However, for Stuart Davis, who had studied with Robert Henri and had worked in his Ash Can style, the Armory Show was an inspirational event. Despite having five of his works exhibited, making him the youngest painter to exhibit at the show, his exposure to the works of modernists such as Matisse, Picasso, Picabia, and Duchamp had a profound effect on his aesthetic as he came under the spell of the French modernists in general and Cubism in particular. "It gave me the same kind of excitement I got from the numerical pre-cisions of the Negro piano players in the Negro saloons, and I resolved that I would quite definitely have to become a 'modern artist,'"[85] he re-called. With *Electric Blub* (1924), Davis subtly reveals the rhythms of the Jazz Age. Not only do the bold colors and forms reflect the energy of the time, but the subject also speaks of American modernism and industrial-ization in the 1920s. It reflected his desire to forge a distinctly American approach, claiming that he painted what he saw in America—the American scene. Inspired by advertisements and posters from in and around the streets and subways of New York, he used words in his paintings in a way that was far bolder than a Picasso or a Braque, and it gave his paintings rhythm that he claimed was inspired by jazz—believing it to be the first American modernism. Both the titles and images of his late 1930s work often reflected the rhythms of the Swing Era, while his murals for the Federal Arts Project of the Works Progress Administration in 1938–39 were also influenced by his love of jazz. The outstanding American artist to work in Cubism, Davis was on his own in American art in the 1930s and 1940s, no American painters caring to embrace modernism so completely.

If modernist fine art and sculpture were encountering resistance from the critics and public at the time of the Armory Show, so too was literary modernism, finding limited outlets through small publishing houses like Mitchell Kennerley or B. W. Huebsch, or through "little magazines" like Harriet Monroe's *Poetry* and Scofield Thayer's *Dial*; big publishing firms like Doubleday's or Scribner's chose to maintain ultraconservative lists. Modernism may have been present in spirit in prewar America, but as Gertrude Stein argued in 1926, it took the violence of the Great War to embolden the modernist ethos. Although she did not ascribe the war as the cause of American modernism, she believed that it was its greatest publicist, writing that it "advanced a general recognition of the expression of the contemporary composition by almost thirty years."[86] By then, the works of Stein and her fellow "lost generation" writers who had relocated to Paris after World War I had begun to gain recognition as a highpoint of American literature, "the moment when it emerged from the monotonous nightmare of naturalism into the daylight of modernism."[87]

## The Reception of Jazz in "Jazz Age" America

Whatever modernist connotations early jazz was acquiring in Europe, they were by no means as forthcoming in the United States. Alarmed at the inroads an Afro-American entertainment was making into dominant white culture, self-appointed moral watchdogs were quick to attack jazz as "a low streak in man's tastes that has not yet come out in civilization's wash."[88] Even the "lack of conventional deportment" displayed by jazz performers was singled out for criticism, such as a piece in the *Literary Digest* in 1917 that spoke of a "group that play for dancing, when colored, seem infected with the virus that they try and instil as a stimulus to others. They shake and jump and writhe in ways to suggest return of the medieval jumping mania."[89] Negative connotations such as these fueled a rising tide of controversy that swirled around the music which was such that in 1918, the *Times-Picayune*, New Orleans's leading newspaper, took the unusual step of disowning jazz by denying that the city was the "birthplace of jazz": "In the matter of jass, New Orleans is particularly interested since it has been widely suggested that this particular form of musical vice had its birth in this city—that it came, in fact, from doubtful surroundings in our slums. We do not recognise the horror of parenthood, but with such story in circulation, it behoves us to be last to accept the atrocity in polite society, and where it has crept in we should make it a point of civic honor to suppress it. Its musical value is nil, and its possibilities of harm are great."[90]

Quite what jazz was, whether it was music at all—"This thing called jazz is positively one of the most awful and most inexcusable of musical sins ever committed against the face of the people," said *Musical America* in 1920[91]—contributed to jazz's "other" status. In 1921, Anne Shaw Faulkner's notorious cover feature "Does Jazz Put the Sin in Syncopation?" in *Ladies Home Journal* berated jazz on racial and political grounds, claiming that the music was "the accompaniment of the voodoo dancer, stimulating the half-crazed barbarian to the vilest deeds," and that it represented the "bolshevik element of licence striving for expression in music."[92] Later that year it continued its attack on jazz with a piece called "Unspeakable Jazz Must Go!"[93] reporting how, in Philadelphia, a Miss Marguerite Walz "was charged with the special duty of supervising public dancing in that city." In a crackdown on public dancing, seventy-five policemen were put at her disposal and were instructed "Not to permit cheek-to-cheek dancing, abdominal contact, shimmy, toddle or the Washington Johnny, in which the legs are kept spread apart."[94] Perhaps not unexpectedly, the religious lobby waded into the debate. In 1922 the *New York Times* reported a claim by Percy Stickney Grant, rector of the Episcopal Church of the Ascension at Fifth Avenue and 10th Street, that "jazz . . . is one of the crying evils of today."[95] Three months later, the same paper continued to maintain pressure on the music with a feature by the Rev. Dr. A. W. Beaven of Rochester headlined, "Primitive, Savage Animalism, Preacher's Analysis of Jazz."[96]

In their study of early recorded jazz, Phillips and Owens make the point that "Whereas there was little distinction between highbrow and lowbrow culture in the 1800s, the influx of non-Anglo immigrants and other developments in the U.S. challenged the old-money elite's social standing, resulting in the construction of rules to institutionalize the purity of highbrow culture and the exclusivity of elite class membership."[97] They cited an unnamed *New York Times* music critic who gave voice to these elite goals: "The way to elevate is elevate, to keep the people face to face with the best by eradicating everything less than best."[98] In the eyes of the elite, jazz was perceived to be primitive, discordant, and troubling by virtue of its vernacular origins and an incitement to promiscuity and licentiousness because of the social dancing it provoked. In a context where the state had already intervened to save the nation from itself by banning the sale, manufacture, and transportation of alcohol with the Volstead Act in 1920, many thought it should be acting again by banning jazz. The Superintendent of Schools in Kansas City proclaimed before an audience of a thousand school teachers, "This nation has been fighting booze for a long time. I am just wondering whether jazz isn't going to have to be legislated against as well."[99] Such sentiments reflected a broad anti-jazz consensus within the educational establishment—for example, at a meeting of the National Educational Association in 1921, Dr. Henry van Dyke claimed, "Jazz music was invented by demons for the torture of imbeciles."[100] *The Etude Music Magazine*, the most popular music teachers' magazine in the United States during the first half of the twentieth century, was also lined up against jazz. For example, the garish cover of its August 1924 edition announced its intention to grapple with "The Jazz Problem," reassuring readers, "We . . . most emphatically [do] *not endorse* Jazz" [*The Etude*'s emphasis].[101]

The anti-jazz lobby in the early 1920s included the following:[102]

*Institutions/Organizations.* Federal Interdepartmental Social Hygiene Board; General Federation of Woman's Clubs; Health Commissioner of Milwaukee; National Association of Masters of Dancing; National Federation of Music Clubs; New York State Legislature; Public Welfare Department of Illinois; United States Public Health Service; State Superintendent of Schools in Kansas City.

*Trade Press. The Etude; The Musical Courier; Musical Leader; The Musician; New Music and Church Review; Talking Machine World; Ladies Home Journal; The Literary Digest (Reader's Digest); New York Herald Tribune; New York Times*

*Prominent Individuals.* Henry Ford; Thomas A. Edison; Mrs. J. P. Morgan; Mrs. Borden Harriman; Mrs. Henry Phipps; Mrs. James

Roosevelt; Mrs. E. H. Harriman; Surgeon General Coming; Virgil
Thomson; John Phillip Sousa

As Phillips and Owen point out: "The elites (along with many in the
upper-middle class) worked against jazz through music and dancing
clubs, women's organizations and public health agencies,"[103] while members of the business elite banned jazz from their plants.[104] There was also a
substantial religious lobby that included the Clericus of the Episcopalian
Church of Louisville, the Salvation Army, and the Catholic Church that
also campaigned vigorously against jazz. Cardinal Begin, the Archbishop
of Quebec, condemned "lascivious" dances and asserted that they must
be combated as moral contagion; a decree of the Synod reproved dances
"such as the 'fox-trot,' the 'tango,' the 'shimmy,' the 'cheek-to-cheek,' the
'turkey trot,' the 'camel trot,' the 'one-step' and others of the same kind."[105]
In 1921, the music section of the General Federation of Woman's Clubs
launched a crusade against jazz, and, at its national convention two years
later, *Music Courier* headlined: "Representatives of 2,000,000 Women,
Meeting in Atlanta, Vote to Annihilate Jazz."[106]

Such was the opprobrium jazz was attracting that in 1921, Senator Sal-
vatore A. Cotillo presented a bill to the New York state legislature on February 24 designed to regulate public dance halls, the passage of which
he said would eliminate "the bunny hug, the alligator glide, shimmy and
other disgraceful dances." According to the *New York Times*,[107] Cotillo asserted that the measure had the support of many welfare organizations
and expressed the hope the public would give favorable attention to his
bill, whose effect was to prohibit public dancing unless a person, association, or corporation intending to hold such a dance had received a permit
costing two dollars from the commissioner of licences. With his new-
found power, the commissioner then promptly banned jazz and dancing
on Broadway after midnight.[108] The *New York Herald* commented: "The
Commissioner of Licenses in New York is to be the dictator of dancing.
He can decide whether the shimmy is immodest; just what kind of fox
trot or turtle slide young girls may dance in public without endangering
their morals and how late youth and greybeard of the metropolis may
dance without risking their health."[109] The result of the bill meant that
dance hall managers in the Broadway area were forced to lower musicians' wages to a level where work there was no longer profitable. Not
all in the House of Representatives agreed with the bill, however. Representative Hackenburg told the *New York Times*: "The Cotillo bill for

the licensing of dance halls is the worst kind of class legislation. It will stop the shimmy in the dance halls of New York City, but any people who have the money can hire the ballroom of the Waldorf-Astoria and shimmy all they please . . . and people who haven't money will go to dives."[110] In Harlem, where the Cotillo bill received lax enforcement, jazz continued to thrive, actually becoming a feature for wealthy white socialites who would finish off an evening's entertainment by heading Uptown to "slum" while taking in a little jazz with their bootleg liquor. Downtown, however, jazz went underground, into the dives and speakeasies, as Representative Hackenburg had predicted, prompting several premature obituaries—the *New York Herald* reported in January 1922: "The decline and fall of jazz, they say, has been going on apace during the present theatrical season,"[111] while a *Musician* feature from May that year was headlined simply "The Decline of Jazz."[112]

The burgeoning recording industry's response to jazz during its early years appears to have been influenced by the jazz debate. Prewar, their response to the dance craze had been to enlist light orchestral or military bands to record dance titles. But as a youthful audience became progressively more engaged with the dance craze, they were on the lookout for contemporary bands directly engaged with a younger public, not least because their following might act as a spur to sales. One band that the Victor Talking Machine Company began to take an interest in was the Original Creole Orchestra from New Orleans, whose tour itinerary in 1915 included Los Angeles, San Francisco, Winnipeg, Salt Lake City, Chicago, a thirteen-week tour for the Western Vaudeville Managers Association of Iowa and Illinois, and New York dates including the Columbia Theater in Times Square, the Bushwick in Brooklyn, and the American in Manhattan. Clearly a band that could command such a busy schedule suggested a demand for their music, which was of interest to Victor: "The itinerary of the Creole Orchestra makes the most likely dates for negotiations towards a recording date . . . December 1915, January 1917 or early 1917," writes Larry Gushee.[113]

What especially interests historians is that this ensemble included the cornet player Freddie Keppard, one of the key figures in the early development of jazz in New Orleans, whose reputation has been conflated with that of Buddy Bolden, a legendary trumpet player who, despite the absence of recorded evidence, has been credited with consolidating the first genuine jazz style. Keppard is an especially interesting figure, since according to clarinetist Sidney Bechet—who would have been about eight or nine years of age when he first heard Bolden—Keppard "possessed [Buddy] Bolden's manner but had a greater talent and imagination."[114] In the event, jazz legend has it that Keppard was responsible for declining any potential recording deal, so making it, as Gushee has suggested, inevitable that he "fills a mythic function in jazz history . . . [that] mines a vein of irony: the Original Creole Orchestra had a chance to record for Victor in 1916 (possibly 1917) but—as most histories have it—Keppard refused because he feared others would then 'steal his stuff.' There are at least two or three other equally plausible but weakly substantiated stories about Keppard's refusal; behind each of them, the idea seems to be that an Afro-American should have been the first to make commercial jazz recordings."[115] When Keppard finally did record, with Cook's Dreamland Orchestra in 1924, history had all but passed him by, since in 1917 the Victor Talking Machine Company turned to the Original Dixieland Jazz Band, which provided them with one of their earliest million-selling recordings. Columbia had actually recorded the Original Dixieland Jazz Band before Victor but hesitated to release the recordings, quite possibly out of fear of being attacked by the elites.[116]

Remarkably, Victor did not follow up on their success with the Original Dixieland Jazz Band to the extent they might have done. For one thing, the band was out of the country between March 1919 and June 1920, and although they recorded the band on its return from England, they chose not to renew the band's contract when it expired in December 1921. Equally, James Reese Europe, who had begun a historic series of recordings for Victor on December 29, 1913, as the recipient of one of the first ever recording contracts given by a major record company to a black musician and the first ever to a black orchestra,[117] was not recorded by Victor on his return from France in 1919, despite his distinguished war service and a hero's welcome down Fifth Avenue. Reese had to record his legendary Hellfighters Band for the relatively obscure Pathé label on nonindustry standard ten-and-one-half-inch discs on March 3 and 14, and May 7, 1919. Although a few sides were subsequently reissued on LP, it was not until Memphis Records reissued the Hellfighter's sides in their entirety in 1996 that Europe's significance in nascent jazz becomes clear—and so too Victor's reason for not exercising any option to record the band. Not only did handbills for a concert tour by the Hellfighters on their Stateside return refer to "The band that set all Europe JAZZ MAD!" but their versions of "Memphis Blues" and "St. Louis Blues" are luminous classics of early jazz.

Instead, Victor opted to set an "example" to the rest of the recording industry by announcing that it would concentrate on high-status singers, conductors, and orchestras from the opera and classical worlds, according jazz low priority. The trade journal *Talking Machine World* concurred: "The future of our industry lies in encouraging the sales of high-priced goods and the best records. It does emphatically not lie in pushing cheap machines and jazz records."[118]

Not only were the recording companies highly visible because of their dominant market position, but their executives were strongly affiliated with the American elite class through educational, matrimonial, and financial ties. "Eldridge Johnson, founder and president of Victor, was top financial contributor to the Republican Party in 1928—whose major contributors also included the Mellons, Rockefellers and Guggenheims. Leon Douglass, Victor's vice president, married into the prominent family that produced Presidents John Adams and John Quincy Adams . . . [while] the founders and executives of Columbia Phonograph included influential attorneys, graduates of prestigious universities and financiers associated with the US Supreme Court and US House of Representatives."[119] Certainly some jazz was recorded during this time, but most was designated "race recordings," a new term for recordings directed at black record buyers. Indeed, after the Original Dixieland Jazz Band's contract with RCA Victor was not renewed, no records were made by the band for a year. At the end of 1922, the General Phonograph Corporation, manufacturers of Okeh records, offered a contract that produced four sides that were listed in the catalogue as "Race Records," indicative of the desire to keep "raucous jazz" away from polite white society. It was against this rising tide of controversy engulfing jazz and the very real threat of the elite's influence and lobbying power to marginalize the music that bandleader Paul Whiteman emerged on the American popular music scene; as George Simon noted, "Whiteman thought big, talked big and, most important of all, acted big."[120]

## Paul Whiteman and Jazz Modernism

Perhaps more than any other figure in American public life, bandleader Paul Whiteman came to personify American musical modernism during the Jazz Age to the American people. Paradoxically, he displayed no singular commitment to jazz, with a repertoire that ran the gamut from light classical music—Louis Armstrong was once witness to a Whiteman performance of Tchaikovsky's *1812 Overture*,[121] for example—through to ambitious, specially commissioned "modernistic" compositions, instrumental novelties, current pop songs, Viennese waltzes, light classical music, and Souza marches. Whiteman's popularity rested on a broad base of music of which jazz was a part, all performed with a high degree of technical precision—since he paid the best salaries to attract the best musicians. Ultimately, it would be his non-jazz, classically orientated musical credentials that became the source of his legitimacy with the anti-jazz elites.

In 1920, Calvin Child, director of Victor's Artists Bureau, brought Whiteman's then nine-piece Ambassador Orchestra into their Camden, New Jersey, recording studio. Their subdued and inoffensive reading of "Whispering" (coupled with "Japanese Sandman") was an enormous hit, selling more than 2 million copies, pushing Whiteman to the forefront of popular music, a position he did not relinquish for over a decade. Victor's Black Label recordings made each tune's purpose clear, with the instruction "For Dancing" clearly printed under the Victor logo to the right of the spindle hole; the implication was that this music was not meant for serious contemplation in the manner of a classical recording, but rather for light-hearted social recreation. To underline the point, each tune title was followed by the appropriate dance-step in parentheses—be it "Waltz," "Fox Trot," "Quick Step," and so on. "Whispering" was designated a "Fox Trot," which was fast overtaking the popularity of the one-step, so aligning it with the popular dance step Vernon and Irene Castle were championing. A 1920 feature in *Talking Machine World* headlined "Why the Fox-Trot Flourishes" attempted to explain the dance's popularity, while also pointing to the then equivocal status of jazz: "It was not so long ago that the fox-trot was an unknown quantity. Shortly after its initial appearance it divided honours about equally with the one-step, but today it seems to have monopolized the dance field. Those who attack this dance are prone to call it 'jazz,' thinking thereby to bring it into disrepute."[122]

Whiteman's orchestra, through his arranger Ferde Grofé, played a pioneering role in "restructuring the dance orchestra which continued (despite numerous modifications) to be fundamental for the next twenty five years and persists even today. By intelligent scoring he managed to make saxophones and brass into principal voices in the dance orchestra . . . and incorporated into dance music many of the most interesting features of jazz."[123] From 1921, Victor released one or two Whiteman recordings per month, many arranged by Grofé. Virtually every year until the mid-1930s, Whiteman scored a No. 1 hit. His early success was such that when he chose to play jazz, it was often the first time many Americans had heard the music, his popularity enabling him to engage top "hot jazz" arrangers of the day to cater for this aspect of his wide-ranging repertoire. Whiteman's popularity, in tandem with the evolution of his orchestra, suggests that his music answered some need in America at that time and, as Max Harrison has suggested, quite apart from his ambiguous effect on jazz, his career has a sociological aspect which gives him a place in the history of those times.[124] His late 1920s ensemble represented the high point of his engagement with jazz thanks to innovative arrangements from the likes of Bill Challis, Matty Malneck, Lennie Hayton, and Tom Satterfield, while in the 1930s his panel of arrangers would include William Grant Still. As Gunther Schuller has pointed out, this music was "designed to make people listen, not dance,"[125] and was often presented in formal concert settings during theater tours around the country. These were "complex, demanding scores that took everything [his] musicians could give";[126] they were not simply functional, but betrayed higher artistic ambition, revealing Whiteman's intent to broaden jazz's expressive sources through technically demanding yet sophisticated arrangements that helped set the pace for big band jazz in the late 1920s.

In March 1923, Whiteman embarked on a hugely successful appearance in England. Performing for royalty and London society as well as an eight-week residency at the London Hippodrome, he became "as big a hit in England as he already was in the United States."[127] To the London *Times* he represented yet more evidence of the inevitable "Americanization" of British culture that was being widely predicted as Britain became increasingly dominated by American capital and ideas, prompting this tongue-in-cheek review of a Whiteman concert: "Whiteman] represents modern American tyranny at its most efficient and devastating development. What are we miserable Europeans today? We are the slaves of America. She has taken us in thrall not merely by the magic of the dollar, but by her terrible efficiency at everything, especially Jazz."[128] On his return to Manhattan in August 13, 1923, Whiteman was greeted by a welcome that involved airplanes, fire-boats, and jazz bands and a welcoming committee comprising city dignitaries and celebrities including Victor Herbert, George M. Cohan, and John Philip Sousa. When he alighted from ss *Leviathan*, his triumphant return to American shores seemed to demand some grand gesture, and the Buescher Band Instrument Company of Elkhart, Indiana—whose instruments Whiteman had just begun endorsing—

coordinated a publicity stunt in which he was "crowned" "King of Jazz." A trade journal reported: "The crown for the coronation was made by the Buescher Band Instrument Co. . . . [and] bore replicas of . . . various instruments, including, of course, the popular saxophone. The coronation address came over the long-distance telephone . . . sent by F. A. Buescher. The golden crown is inscribed 'To Paul Whiteman in appreciation of his art and artistry and his aid to self-determination in the music of the nation.'"[129] The following evening a testimonial banquet costing $7,000, with Whiteman and his musicians as guests of honor, was held at the Waldorf Astoria, an event that moved the bandleader to tears.

Today, the larger significance of Whiteman's cultural symbolism within modernism is usually overshadowed by the debate surrounding his pretensions to the title of "King of Jazz." However, it is important to draw the distinction between "jazz" as the term is understood today, and "jazz" as the term was understood in 1923, since there is a temptation to judge the past by the value systems of the present. To do so is to present an obstacle to understanding, since in the early 1920s "jazz" enjoyed a much broader meaning as an all-purpose adjective that was used to describe almost anything "modern." Clashing colors and loud patterns were dubbed "jazzy"; a play called The Jazz Marriage (1925) was nothing more than a "modern" tale of divorce; retailers stocked "jazz" consumer goods (such as, remarkably, a "jazz" storage jar) and "jazz" clothes; while in Paris there was a drink called a "Jazz Cocktail." Indeed, because the term "jazz" in 1923 was by no means the ideologically charged word it is today, there was little, if any, sense of incongruity expressed at the time at Whiteman's sequestering the title "King of Jazz." Of course, Whiteman's jazz credentials were hardly helped by the Universal motion picture King of Jazz (1930), which had Wilbur Hall performing "Pop Goes the Weasel" and "The Stars and Stripes Forever" on violin and bicycle pump, or Jeanette Loff and Stanley Smith singing "My Bridal Veil." In fact, the whole film was almost entirely disposed toward light entertainment rather than jazz with its revue-style presentation, although it is interesting to see the Whiteman band in feeble Technicolor perform an overproduced version of Gershwin's Rhapsody in Blue with Roy Bargy on piano and Irving Friedman on clarinet—albeit a "slap-tongued" soli by the saxophone section was hopelessly out of date even in 1930, as well as glimpses of Grofé's arranging style wrestling for prominence with the singers. Ultimately, King of Jazz is more of interest to film historians, with its Busby Berkeley–like production numbers, and students of semiotics rather than anybody with more than a passing interest in jazz. It serves to underline how Whiteman's significance was less in his relationship with jazz, however posterity chooses to frame him, but more in the broader sweep of American culture as the main standard bearer of popular American musical modernity in the 1920s.

Whiteman's return to the States was marked by a seven-month run of some 333 performances in the 1923 edition of the *Ziegfeld Follies*. Meanwhile, on November 1 of that year, mezzo-soprano Eva Gauthier gave a recital at the Aeolian Hall in New York, performing works by Henry Purcell, Béla Bartók, Arnold Schoenberg, Arthur Bliss, Claude Debussy, and Charles T. Giffes. In a daring move in the context of the time, she also chose to perform a selection of popular American songs by Jerome Kern, Irving Berlin, and George Gershwin, with Gershwin accompanying her on piano. Perhaps to the surprise of some critics, the recital received a grand ovation and an enthusiastic press, *Musical America* reporting: "Mme. Gauthier, a believer in the value and potentialities of certain jazz essays, had the courage to come before a recital audience in sacrosanct Aeolian Hall and sing a group of Broadway 'hits.' It took courage and one records without reluctance that the audience, far from acting like snobs, enjoyed the songs in all frankness and applauded the singer to the echo."[130]

The event inspired Whiteman, who was in the audience. When he learned that rival bandleader Vincent Lopez was planning a concert at Carnegie Hall in which a symphony orchestra would play a group of classical pieces and the Lopez band would respond by "jazzing" them up, he was galvanized into action. He immediately set about realizing his own ambition to present a concert of modern American music in a concert setting, and booked the Aeolian Hall for the afternoon of February 12, 1924. It was billed as *An Experiment in Modern Music*, and the program notes, written by Hugh C. Ernst, manager of the Whiteman office, betrayed the then controversial status of jazz, even in Whiteman's hands. It asserted: "Most people who ridicule the present so-called jazz and refuse to condone it or listen to it seriously are quarrelling with the name Jazz and not what it represents."[131] Much scholarly hot air has been expended on Whiteman's attempt to "make a Lady out of Jazz," with indignation at the so-called proposition argued from the perspective of the cultural and artistic standing jazz enjoys today, failing to contextualize jazz's equivocal status among the highly influential anti-jazz lobbyists during 1923 and in the run-up to the concert in early 1924.

In the event, the concert program included twenty-six exhausting items, designed, as the program notes state, to demonstrate "the tremendous strides which have been made in popular music from the day of discordant Jazz."[132] Opening with the raucous glissandos of the Original Dixieland Jazz Band's "Livery Stable Blues," intended to portray the perceived excesses of early "discordant jazz," and working through a very varied program designed to show how "the modern jazz-band dance orchestra had advanced to a point where it now had the capability of performing complex and extended works,"[133] the concert culminated in a performance of Edward Elgar's *Pomp and Circumstance* (Number 1 in D major). As Thornton Hagert has noted, "A more respectable piece of establishment music could scarcely have been chosen,"[134] in what was an astute move to placate the elites. Significantly, Whiteman never played the piece again and never recorded it.

Today the concert is remembered for one reason only, the premiere of an ambitious modernistic composition composed during the five weeks leading up to the event and called in the program notes *A Rhapsody in Blue*, performed with its composer, George Gershwin, at the piano. It was programmed in the concert as the penultimate number, and composer Howard Goodall has pointed out: "By the end of its fourteen minutes, the world of music had been changed forever."[135] The ovation that followed its performance was such that Whiteman announced from the stage that there would be repeat performances of the *Experiment in Modern Music* concert on March 7 and April 21. With the passage of time, *Rhapsody in Blue* has become deeply woven into the fabric of Americana, its evocative introduction with its soaring clarinet glissando still able to resonate with contemporary culture—such as in the opening sequence of the Woody Allen movie *Manhattan*. That memorable passage was originally written by Gershwin as a seventeen-note scale, but in rehearsal, Ross Gorman, a brilliant reed player, either out of boredom or whimsy, impulsively smeared the clarinet from the bottom to the top note of the scale, a difficult feat for most clarinetists. Gershwin loved the effect and wrote it into the score, so giving *Rhapsody in Blue* its attention-getting opening.[136] However, it is difficult to imagine the influence of clarinetist Larry Shields of the Original Dixieland Jazzband not playing a part in this. Considering the worldwide impact of their million-selling debut record on RCA Victor (which provided the opening number of the Aeolian Hall concert), it is entirely possible that Shields's outrageous glissandi in solo and ensemble were adapted and perfected by Gorman. Shields was a surprisingly accomplished clarinetist in the context of his time—which can be heard to some advantage on the London recordings of the band (1919–20) for Columbia, where his instrument (for some reason) is forward in the mix—and the extent to which he employed the glissando in these recordings suggests it was integral to his clarinet style.

Press reviews of the Aeolian Hall concert all agreed on two things: that it was sold out and that the audience was delighted. Most of the New York dailies praised the concert as the "finest that season [with] such superlative descriptions as 'admirable results,' 'uproarious success,' 'fresh and new and full of promise,' and 'one long, strong, musical cocktail.'"[137] While *Outlook* magazine noted that Whiteman's concert "was treated seriously by New York musical critics,"[138] there were a couple of reviews critiquing *Rhapsody in Blue*. The *New York Tribune* said: "Recall the most ambitious piece, the *Rhapsody* and weep over the lifelessness of its melody and harmony, so derivative, so stale, so inexpressive."[139] And Olin Downes in the *New York Times*: "It shows a young composer with aims to go beyond those of his ilk struggling with a form which he is far from being master."[140] These reviews reflect the slight queasiness in highbrow circles to the admission of a tunesmith from Tin Pan Alley into the world of "serious music" alongside the likes of Bach, Mozart, and Beethoven that existed for the best part of the twentieth century. Later, Leonard Bernstein would embody the standard criticisms, complaining: "You can't just put four tunes together, God-given though they may be, and call them a composition."[141] However, Larry Starr has pointed out that "*Rhapsody* demonstrates clearly that Gershwin's instrumental music is more thoroughly and shrewdly calculated in melodic, harmonic and formal treatment than one might suspect after reading most of the critical literature on the work. A search for 'tunes' leads not to small, isolated, closed structures but to rich open-ended melodic ideas clearly designed for development over large spans of time—melodic ideas filled with harmonic and formal implications that their composer explored impressively."[142] It is an argument not without force, borne out by the fact that *Rhapsody in Blue* is now one of the standard pieces in every concert orchestra's repertoire and considered an out-and-out modern classic.

Whatever antipathies the elites may have harbored about jazz and jazz-influenced music in the broader debate about jazz in the early 1920s, the one thing Whiteman had on his side after the concert was success—which has always been accorded the highest value in American life.[143] As Whiteman asserted in the *New York Clipper* ten days after the concert: "They can't go on questioning jazz forever. I proved, and it was conceded as such, that the popular highbrow conception of jazz was wrong."[144] By taking jazz and jazz-influenced music into New York's citadel of classical music, where the New York Philharmonic held sway and where classical luminaries such as Sergei Rachmaninoff, Sergei Prokofiev, Ferruccio Busoni, Guiomar Novaes, and Ignacy Jan Paderewski had graced its stage, he turned the debate about the "jazz problem" on its head. The acclaim he enjoyed was not just from the general public, but also from members of New York society; it included "a remarkable collection of conductors, musicians, vocalists, writers, critics, and philanthropists from the world of legitimate music: Frances Alda, Heywood Broun, Frank Crowninshield, Amelita Galli-Curci, Walter Damrosch, Mary Garden, Jules Glaenzer, Alma Gluck, Leopold Godowsky, Jeanne Gordon, Jascha Heifetz, Victor Herbert, Fannie Hurst, Otto Khan, S. Jay Kaufman, Karl Kitchen, Fritz Kreisler, Leonard Liebling, John McCormack, O. O. McIntyre, Sergei Rachmaninoff, Max Reinhardt, Moritz Rosenthal, Pitts Sanborn, Gilbert Seldes, Leopold Stokowski, Joseph Stransky, Deems Taylor, and Carl Van Vechten."[145]

By establishing that his musicians had the skills of classical musicians, Whiteman overcame the objections of the elites to the "discordant jazz," but his orchestra clearly was not a European "classical orchestra," although it could perform classical music, so what was it? To answer this it had to be acknowledged that Whiteman's was an *American* orchestra playing music that was uniquely *American*—including jazz, and music from Broadway and Tin Pan Alley. This had the effect of changing the nature of the discourse, which was now about *modern* music and what constituted modern *American* music. This situated Whiteman's music within a broader debate about what constituted "American-ness" in the arts and how this might be expressed in American national culture. As early as 1892, Antonín Dvořák had been invited to chair the newly founded National Conservatory of Music in New York to encourage Americans—as Emerson had done in *The American Scholar*—to be *themselves*. It was a debate that gathered momentum as the nineteenth century gave way to the twentieth, Charles C. Alexander pointing out that "the vision of a genuinely native, nationally representative artistic expression was the single most significant feature of American cultural commentary in the years after 1900 and up to the Second World War."[146]

Whatever American-ness was, or how it was to be expressed, there was at least a consensus that it should not end up becoming a footnote to, or a mere echo of, European culture. This strongly held belief was reflected in an essay written in 1917 by Van Wyck Brooks in *Seven Arts*, a journal he helped to found, called "Towards a National Culture." In it he argued that America had taken the "best" of other cultures, but now it must create its own "through the elementary experience of living, which alone produced a true culture," endorsing his friend Randolph Bourne's view "that the whole 'melting pot' theory was unsound since it turned immigrants into imitation Anglo-Saxons," and arguing that "America ought to have not narrow European nationalism but . . . become 'the first international nation.'"[147] Whiteman's *Experiment in Modern Music* played directly into this debate, and in the weeks and months that followed the concert came a realization that his musical modernism had much in common with the aspirations and values of a young nation making itself felt in the modern age. As John Andrew Johnson has written: "Shortly after the premiere of *Rhapsody in Blue* . . . Gershwin's name began to appear as a possible, even probable source for 'the great American opera,' for which a dizzying array of possible subjects was offered. One feature of this slurry of news reports is clear and consistent: that an American opera must reflect distinctly American locales, and that the musical idiom of jazz is the logical first choice for such a work."[148] That "great American opera" would be Gershwin's *Porgy and Bess*, premiered not in the concert hall but on Broadway, on October 10, 1935. Meanwhile, five months after the concert, a headline in *Musical America* announced: "Jazz Music Not Such an 'Enfant Terrible' After All," praising Whiteman for his presentation of *Rhapsody in Blue*, which "has its roots in American soil" and whose themes "are American themes . . . [that] at one bound [take] jazz into a new field and a new triumph."[149]

Today, the Aeolian Hall concert is regarded as a defining event of the Jazz Age and of the cultural history of New York City. Encouraged by the success of the concert, Whiteman pursued his modernistic ambitions into the 1930s with a further seven *Experiment in Modern Music* concerts mounted over a fourteen-year period that were designed to present new "modernistic" pieces alongside his own regular repertoire. Among the featured pieces were Bix Beiderbecke's "In a Mist" (with Beiderbecke himself on piano), Gershwin's *Concerto in F* (with Gershwin at the piano), and Ferde Grofé's *Metropolis* and *Grand Canyon Suite*. The eighth and final concert in the series took place December 25, 1938, and included works by six composers—Duke Ellington, Morton Gould, Bert Shefter, Fred Van Epps, Walter Gross, and Roy Bargy—who were invited to contribute one piece each to a forty-minute anthology called "Those Bells." Ellington's contribution would be "The Blue Belles of Harlem," which he would later perform himself in Carnegie Hall on January 23, 1943. As Ellington would later say, "Don't let them kid you about Whiteman. He has been a big man in our music. He's done a lot for it, especially with his concerts where he gave composers a chance to write new, extended works."[150]

In addition, clarinetist Artie Shaw, who had become a household name that year through his hit recording of "Begin the Beguine," guested on a sixteen-minute version of "St. Louis Blues," and Louis Armstrong sang (but played no trumpet) on "Shadrack" and "Nobody Knows the Trouble I've Seen" with the Lynn Murray Singers. Four members of the Raymond Scott Quintette joined the orchestra for "Three Ideas for Quintette and Orchestra," comprising Scott's compositions "Bumpy Weather over Newark," "Suicide Cliff," and "Mexican Jumping Bean." The concert was concluded by revisiting Whiteman's great hit from his first *Experiment in Modern Music* concert, *Rhapsody in Blue*, using Grofé's original orchestration for its debut in Aeolian Hall. As Whiteman's biographer, Don Rayo, has noted,

> Paul Whiteman invested a great deal of time, money and personal energy into these experimental concerts. Was it all worth it? One would have to say, unequivocally, yes. Perhaps more than any other bandleader or conductor of his generation, Whiteman both encouraged modern American composers and gave them a highly-visible platform of exposure for their created works. We would all do to remember that Whiteman didn't have to host these concerts. He was a highly successful and respected bandleader apart from these efforts, and indeed, ventured into them at his own risk. But Paul Whiteman believed in the incipient talent of young American composers and he did everything in his power to nurture and showcase it. Whiteman's contributions are incalculable . . . and contributed greatly to the ascendancy of modern music in this country.[151]

Whiteman's influence on the music scene of his day was considerable, and can be traced in a myriad of ways, not least in how his 1928 "Sweet Sue" anticipated Ellington's "Mystery Song" (1931), how the quasi-oriental device used in his first hit recording of "Japanese Sandman" found echo in Duke Ellington's "Arabian Lover" and Louis Armstrong's "Indian Cradle Song"—indeed, the "classical" piano introduction to Whiteman's "When Day Is Done" bears comparison with Armstrong's "You're Next." More especially, Whiteman's key arrangers, not least Bill Challis, Matty Malneck, Lennie Hayton, William Grant Still, and Tom Satterfield, contributed to expanding the harmonic, melodic, and tonal resources of jazz, something that was in the air during the 1920s to a greater extent than the jazzmen of the time, apart from a few master musicians, are now given credit for.[152] Ultimately, perhaps Whiteman's music should be remembered for helping create an atmosphere in which jazz was able to transcend the claims of the elites and the anti-jazz lobby that the music was merely a vulgar dance novelty. His influence was not just confined to the United States, it extended internationally, including in France with Grégor and his orchestra; Sweden, where Håkan von Eichwald was billed as the "Swedish King of Jazz"; Germany with Efim Schachmeister's Jazz-Symphonie-Ochester and Paul Godwin's Jazz-Symphoniker; and London with the Jack Hylton Orchestra, the Roy Fox Orchestra, and the BBC Dance Orchestra. After seeing Whiteman's band live during the filming of *King of Jazz*, bandleader Roy Fox would later say, "Paul Whiteman was greatly responsible for making popular music what it was in the hey-day of the big band."[153] Although it has been perennially fashionable to diminish Whiteman's role in jazz, one of the few level-headed assessments of his influence on jazz of the 1920s—although obliquely referencing him as a "symphonic jazz exponent"—came in 1964 from Neil Leonard, who pointed out:

> Jazz enthusiasts have ignored the role of symphonic jazz exponents in the advancement of music in America . . . [who] helped greatly to overcome formalism and highbrowism that have done much to constrict the development of music in the United States. Symphonic jazz enthusiasts encouraged composition and performance of music that departed from the European tradition. They were the first Americans with any prestige in official music circles to see that jazz (however much they wanted to change it) should not be dismissed as vulgar dance music, that something in it deserved the attention due art. By reason and ridicule they helped brush aside many prejudices and misconceptions that blocked the way for this recognition. In large measure, it was through their efforts that the term "jazz" became in the twenties and thirties associated less with the brothel and more with the concert hall as a native product of which Americans could be proud.[154]

In many ways, symphonic jazz is revealing of the many ways in which jazz and middlebrow culture overlapped and interacted during the 1920s, reflecting traditional musical values on the one hand and symphonic jazz's promise of modernism and futurity as the way ahead on the other, appealing to the public's desire to be of the modern world and a part of an American future. Yet Grofé's "modernistic" concert-style arrangements for Whiteman were essentially a recombination of existing knowledge using musical techniques borrowed from jazz, classical, and Tin Pan Alley. Typically, Grofé would juggle one, two, and even three separate strains, heralded by an often elaborate introductory passage and linked by developmental passages and interludes; "modernistic" chromaticism and modulatory passages would find resolution in an often elaborate coda.

Grofé's first attempt at writing a symphonic jazz piece after assisting in the preparation of *Rhapsody in Blue* came later the same year with a piece entitled *Broadway at Night*, dated October 11, 1924, but not recorded by Whiteman. It was followed by *Mississippi Suite*, recorded by Whiteman in 1925, albeit excluding the first movement, called "Father of Waters." *Three Shades of Blue* was recorded in 1926, *Metropolis* in 1928, and *Grand Canyon Suite* in 1931. Grofé also arranged pieces for Whiteman composed by others, such as Eastwood Lane's *Sea Burial* and *Persimmon Plucker*, as well as contributing several symphonic jazz arrangements for the Hollywood motion picture *King of Jazz*, in which Whiteman and his orchestra had a major role. Whiteman also commissioned symphonic jazz pieces from, among others, Victor Herbert (*A Suite of Serenades*), Rube Bloom (*Soliloquy*), Matty Malneck (*Midnight Reflections* and *Caprice Futuristic*), and Domenico Savino (*A Study in Blue*). While jazz critics condemned these concert pieces a priori, pointing out the obvious—that they were not jazz—they gave little consideration to what they might be, a brand of popular modernism whose influence spilled out into both popular music and jazz, the most influential of these pieces being *Rhapsody in Blue*. Whiteman recorded *Rhapsody* in abridged form on June 10, 1924, with its composer, George Gershwin, at the piano and again in 1927, also with Gershwin at the piano, when it was conducted by Victor's resident conductor, Nathaniel Shilkret, using the new "Orthophonic" electrical recording process.

In his role as director of light music at the Victor Talking Machine Company, Nat Shilkret used his influence to record a number of symphonic jazz performances under his own name. Being a New Yorker in the 1920s was akin to being surrounded by an advertisement for modernity, since one of the most evocative signifiers of American modernism was the skyscraper: in 1929 and 1930 alone, five major skyscrapers—the Bank of Manhattan Trust, the Chrysler Building, the Chanin Building, the Daily News Building, and the Empire State Building—were finished or in process, symbolizing America's headlong rush into modernity and providing inspiration for at least two modernistic symphonic jazz pieces. In 1929 Shilkret and the Victor Symphony Orchestra recorded his own symphonic jazz piece, called *Skyward*, followed in 1932 by John Alden Carpenter's *Skyscrapers* from his ballet of the same name. Paul Whiteman had sponsored the early concert career of Dana Suesse, who had studied piano with Alexander Siloti and composition, like George Gershwin, with Rubin Goldmark. Suesse carried the banner of symphonic jazz well into the 1950s and provided Shilkret with *Jazz Nocturne*, recorded in 1932, a piece that would later enjoy a second life as "My Silent Love." Thomas Griselle had been to Europe to study with Nadia Boulanger and Arnold Schönberg, and in 1928 Shilkret recorded his *Two American Sketches: Nocturne and March*, from which "Nocturne" would become something of an underground standard in the Big Band Era, recorded by the likes of John Kirby's sextet and Artie Shaw's orchestra.

## 1920s Jazz Modernism

If we dig beneath the established tropes of the Jazz Age (and the Swing Era that followed)—that the music of the 1920s and 1930s was functional, played for dancing, and the more it succumbed to musical exploitation the more equivocal became the position of the jazz musicians in their ranks— the more the range and diversity of modernistic experimentation reveals itself among both large and small ensembles. In what Jeffrey Magee has called "the power of the Paul Whiteman paradigm, which cannot be dismissed as merely a transient commercial alternative,"[155] many bandleaders, both black and white, sought to distance themselves from the "jazz of discord, vulgarity and noise," as well as aspiring to a certain sartorial elegance on the bandstand. When Irving Mills became manager of the Duke Ellington Orchestra in 1926/27, for example, he arranged for several changes of specially tailored stage wear, complete with matching patent leather shoes, for each band member. Several bandleaders used a classical conductor's baton with which to "conduct" their bands, calling their ensemble an "orchestra" rather than a band, "an identifier that signalled a cultivated sound familiar to elites."[156] For a short while, some bands, including Ellington's, added a violinist for the sake of propriety. For many, Whiteman's symphonic jazz was seen as the way of the future, marking "a point on which white commentators intersected with the New Negro press and intelligentsia."[157]

In the early 1920s, one of the first major American jazz ensembles to respond to Whiteman's influence was bandleader Fletcher Henderson through his principal arranger, Don Redman. Although Redman's association with the Henderson band was relatively brief, between 1923 and 1927, his arranging style matured in a remarkably short space of time and gave force to the notion that the arranger could be as much a creative force in jazz as the composer or improviser. Beginning by modifying music publishers' stock arrangements, within four years he was able to produce an arranger's tour de force (and jazz classic) with his treatment of Thomas "Fats" Waller's "Whiteman Stomp," recorded by Henderson in 1927. Writing in the 1940s, Hugues Panassié dubbed Henderson "The Paul Whiteman of the Race."[158] As Henderson biographer Jeffrey Magee explains: "In the case of Henderson we have a black bandleader adapting songs . . . in a style suggestive of Paul Whiteman, the leading white . . . bandleader of the day. And . . . black critics were praising him for doing this."[159]

In using, adapting, and developing techniques deployed by Whiteman's arrangers, Redman (and Henderson) developed and consolidated their approach to arranging for the large ensemble of the time by conscientiously applying Whiteman-esque methodology within a serious jazz context: for example, the skilled use of a three-piece saxophone section in Whiteman's 1922 "Stairway to Paradise" found echo in Henderson's 1924 "Naughty Man." This is kind of creative borrowing is hardly unknown, a time-honored process whereby artists absorb the influence of others in order to help find a route to their own voice. The history of the arts is littered with such examples, such as the composer Johannes Brahms, who venerated Beethoven to the extent that he had a marble bust of the composer adorning his study. When someone suggested to him that the finale of his First Symphony contained a whiff of Beethoven's "Ode to Joy" from his Ninth symphony, Brahms dismissively replied that "any silly ass"—*jeder Esel*—"could see that." Equally, Redman absorbed a range of influences as he developed his own approach to writing for the larger jazz ensemble of which Whiteman's ensemble, the most popular band of the day, was certainly influential; his arrangement of "Words," for example, recorded in 1924 by the Henderson band, follows the then fashionable symphonic jazz trend and, as Magee points out, "pits symphonic gestures against hot jazz in the spirit of Paul Whiteman's 'Experiment in Modern Music' earlier that year."[160] And in the winter of 1924–25, Roger Pryor Dodge recalls hearing Henderson perform a dance arrangement of *Rhap-*

*sody in Blue* at the Roseland Ballroom, and on speaking to Henderson about it later discovered that "[Henderson] thought Gershwin's music outstanding."[161]

Redman was clearly a quick study. His arrangement of "Sugar Foot Stomp" in 1925 provided one of Henderson's best-selling recordings and was ranked by Henderson himself as his favorite recording under his own name. It would become a mainstay of the big band repertoire, with Redman's arrangement providing the template on which others would base their versions. This was a period when Louis Armstrong was briefly in Henderson's band and responsible for the "hot" trumpet solos, posing "a unique negotiation between Armstrong and Whiteman, between orality and written expression."[162] This duality was resolved in 1926–27 in a most spectacular fashion with Henderson's May 16, 1926, recording of "Stampede," which channeled Armstrong's influence into an arrangement that with the rationalization of hindsight affords a glimpse of the kind solo/riff style that became popular in the Swing Era. In early 1927, the intricate yet flowing ensemble passages in Redman's arrangement of "Whiteman Stomp" (with its first piano break alluding to *Rhapsody in Blue*) prompted Jeffrey Magee to note that this performance was "not for dancers but for listeners."[163] This was a crucial distinction, since the band frequently played theaters, and special arrangements such as this were intended for a nondancing public. Whiteman himself would record "Whiteman Stomp" the same year, adapting Redman's arrangement as a feature for clarinetist Jimmy Dorsey. Although Henderson's performance of trumpeter Donald Lindley's modernistic "A Rhythmic Dream" from November 4, 1927, was not issued by Columbia, this modernistic piece reflected the climate of musical curiosity and experimentation that was taking composers and arrangers into the realms of augmented chords and their related whole-tone scales and extended harmonies that would become associated with bebop.

Whiteman's influence also surfaced in the music of Duke Ellington, who at one time billed himself as "The Paul Whiteman of Harlem."[164] Ellington clearly respected Whiteman (and vice versa), something that is well documented not only in his autobiography but also in several biographies[165] and interviews he gave throughout his lifetime.[166] Certainly Ellington's manager at the time, Irving Mills, saw add-on cultural prestige in adapting the extended format of symphonic jazz to elevate his client above the competing claims of rival bandleaders. "We wanted Duke to be recognised as someone more important, and of course I was criticized by a lot of people, they looked down on me because I was a jazz fiend, and so we encouraged him to write more serious works, and little by little he started to get a lot better, bigger arrangements and tunes made," said Mills.[167] This desire to project Ellington as "someone more important" is reflected in an advertising manual prepared by the Mills Office in 1933 called *Irving Mills Presents Duke Ellington*. It was intended for promoters, ballroom operators, theater owners, nightclub owners, and just about anyone who might be in a position to put work Ellington's way. It reveals Mills's remarkably far-sighted marketing strategy, which was concerned with presenting Ellington not just as an entertainer but as something more—an internationally respected artist in the realm of *modern* music: "Do not treat Duke Ellington as just another jazz bandleader . . . Ellington's genius as a composer, arranger and musician [has] won him the respect and admiration of such authorities as Percy Grainger, head of the department of music at New York University . . . [and] Paul Whiteman, whose name is synonymous with jazz."[168] Several sample stories intended to feed the press sought to establish the importance of Ellington as a composer and arranger, far above the jazz milieu, who had been "accepted seriously by many of the greatest minds in the world of music."[169]

Ellington's earliest concert-style work, "Rhapsody Jr.," dates from 1926, Mark Tucker noting that Ellington displays "some of the hallmarks of mid-twenties 'jazz modernism,'"[170] to which John Howland has added: "Whitemanesque modern American music."[171] During this period, Whiteman and Ellington were well known to each other, Ellington recounting in his autobiography how Whiteman and members of his orchestra would call at the Kentucky Club to hear Ellington's band with trumpeter Bubber Miley perform. Ellington would have been keenly aware of Whiteman's work—the scores of *Rhapsody in Blue* and Grofé's *Mississippi Suite* were readily available through Whiteman's music publisher and would have provided an insight into some of the "modern" techniques at work in symphonic jazz. Indeed, *Rhapsody in Blue* was part of Ellington's repertoire during the 1930s (orchestration now in the Smithsonian's Ellington Collection), but he did not record the piece until 1962. In his autobiography, Ellington's son Mercer confirms how Irving Mills wanted Ellington to share with Whiteman the "prestige" of presenting an extended composition "that occupied *both* sides of a ten inch 78 rpm record . . . for a black band it was a major step forward."[172] Ellington's first attempt to break the three-minute time limitation of the 78-rpm record came with Nick La-Rocca's "Tiger Rag," recorded in two parts, on March 28, 1929. This was followed by an original composition called "Creole Rhapsody," again over two sides of a 78 rpm, recorded on May 14, 1931, for Brunswick and on June 11, 1931, for RCA. As Alex Ross has noted:

> What distinguished Ellington from most of his contemporaries was that he set himself the goal of expanding the time frame of the jazz piece, stretching it well beyond the limits of the 78-rpm side and into the realm of the large-scale classical work. *Rhapsody in Blue* was the obvious model, a jazz-based work that had grown into symphonic dimensions. In a 1931 article titled: "The Duke Steps Out," Ellington announced that he was writing "a rhapsody unhampered by any musical form in which I intend to portray the experiences of the colored races in America in the syncopated idiom." It would be, "an authentic record of my race *written by a member of it*"—the italics are Ellington's.[173]

Part of "Creole Rhapsody" was briefly featured in the Paramount short *The World at Large* (1933), where it was described as "Duke Ellington's latest symphonic poem,"[174] to distinguish it from the mainstream of jazz. With "Creole Rhapsody," Ellington was clearly aligning himself with the modernistic implications of symphonic jazz by "encroaching on Whiteman's signature cultural territory,"[175] consciously drawing on the "prestige" a recording spread over two sides of a ten-inch, 78-rpm record implied at the time. "'Creole Rhapsody' has clear ties to *Rhapsody in Blue*," continues Alex Ross. "At one point it alludes directly to Gershwin's opening flourish—the upward scale that turns into a glissando."[176] Ellington would later say how "A Creole Rhapsody" provided the seed from which his other extended works grew.

In 1935 came the more ambitious *Reminiscing in Tempo*, spread over fours sides of two ten-inch, 78-rpm records. The Mills publicity office carefully framed any potential debate about the piece's length in a trade advertisement at the time, calling the work a piece of trailblazing musical modernism and again emphasizing how Ellington should be considered above the jazz milieu, "Only the important things in art and life merit serious discussion and create critical controversy. The mediocre items are ignored by the press and public alike . . . Whatever your musical opinion of this latest work in the modern idiom created by Duke Ellington—trailblazer in newer music—it will not be indifferent."[177] The modernist implications invoked by the Mills office suggest that a work like *Reminiscing in Tempo* should not merely be situated within the world of entertainment, but among the important things in art and life, where it might be contemplated and debated, like all great works of art. This was music to challenge the listener and provoke "serious discussion." Concert-style pieces such as this, with their ad hoc forms, intricate part writing, and harmonic ingenuity went far beyond a functional role of music for dancing but were aimed instead at a listening audience who, in the case of Ellington and Henderson, would often be seated in theaters.

Pieces like *Reminiscing in Tempo* or Henderson's "Whiteman Stomp" were intended to challenge listeners with the kind of musical artistry they would not encounter on the dance floor. It is perhaps surprising, therefore, to learn from the pages of one well-distributed jazz textbook that it was not until the advent of bebop that jazz musicians attempted to "raise the quality of jazz from the level of utilitarian dance music to that of a chamber art form," and that it was bebop musicians who were "trying to raise the status of the jazz performer from entertainer to artist."[178] One glance at the film short *Symphony in Black* (1934) featuring Ellington that presented the second of his extended symphonic suites might put this often repeated trope to bed once and for all. Ellington is portrayed as a composer commissioned to write an important symphonic jazz work to deadline. When the music is premiered, we see the full Ellington orchestra in a concert hall setting from the perspective of a member of the audience. The orchestra, immaculately attired in tuxedos and bow ties, has been augmented for the performance, comprising a six-man saxophone section and a ten-man brass section. There are two rhythm guitars, two double basses, a percussionist, a timpanist, and a drummer, with Ellington out front conducting from the piano. This formal, concert-style presentation of his music and the aesthetic ambition it displays is clearly not "a primitivist spectacle for the entertainment of a well-heeled clientele seeking the exotic,"[179] although why the "Jungle" music of Ellington's Cotton Club period should be considered mere entertainment and thus not modernistic, while *La Création du monde*—a primitivist spectacle if ever there was one—remains an undisputed classic of early modernism, remains unclear.

In October 1935, George Gershwin's *Porgy and Bess* premiered on Broadway, and around this time Ellington began work on his own opera/concerto, provisionally titled *Boola*. This was never completed, but sketches did emerge, from which the majestic "Ko-Ko," recorded on March 6, 1940, represents a musical highpoint of Ellington's career. This is perhaps the epitome of jazz modernism, its musical disposition still sounding ahead of its time today—for a start the piece is themeless, and what might be variously described as a twelve-bar blues in E-flat minor, or a piece derived from the E-flat minor Aeolian scale, hardly does justice to what has been described as one of the "undisputed masterpieces of orchestral jazz."[180] A combination of dissonance and whole-tone rootlessness held together by a sustained pedal, the piece reaches a climax in the fourth blues chorus (which begins at bar 77) with its concentration of dissonance in the brass section, the like of which had never been heard in any "dance orchestra." Ellington himself, at bar 45, splashes bitonal clashes and whole-tone flurries in a way that points to the playing of Cecil Taylor (who has acknowledged Ellington's influence). Here Ellington shows his prowess as a composer and arranger without giving his audience anything in the way of a singable tune, in what on the one hand is one of the major musical events of the twentieth century, and on the other what Mark Tucker has described as "one of Ellington's most inspired and successful creations."[181] Also derived from Ellington's *Boola* notebook was the forty-five-minute *Black, Brown and Beige*, premiered in Carnegie Hall in January 1943 in front of a black-tie audience. A jazz concerto grosso that included several pieces that now stand alone as great pieces of Ellingtonia—"Work Song," "The Blues," and "Come Sunday"—*Black, Brown and Beige* was a major work, perhaps following Gershwin, as Alex Ross has suggested, albeit in Ellington's inimitable way. If he was disappointed in the criticism at the time, he was undaunted, continuing with long-form compositions for the rest of his life, including memorable works such as *The Liberian Suite, The Harlem Suite, Anatomy of a Murder, A Drum Is a Woman, Such Sweet Thunder, My People, Far East Suite*, and *New Orleans Suite*.

In the broader sweep of 1920s American popular culture, a fad for being "modernistic" had become the height of fashion. It is not generally acknowledged the number of artists, writers, musicians, and popular artists during this period who actively sought to be associated with the trend. In 1929/30 pianist James P. Johnson, who had earlier scored a huge hit with his composition "The Charleston," recorded his composition "You Got to Be Modernistic" twice, including a solo version, recorded on January 21, 1930, that is one of the highlights of his recorded repertoire. Another version, billed on the Victor recording as Jimmie Johnson and His Orchestra and recorded on November 18, 1929, had a vocal refrain by the Keep Shufflin' Trio, who sang "When you start to play modernistic, don't forget to be futuristic," suggesting the extent to which modernism and Futurism had become linked in the public imagination. Certainly, for the record-buying public, modernism in jazz represented something that sounded "ultramodern" and "of the future"—the latest thing in jazz. This was expressed in a variety of ways, including "daring" harmonies—in the case of Johnson's "You Got to Be Modernistic," it took the form of whole-tone (augmented) ninth and diminished chords predominating in the first two strains[182]—classical allusions, harmonic ambiguity, suggestions of dissonance, and asymmetric melodic lines.

Johnson was sufficiently inspired by Whiteman's performances of works by Gershwin and Grofé to explore musical modernism himself, his best-known composition being *Yamacraw—A Negro Rhapsody* from 1927,[183] a twelve-minute portrait of a black community in Savannah, Georgia. John Howland has noted how it opened "a valuable window on the vibrant legacy of the 1920s symphonic jazz idiom as it existed beyond the George Gershwin and Paul Whiteman circle."[184] In April 1928, W. C. Handy hosted a concert at Carnegie Hall that featured *Yamacraw*, orchestrated by William Grant Still. According to the *Music Trade Review*, "The program included a negro rhapsody entitled *Yamacraw*, composed by James P. Johnson, in which Thomas Waller played the piano solos."[185] In 1930, Vitaphone made a movie short of *Yamakraw*, orchestrated by Hugo Marianni, former head of conducting staff at NBC. Johnson's four-movement *Harlem Symphony*, from 1932, a musical portrait of Harlem, turned out to be his most performed concert work, receiving its premiere on March 11, 1939, by the Brooklyn Civic Orchestra conducted by Dr. Paul Kosok and broadcast over WNYC, New York. In 1934 came *Jazzamine Concerto*—also known as *Concerto Jazz a Mine*—which Johnson finally recorded as a piano solo in 1945 which was effectively a stride piano concerto, and in 1935 came his *Symphony in Brown*. "Modernistic" experiments such as these have tended to be overlooked in the thrust of jazz histography, or if acknowledged at all regarded as instrumental "novelties." Yet many represented a kind of sotto voce avant-gardism, such as the musical experimentation of cornetist Bix Beiderbecke. As Max Harrison has pointed out, even from his first recordings we hear "not only a striking technical assurance but a certainty of expressive aim, a clearly focused emotional content, that is almost disquieting in one so young."[186]

As the British critic Benny Green observed, Beiderbecke was a modernist, inasmuch as modernism was not so much a style but an attitude, and there is no shortage of anecdotes and accounts of Beiderbecke's fascination with advanced harmonies. Indeed, on his final recording session with the Wolverines band (1924) he played piano on "Big Boy," mischievously dabbling in dissonance; on the first recording as a leader, as Bix and His Rhythm Jugglers, he produced a masterpiece in "Davenport Blues," recorded in December 1924, where his subtle harmonic inflections included flatted fifths, altered elevenths and thirteenths, and whole-tone scales that were subordinated to the emotional climate and overall melodic unity of his solo. On his celebrated piano composition "In a Mist" (1927) he "uses a chromatic language beyond that of most jazzmen at the time,"[187] a series of modernistic piano episodes using sequential ninth chords and shifting tonal centers whose coda Richard Hadlock suggests was derived from the codas that arranger Bill Challis had written for Whiteman and Jean Goldkette.[188] Hadlock also points out that the final sheet music version of "In a Mist" was put together for Beiderbecke by Bill Challis, differing from the recorded version.[189] It is a piece that reflected his growing interest in composers such as Ravel, Debussy, and Stravinsky, expressed by frequent visits to the symphony to hear modernistic pieces while living in St. Louis in 1926/27. As clarinettist Pee Wee Russell recalled, "We would often order a score of a new classical work, study it, and then request it from the St. Louis Symphony. And we'd get ourselves a box for those concerts when they did a program we all liked . . . stuff like the *Firebird Suite*."[190] Later, during his tenure in the Paul Whiteman Orchestra, his immediate musical and social circle included people like Bill Challis, Ferde Grofé, and Fud Livingstone, to whom he was able to turn in order to expand his musical knowledge. When Ravel came to New York in 1928, he attended a Paul Whiteman recording session with Beiderbecke in the trumpet section. Especially for Ravel's benefit, Whiteman kept the band on after the record date to play through Grofé's *Metropolis* and Victor Herbert's *Suite of Serenades*. That evening, Beiderbecke and several bandmates went to see Ravel conduct the New York Philharmonic and were later surprised to encounter Ravel in a speakeasy after the performance. Beiderbecke introduced himself, and was soon engrossed in deep conversation, "It is not certain whether the two men saw one another again, though at least one account has Ravel visiting Bix's flat in 1931 to listen to him play his own piano works."[191]

One of Beiderbecke's close bandmates in the Whiteman orchestra was saxophonist Frankie Trumbauer, who recorded a series of pieces with the cornetist in 1927 that were both self-consciously modernistic in ambition and noncommercial in conception—such as the Bill Challis arrangement of "Three Blind Mice (Rhythmic Theme in Advanced Harmony)," Don Murray's arrangement of "Krazy Kat (Tone Poem in Slow Rhythm)"—no connection to John Alden Carpenter's *Krazy Kat* ballet of 1922 and, one might add, a fast-moving chord sequence unusual in jazz at that time—and Fud Livingstone's arrangement of his own composition "Humpty Dumpty," the latter, as Schuller points out, "a piece that featured chromatic progressions imitative of Whiteman's stylings, but otherwise way beyond that of real jazz orchestras, including those of Henderson and Ellington."[192]

Perhaps Beiderbecke's masterpiece with Frankie Trumbauer and His Orchestra was "Singin' the Blues," recorded on February 4, 1927, which proved to be the first "ballad" interpretation in recorded jazz,[193] and which trumpeter and historian Digby Fairweather called "the true emblem of 1920s modernism."[194] Beiderbecke's solo, incorporating the ninth degree of the scale and augmented chords within his solo's overall architecture without disjunction or artifice, has continued to impress succeeding generations of musicians with its structural unity and musical logic, to the extent that the solo stands as an almost perfect composition in its own right. Similar qualities can be discerned in his solo on "I'm Coming Virginia," recorded three months later, which prompted the following observation from Charles Fox: "Unlike Armstrong, who sometimes made mistakes because of the sheer effrontery of his genius, Beiderbecke aimed at perfection of detail as well as overall plan. His approach corresponded to the enclosed lyricism found in classic ragtime (the kind of thing, too, that a good sonnet writer aims at), rather than the open-ended adventuring that goes, say, with taking innumerable choruses on a twelve bar blues."[195] The close musical inter-relationship between Beiderbecke's lead and solo work with the finger-picked accompaniment of guitarist Eddie Lang on both pieces is a minor marvel of musical unity and invention that would be echoed in the 1970s with the playing of cornet player Ruby Braff and guitarist George Barnes in the Ruby Braff George Barnes Quartet.

In 1928, Paul Whiteman commissioned Bill Challis to produce an arrangement of "Singing the Blues" to feature Beiderbecke, who scored Trumbauer's C-melody saxophone solo as a saxophone *soli*. Although Whiteman did not record the piece, it was successfully re-created by the New Paul Whiteman Orchestra featuring Dick Sudhalter in 1975, the original arrangement having been made available for performance by the Paul Whiteman Collection, Williamstown, Massachusetts. The influence of Beiderbecke on Whiteman's ensemble during his tenure with the band was considerable, and examples of this can be heard in the Bill Challis arrangement of "San," in which Beiderbecke takes the opening solo chorus, while the subsequent *soli*—first by the strings and then by the brass—are pure orchestrated Beiderbecke, just as the trumpet *soli* is on Matty Mal-neck's arrangement of "From Monday On." But Beiderbecke's influence was not confined just to his immediate circle within the Whiteman band. For example, on April 25, 1931, Rex Stewart paid tribute to Beiderbecke during his solo on the Fletcher Henderson version of the song, which also used Trumbauer's solo scored as a saxophone *soli*. Stewart later reflected: "Admiring Bix as I did, it was not difficult for me to attempt to copy his memorable solo on 'Singing the Blues' . . . in my book Bix was a once-in-a-million artist. I doubt if what he played will ever be surpassed on trum-pet. He was one of the all-time giants, and I feel that his gifts remain today as unsullied and strikingly refreshing as when he lived." Cabaret singer Marion Harris's version of the song, recorded on August 2, 1934, may well be one of the first recorded examples of vocalese, when she set lyrics to Beiderbecke's solo, and on February 1, 1940, a short-lived big band led by cornetist Bobby Hackett recorded the song, with Hackett paying elegant tribute to Beiderbecke's work of almost exactly thirteen years before.

In 1938, seven years after Beiderbecke's death, Benny Goodman played tribute to Beiderbecke in a brief cameo called "Twenty Years of Jazz" at his famous Carnegie Hall concert of Sunday, January 16, 1938. In the short time since the remarkable "Young Man with a Horn's" death, he had al-ready passed into jazz legend, his acclaimed solo on "I'm Coming Virginia" re-created in Carnegie Hall by Bobby Hackett on cornet, with guitarist Allan Reuss playing the Eddie Lang guitar break near the end. Later in the year, the Robbins Music Corporation of America published a folio of Beiderbecke compositions that included his piano compositions "In a Mist," "Candlelights," "Flashes," and "In the Dark" that revealed an inter-est in pandiatonicism—a use of whole-tone scales and parallel seventh and ninth chords.

Far from being the misunderstood genius driven to drink, Beiderbecke was greatly admired among musicians in the 1920s, as contemporane-ous accounts attest. Pianist and composer Hoagy Carmichael was one of many who recognized in Beiderbecke a unique talent whose influence and inspiration spilled into his own work. Carmichael's recording debut was for the Gennett label in Richmond, Indiana, on May 19, 1925, with Hitch's Happy Harmonists, where he played piano and directed the date for the session's nominal leader, Curtis Hitch. Of the two Carmichael numbers recorded that day, one, a stomp called "Boneyard Shuffle," had an ABACAA form that, as Richard Sudhalter notes, bristled with "'mod-ernistic' touches: whole tone scales, unexpected chordal turns, irregular thematic structures—even an elision: bringing in the 'C,' or secondary theme, a bar early foreshortening the tenor sax solo."[196] As a "hot" specialty, "Boneyard Shuffle" was "an innovation . . . little in the output of either white or black bands compares with its way of making the unconventional seem perfectly natural."[197] Perhaps the now forgotten Hitch deserves a place in jazz history, since an earlier February 23, 1924, session with his Happy Harmonists yielded a piece called "Ethiopian Nightmare," which, as Max Harrison reminds us, is "one of the earliest instances recorded of the later quite widespread practice of basing a jazz piece on the chords of a popular song, in this case those of 'Alexander's Ragtime Band.'"[198] It is perhaps worth laboring this point in the context of this chapter, since the use of contrafacts (new melody lines to pre-existing harmonies) became a feature of the bebop repertoire, yet it is not generally acknowledged how far back in jazz history this practice extends.

On August 3, 1925, Ross Gorman and His Orchestra recorded a piece called "Rhythm of the Day," their feature number in the third *Earl Carroll's Vanities* revue at the New Amsterdam Theater on Broadway. Although a standard thirty-two-bar song, it has an ABAC form with the A sections based on the rootless, harmonically ambiguous quality of augmented chords whose whole-tone melodic passages anticipated Fletcher Henderson's experimental "Queer Notions" by about eight years. Trombonist Miff Mole executes an impressive thirty-two-bar solo based on the whole-tone, rather than diatonic, scale whose musical adventurousness was widely admired by musicians at the time. In 1926, the Original Memphis Five executed the shifting tonal centers of "The Chant" with ease, while the Charleston Chasers, a pick-up band that existed only in the recording studios, recorded several ambitious modernistic pieces including "Delirium," an original by their pianist, Arthur Schutt, recorded on May 18, 1927. Using whole-tone scales and interesting harmonic substitutions, Schutt's atonal piano solo grabs the attention, which was not only daring but also ahead of its time.

On August 30 of that same year, Miff Mole and his Little Molers recorded "Imagination" and "Feelin' No Pain" for Okeh.[199] Both these titles were written and arranged by saxophonist and clarinetist Fud Livingstone, a modernist whose approach here and with Bix Beiderbecke derives much from the work of the French Impressionists by embodying the use of augmented chords and their underlying whole-tone scales and extended harmonies more associated with the advent of bebop in the 1940s. "Imagination" is full of shifting tonal centers and has a twenty-eight-bar theme based on descending whole tones, while "Feelin' No Pain," which would be recorded another three times by musicians in the Nichols/Mole circle, "even displays a touch of *Klangfarbenmelodie*. That device so beloved of followers of twelve-tone European music, brings different tone colors (represented by different instruments in different registers) to bear on the same pitch or sequence of pitches; the result is a 'melody' constructed as much out of textures as pitches."[200]

Vocalist Cliff Edwards drew on the talents of quiet experimenters such as Red Nichols, Miff Mole, and Arthur Schutt for his "Hot Combination," which recorded for the Pathé label between 1923 and 1927. As Will Friedwald has pointed out, Edwards was among the first vocalists to display a genuine jazz virtuosity: "Besides constructing scat solos that predict Leo Watson and Ella Fitzgerald, Edwards had a remarkable gift for using jazz techniques to make a jazz point."[201] On "Dinah" (1925) he and cornetist Red Nichols engage in a chase chorus of remarkable interplay for its time, while his vocal on "Sunday" (1926) continues the vocalist's easy rapport with his supporting musicians. In terms of the 1920s, scat was widely seen as an aspect of American jazz modernism, especially at the hands of Louis Armstrong, who developed the style much further than Edwards in his almost Dada-esque deconstruction of the popular song. Armstrong was billed for a while as "Master of Modernism" in the 1920s, and, as Alfred Appel has noted, was a modernist who has "jazzed the ordinary and given it new life."[202]

This chapter, however, does not seek to add to the already voluminous writing about Armstrong, save to acknowledge his enormous influence in the music, but rather to explore areas of jazz modernism that have been less zealously documented in the broad teleological sweep of jazz history. One such ensemble was the Boswell Sisters, who in the context of their time were startlingly modernistic. Indeed, what this vocal group achieved had no precedent in jazz. They were far in advance of their time, and even in the early years of the new millennium still remain sui generis. Connie Boswell, the trio's lead singer, was also its arranger, albeit such was the three sister's mutual empathy that no vocal parts were ever written down—only those of their accompanists, who were among the top-notch studio musicians of the day, including Bunny Berigan, Tommy and Jimmy Dorsey, Joe Venuti, Eddie Lang, and Carl Cress. By any standards, Boswell was and remains an extraordinarily imaginative and resourceful arranger. What is even more remarkable is that many of their recordings—their finest were recorded while they were signed to the Brunswick label between 1931 and 1936—were simplified for the record-buying public at the insistence of producer Jack Kapp. "You should have heard the things we weren't allowed to record," said Connie to an interviewer in the 1950s.

Even so, what we do have is a startling legacy of recordings that were audaciously conceived and brilliantly executed. The sisters' first Brunswick release was "Wha'dja Do to Me" coupled with "When I take My Sugar to Tea," and it caused a sensation. A hallmark of the Boswells' recordings is their ability to handle abrupt tempo changes, sometimes as many as six or seven in the three-minute recording, such as in the dazzling "Roll On, Mississippi, Roll On." But the Boswells were not content with mere tempo changes. They might change the tonality of a song from major to minor, reharmonize passages, interpolate lyrics and passages from other songs, launch out on wordless scat improvisations, insert transitions of their own, opt for unexpected modulations into remote keys, introduce elements of gospel and blues, or break free of the underlying groundbeat and demonstrate a complete rhythmic ease—freedom within form—within the popular song. They were unique in the context of their time, since song publishers and their pluggers were usually insistent that recordings be an accurate rendition of the songwriter's intent.

In the Boswells' hands, song after song became virtual tours de force of the vocal art, musical fantasias informed by a thorough understanding of jazz improvisation. Nothing sounded forced, yet each song became a musical journey in its own right, such as their stunning version of "Forty-Second Street" or the dizzying concept of "Everybody Loves My Baby." As Richard Sudhalter has written: "There is hardly a Boswell Sisters record that does not yield some audacious dismantling and reassembling of the component parts of their materials, often with a result far richer and more provocative by far than the original."[203] This was music from fertile and imaginative musical minds, its function not dance music but music to contemplate (and wonder at) either at home with the recording or when performed in theaters, concert halls, on the radio, or in the movies. If one of the characteristics of bebop in the 1940s was to challenge the dancing public with "listening music," then this ethos was most assuredly shared by the Boswell Sisters' music in the early 1930s. Adventurous, modernistic—even avant-garde—this music has been virtually ignored by a patriarchal construction of jazz history that has considered their work barely worthy of a footnote; indeed, in Gunther Schuller's otherwise laudable *Swing Era*, that is all they get.

## 1930s and 1940s Jazz Modernism

One aspect of the art/entertainment dichotomy of jazz during the 1920s and 1930s has been the failure to recognize these decades as the period of radical change they were: the move from head arrangements by (largely) nonreading, autodidactic musicians in small ensembles typically comprising trumpet, clarinet, trombone, piano, banjo, bass (or tuba), and drums, to sophisticated, written arrangements for larger ensembles, typically comprising three trumpets, two trombones, two alto and two tenor saxophones, piano, bass, guitar, and drums was, in terms of evolution, a massive step that occurred in a relatively short space of time. It had the effect of totally reinventing the original loose, freewheeling polyphony of the small New Orleans and Chicago ensembles with the precise antiphony of larger ensembles of schooled musicians reading often complex, written arrangements. Trombonist Clyde Bernhardt recalled: "If you didn't read by 1927 or 1928, you got left out. No place for you in a quality band."[204] This was a significant change in the music, a virtual reorientation of the music from smaller to larger ensembles that caused massive dislocation among the hitherto established jazz masters of smaller band jazz, sidelining players of the stature of Joe "King" Oliver and "Jelly Roll" Morton. Small wonder that this polarized jazz debate at the time, with proponents of small New Orleans–inspired jazz claiming that theirs was "the real jazz" and that the music of the big bands was something else.

The 1930s were a decade when the arranger came of age, setting the sound signature of the band so essential to differentiate it from its competitors when broadcasting on radio or in live performance. What is significant is that commercial pressure did not emasculate musical curiosity and creativity; it is perhaps overlooked that consumer choice and market forces at work during the pre-bop era provided a powerful creative spur to musicians, who responded within the then-prevailing entertainment infrastructure. The strictures of that infrastructure—playing music for dancing, the three-minute limit imposed on recordings because of the ten-inch 78 rpm, and so on—were precisely the kind of obstacles that needed inspiration to transcend them, so perhaps Jeffrey Magee's apposite comment, "The bromide that jazz becomes an art music with the advent of bebop,"[205] should be seen in this context.

Today we have lost sight of how musicians in the pre-bop era were already experimenting with extended harmonies, augmented and diminished chords and the whole-tone scales derived from them, and chords such as the minor ninth and intervals such as the eleventh and thirteenth, all elements we more commonly associate with bebop. In fact, it is remarkable how much experimental music actually got onto record, since by definition it was, by the standards of the time, uncommercial. For the musicians who made these recordings, modernism meant experimentalism, music for music's sake rather than commercial ends. An example is a Red Norvo date in November 1933 with Benny Goodman playing bass clarinet that produced two classic modernist performances: a "definitive"[206] reading of Beiderbecke's "In a Mist" and the tonally ambiguous "Dance of the Octopus" that was, as Gunther Schuller points out, "in no sense 'dance' or entertainment music."[207]

After Don Redman left Fletcher Henderson he was persuaded to take over the leadership of McKinney's Cotton Pickers before forming his own big band, whose repertoire included the modernistic composition "Chant of the Weed" (1931) with its futurist introduction and parallel whole-tone chords in the first four bars of the A section of the AABA structure. It perhaps inspired the modernistic Coleman Hawkins composition for the Fletcher Henderson Orchestra, "Queer Notions" (1933), with its parallel augmented chords and whole-tone clusters and an arresting whole-tone trumpet solo by Henry Allen. Bandleader Eddie Condon would frequently call upon saxophonist Bud Freeman to perform his original composition "The Eel," first recorded October 21, 1933, which made its appeal through a chromatically and harmonically suggestive melody that sounded modernistic in conception—as did David Rose's "Shadows," written for his own orchestra in 1933.

British bandleader Spike Hughes wrote several Ellington-inspired originals that were recorded in 1933 by his "All American Orchestra" in New York that included the modernistic disposition of "Arabesque." Many bandleaders included one or two "modernist" numbers in their books, such as the play on words of Jimmy Dorsey's "Murdersitic," Jan Savitt's "Futuristic Shuffle," or Ambrose and His Orchestra's "Streamline Strut." In 1939, the former Henderson arranger and saxophonist Benny Carter used chromaticism in "Shufflebug Shuffle" in a way that actually takes us up to the door of bebop, Gunther Schuller noting how Carter employs "very 'modern' chromatically shifting changes of the kind that would become thrice familiar in the bebop period with pieces like Dizzy's 'Night in Tunisia' and Pete Rugolo's 'Artistry in Rhythm.'"[208]

Xylophonist Red Norvo had experienced musical modernism at first hand while a member of Paul Whiteman's orchestra. He was particularly impressed by William Grant Still's arrangements that featured his future wife, vocalist Mildred Bailey, then also a member of the Whiteman orchestra. "Some of the backgrounds that were written for Mildred by William Grant Still were very dissonant and involved," he recalled in an interview in 1968. "Beautiful backgrounds. Harmonically, they were very advanced."[209] Ever forward looking, he was probably the first to use "Swing" in a band's name on a record label, in 1933–34, when he recorded a series of sessions using top New York freelance musicians under the name Red Norvo and his Swing Septet—at that time "swing" was not a word in common use among the general public. When he came to form his own mid-band in the late 1930s, he remained ever the quiet experimenter. With Julliard graduate Eddie Sauter's ingenious arrangements and Bailey's vocals, his band earned many admirers within the music business. Their first recording session produced a subtly modernistic slant on what was already a modernistically inclined James P. Johnson composition, "A Porter's Love Song to a Chamber Maid." Later recordings, such as "Smoke Dreams," embrace musical modernism with its momentary dissonances and polytonality, while Sauter's arrangement of "Remember" is widely regarded as a minor masterpiece of the Swing Era with its clever modulations and dissonant textures. Sauter also employed a decidedly modernistic introduction to "Tea Time" that presages a *mysterioso* performance that was greatly admired by musicians at the time, but the band would eventually dissolve because of friction between Norvo and his wife.

Bassist John Kirby's sextet, one of the exemplary small bands of the Swing Era, was once amusingly described by the poet Philip Larkin, in *All What Jazz*,[210] as a "tight arsed" little band because of its inch-perfect ensemble cohesion, immaculate articulation, and precise intonation—even at the fastest of tempi. Kirby's "jazzing the classics" was perhaps a less subtle approach to musical modernism than a handful of subtly modernistic compositions that stand out among their tightly swinging repertoire—such as the programmatic feel of "Dawn on the Desert" or modernist composer Thomas Griselle's "Nocturne." It is tempting to say that the Kirby Sextet displayed several stylistic characteristics that anticipated bebop: complex ensemble passages; a trumpet/clarinet/alto sax front-line able to handle such complexity; pianist Billy Kyle's harmonic substitutions that anticipated early bebop pianists such as Clyde Hart; O'Neill Spencer's sophisticated drumming that anticipated (and influenced) the work of the great bebop drummers; and several aspects of the work of trumpeter Charlie Shavers, who in 1939 was "closer to becoming

Dizzy Gillespie than Gillespie." It contained harbingers of the new music, bebop, since Shavers was developing "precisely along Gillespie's contemporary rhythmic and harmonic lines [and] had secured much better control of his instrument."[211] An example of how close the Kirby Sextet was to bebop was revealed—ironically—after Kirby's death in 1952. In 1955, Charlie Shavers led a recording session for Bethlehem Records with surviving members of the sextet—Buster Bailey, Russell Procope (then with Duke Ellington), and Billy Kyle (then with Louis Armstrong). Aaron Bell (also with Duke Ellington) replaced the late John Kirby, and Specs Powell replaced the late O'Neil Spencer (who had died in 1944). On Kirby's theme song, "Flow Gently, Sweet Rhythm," it is clear that the musicians had made minor adjustments to their style to reflect the ubiquity of bebop, but nevertheless with Powell's bebop-influenced drumming (his bass drum "bombs," for example) and the tight ensemble passages that gave ample space to soloists, the correlation with bebop becomes much clearer.

In 1940, Kirby recorded "Twentieth Century Closet" (which he once announced tongue-in-cheek from the bandstand as "In a Twentieth Century Outhouse"),[212] which was actually a swinging parody of the Raymond Scott Quintet's (sometimes spelled "Quintette") baroque-pastiche "In an Eighteenth Century Drawing Room." Scott's Quintet was Kirby's main competitor, and the bassist's ensemble occasionally betrayed Scott's influence of musical complexity for complexity's sake—such as the opening ensemble passage of "Sweet Georgia Brown" (Matrix 24678-A, as opposed to Matrix 24678-B). When Kirby's original sextet was forced to break up when Russell Procope and Billy Kyle were drafted for war service, Kirby found work in the band Scott led at CBS. Scott had begun his career as a staff pianist for the CBS house band, which his brother conducted and who encouraged him to contribute originals. A broadcast of "Confusion among a Fleet of Taxicabs upon Meeting with a Fare" in March 1935 with a twelve-piece ensemble that probably included Artie Shaw and Bunny Berigan presents under its programmatic guise dissonance unusual in popular music or jazz of the period, an interlude that uncannily anticipates free jazz.

The following year, on December 26, he debuted his quintet on *Saturday Night Swing Club* on the CBS radio network with "The Toy Trumpet" and began to enjoy considerable popularity in the late 1930s, becoming a regular on *Your Hit Parade* and appearing on programs such as *This Is New York* and *The Rhythm Roundup*. When Scott and members of his band appeared on Paul Whiteman's final "Experiment in Modern Music" concert in December 1938, Whiteman had already commissioned seventeen full orchestral arrangements of Scott originals for his orchestra, including "Christmas Night in Harlem," which became a Whiteman hit (although not recorded commercially by Scott himself). Whiteman was not alone in adding Scott originals to his repertoire, and several famous and not-so-famous big band leaders followed Whiteman's example. Columnist Walter Winchell called Scott's music "instrumental literature," describing the quintet as "positively *zzymzzy*," meaning "the last word."[213]

Scott's musical conception was above all modernistic, complex, intriguing, painstakingly intricate, and as unusual in the 1930s as it is today. Although billed as a quintet, Scott's group was actually a sextet; he preferred the title "quintet" to "sextet" because he believed it had a "crisper" sound. And sound was important to Scott; he was one of the first musicians to sit in the recording booth to monitor and control sessions. As *Billboard* noted in 1937: "[He] hears things in there that completely escape [other bandleaders'] ears."[214] Scott recorded most rehearsal sessions and almost all radio broadcasts—most of which have survived and are today in the Raymond Scott Archives at the University of Missouri, Kansas City—which he would later carefully study in his quest for perfection. The music for his group was not written down but dictated from the piano by Scott— "There's a tremendous difference in performance if you skip the eyes," he explained[215]—and selections were given intriguing programmatic titles such as "Dinner Music for a Pack of Hungry Cannibals," "Reckless Night on Board an Ocean Liner," "Bumpy Weather over Newark," "Careful Conversation at a Diplomatic Function," and, as mentioned, the delightfully titled "Confusion among a Fleet of Taxicabs upon Meeting With a Fare." Often, titles such as "Powerhouse," "Girl at the Typewriter" (shades of typewriter sounds à la Erik Satie's *Parade*), and "Oil Gusher" reveal him to be a child of the Machine Age, his compositions representing a confluence of modernistic influences evoking the modern production line, the automobile, the jagged imagery of skyscrapers then transforming the New York skyline, and, perhaps significantly, the fast-evolving radio and phonograph technology—the latter an especial interest—and electrical power. Indeed, the introduction to "Powerhouse" is impressive in its programmatic expressionism suggesting hydroelectric power.

Ultimately, however, Scott's compositions often had a mechanical feel to them; he never wrote of human emotion, and his portrayals of the human condition seem to have been undertaken from a distance with no possibility of emotional entanglement. And while some believe external impression and internal emotion both have a perfect right to be expressed in musical works, in Scott's case emotional engagement with his music is often difficult to discern—an example of the "heart/head" dichotomy in extracting meaning from music. Perhaps this lack of emotional appeal made his music attractive to Carl Stalling at Warner Bros., who began using Scott's compositions in their *Looney Tunes* and *Merrie Melodies* animation. In more contemporary times, his music was used on the long-running animated series *The Simpsons*. It has meant that although he may be a footnote in jazz history today, Scott's music has been heard by millions. Given his music's deliberate complexity and the impossibility of its functioning as dance music—Scott called it "Descriptive jazz"—with its ad hoc forms, tempo changes, its sometimes awkward melodic content, its accelerando and ritardando passages, it is perhaps surprising today how popular his music was in its time, attracting a huge radio audience and his recordings selling millions of units. In 1937 the *New York Times* described his music as, "A brand of music that is at one and the same as free as a jam session and as authoritatively formal as a Debussy cake walk— and not unacquainted with the humor of both."[216]

Two years later Scott expanded his music for the broader palette of a big band and going out on tour, where he was billed as "America's Foremost Composer of Modern Music." In 1942 he returned to a staff job with CBS and formed the first inter-racial radio network studio orchestra, attracting such names as Coleman Hawkins, Ben Webster, Charlie Shavers, Cozy Cole, Benny Morton, Emmett Berry, and from time to time bassist John Kirby to play his music. Forward-looking and futuristic, the inherent complexities of his writing posed a challenge to jazz machismo. Reporting for *Metronome* magazine in 1948, George Simon described a Scott rehearsal: "His [then new] group was running through one of his compositions called 'Siberian Sleighride.' Suddenly one of the men exclaimed, 'Hey, that's taken right out of Dizzy [Gillespie]!' 'Could be,' answered Ray, 'only I wrote this thing fourteen years ago.'"[217]

In 2012 a documentary film of his life was made by his son Stan, *Deconstructing Dad: The Music, Machines and Mystery of Raymond Scott*, in which, in his single-minded pursuit of his off-beat musical vision, he is likened to Frank Zappa. The *New York Times* commented: "Musicians as diverse as the composer and conductor John Williams whose father was a drummer in Quintette; Mark Mothersbaugh, a co-founder of Devo; and Paul D. Miller, a. k. a. DJ Spooky, call Scott a significant influence on contemporary music. One talking head cites his early '60s album 'Soothing Sounds for Baby' as a precursor to the work of Brian Eno and Philip Glass."[218] Today, it matters less whether Scott's music was "jazz" or not, more how the avowedly modernistic stance of his music influenced jazz musicians with its inherent complexity and Futurist aspirations which fed into a range of influences that surrounded forward-thinking jazz experimenters in the fast-evolving musical scene in the 1940s. Drummer Art Blakey noted in a *Downbeat* interview: "This big show came in from New York—Tondelayo and Lopez. They had this special music written by Raymond Scott. It was called 'Powerhouse.' Really impressive stuff."[219]

The British pianist and composer Reginald Foresythe (1907–58) may be an obscure figure in jazz history today, but his modernistic compositions were recorded by Paul Whiteman, Earl Hines, Louis Armstrong, Adrian Rollini, Fats Waller, Hal Kemp, Benny Goodman, the Casa Loma Orchestra, and Lew Stone, among others. In 1959, *Melody Maker* magazine described his music as "more futuristic than modern [whose] strength lay in the originality of its compositions."[220] Foresythe's father was a Yoruban lawyer and his mother an Englishwoman with Scottish/German antecedents. He grew up in privileged circumstances in west London and early on displayed a gift for both music and linguistics. He originally began work as a linguist by day but was soon playing in professional dance bands at night, his first significant break coming when he was hired in 1929 as an accompanist for the blues singer Zaidee Jackson, a performer hugely popular among the Parisian set. Another job as accompanist saw him touring Australia, from where he visited Hawaii, ending up in California, where his cultured demeanor, good looks, and obvious musical ability saw him enter privileged musical circles, recording with Paul Howard, meeting Duke Ellington, and contributing music to film director D. W. Griffith's *Abraham Lincoln*. Moving on to Chicago in 1930, he was introduced to Earl Hines: "He stayed with us several months," recalled Hines. "He and I wrote [my] band's theme song together—'Deep Forest.' . . . This was about the time Paul Whiteman was appearing at one of the big, fine hotels. He often used to come down to the Grand Terrace with Mildred Bailey . . . anyway, I introduced Reginald to Paul Whiteman and Paul took to him straight away because he was a very good, well trained musician. He could play any overture you wanted to hear and he had memorized works like 'Rhapsody in Blue' . . . and for a time he did very well with Whiteman, who recorded 'Deep Forest.'"[221]

"Deep Forest" was recorded by Hines in June 1932 and initially appears as an exotic fantasia evoking "St. James Infirmary," which is somewhat contradicted by the pianist's urge to swing and escape from the prevailing mood of the piece. In contrast, Whiteman's version, arranged by Foresythe and recorded in December 1934, is a better realization of the atmospheric potential of the piece, underlined by the emergence of a clarinet choir after the introduction that is followed by a brass passage with strings adding a sustained high pedal that eerily, but masterfully, heightens the mood. It is claimed that, while in America, Foresythe also contributed arrangements to Duke Ellington,[222] while Richard Sudhalter writes that he arranged for a band to be led by Wild Bill Davison and Frank Teschemacher: "[They] had gotten a band together for an engagement at Guyon's Paradise Ballroom. With hand-picked personnel and arrangements by West Indian [sic] composer Reginald Foresythe, it seemed a sure winner."[223] However, on February 29, 1932, en route to the engagement, Davison was involved in a motor accident in which his passenger, Teschemacher, was killed, and nothing became of the enterprise. Foresythe's American visit was completed in New York, where he met lyricist Andy Razaf with whom he wrote "Mississippi Basin," later recorded by Louis Armstrong, Adrian Rollini, and John Kirby.

Back in England in 1933, he formed Reginald Foresythe's New Music, in this case "new" having subtle modernistic implications, and opened at London's Café de la Paix with a line-up that included saxophones, two clarinets, and a bassoon. Although his original music did not go down particularly well with a society set who demanded uncomplicated, inoffensive dance music, many of his modernistic compositions written for this engagement were recorded by his English ensemble, beginning with a session on October 14, 1933, that produced "Serenade for a Wealthy Widow" and "Angry Jungle." The former title, when published as sheet music, sold remarkably well at a time when such sales were more important than sales of recordings, and it was recorded by, among others, Stuff Smith, Fats Waller, and Paul Whiteman. Two sessions, in February and September, included titles such as "The Duke Insists," "Garden of Weed," and "Deep Forest"—the latter presented by Foresythe as the first part of a two-part tone poem called *Hymn to Darkness* (the second part called "Hymn for Congo").

Lew Stone, one of the top British bandleaders of the day, was impressed by Foresythe's work, recording definitive versions of his "Serenade for a Wealthy Widow" and "Garden of Weed" with an orthodox big band instrumentation in 1934. In 1933, after hearing Foresythe's recording of

"Serenade for a Wealthy Widow," Theo Uden Masman, the leader of the Ramblers Orchestra in the 1930s, which at various times welcomed both Coleman Hawkins and Benny Carter as sidemen during their European sojourns, wrote: "This is a record that should not be ignored; it is simply an entirely new way of making music . . . it's obvious that Foresythe did not compose and play this music with profit motive in mind."[224]

In January 1935 Foresythe was back in New York, where he recorded four titles with an American version of his New Music ensemble on January 23. As Benny Goodman's biographer/discographer D. Russell Connor noted: "The Reginald Foresythe session [was] an event [Gene] Krupa recalls with clarity and great relish. Gene remembers that Benny, he and the other BG sideman admired Reggie Foresythe, and given the chance to record some of his compositions they leapt at it."[225] To place this in context, this session was sandwiched between Goodman's weekly NBC radio program, called *Let's Dance*, which presented the attendant problem of rehearsing his recently formed big band with new material the weekly program demanded; indeed, the next *Let's Dance* broadcast was just three days after the Foresythe session. Goodman's role in the *Let's Dance* radio show is now generally regarded as the opening chapter of the Swing Era of the 1930s. It represented a break of enormous importance in Goodman's burgeoning career, and his willingness to perform as a sideman for a flat session fee offered him no pecuniary advantage. Rather, it speaks of modernism's appeal as a musician's music, Goodman acceding to the old maxim that you always find time to do the things that you really want to. Four titles were recorded: "The Melancholy Clown," "Lullaby (For Mildred Bailey)," "The Greener the Grass," and "Dodging a Divorcee."

In April 1935 the Hal Kemp Orchestra also recorded "Dodging a Divorcee," followed by Paul Whiteman in July the same year. Whiteman's version—arranged by Foresythe—is yet another example of a big band playing music that was not intended for dancing; this is modernistic experimentation including a fugue section featuring clarinet and cor anglais. The only acknowledgment the arrangement makes to the prevailing climate of dance music is a shout chorus that acts as a coda. Equally, Whiteman's version of "The Duke Insists" is taken at a faster tempo than Foresythe's London band, and his elegant writing here reveals Foresythe's artistic growth. Whiteman's version of "Garden of the Weed" begins by encroaching on Cab Calloway's signature "Moocher" territory (in a way that Foresythe's London recording of the piece did not) before making its modernistic mood clear with a wonderfully surreal use of strings and a bowed bass used to underpin the ostinato interlude. Foresythe's orchestrations for Whiteman number among the American bandleader's best work in the 1930s, and the regard in which Whiteman regarded him was reflected by the fact that he appeared as a featured soloist with his orchestra in 1934, a significant achievement for a black artist of the time.

Benny Goodman's initial success in the Swing Era was largely shaped by the arrangements of Fletcher Henderson's masterful antiphonal style of writing, which became the musical template that helped define the Swing Era. One notable deviation from the prevailing musical status quo was his recording of the blind Welsh pianist Eric Templeton's arrangement of "Bach Goes to Town" for RCA on December 15, 1938. A decidedly modernist gesture, the piece is a cleverly conceived fugue written in a "swing" style. However, by 1940 Goodman was aware that despite his great love of and respect for Henderson's charts, the musical competition had caught up with him, and there was a need to exorcise his predilection for mechanical Hendersonian call-and-response patterns that had become the industry norm so as to differentiate the sound of his band from the musical milieu around him. To do this he turned to former Red Norvo arranger Eddie Sauter. By any standards, several of Sauter's arrangements for Goodman move from the realms of functional "dance music" to jazz performances more appropriate for the concert platform. Indeed, Goodman tacitly acknowledged this, since several Sauter arrangements, having been rehearsed and recorded, were seldom played for his dancing public.

Sauter's growing reputation as an innovative arranger preceded him when he began working for Goodman in 1939. An arranger who was less concerned with the antiphonal style popularized by Henderson (although he could write effectively in that style when needs must, such as his arrangement for Goodman of "How High the Moon"), Sauter wrote linearly and contrapuntally and realized a profound change in the sound and style of the Goodman orchestra. The extended composition "Superman," for example—a feature for trumpeter Cootie Williams, which appeared on one side of a twelve-inch 78-rpm recording—consists of seven sections of six-, seven-, and twelve-bar lengths, and even some of these are divided asymmetrically. An example is the opening ten-bar passage in which the soloist, Cootie Williams, plays over the band for three bars and exchanges phrases with the trombones for seven. Equally, pieces like "Clarinet a la King" and "Benny Rides Again" are best thought of as miniature clarinet concertos rather than dance music per se, while pieces such as "Moonlight on the Ganges," "La Rosita," "Love Walked In," "The Man I Love,"

"How Deep Is the Ocean," "My Old Flame," and "More Than You Know" added, as George Avakian has noted, "depth and richness previously unknown in Benny's music—or anybody else's for that matter, for Sauter was breaking new ground."[226]

What dancers made of Sauter's stunning introduction to "Intermezzo" or the intro and coda of "Soft as Spring" can only be a matter of speculation, since there is nothing else in jazz music of the time for his audience to establish their musical bearings with. Indeed, it is perhaps here, in Sauter's introductions, modulations, and codas that his great gift was realized—even if Goodman felt he had to edit some of Sauter's ideas. Gunther Schuller has written that he does not think "there ever has been a master of harmonic modulation in jazz to equal Sauter. His skill in this respect is certainly equal to Richard Strauss's in classical music, and it has not been matched in jazz in its deftness, economy and chameleon-like quick-change artistry. In no time one key disappears under one's eyes (and ears) and in an instant one is in another harmonic world."[227] The best of Sauter's work for Goodman represents a highpoint of jazz modernism—modern jazz without being bebop; examples abound in his work for Goodman, such as modulation from D to G-flat midway through "The Hour of Parting," which employs "the IIb method of getting to the tonic chord—in effect the 'flat five' tritone related substitute for the dominant chord—[that] was in 1940 still a relatively 'advanced' and rare harmonic usage."[228]

The technical complexity of some of Sauter's background figures for saxophones, seemingly throw-away lines, are nevertheless rich in inner detail and meticulously crafted, demanding musicians with a high degree of executive skill to realize. It is perhaps worth mentioning that these pieces were recorded at a time when jazz education and conservatoire training for jazz musicians was unheard of. Yet Sauter's challenging scores demanded musicianship of conservatoire standard which Goodman's young band aspired to, with Skippy Martin's pluperfect lead alto bringing astonishing definition to Sauter's lines with his inch-perfect articulation, intonation, and sense of dynamics. As Schuller has pointed out, "During these years of the early forties, the Goodman band—and Goodman himself—played with a dazzling brilliance that was the envy of all the other bands. The emphasis was not on soloists—as with Basie, for example—but on the orchestra, and on jazz *as* arrangement and composition."[229] It says much of Goodman's skill as a bandleader—much caricatured in later years—that he was able to realize the potential of Sauter's often complex writing, which represents some of the most imaginatively constructed, expertly executed, and emotionally serious music to emerge from the pre-bop period to stand alongside Ellington's work as the highlight of an era. Not without good reason, Sauter's work from this period has variously been described as "modernistic," while singer Mel Tormé called it "Futuristic."[230]

Clarinetist Artie Shaw maintained a continuum with the symphonic-modernist jazz tradition through the 1930s and into the 1940s. When he premiered an original piece called "Interlude in B Flat" with two violinists, a violist, a cellist, guitar, bass, and drums at the Imperial Theater in New York in the summer of 1935,[231] his unexpected success—the ovation for his performance was such that he was called back to play an encore—led directly to his becoming a bandleader in his own right. The performance was as a part of "A Swing Concert" mounted by Joe Helbock, then owner of the Onyx Club on 42nd Street, as a benefit for the American Federation of Musicians, Local 802. Shaw's first ensemble, called Art Shaw and his New Music, was a big band with strings that quickly proved to be a financial disaster after a run at New York's Hotel Lexington in 1936, prompting him to ditch the strings and work with an orthodox big band that made its breakthrough with the million-selling "Begin the Beguine" in 1938. Shaw's theme song was the avowedly modernist "Nightmare," an original composition arranged by Jerry Gray that first surfaced in part on Shaw's 1936 recording of "Skeleton in the Closet." Recorded on July 24, 1938—a session that produced two million-sellers in "Begin the Beguine" and "Back Bay Shuffle"—"Nightmare" is a dissonant piece in A minor that has been described as both cantorial and Hassidic—Shaw himself said he could not deny the influence of his Russian-Jewish-Austrian ancestry during his solo.[232] It is a song that makes no concessions to populism yet remains one of the Swing Era's most memorable themes, and which still has currency in contemporary culture since it is an acknowledged influence on John Barry's memorable orchestration of Monty Norman's title theme for the *James Bond* movies, one of the most famous melodies in the consumerist world. Go below guitarist Vic Flick's melody line in the A sections, and the writing for trombones and French horns is clearly influenced by "Nightmare." Shaw quickly became one of the most popular bandleaders in the United States but famously turned his back on success on November 18, 1939, when he walked out on his band and headed to Mexico to recuperate from the stress that superstardom had thrust upon him.

Under pressure to fulfill his recording contract with RCA Victor, he entered the recording studio again on March 3, 1940, with a twenty-one-

piece studio ensemble that was essentially an orthodox big band augmented by a bass clarinet, French horn, flute, oboe, eight violins, three
violas, and two celli. The line-up included three former Whiteman sidemen: Charlie Margulis on trumpet, Bill Rank on trombone, and Mischa
Russell on violin. The arrangements were provided by another former
Whiteman employee, the celebrated Afro-American composer William
Grant Still, whose accomplishments included four symphonies including his *Afro American Symphony* (1930), ballet music, and *The Lennox Avenue Suite* (a work for Radio Announcer, chorus, and orchestra). Probably
not coincidentally, Shaw also chose to record the Paul Whiteman–Jack
Meskill–Joan Edwards composition "My Fantasy" (based on a theme by
Borodin). To everyone's surprise, including Shaw himself, Still's arrangement of "Frenesi" became a runaway million-seller. "'Frenesi' was an experimental record," said Shaw in 1992. "I wanted to see if you could use
strings in a big band jazz context. The experiment worked: it taught me
what to do."[233] Also from the same March 3 session came Still's arrangement of composer Edward A. MacDowell's "Deserted Farm" from his
*Woodland Sketches* and a haunting version of "Gloomy Sunday," providing
further evidence of the clarinetist's modernist impulses. The success of
"Frenesi" prompted Shaw to resume a full-time musical schedule with an
enlarged orchestra with strings, opening at the Palace Hotel in San Francisco on September 12, 1940.

A regular working ensemble demanded a sizable repertoire, and Shaw
turned to—among others—former Whiteman arrangers Bill Challis, who
among other arrangements produced an imaginative framing of "Blues
in the Night," and Lennie Hayton, coarranger with Shaw on "I Cover the
Waterfront," with its haunting introduction evoking film noir's moody
soundtracks being recorded on Hollywood soundstages around the same
time. After working with Shaw, Hayton would go on to become musical
director at MGM, a position he held until 1953. His achievements during
this period included *On the Town* and *Singin' in the Rain*. "Lennie Hayton
and I used to do a lot of work together," said Shaw. "'I Cover the Waterfront' was Lennie's arrangement, with me. Like the arrangement of 'Star
Dust' that sold really big and is in the Hall of Fame, that was his, but I
would write a sketch—this is who starts here and who plays there—and
he would orchestrate. 'I Cover the Waterfront' he made a beautiful introduction, a nice modulation after the first chorus; the rest was more or less
from my sketch. A good song; it came from a movie that has been long
since forgotten."[234]

Shaw's "Stardust" is one of the classic recordings of the Swing Era, an elegant balance of inspired solos and ensemble writing; Jack Jenny's solo, for example, is a small trombone masterpiece of nine bars that immediately wrote itself into the history books with its supreme technical artistry allied to expressivity. Gunther Schuller noted: "The performance of Lennie Hayton's arrangement of 'Stardust' was near perfect."[235] Hayton also provided the arrangement of "Sometimes I Feel like a Motherless Child," featuring Hot Lips Page. Other pieces that show this important, if overlooked, ensemble to best advantage include Ray Conniff's arrangements of "To a Broadway Rose" and "Prelude in C Major." ("Before he went over to the lady singers and lived happily ever after Ray was a very talented writer and a damn good trombone player," Shaw recalled.)[236] Shaw's own arrangement of "Beyond the Blue Horizon," Still's arrangements of "Blues (Parts I & II)" from his own *Lenox Avenue Suite*, "Danza Lucumi," "Gloomy Sunday," "My Fantasy," "Don't Fall Asleep," "Old, Old Castle in Scotland," and "Chantez-les Bas," a recording with an inspired coda that enjoys a second life in the memory. "Chantez-les Bas literally means 'swing 'em low,'" recalled Shaw. "The arrangement is by William Grant Still, who was the first black symphonic conductor-composer in America. He's the guy who worked with me on the arrangement of 'Frenesi,' but I like this one much better, even though 'Frenesi' was the record that took off. This is a very nice example of the use of strings with a jazz band, and again it hasn't been heard enough."[237]

Little is known of arranger and composer Paul Jordan, whom Shaw met in October 1941 when he and his orchestra played Chicago, where he was introduced to the young composer who had gained a strong reputation locally leading a rehearsal band. "A highly skilled black musician, he was equally at home with jazz and concert music," said Shaw. "I was impressed by his training and depth of interest in *music*—not just jazz—and his ability to use what he knew and felt in an unpretentious and telling manner."[238] There was a meeting of minds, albeit Jordan's only claim to fame remains his work with Shaw, who recorded four of his originals—"Suite No. 8," "Two in One Blues," "Hindustan," "Evensong," and "Carnival"—despite strong indifference from RCA Victor executives. Jordan's contributions to Shaw's ensemble were far removed from commerce and the demands of a dancing public, and came close to realizing Shaw's dream of combining quality jazz with serious contemporary composition. "'Suite No. 8' starts with strings stating a theme and then they go into a fugue," explained Shaw. "It's a record that's not been heard sufficiently

. . . 'Two in One Blues' is one of the finest pieces of music my band ever played, quite remarkable for its day." It took, he argued, "some sophistication to hear what we were doing," while "Carnival" sounds "very much as if it came right out of Stravinsky."[239] As Schuller has pointed out, "Jordan's 'Evensong' and 'Suite No. 8' were real 'compositions,' strongly influenced by classical forms and techniques, though at the same time thoroughly grounded in certain jazz traditions (Ellington) and sound concepts. These pieces were far removed from the world of 'arrangements' and dance numbers and pop tunes."[240]

Jerry Sears's arrangement of "Nocturne" by Thomas Griselle reveals a rounded conception of integrating strings within a jazz ensemble, Shaw explaining: "'Nocturne' is not a tune, it's a composition that won a prize for best American composition written in the 'jazz idiom' [in 1928]. It was a very pretty piece of music and we recorded it. Not a dance piece, by the way." Shaw's instinct and ambition at this point were leading him toward concert performances. "In those days nobody thought of having a dance band do concerts, but that's what we were doing," he said. "Half the time there'd be, let's say 9,000 people in the Palomar [Ballroom in California] and probably 75 of them out there dancing. The rest were watching and I used to say, 'Why don't we give them chairs?' Anyway, I used to play this in theaters and the audience would sit there in a trance and when it was finished there would be a momentary hush and then they would go crazy. So we were obviously doing something they liked."[241]

Shaw's own arrangement of "Concerto for Clarinet" was framed as a concert presentation and was surely the culmination of a journey that began in 1935 with "Interlude in B flat," progressing through "The Blues March Parts I & II" from 1937, Irving Szathmary's arrangement of "St. Louis Blues" (which Shaw performed as guest soloist with the Whiteman orchestra expanded to twenty-nine musicians at Carnegie Hall on December 25, 1938), "Summit Ridge Drive"—a blues in C—from September 3, 1940, "Chantez Les Bas" from September 7, 1940, and William Grant Still's "Blues (Parts I & II)," recorded a week before "Concerto," in December 1940. "'Concerto for Clarinet' was done for a movie called *Second Chorus*, which had some awfully good people in it—there was Fred Astaire and Paulette Goddard and Charlie Butterworth who's one of my favorite funny men—but was one of the most preposterous movies ever made," recalled Shaw. "There's a portion in it where we're supposed to be rehearsing for a concert. In those days, dance bands didn't play concerts, and the film concerns itself with this in a stupid, superficial way. But I wanted to record this to show the band spreading out a little and doing things that were not altogether standard dance-band fare. It was done on two sides of a 12 inch record, which doomed it to instant oblivion in those days. But it's a good showpiece for the clarinet and for the rest of the band and I thought everyone swung like crazy on it. My part was entirely improvised."[242] Taken together, the recordings Shaw made with his big-band-with-strings between 1940 and 1942, after which he enlisted for war service, continue to enhance his reputation and stand today as a continuum of Whiteman-esque symphonic jazz that in Shaw's hands at least, obliquely demonstrated that art and commerciality need not necessarily be incompatible.

In 1944, after two years of military service, Artie Shaw formed a new big band, turning to several arrangers, including Eddie Sauter, who provided the band with two outstanding arrangements, an extended version of "Summertime," recorded on April 17, 1945, with its startling writing for clarinets toward the end of the piece, and "Maid with the Flaccid Air" recorded on July 19, 1945. In 1946 and 1947, Sauter wrote several arrangements for Ray McKinley's orchestra,[243] and pieces such as "Sandstorm" and "Tumble Bug" bear his distinctive modernistic imprimatur. In April 1952, Sauter teamed up with former Glenn Miller arranger Bill Finegan to form the Sauter-Finegan Orchestra that in some ways represented a contemporary update and reframing of Paul Whiteman's 1920s orchestra in a contemporary 1950s context. Effectively a jazz-influenced concert orchestra that offered a startling new dimension to the conventional big band instrumentation by incorporating harp, flutes, oboes, fifes, toy trumpets, and even kazoos, their repertoire was wide ranging and ambitious. The distance the Sauter-Finegan orchestra had traveled from Whiteman's band of the 1920s while remaining wedded to the concept of ambitious, modernistic writing is illustrated on Eddie Sauter's arrangement of "Avalon,"[244] a best-seller for Whiteman in the mid-1920s. Whiteman used a musical saw in his recording; the Sauter-Finegan recording is altogether more dynamic, thanks to a powerful brass section for which the piece is a virtual feature.

On their 1955 album *Concert Jazz*, complete with a modernistic album cover designed by Jim Flora, the band experimented with Impressionism ("Sleepy Village") and programmatic writing ("Pictures from Sauter-Finegan Land," "The Loop," "Madame X"), along with an imaginative recasting of "Where or When" using Sally Sweetland's voice, and a piece based on the second movement of Gershwin's *Concerto in F*. Another striking example of Jim Flora's modernistic cover art announces *Inside Sauter-Finegan*, with less emphasis on ensemble writing, more on creating a context to feature the wide-ranging solo talent within the band. Ultimately, however, it was the imaginative ensemble writing by the co-leaders that is remembered today, such as their bravura arrangement of Prokofiev's "Midnight Sleighride" from *The Lieutenant Kije Suite*. The band toured extensively, playing both dance and concert venues, and enjoyed radio exposure on Camel Caravan broadcasts and the NBC Bandstand program, among others. As George T. Simon has noted: "These two men were utterly dedicated, and not prepared to change their ideas to satisfy the public, producers, managers and the more commercially minded."[245] The band was eventually wound up in 1957: the sheer cost of running such an ensemble full time and the diminishing number of venues able to employ an orchestra of its size were given as reasons for its relatively short life span. In 1957, Sauter composed and arranged the album *Focus* for tenor saxophonist Stan Getz. Using a string orchestra with bass and drums accompaniment, this album is far removed from the prevailing bebop/hard bop hegemony yet resolutely modernistic in its creative rigor; it stands alone; it had hardly any ancestors and virtually no progeny (other than the somewhat fragmented collaboration with Getz on the soundtrack music for the motion picture *Mickey One* in 1965 with a large orchestra) yet numbers among the finest recordings in jazz. Sauter's imaginative writing on pieces such as "Night Rider," "Pan," and "I'm Late — I'm Late" prompts some exceptional improvisation from Getz, who was free to create his own part within the music. In May 1957, Sauter accepted an invitation from the Südwestfunk (South-West Radio) in Baden-Baden, Germany, to become leader of their radio big band. On October 27, 1957, he recorded two impressive pieces with the orchestra that are captured on the album *The Historic Donaueschingen Jazz Concert 1957*. Both "Tropic of Kommingen" and "Kinetic Energy" reflect Sauter's studies with Stefan Wolpe and appear distant relatives of Wolpe's *Quartet for Trumpet, Tenor Saxophone, Piano, and Percussion* of 1950–54, the former featuring an impressive Hans Koller on tenor saxophone and the latter, whose cellular structure was described by Sauter as "microcosmic particles in constant rotation," indicative of an artist not content to stand on past accomplishment.

The advanced musical ideas of Eddie Sauter could hardly be said to have flowed from bebop, but was more a continuum of musical modernism, something that might also be said of the Boyd Raeburn and Stan

Kenton orchestras. As George T. Simon said of the Boyd Raeburn Orchestra, "So far as musicians were concerned, one of the truly great bands of the mid-forties was Boyd Raeburn's. But so far as the public was concerned it was just another modern-sounding outfit that wasn't very good to dance to."[246] Raeburn had led a big band since 1942, but in 1945 he formed a new ensemble with arrangements provided by a twenty-four-year-old George Handy that took the band to the forefront of what can only be described as avant-garde jazz of the period. "The new scores emitted flashes of Stravinsky, Bartók, Debussy and Ravel. To musicians such deployments on classical Modernists and Impressionists were completely dazzling," continued Simon.[247] Raeburn's music attracted to his band some of the brightest and best emerging young musicians of the period, such as saxophonists Al Cohn, Serge Chaloff, Jimmy Guiffre, Buddy DeFranco, Johnny Bothwell, Hal McKusick, and Frank Socolow; trumpeters Roy Eldridge, Conte Candoli, Sonny Berman, and Bernie Glow, and, for his January 7, 8, 9, 1945, sessions, trumpeters Dizzy Gillespie, Benny Harris, and Stan Fishelson. Other forward-looking young musicians included pianist Dodo Marmorosa; guitarist Dave Barbour; drummers Don Lamond, Irv Kluger, and Jackie Mills; and trombonists Earl Swope, Milt Bernhart, Si Zentner, Ollie Wilson, and Britt Woodman (who would later join Duke Ellington on the recommendation of band agent Cress Courtney, who was booking the Raeburn band in 1946).

The best Raeburn of this period appeared on three volumes of ten-inch LPs on the Savoy label, with the title track of the second album *Boyd Meets Stravinski* [sic], arranged by the somewhat orthodox Ed Finckel that owed much to Woody Herman's First Herd in terms of energy and Don Redman's "Chant of the Weed" in musical conception. Finckel's arrangement of "Tonsillectomy" submitted to the prevailing bebop influences with its use of flatted fifths, but it was Handy's writing for the band that catches the ear today. For example, his introductions to "Temptation" and "Forgetful," with vocals by Ginny Powell and David Allyn, respectively (the latter a fine if underrated ballad singer in the same league as Sinatra, Haymes, and Bennett of the period), were exacting musical obstacle courses that had little precedent in jazz, while "Man with a Horn" boasts another brilliant opening that gives way to Bill Starkey on English horn. Handy's arrangements of "Dalvatore Sally" (which became the band's theme song) was written as the first part of a suite that included "Hey, Look I'm Dancing," "Grey Suede," "Special Maid," and "Keef" (all recorded on V-Disc). "Dalvatore Sally" manages to impress even today with its starkly modernistic disposition of contrasting mood swings and a brilliant trumpet flourish in the coda. Handy arranged the first part of "Body and Soul" for Ginny Powell's vocal but did not finish the piece, a task that fell to Johnny Richards; quite what the dancing public made of their joint version of Buddy Green's enduring standard is in part answered in a review of the band by critic Barry Ulanov, one of the band's boosters, who wrote in *Metronome* magazine: "This Raeburn band is by no means a dance organization. The music it plays is designed for listening; it's modern music, cast in new molds out of classical forms and jazz rhythms and harmonies."[248]

No band leader in jazz pursued the elusive goal of modernism with such tenacity as Stan Kenton. Although in his orchestra's early years he set the style of the band with his own arrangements, he soon handed the destiny of his orchestra to a series of composers and arrangers, so at this distance his repertoire appears to show little or no unity. Indeed, there were occasions when some ideas and ideals were not only wildly different but also incompatible. Yet despite this apparent lack of focus, Kenton's faith in modernism and Futurism produced some music that was excellent, and some that was even importantly original in a career that his biographer Michael Sparke characterized as embracing "more triumphant achievements and more humiliating failures than most people would encounter in a dozen lifetimes."[249]

Kenton initially established a reputation at the Rendezvous Ballroom in Balboa Beach, California, in the early forties, where Count Basie, on having heard a broadcast by his band in 1941, told his band, "That will be the new king!"[250] Kenton gave his all to his music, and his musicians responded with the zeal of men on a mission rather than working for a weekly paycheck. But the transition from dance band music to existentialism clearly required something more than new arrangements, however inspired. It needed a vision that saw beyond the jazz conventions of the day. Here Kenton was helped by the likes of composers and arrangers Pete Rugolo, Bill Russo, Bill Holman, Shorty Rogers, Johnny Richards, and, briefly, Gerry Mulligan. Various editions of his band came and went through the 1940s and into the 1970s, often pioneering challenging new directions for the large jazz orchestra and advancing the art of big band jazz in the process: the *Artistry in Rhythm* band, the forty-piece *Innovations Orchestra* that included a string section, the "Progressive Jazz" of the *New Concepts in Artistry in Rhythm* band, and, indicative of his continued pursuit of modernism, his *New Era in Modern Music* band of the 1960s.

Among the most interesting works of his large discography is the modernist disposition of his Innovations band of 1950–51, whose repertoire divides neatly into two parts: the music written and arranged by Shorty Rogers, Pete Rugolo, and Johnny Richards, and that written and arranged by Robert Graettinger; it is the latter's contribution that appears the most rewarding today. Graettinger was one of countless young musicians who owed their reputation in jazz to Kenton, who was, perhaps surprisingly, a reluctant leader, considering himself too tall, awkward, and tongue-tied to front a band. But charisma, infectious enthusiasm, and his sheer physical presence made him a natural for the role. If the new and different were Kenton's guiding lights, then no piece of music exemplified this more than Graettinger's *City of Glass*, comprising four movements. "Although by the filibustering standards of some later jazz it is brief, the four movements together lasting less than 17 minutes, it is highly concentrated. So much happens in that short span," wrote Max Harrison.[251] *City of Glass* is one of the great, if misunderstood, extended compositions in jazz. Neither low-brow, middle-brow, nor high-brow, but aimed well over the heads of most people, it was predictably berated by the critics for its "classical" aspirations when Kenton debuted this ambitious piece at the Chicago Civic Opera House in 1948. A capacity audience greeted the piece in stunned silence until Kenton, with remarkable presence of mind, leaped in front of his band and with a dramatic gesture signaled for his band to take a bow. The baffled audience responded with a huge ovation. This uniquely conceived piece of music had no precedent in either classical music or jazz, so there was no context in which to situate it at the time. The endorsement by many great jazz musicians—Coleman Hawkins was one—made tart contrast to the critics' instant dismissals. In fact, *City of Glass* is strikingly original, and in its multilayered complexity, textural density, and in its at times nontonal language, Graettinger actually anticipates many of the European and American avant-garde jazz experimenters of the 1950s and 1960s. Yet as Harrison has observed, "This music signalled no 'revolution,' as was inevitably claimed; nor did it 'bridge the gap between jazz and the classics,' as was more predictably asserted. It is just itself. And that is enough."[252]

The Claude Thornhill Orchestra might be said to have occupied the opposite end of the sound spectrum from Kenton; where the latter made a wall-of-sound appear fashionable some two decades before producer Phil Spector, Thornhill specialized in delicate, filigree piano solos framed by sotto voce ballads. However, his repertoire did include the modernist disposition of the up-tempo "Portrait of a Guinea Farm," which he composed and arranged and which was described by George T. Simon as "one of the most fascinating instrumental originals ever recorded by any band."[253] This piece owed little to prevailing conventions of big band music, its sweeping orchestral tone colors more modernistic jazz than modern jazz. From late 1941 one of the band's chief arrangers was Gil Evans, and although he would acknowledge the importance of bebop with arrangements of "Yardbird Suite," "Anthropology," and "Donna Lee," his greatest contributions to the Thornhill repertoire had little to do with bebop at all. His adaptations of "La Paloma," Tchaikovsky's "Arab Dance," and Mussorgsky's "The Old Castle" from *Pictures at an Exhibition*—the latter described by Max Harrison as "Vividly original"[254]—stand today as eloquent examples of jazz modernism: more concerned with ends rather than means in their disregard for the post-Henderson antiphonal writing, on the one hand, than the conventions of bebop, on the other, and imaginatively drawing on the instrumental resources of the orchestra, which included up to seven clarinets who doubled on piccolos, plus flutes, tuba, French horns, trumpets, and trombones.

Other examples of how jazz continued to be influenced by the modernist ethos during the 1940s might include guitarist George Barnes's octet, described by Richard Sudhalter as "one of the most inventive, musically refreshing jazz chamber groups,"[255] which comprised four woodwind players playing, variously, bass saxophone, bass clarinet, bassoon, oboe, A clarinet, B-flat clarinet, flute and piccolo, two guitars, bass, and drums; also Woody Herman's performance of "Dancing in the Dawn" from 1943 (with shades of "Song of the Dawn" from the Paul Whiteman motion picture *King of Jazz*) and his striking debut of Stravinsky's "Ebony Concerto" at Carnegie Hall on March 25, 1946; Dennis Sandole's composition "Dark Bayou" for the Charlie Barnet Orchestra, also from 1946; Mel Tormé's *California Suite* from 1949; the experiments of Gunther Schuller and John Lewis including *The Modern Jazz Society Presents a Concert of Modern Jazz* (1955), *Music for Brass* (1956), and *Modern Jazz Concert* (1957) that marked a brief period of experimentation called Third Stream; Matyas Seiber's and Johnny Dankworth's collaboration that produced *Improvisations for Jazz Band and Symphony Orchestra* in 1959; and from the 1990s, Randy Sandke's *Awakening* album, which included an orchestral version of Bix Beiderbecke's unrecorded piano composition "Clouds" and a Charles Ives composition from 1906 called "Unanswered Question" with the Bulgarian National Symphony. All these creations were modernistic in a way that owed little to bebop. A partial list such as this simply serves to illustrate how modernism's belief in searching for new ideas and different approaches, unusual melodies, harmonies, and instrumentation, and a desire to raise the standard of jazz performance from an entertainment to an art form was not the exclusive province of bebop. It had a long history within jazz before, during, and after the bebop era.

One reason, perhaps, that jazz in its pre-bop stages has not been recognized as a modernist music is that the breadth and diversity of the highly individual experimentation going on beneath the surface of the Jazz Age and the Swing Era by the jazz modernists did not fall into any convenient stylistic groupings around which jazz history could be constructed—such as "New Orleans," "Chicago," "Stride," or "Swing"—essential to producing a coherent teleological history of jazz. Developments at the perceived margins of the music simply deflect from the construction of a coherent master narrative and have often been ignored or restricted to the recognition that an individual player might achieve for a specific work or works, rather than the collective impact a community of similarly orientated and competing artists performing in a single coherent style might achieve. It has meant that the absence of a single dominant style so essential for music marketing, media validation, and canon construction has minimized the importance of the pre-bop jazz modernists within the overall thrust of jazz history, creating an unusual paradox whereby their very originality has mitigated against their very real achievements.

As this chapter seeks to illustrate, there was no shortage of "experiment and a sense of risk—innovation for its own sake in the cause of advancing the music,"[256] cited as the sine qua non of bebop, in pre-bop music. Yet what is often overlooked is that jazz modernism, particularly in the pre-bop eras, however fragmented, represented the avant-garde jazz of its day; claims that bebop was "the first authentically modern phase of jazz" because it "challenged both the entertainment industry and the dancing public and confronted them with an artistically self conscious listening music"[257] are clearly wide of the mark when held up to scrutiny.

## Bebop, Modernism, and Modern Jazz

In the 1940s, the burgeoning bebop movement provided simple and direct correlations with modernism. Though it was often portrayed as a "revolution," the musicians themselves were inclined to view it in less polemical terms. Nevertheless, the music was presented with a certain creative rigor that separated it from the big bands then popular with the American public. One of the key arguments used to differentiate bebop from pre-bop takes the form: "Bebop was the first authentically modern phase in jazz. Experiment and a sense of risk—innovation for its own sake in the cause of advancing the music—marked this development. It also challenged the entertainment industry and the dancing public and confronted them with an artistically self-conscious listening music."[258] This suggests a willingness to let the music stand or fall on its artistic merit, by creating a music to be listened to, rather than to fulfill the criteria as a music for dancing. But as John Howland has argued, this conforms to a long-standing, bifurcated view of American culture as either "art" or "entertainment."[259] But "life or art" has never been a choice between two moral absolutes, between black and white; it is about the infinite number of shades of gray in between. Readings of jazz that move toward a separation of the jazz tradition from popular entertainment, seeming to exclude the possibility of great art being created within the broader conventions of the entertainment infrastructure, surely represent a distortion of the music's history.

The demonization of commercialism as a corrupting influence is a persistent theme that runs through much jazz commentary. But as Brian Priestly demonstrated in his essay "Charlie Parker and Popular Music": "Parker's work, no less than his career, was crucially embedded in the popular music of his day,"[260] pointing out that almost all of Parker's official studio recordings were produced with a pre–long play mindset, and with just a couple of exceptions for the Verve label, all were released as 78-rpm or 45-rpm recordings competing for the same radio exposure, jukebox space, and retail sales as popular music. Thus it is perhaps misleading to suggest that Parker's work (and that of Dizzy Gillespie) remained somehow remote from the entertainment milieu. As Priestly points out, recordings such as "Just Friends," "My Little Suede Shoes," and "Autumn in New York" actually sold quite well. Priestly might have profitably added that both Parker and Gillespie were from time to time members of Norman Granz's *Jazz at the Philharmonic* troupe, perhaps the most commercially successful concert hall presentation of jazz during the late 1940s and 1950s, whose appeal exploited the lowest common denominator in music-making by way of "cutting contests" that were frequently resolved by who could play the loudest, the fastest, and the highest, or, in the case of drum battles, the loudest, to the delight of the baying fans. "Connecting with the public, however, is not an idea that concerns most fans of this music," continues Priestly. "It strikes me as no coincidence that by the end of the 1940s both Parker and Gillespie in their differing ways were seeking rather desperately for ways to bring their talents before a wider audience . . . Like the showmen of an earlier generation, bandleaders Parker and Gillespie had to court their listeners with whatever strategies were to hand . . . We listeners on the other hand have bought into the idea that bebop was deliberately designed to be difficult and alienating and have treasured such statements by the participants as seem to back up our preconceptions."[261]

The continued insistence that bebop was anticommercial fits the way jazz history has been constructed and so suits the need in jazz discourse to make a separation between jazz as a commercial endeavor and jazz as an "art form." That is despite annoying reminders to the contrary, such as Dizzy Gillespie's big bebop band of the period catering to dancers by commercially framing and presenting bebop in numbers such as "Oll-Ya-Koo," "Oooh Bop Sha'bam," "He Beeped When He Should Have Bopped," or "Hey Pete! Let's Eat More Meat." Equally, the continued presence of bebop stars in Norman Granz's *Jazz at the Philharmonic* touring ensembles that delighted large audiences with bebop anthems such as "How High the Moon," or the commercial success of Woody Herman's "First Herd" are typically overlooked. As the cultural critic Andrew Ross has pointed out: "Commercial and contractual relations enter into *all* forms of musical entertainment, or at least whenever the music is performed in order to make a living."[262] As we have seen, the art/entertainment dichotomy seems at odds with the original precepts of modernism; Les Six in Paris, for example, wanted to *close* the gap between artistic and everyday discourse, to fuse art and the everyday, to become *popular*; Cubism's use of collage was a way of strengthening the link between art and the real world, the everyday. Indeed, no other jazz artist in the twentieth century straddled the worlds of art and entertainment as successfully as Louis Armstrong; Ralph Ellison saw no disjunction in drawing a correlation between T. S. Eliot's *Waste Land*, a classic of modernist literature, and the "rowdy poetic flight"[263] of "West End Blues."

Whatever else it was, bebop nevertheless "sounded" modern in the context of its times, and was soon being referred to in the press as "modern jazz" to distinguish it from styles of jazz that had preceded it. During the 1950s and 1960s this association with modernism did jazz no harm; indeed, modernity became symbiotically associated with all new forms of post-1945 jazz during the 1950s and 1960s when the media collectively referred to bop, hard bop, cool jazz, and later free jazz under the rubric "Modern Jazz."[264] It was also a useful term for music marketers, since it played into the consumerist ethos of buying into the always new, the "modern," and the "up to date." Some classics of West Coast jazz appeared on the album *Modern Sounds*, an album title deliberately chosen to strengthen its link with "modern" jazz, when trumpeter Shorty Rogers and his group the Giants and the Gerry Mulligan Tentet each shared one side of a twelve-inch LP. Rogers's albums *Cool and Crazy* and *Courts the Count* were modernistic in the sense of being modern jazz without being bebop. However, his most successful album was *The Swinging Mr. Rogers*, which included "Martians Go Home," whose success resulted in, as Ted Gioia, author of *West Coast Jazz*, has pointed out, "A steady string of related titles: 'Planetarium,' 'Martian's Lullabye,' 'Saturnian Sleigh Ride,' 'March of the Martians,' and 'Astral Alley,' to cite a few examples. Somehow, the modernistic notions surrounding outer-space implied, at least in the 1950s, that any music related to it would be equally modernistic."[265]

Consumers of jazz during this period may have been engaging with jazz music, but they were also engaging with "the state of being modern," reinforced by album cover art that often depicted modernistic exterior and interior designs, streamlined cars, modern art, and modern artifacts such as hi-fi's being used and consumed by young, clean-cut snappily dressed fans. For example, the cover art for Duane Tatro's *Jazz for Moderns* LP came with a photo of a very futuristic Firebird II motorcar, while a modernistic art theme was taken up by several record labels that hired design artists to provide suitable cover art, such as Columbia's Alex Steinweiss, Jim Flora, and Jim Amos. Additionally, modernistic artists were commissioned to provide customized cover art, most famously David Stone Martin for the Verve label and Andy Warhol, then a freelance commercial artist, whose cover art included *Count Basie* for RCA, the *Cool Gabriels* for the Groove label, and album covers for the Blue Note label such as *Blue Lights* by Kenny Burrell and *The Congregation* by Johnny Griffin.

Other labels secured the necessary permissions to reproduce photographic images of paintings by modernism's established artists, the most famous examples being Jackson Pollack's *White Light* for Ornette Coleman's historic album cover *Free Jazz*, and Joan Miró's *Painting: 1925* for Dave Brubeck's *Time Further Out*. "Joan Miró's *Painting: 1925* fascinated me as a visual representation of my quartet's rhythmic explorations," recalled Brubeck in 1996. "Actually, I wanted to use it for the cover of our very first experimental album, *Time Out*. We could not obtain the necessary permissions in time for the release date, so the now-familiar Neil Fujita painting was used for the cover. Meanwhile, through the help of Xenia Cage and the Matisse Gallery, I located Miró, who was sailing in a yacht in the Mediterranean. I was prepared to be disappointed. But instead of the resounding 'No' I anticipated, or the exorbitant fee I was told he would charge, I received a friendly cabled reply: 'It would be an honor.' Thus began a series of quartet recordings with contemporary paintings."[266]

Neil Fujita, who provided the cover art for Brubeck's best-selling *Time Out* album, had in fact been influenced by Picasso, Georges Braque, Paul Klee, and Miró, while *Time in Outer Space* used artwork by Franz Kline, and *Time Changes* used artwork by Sam Francis. Probing beneath Brubeck's iconic album covers it is now clear that his music is more comfortably viewed through the prism of modernism than by trying to make his music fit into any particular post-1950s stylistic category or genre. The great paradox of Brubeck's music is that he was playing "modern jazz," but it was not in the prevailing hegemonic style of bebop-into-hard bop—something critics in the 1950s and 1960s found difficult to forgive. The key to his musical philosophy was the modernistic influence of Darius Milhaud (one of Brubeck's sons was named Darius in the composer's honor), whose personal encouragement meant much to the young, aspiring pianist's development.

After Brubeck graduated from the College of the Pacific with a bachelor of music degree, World War II intervened, and on volunteering for the army he was posted to Europe, returning home in January 1946. Taking advantage of the GI Bill he again entered college, this time to study under Milhaud. "Pete Rugolo and my brother were two piano majors and they were the first graduate students of Darius Milhaud to come out of Mills College," recalled Brubeck.

> Mills College was a girls school, and they allowed my brother and Rugolo to come and stay with Milhaud because Milhaud had started teaching there, and then they allowed GI's after the war to come and study at this girls school with Darius Milhaud. So that's when my octet was formed—with students of Milhaud. It was formed by five guys that were Milhaud students—Bill Smith, David van Kriedt, Dick Collins, Jack Weeks, and me—that's the five of the eight. Then Paul Desmond came over from San Francisco State because he was friends with these guys and Cal Tjader was also from San Francisco State. And then Milhaud suggested that we play for the assembly of the girls in the audito-

rium and the first octet concert was at his suggestion at Mills College. The second was at the College of the Pacific where we graduated, and we went up there and played, and then we played at the University of California. This would have been '46, '47.[267]

Brubeck's octet put into practice some of the concepts of counterpoint, fugue, and composition he and his fellow students were studying under Milhaud. What these recordings reveal is how these musicians were pursuing the goal of modernism in their own highly characteristic way, actually anticipating some of the textures and techniques more famously explored in the Miles Davis *Birth of the Cool* sessions of 1949–50 for the Capitol label. "Counterpoint, which had become almost dormant in the Swing Era and is now a commonly accepted device in modern jazz was the distinguishing feature of the Octet," explained Brubeck in May 1956. "Along with polytonality it was the unifying quality in the varying styles of the group's arrangers. We explored polytonality, polyrhythms, various rhythms, and new forms. Dave van Kriedt's fugues were among the first, I believe, to come from a jazz musician."[268] In fact, as Max Harrison has pointed out, van Kriedt's "Fugue on Bop Themes" "may be the most thoroughgoing and effective use of a fugue ever recorded by a jazz composer."[269]

The octet recordings brought Brubeck and alto saxophonist Paul Desmond together for the first time on record, an association they would renew when Brubeck formed a quartet in 1951. It was during these years that Brubeck emerged as a major jazz star and the standard bearer of a brand of sleek modern jazz that seemed to reflect the sunny optimism of the Eisenhower Era. Two albums stand out from this period: *Jazz at Oberlin* from March 1953 and *Jazz at the College of the Pacific* from December 1953. The Oberlin date has Ron Crotty on bass and Lloyd Davis on drums, and of especial interest is the performance of "The Way You Look Tonight," which was adapted from Brubeck's arrangement of the song for the octet, revealing of just one aspect of Milhaud's continuing influence within the quartet context. On the College of the Pacific date Joe Dodge replaces Davis. On both occasions Desmond played as well as he did at any point in his career. "Paul is fantastic in this concert," says Brubeck. "Of the many, many years I've enjoyed Paul's playing some of my favorite up-tempo work by him comes from those dates, his ideas just flowed."[270]

In 1954, after releasing several successful albums on the Fantasy label, Brubeck was signed by record giant Columbia. Their first studio album was released in 1954, the cover art adapting Boris Artzybasheff's original portrait of Brubeck for the cover of *Time* magazine for an album called, perhaps unsurprisingly, *Brubeck Time*. However, the most important single event in the history of what was to become known as the "classic" Dave Brubeck quartet was the addition of drummer Joe Morello in 1956. The rhythmic spring that Morello brought to the quartet is immediately apparent on *Jazz Goes to Junior College*, recorded at concerts at Fullerton and Long Beach junior colleges in California. Morello was the first non–West Coast member of the quartet, and he brought with him the accomplishment of a thoroughly trained percussionist and added a new dimension to the quartet with his virtuoso technique, fluency with polyrhythms, and a willingness to become a third solo voice within the group. With the addition of Gene Wright on bass at the end of 1957, the group was poised to make its greatest impact on jazz. In 1958, the group made the first of many international tours sponsored by the US State Department, with Brubeck performing the role of a Goodwill Ambassador for his country with distinction.

When they went into the Columbia recording studios at 30th Street in New York City on July 1, 1959, none of the quartet realized that this would turn out to be the most important session in the history of the Dave Brubeck Quartet. The concept of *Time Out* was a series of originals, each with a different time signature. "For a number of years the Quartet frequently used a polyrhythmic approach within improvised solos," wrote Brubeck in 1996.

> In 1958 we shared the experience of travelling in the Middle East and India and playing with musicians from those countries, where folk music wasn't limited to $\frac{4}{4}$ . . . I felt immediately intrigued with the $\frac{9}{8}$ rhythm I heard on the streets of Istanbul. Combining the Turkish $\frac{9}{8}$ pattern with the classical rondo form and the blues resulted in "Blue Rondo a la Turk," the flip side of "Take Five" which was the hit single that finally emerged from *Time Out*. The album defied all expert predictions, and instead of becoming an experimental "dud," of interest only to other musicians, "caught on" with the general public, despite lack of interest by the record company and a generally hostile reaction by jazz writers and critics.[271]

Other than Tchaikovsky's use of $\frac{5}{4}$ in the second movement of the *Pathétique* symphony, "Take Five" is now probably the most famous use of this asymmetrical time signature in Western music. The single featured on the *Billboard Hot 100* chart for more than two years, repeating pop chart success in the United Kingdom when it was released in 1961, reaching No. 6 in the UK chart. For a large section of the public it came to represent the epitome of hip, "modern" jazz, appearing on the soundtracks of countless films and television programs when the scene called for music that suggested the up to date, trendy, fashionable, modern, and futuristic. The song, written by Paul Desmond, has been covered by almost forty artists from singer Al Jarreau to the Swedish rock band Plankton. It was even used as the signature tune for the NBC *Today* program in the 1960s, helping to secure an enduring relationship between Brubeck and middle America.

Brubeck's contract with Columbia called for a remarkable three albums a year, which he fulfilled and sometimes exceeded. Among the highlights were a series of *Jazz Impressions* albums that reflected the inspiration of the music of the Middle East, Europe, the United States, Japan, and Mexico as refracted through Brubeck's compositional prism. A more ambitious project was realized with *The Real Ambassadors* from 1962, described on the album sleeve as "An Original Musical Production by Dave and Iola Brubeck." Featuring Louis Armstrong, Carmen McRae, the vocal trio Lambert, Hendricks, and Ross as well as the Brubeck Quartet, it was a musical play concerned with the use of jazz as a medium of international goodwill by the State Department—"The State Department has discovered jazz / It reached folks like nothin' ever has / Like when they feel that jazzy rhythm / They know we're really with 'em / That's what we call cultural exchange."[272] This album, together with his 1962 album *Brandenburg Gate*, reflected his growing skill as a composer, the latter taking its name from a track from *Jazz Impressions of Eurasia* that presented five Brubeck originals in a fuller orchestral form.

In 1967, the quartet, nearing the end of its seventeen-year run, visited Mexico for a series of sold-out concerts that resulted in *Bravo! Brubeck*, their second to last album, which bubbles with exuberance. The quartet's final concert took place in Pittsburgh on Boxing Day that year and was finally released in 2012 as *Their Last Time Out*. In all, Brubeck recorded some fifty albums for Columbia, a reflection of his and the quartet's creativity, since they are all of uniformly high standard; yet, while they are indisputably "modern jazz," they do not share characteristics in common with the then dominant form of jazz modernism dominated by bop and hard bop. In the 1950s, critics believed that the sine qua non of jazz was swing, yet Brubeck swam against the prevailing current by experimenting with odd time signatures and polyrhythms. "The way I want to swing is the most difficult," he explained in 1961. "To superimpose over what the bass and drums are doing. And the polyrhythmic qualities that should be inherent in jazz are only going to be attained through the idea the bass and drums are playing together and the pianist is a superimposition over this—which is a very African approach."[273] And as if to confuse matters even further, his pursuit of modernism also saw him experimenting polytonally—the use of two or more tonalities simultaneously. The impact of his experimentation was such that by 1957, Brubeck was able to say, "Polytonality and polyrhythms would be two avenues that I think we opened up more than any other group [in jazz] . . . There's so few people that will stick their necks out and *do* something different because you're going to get it cut off if you stick it out. And that is what I've been willing to do."[274]

While Brubeck's career seemed to be conducted in the full glare of the public spotlight, the career of pianist and theorist Lennie Tristano might be said, in comparison, to have been conducted in the glare of candlelight. Like Brubeck, Tristano was very much a modern jazz musician who did not play in the prevailing modern jazz style of bebop-into-hard bop, even though, paradoxically, he had mastered the idiom and was fascinated by what musicians such as Charlie Parker (he was a pallbearer at Parker's funeral) and Fats Navarro had achieved within the style. However, his own harmonic concepts extended beyond the complexities of bebop; a pianist with a prodigious technique who in his early years had mastered Art Tatum's style, he delighted friends by performing Tatum's showcase "Elegy" faster than the original recording.[275]

He was also a pedagogue who opened his own teaching studio in June 1951 on East Thirty-second Street in Manhattan, attracting a number of musicians who became known as the "Tristano School" in order to distinguish their music from the prevailing "bop," "cool," and "hard bop" schools. Stated simply, the bulk of Tristano's finest music was recorded on two LPs for the Atlantic label that appeared during his lifetime, *Lennie Tristano* (1956) and *The New Tristano* (1962), and two LPs released by the label three years after his death as *The Lennie Tristano Quartet* (1981). His early work for the Keynote label in 1947 showed his concern for linear development, while his Capitol sides, recorded in 1949, represent an important body of work that brings together key collaborators (and students) in Lee Konitz (alto saxophone) and Warne Marsh (tenor saxophone). Of the seven recordings Tristano made for Capitol, two tracks, "Yesterdays" and "Intuition," accurately prefigured free jazz improvisation of the late 1950s by abandoning preset chord sequences, melody, or key centers. A key aspect of Tristano's music on the other Capitol sides was the use of counterpoint, hardly unknown in jazz but here taken to a degree of spontaneous sophistication that was unique in jazz then as much as it is now. "It was one of the things we did very well together," recalled Konitz, "one of the things I used to enjoy doing with that group. I don't know what kind of effect it had. The only immediate effect I know about was on Dave Brubeck, who watered it down enough to make it acceptable at the right time."[276]

In 1956, Atlantic released *Lennie Tristano* to immediate controversy, since the tracks "Line Up" and "East Thirty-Second" involved speeding up the sound of the piano to match the prerecorded sounds of bass and drums. Such sonic legerdemain offended purists at the time, who wanted recordings to be a virtual sound "photograph" of the actual event. Today the piano sounds slightly similar to a "prepared" piano, and seems to emphasize Tristano's somewhat austere approach to improvisation, as demanding to the player in sustaining such long lines of invention as it is for the listener to engage with. "Turkish Mambo" involved multitracking three lines, one moving from $7/8$ to $7/4$, another from $5/8$ to $5/4$, and the third from $3/8$ to $4/4$, but the mixing is done in a way that the leading line is not crowded out by the subsidiary lines, which could have contributed to a feeling of congestion.

Today this futuristic track still sounds remarkably modern, while the moving "Requiem," a solo piano blues performance with a profound, almost stately introduction, reveals Tristano's ability to "play" silences, before the exposition of a twelve-bar blues mourning Charlie Parker's death. It includes an embellished reference en passant to a blues riff Parker presented to the public domain on "Hootie Blues" with bandleader Jay McShann in 1941—two descending figures that begin on the tonic and drop an octave below that appear in bars seven and eight of Parker's one-chorus solo. "Requiem" also had subtle, overdubbed piano accompaniment, and what critics at the time failed to appreciate about postproduction techniques (now commonplace) was not the means used to create the end, but what the end achieved that mattered. And that end was truly modernistic in its conception and presciently forward looking, since at the core of these performances was an intensity and a masterful compression of ideas and motifs into small spaces that make this music so compelling, *Metronome* magazine noted that "Line Up" was "'All of Me' improvised until the stuffing fell out."[277] In 1962, Atlantic released *The New Tristano*, comprising seven solo piano tracks, and this time the liner notes specifically pointed out: "No use is made of multi-tracking, overdubbing or tape speeding on any selection."[278] As Ira Gitler notes, this album is "a remarkable tour de force,"[279] not least for the remarkable "C Minor Complex," a contrafact of "You'd Be So Nice to Come Home To," that a cursory audition might ascribe to multitracking and tape speeding, such is the intensity of ideas and the fluency of their execution. Liner note writer Barry Ulanov was moved to note that this six-minute piece had such "concentrated feeling [it] reminds one of nothing so much as the *D minor Chromatic Fantasy and Fugue* of Bach."[280]

On June 11, 1955, Atlantic recorded Tristano live at the Sing Song Room of Manhattan's Confucius Restaurant 1955 with Lee Konitz (alto saxophone), Gene Ramey (bass), and Art Taylor (drums). Five tracks were originally released on the 1956 album *Lennie Tristano*, and in 1981 Atlantic released a further thirteen tracks from this session as a two-album set entitled *The Lennie Tristano Quartet*. Taken together, these tracks represent exemplary small-group playing, Konitz, like his mentor Tristano, intent on improvisations that cut to the bone: stripped of ornament and repetition, they probed to the very heart of each song.

Despite sharing the same instrumentation as the Dave Brubeck Quartet, the music could hardly have been more different in both concept and execution. Whereas Brubeck epitomized the sunny optimism of the Eisenhower Era, Tristano's group had an earthy intensity—although, like Brubeck, Tristano enjoyed polyrhythms and deploying different time signatures over a basic ¼ pulse, whose possibilities, he claimed, were "practically infinite, endless even in the most simple forms. You are constantly creating form on form, a multiplicity of lines, a great complex of forms."[281] These performances, comprising over eighty minutes of music, reveal what a masterful pianist Tristano was, improvising with the concept of time, superimposing new time signatures over the basic ¼ pulse, even improvising with the underlying chord progressions. In an interview he gave in 1964, he said, "I want jazz to flow out of the id,"[282] the id being the set of uncoordinated instinctual trends that form a part of Sigmund Freud's model of the psyche.

Today, musicians instead refer to "getting into the zone" when they improvise, which goes to the heart of the improvisational process, as Sonny Rollins explained:

> When I am working with a piece of music, I will study the music and learn the melody and the chord progression in preparation for my in-

strumental improvisation. Now, when I improvise after formally learning these things, I forget them. I don't go up on the stage and think of
them, I forget them and that's where the creativity comes in. That little area is quite mysterious. Music is magical, we all know that, and
that area where you create and your subconscious is at work, you
don't know what you're playing. Often I play things, if I'm in the right
groove, I'll play things that I surprise myself with, those are things that
are deep in my subconscious and they come out during my improvisation, but they are not things I went into the song thinking about. And
this is why in improvisation it is so top of the field when it comes to artistic expression, to me, because there is so much skill involved in playing music, and yet it has got to be free and loose—the skill is there, you
learn the skill and you forget it. In a way improvisation is making the
mind blank, when I'm playing I'm just in a trance. So that's what I have
learned about music, about improvisation, and it's beautiful.[283]

Somehow, the modernistic clock seemed to have gone full circle, back to
Robert Goffin's reaction to early jazz when he argued, "Jazz was the first
form of Surrealism,"[284] and certainly there were those in Europe during
the 1950s who argued Ornette Coleman was a manifestation of this. In
contrast, John Coltrane's modernistic path, driven by a desire to exhaust
the potentialities of any harmonic situation by seeking to reveal all sides
of a harmonic situation and crowding in every conceivable chord substi-
tution, was perhaps more analogous to the cubist artist's desire to simultaneously reveal every aspect of the subject matter at hand.

In more recent times, Wynton Marsalis signified on modernism with
his use of Henri Matisse's *Icarus* as cover art for his album *The Majesty of
the Blues* (1989). Matisse, who quite probably saw Satie's *Parade* in 1918,
began using paper cut-outs in 1931, announcing that he was dissatisfied
with the scope of painting as a medium. In 1947 his work *Jazz* was published in book form, with *Icarus* as plate 7 among twenty prints of his
paper cut-out images on colored backgrounds. Matisse realized that re-
ducing images to bare outlines intensified the simplicity of both the composition and the purity of the colors used. Handwritten texts in his large,
flowing handwriting provided a counterpoint to the images, and the relatively small print-run by the publishing company Editions Verve did not
stop *Jazz* from being well received. Praised for its spirit and immediacy,
it was said to invoke connotations of the music to be heard in the jazz
bars in Saint-Germain-des-Prés. In fact, Matisse's original working title

for the twenty prints had been *Circus*, and all but four of the cut-outs had been completed by 1943. *Circus* provided inspiration for more than half the motifs, while *Icarus*, *The Wolf*, *The Heart*, *Forms*, and *Pierrot's Funeral* were all metaphors for life. Modernist and primitivist (*Toboggan*, *Destiny*, and *Lagoon* evoke a trip the artist had made in 1930 to Tahiti, like Gauguin before him), Matisse's cut-outs, with their use of abstract designs and intense, reduced colors, seemed like an explosion of expression when they first appeared in 1947.

Yet Marsalis's choice of *Icarus* for the cover of *The Majesty of the Blues* represented more than a passing interest in modernism. As the *Guardian* newspaper has pointed out, Marsalis had come to see all jazz as modern: "Musicians believe in a separation between the old and new," he said, "post–Charlie Parker, or everything before. But once I discovered it wasn't the case, I felt an artistic responsibility to learn more."[285] It was reflected in a wide range of albums including extended, larger scale works whose genesis can be traced back to the inspiration of Duke Ellington and are probably better understood as jazz modernism; *A Fiddler's Tale*, for example, was inspired by Igor Stravinsky's *A Soldier's Tale* in a work that combined the talents of Lincoln Center's Chamber Music Society with those of Jazz at Lincoln Center. "In some cases I used his actual forms and harmonies," said Marsalis. "Much of Stravinsky's music was so complicated that the only action I could take was to swing."[286] Marsalis's *All Rise*, a twelve-part millennial composition for choir, jazz and symphony orchestras drew on "inspiration from Bartók and Stravinsky as well as African-American music from gospel to jazz."[287] Premiered in 1999, the CD was conducted by Los Angeles Philharmonic's Esa-Pekka Salonen, who described it as "Mahlerian in spirit."[288] Marsalis's magnum opus was the jazz oratorio *Blood on the Fields*, premiered on April 1 and 2, 1994, which culminated in a Pulitzer Prize for the composer in 1997. Impressive in scale, it was a performance unique in its time, in many ways displaying the ambitions of early jazz modernism, a milieu in which jazz originally defined itself, and, like Matisse's modernistic cut-outs, forcing the audience to reconsider the parameters of the art form. It was also a reminder, with its echoes of Ellingtonia, of how much jazz's cultural capital is enhanced when we consider all of it a modernist music.

# Notes

## Preface

1. *Congressional Record—House*, September 23, 1987, H7825–27, quoted in *Keeping Time: Readings in Jazz History*, ed. Robert Walser (New York: Oxford University Press, 1999), 333.

2. *Downbeat*, May 2006, 36. The magazine's cover featured e.s.t., or the Esbjörn Svensson Trio, the first time in the magazine's then seventy-two-year publishing history that a European jazz band had achieved that honor.

3. Wolfram Knauer and Arndt Weidler, eds., *Wegweiser Jazz* (Darmstadt: Jazzinstitut Darmstadt, 2009), 20.

4. *Congressional Record—House*, September 23, 1987, H7825–27, quoted in Walser, *Keeping Time*, 333.

5. Neal Gabler, *An Empire of Their Own: How Jews Invented Hollywood* (New York: Anchor Books, 1988), 432.

6. John O'Sullivan in *National Review* 44, no. 1 (1992): 6.

7. Duncan Webster, *Looka Yonder! The Imaginary America of Popular Culture* (London: Routledge, 1988), 228.

8. Thelonious Monk Institute, Jazz in America, *What Is Jazz? IV: Jazz—America's Music*, www.jazzinamerica.org/LessonPlan/11/1/130.

9. Hannah Arendt, "The Crisis in Culture," in *Between Past and Future* (New York: Penguin, 1977), www.scribd.com/doc/87670611/Arendt-The-Crisis-in-Culture-1968.

10. Mary Kaldor, "Nationalism and Globalisation," *Nations and Nationalism* 10, nos. 1/2 (2004): 161.

11. "Delving into the Genealogy of Jazz," *Current Opinion*, August 1919, 97, quoted in *Riffs and Choruses: A New Jazz Anthology*, ed. Andrew Clark (London: Continuum, 2001).

12. Jed Rasula, "Jazz as a Decal for the European Avant-Garde," in *Blackening Europe: The African American Presence*, ed. Heike Raphael-Hernandez (New York: Routledge, 2004).

## 1. Jazz and the Perfect Storm

1. Michael H. Hunt, *The American Ascendancy: How the United States Gained and Wielded Global Dominance* (University of North Carolina Press, 2007), 322.

2. Ronan Guilfoyle, *Mostly Music*, http://ronanguil.blogspot.co.uk/2010/02/grim .html.

3. Ibid.

4. Nate Chinen, "Doomsayers May Be Playing Taps, but Jazz Isn't Ready to Sing the Blues," *New York Times*, August 19, 2009.

5. Kurt Ellenberger, "If Not Jazz Education, What Will Rebuild Jazz Audiences?" *A Blog Supreme*, May 14, 2012, www.npr.org/blogs/ablogsupreme/2012/05/14 /151962816/if-not-jazz-education-what-will-rebuild-jazz-audiences#more.

6. "Recession's Effect Hit Majority in U.S.," *USA Today*, September 26, 2010.

7. "The Long-Term Effects of America's Great Recession for America's Youth," *Brookings*, September 3, 2010, www.brookings.edu/up-front/posts/2010/09/03-jobs -greenstone-looney.

8. Ted Gioia, introduction to "Is the Jazz World Recession Proof?" *jazz.com*, February 15, 2009.

9. Chinen, "Doomsayers May Be Playing Taps."

10. Jared Pauley, *Is the Jazz World Recession Proof? Jazz.com*, February 15, 2009.

11. Chinen, "Doomsayers May Be Playing Taps."

12. Bob Belden, interview with author, August 2008.

13. Darcy James Argue, "Dispatches from the Jazz Wars," *NewMusicbox*, July 16, 2008, www.newmusicboxorg/printerfriendly.nmbx?id=5635.

14. Mark Turner, interview with author, March 18, 2009.

15. Craig Taborn, interview with author, May 16, 2013.

16. Andrew Collier, *Jazz Global Connections, West View News: The Voice of the West Village*, May 2012, http://westviewnews.org/2012/05/jazz-global-connections.

17. Ibid.

18. Ibid.

19. Ronan Guilfoyle, quoted in Patrick Jarenwattananon, "NYC vs. the U.S.," *A Blog Supreme*, January 20, 2011, www.npr.org/blogs/ablogsupreme/2011/01/20 /133088318/nyc-vs-the-us. Quotation from Guilfoyle's *Mostly Music* blog, http:// ronanguil.blogspot.co.uk.

20. John Abercrombie, interview with author, February 24, 2004.

21. Patrick Jarenwattananon, "How Do Jazz Musicians Make Money?" *A Blog Supreme*, October 4, 2011, www.npr.org/blogs/ablogsupreme/2011/10/04/141061716 /how-do-jazz-musicians.

22. Joe Bowie, author interview, November 6, 2006.

23. "Jazz Musicians and Money from Music," Future of Music website, http://money.futureofmusic.org/jazz-musicians.

24. Jean Cook, quoted in Jarenwattananon, "How Do Jazz Musicians Make Money?"

25. Frøy Aagre, *Life on the Road: The Journal of a Travelling Jazz Musician*, ed. Stuart Nicholson, www.jazz.com.

26. Chinen, "Doomsayers May Be Playing Taps."

27. Guilfoyle, "NYC vs. the U.S."

28. Kurt Ellenberger, "Jazz in Crisis, Part II," http://frakathustra.wordpress .com/2010/06/08/jazz-in-crisis-part-ii-2.

29. Mark Christman, interview with author, September 30, 2008.

30. Michael J. West, "Jazz Education Network: Miracle Workers," *Jazz Times*, September 14, 2010.

31. Jazz Arts Group Multi Site Survey of Current and Prospective Jazz Ticket Buyers, June 2011, www.jazzartsgroup.org/wp-content/uploads/2011/06 /JAITicketBuyerStudy_ExecutiveSummary.pdf.

32. Terry Teachout, "Can Jazz Be Saved?" *Wall Street Journal*, August 9, 2009.

33. Jazz in America, "Jazz Education, part 2: The Rise in Formal Jazz Education," www.jazzinamerica.org/JazzResources/JazzEducation/Page/163.

34. Ibid., "Jazz Education, part 3: Jazz Education Today," www.jazzinamerica.org /JazzResources/JazzEducation/Page/164.

35. Hannah Arendt, "Crisis in Culture," www.scribd.com/doc/87670611/Arendt -The-Crisis-in-Culture-1968, 211.

36. Ibid., 207.

37. Tessa Blackstone, quoted in Martin Smith, "Arts Funding in a Cooler Climate: Subsidy, Commerce and the Mixed Economy of Culture in the UK," pamphlet, 12, www.wbceurope.com/downloads/ab_funding_in_cooler_climate_8.pdf.

38. Arendt, "Crisis in Culture," 207.

39. Ray B. Browne and Pat Browne, *A Guide to United States Popular Culture* (Madison: University of Wisconsin Press, 2001).

40. Krin Gabbard, "The Jazz Canon and Its Consequences," in *Annual Review of Jazz Studies* 6, ed. Edward Berger, David Cayer, and Dan Morgenstern (Metuchen, NJ: Scarecrow Press, 1993).

41. Max Harrison, "Review: 'The Jazz Cannon and Its Consequences' by Krin Gabbard," *Annual Review of Jazz Studies* 6 (1993), in *Journal of the International Association of Jazz Record Collectors* (Winter 1995): 76.

42. Ibid.

43. Gabbard, "The Jazz Canon and Its Consequences."

44. Harrison, "Review: 'The Jazz Canon and Its Consequences,'" 76.

45. Andrew Ross, *No Respect: Intellectuals and Popular Culture* (New York: Routledge, 1989), 187.

46. Arendt, "Crisis in Culture," 207.

47. Nicholas Payton, *The Cherub Speaks*, November 27, 2010, http: //nicholaspayton.wordpress.com/2011/11/27/om-why-jazz-isnt-cool-anymore.

48. Victor Fiorillo, *The Philly Post Blog*, January 10, 2012, http://blogs.phillymag .com/the_philly_post/2012/01/10call-jazz-call-black-american-music.

49. Ibid.

50. Ibid.

51. Christian Scott, liner notes, *Christian Scott: Christian Atunde Adjuah* (Concord Jazz 0888072332379).

52. Robert Glasper, quoted in Chris Barton, *Robert Glasper's "Black Radio": Is All That Jazz? LATimes.com*, March 22, 2012, http://latimes.com/entertainment/news /la-et-robert-glasper-20120322,0,407125.story.

53. Alison Crockett, "The Black Audience Question," *Independent Ear*, January 13, 2012, www.openskyjazz.com/2012/01/the-black-audience-question.

54. Marc Myers, *Jazzwax*, June 9, 2012, www.jazzwax.com/2012/06/weekend-wax -bits.html.

55. Will Layman, "Jazz Ain't Dead, But Charlie Parker Is—So Let's Move On, Shall We?" *Popmatters.com*, June 29, 2010, www.popmatters.com/pm/tools/print/126714.

56. Myers, *Jazzwax*, June 9, 2012.

57. "Drug Round-up Nets 131 in 24 Hours," *New York Post*, May 29, 1957.

58. James Lincoln Collier, *The Making of Jazz* (London: Granada Publishing, 1978), 407.

59. Ellenberger, "Jazz in Crisis, part I," May 30, 2010, http://frakathustra .wordpress.com/2010/05/30/jazz-in-crisis/.

60. Steven Graybow, "Jazz Notes: 2002 in Review," *Billboard*, December 28, 2002, 23.

61. Ibid.

62. Dan Ouellette, "The Year in Music and Touring 2007: Vocal Majority— Singing Scores the Sales in Jazz," *Billboard*, December 22, 2007, 76.

63. Ibid.

64. Elon University's Imagining the Internet Center and the Pew Research Center's Internet & American Life Project, 2012 report, www.elon.edu/e-web /predictions/expertsurveys/2012survey/future_generation_AO_2020.xhtml.

65. Ibid.

66. Jack DeJohnette, interview with author, June 2006.

67. "How Social Media Is Ruining Our Minds," *Assisted Living Today*, December 13, 2011, http://assistedlivingtoday.com/p/resources/social-media-is-ruining-our -minds-infographic.

68. John Storey, *An Introduction to Cultural Theory and Popular Culture* (New York: Longman, 1997), 188.

69. The experiments of Daniel Berlyne, Paul Vitz, Tuomas Eerola, and Adrian North are dealt with in greater length in Philip Ball, *The Music Instinct* (London: Bodley Head, 2010), 344–46, from which this information has been taken.

70. Carlos Santana, *Angels and Demons*, directed and produced by Jeremy Marre, BBC Productions, 2011.

71. Elon University's Imagining the Internet Center and the Pew Research Center's Internet & American Life Project, 2012 Report, www.elon.edu/e-web /predictions/expertsurveys/2012survey/future_generation_AO_2020.xhtml.

72. Branford Marsalis, interview with author, June 7, 2012.

73. Gary Burton, interview with author, March 14, 2013.

74. Branford Marsalis, interview with author, June 7, 2012.

75. Joe Lovano, interview with author, May 2009.

76. Ibid.

77. Christian McBride, interview with author, June 19, 2013.

78. Dan Nicholls, interview with Peter Bacon, *The Jazz Breakfast*, http: //thejazzbreakfast.com/acrossthetable/.

79. Francis Davis, *Bebop and Nothingness: Jazz and Pop at the End of the Century* (New York: Schirmer Books, 2001), 183.

80. Branford Marsalis, interview with author, June 7, 2012.

81. Ibid.

82. Chia-Jung Tsay, "Classical Music Competitions Judged by Sight Not Sound," *UCL News*, August 20, 2013, www.ucl.ac.uk/news/news-articles/0813/130820 -Classical-music-competitions-judged-by-sight-not-sound.

83. Bob Belden, interview with the author, July 4, 2012.

84. Bob Karlovits, "Beware of Those Blasts from the Past," *Pittsburgh Tribune-Review*, July 12, 2009, http://pittsburghlive.com/x/pittsburghtrib/ae/music/print _632797.html.

85. Joe Klopus, "Too Many Jazz Tribute Shows Leave Little Room for Innovation," *Kansas City Star*, July 29, 2009, www.kansascitystar.com/entertainment/v-print/story /1351685.html.

86. Gary Giddins, "Brand New Old Music," *Jazz Times*, December 2005, 24.

87. For example, at the 33rd International Association for Jazz Education convention held in New York City in 2006, one delegate (who prefers anonymity) was present at an informal discussion among a small number of jazz educators that centered on how important they felt the meeting was for them, since it was the only time they got to see live jazz, other than the undertakings of students at their respective institutions.

88. Pat Metheny, interview with author, October 21, 2004.

## 2. Does Jazz Have a Universal Meaning?

1. H. O. Brunn, *The Story of the Original Dixieland Jazz Band* (London: Jazz Book Club, 1963), 56.

2. Burnet Hershey, "Jazz Latitude," *New York Times Book Review and Magazine*, June 25, 1922, 8–9, quoted in *Keeping Time: Readings in Jazz History*, ed. Robert Walser (New York: Oxford University Press, 1999).

3. Felix Belair, Jr., "The United States Has Secret Sonic Weapon—Jazz," *New York Times*, November 6, 1955, 1.

4. Willis Conover, liner notes, Kenny Clarke—Francy Boland Big Band, *Jazz Is Universal* (London: Atlantic HA-K 8085).

5. American Jazz Institute, http://amjazzin.com.

6. J. T. Titon and M. Slobin, "The Music-culture as a World of Music," in *Worlds of Music: An Introduction to the Music of the World's Peoples*, ed. J. T. Titon (New York: Schirmer Books, 1996), 1.

7. Ian Cross and Elizabeth Tolbert, "Music and Meaning," in *The Oxford Handbook of Music Psychology*, ed. Susan Hallam, Ian Cross, and Michael Thaut (New York: Oxford University Press, 2008).

8. German Marshall Fund, Transatlantic Trends 2003, "Topline Data," http: //transatlantictrends.org, 49.

9. Igor Stravinsky and Robert Craft, *Expositions and Developments* (London: Faber and Faber, 1962), 101–3.

10. Leonard B. Meyer, *Emotion and Meaning in Music* (Chicago: University of Chicago Press, 1961), 265.

11. Ibid., 59.

12. Ibid., 155.

13. Ibid., 32.

14. Patrik N. Juslin and Daniel Västfjäll, "Emotional Responses to Music: The Need to Consider Underlying Mechanisms," *Behavioral and Brain Sciences* 31 (2008): 562.

15. Ibid., 559–75.

16. Ibid., 564.

17. "Rhythmic Entrainment" appears in adapted and edited form and is taken from Patrik Juslin, *Music and Emotion: Seven Questions, Seven Answers*, www.psyk.uu .se/digitalAssets/31/31196_Chapter.pdf.

18. Juslin and Västfjäll, "Emotional Responses to Music," 564.

19. Ibid., 565.

20. Patrik Juslin, "Communicating Emotion in Music Performance: A Review and a Theoretical Framework," in *Music and Emotion: Theory and Research*, ed. P. Juslin and J. A. Sloboda (New York: Oxford University Press, 2001), 309–37.

21. Juslin and Västfjäll, "Emotional Responses to Music," 566.

22. Ibid., 567.

23. Ibid., 568.

24. Ibid.

25. Ibid., 572.

26. Meyer, *Emotion and Meaning in Music*, 11.

27. Roy M. Prendergast, *Film Music: A Neglected Art* (New York: W. W. Norton, 1992), 222.

28. Meyer, *Emotion and Meaning in Music*, ix.

29. "Border Drug War Is Too Close for Comfort," *Los Angeles Times*, February 19, 2009.

30. Meyer, *Emotion and Meaning in Music*, 262.

31. Juslin and Västfjäll, "Emotional Responses to Music," 569.

32. Patrik N. Juslin, "Are Musical Emotions Invariant across Cultures?" *Emotion Review* 4, no. 12 (July 2012): 283.

33. Meyer, *Emotion and Meaning in Music*, 262.

34. Ibid.

35. Janet Wolff, *The Social Production of Art* (New York: New York University Press, 1989), 40.

36. Constant Lambert, *Music Ho!* (London: Hogarth Press, 1985), 154–55.

37. Wolff, *The Social Production of Art*, 4.

38. Joost Smiers, *Arts under Pressure: Promoting Cultural Diversity in the Age of Globalisation* (London: Zed Books, 2003), 82.

39. Clotaire Rapille, *The Culture Codes: An Ingenious Way to Understand Why People around the World Live and Buy as They Do* (New York: Broadway Books, 2006), 5–6.

40. T. Dowmunt, ed., *Channels of Resistance: Global Television and Local Empowerment* (London: British Film Institute, 1993).

41. Stuart Hall, "Encoding/Decoding," in *The Cultural Studies Reader*, ed. Simon During (New York: Routledge, 1999), 513.

42. Ibid., 516.

43. Ibid.

44. Ibid., 517.

45. R. W. S. Mendl, *The Appeal of Jazz* (London: Phillip Allan and Co., 1927), 96.

46. Ibid., 97, 98.

47. Ibid., 98.

48. Ralph Ellison, *Living with Music: Ralph Ellison's Jazz Writings*, ed. Robert G. O'Meally (New York: Modern Library, 2001), 58.

49. Ibid.

50. Ibid.

51. Donald Sassoon, *The Culture of the Europeans: From 1800 to the Present* (London: Harper Press, 2006), 935.

52. However, London ceased to be a market for American players after the 1935 Musicians Union ban, which was not lifted until the early 1960s. This meant that for British fans at least, live American jazz was denied them for more than twenty years.

53. Francis Newton, *The Jazz Scene* (London: Jazz Book Club, 1960), 246.

54. Ernest Borneman, *Harper's*, March 1947.

55. Kathy J. Ogren, *The Jazz Revolution: Twenties America and the Meaning of Jazz* (New York: Oxford University Press, 1989), 5.

56. Christina L. Baade, *Victory through Harmony: The BBC and Popular Music in World War II* (New York: Oxford University Press, 2012), 105.

57. *Metronome*, quoted in *Melody Maker*, August 5, 1944, 4.

58. Paul Wilson, interview with author, November 3, 2011.

59. Sir John Dankworth, interview with author, July 4, 2007.

60. Dave Brubeck, quoted in the liner notes of *In Concert: The Jazz Couriers* (Tempo TAP 22), one of many sources for the quotation that apparently originally appeared in *Melody Maker* magazine.

61. Named for the former British bandleader Geraldo, who after the war ran an agency booking bands for the Cunard Line.

62. Johnny Dankworth Club XI Quartet, "Second Eleven," on *Bop at Club Eleven* (Esquire S315).

63. Johnny Dankworth and his Orchestra, *Bundle from Britain*, Top Rank RS614.

64. *Downbeat*, August 6, 1959, 13–14.

65. Hall, "Encoding/Decoding," 513.

66. Ibid., 516.

67. "Jazz around the World," *Metronome Yearbook 1957* (New York: Metronome Corp, 1957), 54.

68. Peter J. Martin, "The Jazz Community as an Art World," in *The Source: Challenging Jazz Criticism 2*, ed. Tony Whyton (Leeds, UK: Leeds College of Music, 2005), 8–9.

69. Susan Marling, *American Affair: The Americanisation of Britain* (London: Boxtree Limited, 1993), 9–10.

70. Norman Granz, "Norman's Tale of Europe," *Downbeat*, June 4, 1954, 17.

71. Belair, "The United States Has Secret Sonic Weapon—Jazz," 1.

72. Hall, "Encoding/Decoding," 517, although I do suggest a broad application of Hall's principle rather than a semantic application.

73. Quoted in Keith Hatschek, "The Impact of American Jazz Diplomacy in Poland during the Cold War Era," *Jazz Perspectives* 4, no. 3 (December 2010): 256.

74. It is worth noting that Ray McKinley directing the Glenn Miller Orchestra played in Warsaw in 1957, while clarinettist Albert Nicholas played the 2nd Sopot Jazz Festival (in Poland) the same year, but neither *toured*. Brubeck was the first American jazz musician to tour behind the so-called Iron Curtain.

75. Quoted in Hatschek, "The Impact of American Jazz Diplomacy in Poland during the Cold War Era," 256.

76. U.S. Department of State, Bureau of Educational and Cultural Affairs website, http://exchanges.state.gov/culture/music.html.

77. S. Frederick Starr, *Red and Hot: Jazz in the Soviet Union* (New York: Oxford University Press, 1983), 209.

78. Juslin and Västfjäll, "Emotional Responses to Music," 569.

## 3. Jazz and American Cultural Power

1. Joseph S. Nye, Jr., *Bound to Lead: The Changing Nature of American Power* (New York: Basic Books, 1990), 267.

2. Ibid., 193.

3. Ibid., 194.

4. Derek Ellwood, "American Soft Power Comes through Its Culture," *The European* (Spring 2007).

5. John Rockwell, "Pop Culture, the New Colossus: American Culture as Power Export," *New York Times*, January 30, 1994.

6. Reinhold Wagnleitner, "The Idea of America: Pop Culture and Geopolitical Aesthetics," 7, www.ejournal.at/Forum/americanfun.html.

7. Joseph S. Nye, Jr., *Soft Power: The Means to Success in the World of Politics* (New York: Public Affairs, 2004), 97.

8. Maoz Azaryahu, "McIsrael? On the 'Americanization of Israel,'" *Israel Studies* 5, no. 1 (Spring 2000): 45.

9. Victoria de Grazia, *Irresistible Empire: America's Advance through 20th Century Europe* (Cambridge, MA: Belknap Press of Harvard University Press, 2005), 470; italics in the original.

10. Saritha Rai, "Tastes of India in U.S. Wrappers," *New York Times*, April 29, 2003, W1.

11. Eric Hobsbawm, *Globalisation, Democracy and Terrorism* (London: Little, Brown, 2007), 45.

12. Henry R. Luce, quoted in Geir Lundestad, *The United States and Western Europe since 1945* (New York: Oxford University Press, 2009), 24.

13. See Hobsbawm, *Globalisation, Democracy and Terrorism*, 68.

14. Ibid.

15. George Ritzer and Michael Ryan, "Americanisation, McDonalisation and Globalisation," in *Issues in Americanisation and Culture*, ed. Neil Campbell, Jude Davies, and George McKay (Edinburgh: Edinburgh University Press, 2004), 47–48.

16. Arthur Miller, *The Price: A Play* (New York: Penguin, 1968).

17. Lundestad, *The United States and Western Europe since 1945*, 1.

18. J. Bradford De Long and Barry Eichengreen, *The Marshall Plan as a Structural Adjustment Program*, www.j-bradford-delong.net/pdf_files/Marshall_Small.pdf.

19. Nye, *Soft Power*, 48–49.

20. Richard Kuisel, *Seducing the French: The Dilemma of Americanization* (Berkeley: University of California Press, 1996), 3.

21. Tony Judt, *Postwar: A History of Europe since 1945* (London: Pimlico, 2007), 338.

22. Ibid.

23. Richard Pells, *Not Like Us: How Europeans Have Loved, Hated, and Transformed American Culture since World War II* (New York: Basic Books, 1997), 241.

24. Judt, *Postwar*, 347–48.

25. Jimmy Page, *Legends: Roll over Beethoven, The Chess Records Saga*, produced and directed by James Maycock (BBC Wales, MMX).

26. George Melly, *Revolt into Style: Pop Arts in Britain* (London: Penguin Books, 1972), 8.

27. Rob Kroes, "Advertising and American Icons of Freedom," in *Here There and Everywhere: The Foreign Politics of American Culture*, ed. Reinhold Wagnleitner and Elaine Tyler May (Hanover, NH: University Press of New England, 2000), 274.

28. Ibid., 275.

29. Ibid., 276.

30. Judt, *Postwar*, 351.

31. For example, in Britain, Francis Williams was disturbed by the threat the "American way" posed to "Englishness" itself, complaining in his book *The American Invasion* (New York: Crown, 1962) that the British were accepting "more American culture than it is possible for society to assimilate and still remain true to its own virtues." In Italy, Michele Bottalico wrote in "A Place for All: Old and New Myths in the Italian Appreciation of American Literature," in *As Others Read Us: International Perspectives on American Literature*, ed. Huck Guttman (Amherst: University of Massachusetts Press, 1991) that "the more we import and absorb American cultural models, the more we should be scared of them, since . . . we risk losing our own cultural identity." In France, Jean-Jacques Servan-Schreiber expressed concern in his book *The American Challenge* (New York: Atheneum, 1968) at the implications of both American economic and cultural dominance on French culture.

32. Gülriz Büken, "Backlash: An Argument against the Spread of American Popular Culture in Turkey," in *Here There and Everywhere: The Foreign Politics of American Culture*, ed. Reinhold Wagnleitner and Elaine Tyler May (Hanover, NH: University Press of New England, 2000), 242.

33. Francis Fukuyama, *The End of History and the Last Man* (London: Hamish Hamilton, 1992), 126.

34. Reinhold Wagnleitner, "The Empire of the Fun, or Talkin' Soviet Union Blues: The Sound of Freedom and U.S. Cultural Hegemony in Europe," *Diplomatic History* 23, no. 3 (Wiley Online Library, Summer 1999), 512.

35. John Fraim, *Battle of Symbols: Emerging Global Dynamics of Advertising, Entertainment and Media* (London: Daimon Verlag, 2003), see ch. 8.

36. Joost Smiers, *Arts under Pressure: Promoting Cultural Diversity in the Age of Globalisation* (London: Zed Books, 2003), 34.

37. *Propaganda in Motion Pictures*, U.S. Congress, Senate Committee on Interstate Commerce, 1942, 423.

38. "Draft Outline of a Directive on Projection of America," Office of War Information, November 30, 1944, quoted in T. A. Wilson, "Selling America via the Silver Screen," in *Here, There and Everywhere: The Foreign Politics of American Culture*, ed. Reinhold Wagnleitner and Elaine Tyler May (Hanover, NH: University Press of New England, 2000), 84.

39. Emily S. Rosenberg, *Spreading the American Dream* (New York: Hill and Wang, 1982), 208.

40. J. Wasko, "Jurassic Park and the GATT: Hollywood and Europe: An Update," in *Democracy and Communication in the New Europe: Change and Continuity in the East and West*, ed. F. Corcoran and P. Preston (Cresskill, NJ: Hampton Press, 1995), 166.

41. Smiers, *Arts under Pressure*, 35.

42. Judt, *Postwar*, 230.

43. Brian Glasser, e-mail to author, January 25, 2012.

44. Judt, *Postwar*, 353.

45. Kroes, "Advertising and American Icons of Freedom," 278.

46. Jean-Michel Valantin, *Hollywood, the Pentagon and Washington* (London: Anthem Press, 2005), 13.

47. Brian Glasser, e-mail to author, January 25, 2012.

48. Valantin, *Hollywood, the Pentagon and Washington*, 13.

49. Ibid., 18.

50. Ibid.

51. Ibid., 21.

52. Ibid., 23.

53. For example, *Blackhawk Down*, *Pearl Harbor*, *Apollo 13*, *True Lies*, *Executive Decision*, and *Air Force One*.

54. David L. Robb, *Operation Hollywood: How the Pentagon Shapes and Censors Movies* (New York: Prometheus Books, 2004), 343.

55. Jonathan Turley, quoted in Robb, *Operation Hollywood*, 13–14.

56. Ibid., 17.

57. Valantin, *Hollywood, the Pentagon and Washington*, 137.

58. Matthew Alford and Robbie Graham, "An Offer They Couldn't Refuse," *Guardian Film and Music*, November 14, 2008, 3.

59. Ibid.

60. Ibid.

61. Ibid.

62. Neal Gabler, *Life: The Movie* (New York: Vintage Books, 1998).

63. Sam Blumenfeld, *New American*, www.newamerican.com, March 3, 2011.

64. Zbigniew Brzezinski, *The Choice: Global Domination or Global Leadership?* (New York: Basic Books, 2004), 185.

65. Wagnleitner, "The Idea of America," 2.

66. Rob Kroes, "American Empire and Cultural Imperialism: A View from the Receiving End," conference at the German Historical Institute, Washington, DC, March 25–27, 1999, 3, http://webdoc.sub.gwdg.de/ebook/p/2005/ghi_12/www.ghi-dc.org/conpotweb/westernpapers/kroes.pdf.

67. Ibid., 5.

68. Keith Hatschek, "The Impact of American Jazz Diplomacy in Poland during the Cold War Era," *Jazz Perspectives* 4, no. 3 (December 2010): 253.

69. See http://photos.state.gov/libraries/cambodia/30486/Publications/what_is_american_culture.pdf.

70. *Congressional Record—House*, September 23, 1987, H7825–27, quoted in *Keeping Time: Readings in Jazz History*, ed. Robert Walser (New York: Oxford University Press, 1999), 333.

71. Lawrence W. Levine writes that "jazz is an integral part of American culture" in "Jazz and American Culture," in *The Jazz Cadence of American Culture*, ed. Robert G. O'Meally (New York: Columbia University Press, 1998), 432.

72. And project a positive image they did as harbingers of jazz modernism—local musicians were convinced they had "special" instruments to make possible some of the remarkable instrumental techniques the band displayed.

73. Reid Badger, *A Life in Ragtime: A Biography of James Reese Europe* (New York: Oxford University Press, 1995), 89.

74. Ibid., 192.

75. James Reese Europe with Hellfighters, newsreel footage in France 1918, French television documentary *Harlem in Montmartre* (2009, WNNET.ORG Properties LLC., Vanguard Documentaries). However, www.youtube.com/watch?v=j -nCIGtIuj4 includes an extended shot of the band marching through a French village shown in part in the above, but only black and white stills of the Paris concert. There is also additional footage of the Hellfighters' embarkation for France, playing on the deck of the troopship.

76. This would be at the insistence of the US authorities, since segregation was not practiced in France, and especially not so in Paris, where black performers discovered a racial climate quite unlike the one they were used to at home. As a result, several had already settled in Paris, and more would do so after hostilities ceased in 1918.

77. Badger, *A Life in Ragtime*, 170.

78. Emmet J. Scott, *Official History of the American Negro in the World War* (Washington, DC, 1919), 304, quoted in William A. Shack, *Harlem to Montmartre* (Berkeley: University of California Press, 2001), 18.

79. Derek Jewell, "Sound of the Forties," *Sunday Times Magazine*, provenance uncertain, probably ca. 1968, 14.

80. Ibid.

81. Joseph S. Nye, Jr., *Bound to Lead: The Changing Nature of American Power* (New York: Basic Books, 1990), 32.

82. Geoffrey Butcher, liner notes, *Glenn Miller: The Lost Recordings* (Happy Days CDHD 401/2).

83. *Downbeat*, August 27, 1952.

84. Ibid., 1.

85. "Acceptance and Solidification Could Summarize the History of the Year," in *Metronome Year Book 1957* (New York: Metronome Corp, 1957), 52.

86. Hatschek, "The Impact of American Jazz Diplomacy in Poland during the Cold War Era," 270.

87. "Acceptance and Solidification Could Summarize the History of the Year," in *Metronome Year Book 1957*, 11.

88. *Downbeat*, July 10, 1958, 5.

89. Ibid.

90. Art Buchwald, quoted in ibid.

91. *New York Times*, May 5, 1958.

92. "Goodman Men Sound Off about Soviet Tour," *Downbeat*, August 30, 1962, 12–13.

93. Bill Crow, "To Russia, without Love," Part 1, Part 2, Part 3, Part 4, *The Note*, vols. 22, 23, 24, 25 nos. 56, 57, 58, 59, 2011–13. This account was first published in 1986 in the *Gene Less Jazzletter* and can be seen on Bill Crow's website, www .billcrowbass.com.

94. Tomasz Stanko, interview with author, March 7, 2001.

95. *Washington Post*, April 6, 2008.

96. P. M. von Eschen, "Satchmo Blows Up the World: Jazz, Race and Empire during the Cold War," in *Here, There and Everywhere*, 166.

97. Pells, *Not Like Us*, 84.

98. *Downbeat*, January 17, 1963, 18.

99. Von Eschen, "Satchmo Blows Up the World," 174.

100. Laurence Bergreen, *Louis Armstrong: An Extravagant Life* (London: Harper Collins, 1997), 461.

101. Dizzy Gillespie with Al Fraser, *Dizzy: To Be or Not to Bop* (London: W. H. Allen, 1980), 425.

102. Cynthia P. Schneider, "Discussion Papers in Diplomacy No. 94: Culture Communicates: US Diplomacy That Works," Netherlands Institute of International Relations, Clingendael, September 2004, 9.

103. *Washington Post*, April 6, 2008.

104. Arch Puddington, *Broadcasting Freedom: The Cold War Triumph of Radio Free Europe and Radio Liberty* (Lexington: University Press of Kentucky, 2000), 188.

105. Gene Lees, *Friends along the Way* (New Haven, CT: Yale University Press, 2003), 253.

106. *Downbeat*, January 31, 1963, 20.

107. Quoted in Schneider, "Discussion Papers in Diplomacy No. 94: Culture Communicates," 8.

108. Hatschek, "The Impact of American Jazz Diplomacy in Poland during the Cold War Era," 253.

109. Schneider, "Discussion Papers in Diplomacy No. 94: Culture Communicates," 10.

110. Gillespie with Fraser, *Dizzy*, 413–27.

111. Dave Brubeck, *Moscow Nights* (Concord CJ-353), liner notes, "The Success of this tour could not have been possible without the tremendous efforts made on our behalf by the foreign service officers stationed in the USSR."

112. Charles Z. Wick, quoted in Andrew Ross, *No Respect: Intellectuals and Pop Culture* (New York: Routledge, 1989), 8.

113. Jason Rabin, "This Year's Messengers on the Rhythm Road," *Jazz Times*, March 15, 2011.

114. Wagnleitner, "The Empire of the Fun, or Talkin' Soviet Union Blues," 506.

115. *Prospect*, no. 41 (May 20, 1999), www.prospectmagazine.co.uk.

116. Quoted in Ed Vulliamy, *1989 and All That: Plastic People of the Universe and the Velvet Revolution*, *The Observer*, September 6, 2009.

117. *Prospect*, no. 41 (May 20, 1999).

118. Bill Nichols, "How Rock n'Roll Freed the World," *USA Today*, November 6, 2003.

119. Nye, *Soft Power*, 49.

120. "A Nation Hails Its New General as Clinton Puts Faith in Soft Power," *Guardian*, December 21, 2011, 18–19.

121. Nye, *Soft Power*, 107–10.

122. Ibid., 127.

123. Ibid., 112.

124. Stuart Nicholson, *Is Jazz Dead (Or Has It Moved to a New Address)?* (New York: Routledge, 2005), 230.

125. "BBC's World Service," *Guardian*, January 20, 2005.

126. Bruce Stokes and Richard Wike, "World to America: We Want Soft, Not Hard Power," CNN World, http://globalpublicsquare.blogs.cnn.com/2012/08/09/world-to-america-we-want-soft-not-hard-power.

127. The Free Dictionary, www.thefreedictionary.com/halo+effect.

128. "Apple Shares Surge on Big Profits," http://news.bbc.co.uk/1/hi/business/4172211.stm.

129. Neal M. Rosendorf, "Social and Cultural Globalization: Concepts, History, and America's Role," in *Governance in a Globalizing World*, ed. Joseph Nye and John D. Donahue (Washington, DC: Brookings Institution, 2000), 123, quoted in Nye, *Soft Power*, 12. Interestingly, Nye concedes that "films that make the United States attractive in China or Latin America may have the opposite effect and actually reduce American soft power in Saudi Arabia or Pakistan." But "[in] some cases, such as Iran, the same Hollywood images that repel the ruling mullahs may be attractive to the younger generation. In China, the attraction and rejection of American culture among different groups may cancel each other out" (12–13).

130. For example, at the time of writing (2011), as far as I can trace no UK university, conservatory, or college offering jazz degree courses includes courses on the history of jazz in the United Kingdom, despite the United Kingdom's having produced many world-class musicians and world-class recorded performances, not least by the likes of Michael Garrick, Mike Westbrook, Evan Parker, John Surman, Joe Harriott, Ian Carr, Stan Tracey, John Dankworth, Cleo Laine, Norma Winstone, John Taylor, Kenny Wheeler, Tony Oxley, John McLaughlin, George Shearing, Victor Feldman, Tubby Hayes, Tony Coe, Derek Bailey, and many more. Significantly, the United Kingdom is not alone in this.

131. E. Taylor Atkins, "Toward a Global History of Jazz," in *Jazz Planet*, ed. E. Taylor Atkins (Jackson: University Press of Mississippi, 2003), xxiii.

132. Among many European jazz musicians to suffer this fate, the British pianist Stan Tracey springs to mind, while on the other side of the globe, in Australia, so does pianist Mike Nock. There are, of course, hundreds of others.

133. John Dankworth, "Our Jazz Is British!" *Melody Maker*, December 7, 1963, 3.

134. Richard E. Nisbett and Timothy DeCamp Wilson, "The Halo Effect: Evidence for Unconscious Alteration of Judgments," *Journal of Personality and Social Psychology* 35, no. 4 (April 1977): 250–56.

135. Todd Gitlin, in Kuisel, *Seducing the French*, 230.

## 4. The Globalization of Jazz

1. Tom Murse, "How Much U.S. Debt Does China Really Own?" at http://usgovinfo.about.com/od/moneymatters/ss/How-Much-US-Debt-Does-China-Own.htm.

2. See World Health Organization, www.mrglobalization.com/globalisation/252-globalization--origin-of-the-word.

3. John Tomlinson, *Globalization and Culture* (Chicago: University of Chicago Press, 1999), 2.

4. Mary Kaldor, "Nationalism and Globalization," *Nations and Nationalism* 10, nos. 1/2 (2004): 161.

5. For example, Charley Gerard, "Battling the Black Music Ideology," in *Riffs &*

*Choruses*, ed. Andrew Clark (London and New York: Continuum, 2001), 201, in which Gerard points out that Amri Bakara "has successfully proved . . . change [in jazz] is not the result of musical developments *per se* but of socio-political events."

6. Ted Gioia in *The Future of Jazz*, ed. Yuval Taylor (Chicago: A Capella Books, 2002), 154–55.

7. Tom Hanahoe, *America Rules* (Dingle, Ireland: Brandon, 2003), 13.

8. Ibid.

9. World Development Movement, "Developing Alternatives: A Discussion Paper," 2, accessed April 2013, www.wdm.org.uk.

10. Raymond Williams, *The Long Revolution* (Harmondsworth: Penguin, 1965), 66.

11. J. N. Pieterse, "Globalization and Culture: Three Paradigms," in *McDonaldization*, ed. G. Ritzer (London: Pine Forge Sage, 2006), 278–83.

12. *Globalizing Cultures: The Question of Cultural Diversity*, accessed May 2011, https://globalsociology.pbworks.com/w/page/14711190/Globalizing%20Cultures%3A %20The%20Question%20of%20Cultural%20Diversity.

13. Thomas L. Friedman, *The World Is Flat* (London: Penguin Books, 2006), 477.

14. Arjun Appadurai, "Disjuncture and Difference in the Global Cultural Economy," in *The Cultural Studies Reader*, ed. Simon During (London and New York: Routledge, 1993), 220–30.

15. Ibid., 221.

16. Ibid.

17. Roland Robertson, "Globalization: Time-Space and Homogeneity-Hetrogeneity," in *Global Modernities*, ed. M. Featherstone, S. Lash, and R. Robertson (London: Sage, 1995), 27.

18. Appadurai, "Disjuncture and Difference in the Global Cultural Economy," 220–30.

19. Neil Campbell, Jude Davies, and George McKay, eds., *Issues in Americanisation and Culture* (Edinburgh, UK: Edinburgh University Press, 2004), 10.

20. D. Towers, *Wal-Mart: A Glocalized Company* (2004), www.towers.fr/essays/Wal -Mart%20a%20Glocalised%20company.pdf.

21. Roland Robertson, *Globalization: Social Theory and Global Culture* (Newbury Park, CA, and London: Sage, 1992).

22. Luciana Ferreira Moura Mendonca, "The Local and the Global in Popular Music: The Brazilian Music Industry, Local Culture and Public Policies," in *Global Culture*, ed. Dina Crane, Nobuko Kawashima, and Ken'ichi Kawasaki (New York: Routledge, 2002), 107.

23. Russell White, "Sign of a Black Planet: Hip-Hop and Globalization," in *Issues in Americanisation and Culture*, ed. Neil Campbell, Jude Davies, and George McKay (Edinburgh, UK: Edinburgh University Press, 2004), 173–74.

24. F. Lerdahl and R. S. Jackendoff, *A Generative Theory of Tonal Music* (Cambridge, MA: MIT Press, 1983).

25. *Congressional Record—House*, September 23, 1987, H7825–27.

26. B. B. Kachru, *English in the World: Teaching and Learning the Language and Literatures* (Cambridge, MA: Cambridge University Press, 1985), 30.

27. Billy Taylor, *Jazz Piano: A History* (Dubuque, IA: Wm. C. Brown Company, 1982), 6–7.

28. Keith Wood, introduction to the opening of the 2013 Six Nations Rugby Championship, BBC Television, BBC1, February 2, 2013.

29. Tomlinson, *Globalization and Culture*, 270.

30. S. Strange, *The Retreat of the State: The Diffusion of Power in the World Economy* (Cambridge, MA: Cambridge University Press, 1996), 4.

31. S. Strange, "The Declining Authority of States," in *The Global Transformations Reader: An Introduction to the Globalization Debate*, ed. David Held and Anthony McGrew (Cambridge, MA: Polity Press, 2003), 133.

32. Zbigniew Brzezinski, "The Dilemma of the Last Sovereign," *American Interest* 1, no.1 (Autumn 2005).

33. Christian von Campe, "Globalization and Its Effects on Nationalism," www .atlantic-community.org/app/webroot/files/articlepdf/Globalisation%20and %20Nationalism.pdf.

34. Liah Greenfield, *Nationalism: Five Roads to Modernity* (Cambridge, MA: Harvard University Press, 1992), 10–11.

35. Tony Whyton, "Europe and the New Jazz Studies," in *Eurojazzland*, ed. Luca Cerchiari, Laurent Cugny, and Franz Kerschbaumer (Boston: Northeastern University Press, 2012), 370; italics added.

36. Robertson, *Globalization*, and "Globalization Theory 2000+: Major Problematics," in *Handbook of Social Theory*, ed. George Ritzer and Barry Smart (London: Sage, 2001), 458–71.

37. Brian Large, *Smetana* (London: Duckworth, 1970), 250.

38. John Clapham, "Dvořák, Antonín (Leopold)," in *The New Grove Dictionary of Music and Musicians, Vol. 5*, ed. Stanley Sadie (London: MacMillan, 1995), 765.

39. Given America's desire to assert its own unique national culture within music, should it come as a surprise that jazz musicians beyond Manhattan Island should seek to do the same?

40. Eric Hobsbawm, *On History* (London: Abacus, 2002), 358.

41. Tony Whyton, *Jazz Icons: Heroes, Myths and the Jazz Tradition* (Cambridge, MA: Cambridge University Press, 2010), 116. As an aside, we assume Holiday was not actually in a basket while eating chicken, as Whyton appears to claim.

42. Hobsbawm, *On History*, 358.

43. Ibid., 358.

44. Ibid., 360.

45. Whyton, "Europe and the New Jazz Studies," 367.

46. Krin Gabbard, "Signifyin(g) the Phallus: *Mo' Better Blues* and Representations of Jazz Trumpet," in *Representing Jazz*, ed. Krin Gabbard (Durham and London: Duke University Press, 1995), 104–30.

47. Randall Sandke, "Unforgivable Whiteness," *Journal of Jazz Studies* 7, no. 1 (Spring 2011): 116.

48. Ibid., 117.

49. Ibid., 109.

50. Krin Gabbard, *Hotter than That: The Trumpet, Jazz, and American Culture* (New York: Faber and Faber, 2008), 199.

51. Sandke, "Unforgivable Whiteness," 118.

52. Ibid., 119.

53. Whyton, "Europe and the New Jazz Studies."

54. Steven Vertovek, *Transnationalism* (New York: Routledge, 2009), 13.

55. Ibid., 18.

56. Ibid.

57. Paul Gilroy, *The Black Atlantic: Modernity and Double Consciousness* (New York: Verso, 1993), 15.

58. L. Basch, N. Glick Schiller, and C. Szanton Blanc, eds., *Nations Unbound: Transnational Projects, Postcolonial Predicaments and Deterritorialized Nation States* (Basel, Switzerland: Gordon and Breach, 1994).

59. Gilroy, *The Black Atlantic*, 58.

60. Ibid., 1–2.

61. Paul Gilroy, "Diaspora and the Detours of Identity," in *Identity and Difference*, ed. Kathryn Woodward (Milton Keynes, UK: Open University, 1997), 329.

62. Ibid., 334.

63. Ibid., 329.

64. John McLeod, "Diaspora and Utopia: Reading the Recent Work of Paul Gilroy and Caryl Phillips," in *Diasporic Literature and Theory: Where Now?* ed. Mark Shackleton (Cambridge, MA: Cambridge Scholars Publishing, 2008), 17.

65. Ien Ang, "Together in Difference: Beyond the Diaspora, into Hybridity," *Asian Studies Review* 27, no. 2 (2003): 141–54.

66. Dr. Tony Whyton, "Jazz as National and Transnational Practice," lecture, April 2012. It is perhaps unsurprising that in order to explain jazz's international presence it is described as a transnational practice, since it conforms to Gilroy's diaspora/transnational theories. But as Steven Vertovek has pointed out in his study *Transnationalism* (New York: Routledge, 2009), since "transnationalism is a manifestation of globalization, its processes and outcomes are multiple and messy," suggesting that such brash alignment between jazz and transnationalism must be approached with caution. Although in the popular press words like "global," "international," "transnational," and "multinational" appear interchangeable, globalization theorists make a careful distinction between the international and the transnational. Much research has been conducted in the global economy that specifically avoids the conflation of transnational and international processes. In his book *Globalization and the Nation State* (London: Palgrave, 2011), Robert J. Hilton points out that "international" is understood to mean relationships *between* nation states. So, despite jazz's international presence, it does not follow that it is a "transnational" music; rather it is an international music with its origins in one country (the United States) that is/has been communicated/exported to other countries through the trade routes of the global cultural economy.

Certainly jazz was not communicated to the rest of the world through transnationalism or diasporic migration. Donald Sassoon has noted in *The Culture of the Europeans: From 1800 to the Present* (London: Harper Press, 2006, 935) that "the spread of jazz to Europe in the 1920s was the first great trend in music history *to occur mainly through recording*" [author's italics]. It might be said that jazz is a genre of music that operates through multilayered structures involving three dimensions: the international, the national, and the local. Transnational, however, stands *above* national determination and control—for example, the integration of the world's financial markets that in 2007 saw trading reach $3 trillion *per day*, which is clearly beyond any single nation's ability to control or regulate. From "international" to "transnational," then, involves a significant qualitative change in strategic orientation and thinking. For example, General Motor's Opel brand is transnational in scope. The Opel Agila was badge engineered for sale around the world, a transnational product sold in a wide range of global markets. In the IT world the products of Microsoft, Sun Microsystems, and Apple may be said to be transnational, whereby the characteristics of the product, like the Opel Agila, remain the same wherever purchased. This has advantages of brand recognition for consumers—wherever they are in the world, they know they can turn to the brand reliability of, say, a Coca-Cola, since it is a transnational product maintaining the same characteristics wherever purchased.

Transnational fast food outlets operate on the same premise—for example, a McDonald's hamburger tastes the same in Times Square as it does in Red Square. Thus when Whyton argues that jazz is a "transnational practice," he appears to be arguing in favor of the hamburgerization of jazz—the same product with the same characteristics irrespective of location, so that a jazz ensemble in the Blue Note jazz club in Manhattan sounds the same as a jazz ensemble in the Blue Note jazz club in Milan. This argument, of course, presents a neat symmetry with Gilroy's diaspora/transnationalism theory, which blots out cultural differentiation, since diaspora presents an alternative to the conception of "absolutely distinctive cultures."

67. Whyton, "Europe and the New Jazz Studies," 366–80.

68. Ibid., 376.

69. Gilroy, "Diaspora and the Detours of Identity," 334.

70. Campbell, Davies, and McKay, "Issues in Americanisation and Culture," 24.

71. Gilroy, "Diaspora and the Detours of Identity," 328.

72. Ibid.

73. Ien Ang, "Together-in-Difference: Beyond Diaspora, into Hybridity," *Asian Studies Review* 27, no. 2 (2003): 141–54. www.uws.edu.au/__data/assets/pdf_file /0006/156957/Ang_Together-In-Difference_ICS_Pre-Print_Final.pdf.

74. Gilroy, "Diaspora and the Detours of Identity," 334.

75. Ibid., 328.

76. By the time of his seventieth birthday, for example, the Finnish nationalist composer Jean Sibelius was the most popular living composer in the United States and Britain.

77. Whyton, "Europe and the New Jazz Studies," 370.

78. Indeed, nobody has ever dismissed Fauré's music in this way. Insofar as jazz musicians creating music that reflects their own cultural identity, the end they have achieved has in many cases resulted in laudatory reviews and success in critics' polls in jazz magazines such as *Jazzwise, Jazznytt, Jazz Special, OJ, Jazzthing, Musica Jazz, Jazzit, Jazzthetik,* and more.

79. Whyton, "Europe and the New Jazz Studies," 376; author's italics.

80. Gilroy, "Diaspora and the Detours of Identity," 328.

81. Ibid.

82. Whyton, "Europe and the New Jazz Studies," 376.

83. Kenan Malik, "Between Camps," *Independent on Sunday*, June 11, 2000.

84. Philip Ball, *The Music Instinct* (London: Bodley Head, 2010), 383; author's italics.

85. Ibid., 399.

86. Peter J. Burkholder, Donald Grout, and Claude Palisca, *A History of Western Music* (London: W. W. Norton, 1996).

87. Aniruddh Patel's study of language patterns of rhythm and melody cited in Ball, *The Music Instinct*, 359.

88. Ibid.

89. Antony Hopkins, *Understanding Music* (London: J. M. Dent and Sons, 1979), 31.

90. Danlee Mitchell and Jack Logan, "Basic Element of Music: Melody," www .cartage.org.lb/en/themes/arts/music/elements/elemofmusic/melody/melody.htm.

91. Michael Wollny, interview with author, April 25, 2006.

92. Jef Neve, interview with author, November 9, 2006.

93. Nils Lindberg, interview with author, November 2002.

94. Lera Boroditsky, "Lost in Translation," *Wall Street Journal*, July 23, 2010.

95. Frances Simon, "How Language Influences Culture," March 15, 2009, www .helium.com/items/1376376-how-language-influences-culture-cultural-identity.

96. Clotaire Rapaille, *The Culture Code* (New York: Broadway Books, 2006), 10–11.

97. Richard Dawkins, "Postmodernism Disrobed," *Nature* 394 (July 9, 1998): 141–43.

98. Margaret Mead, *Keep Your Powder Dry: An Anthropologist Looks at America* (New York: William Morrow and Company, 1942/43), 21.

99. Marjane Satrapi, interview at www.lesinrocks.com/2007/06/26/cinema /actualite-cinema/entretien-marjane-satrapi-et-vincend-paronnaud-persepolis-0607 -1159944.

100. Krin Gabbard, "The Jazz Canon and Its Consequences," *Annual Review of Jazz Studies* 6, ed. Edward Berger, David Cayer, and Dan Morgenstern (Metuchen, NJ: Scarecrow Press, 1993).

101. Dawkins, "Postmodernism Disrobed," 141–43.

102. Whyton, *Jazz Icons*, 148. Yet despite these high aspirations, Whyton gives every indication of being somewhat divorced from reality and any kind of methodology when he asks: "How vibrant would the European jazz scene be if we had . . . musicians playing 'carbon neutral jazz' or 'vegan jazz,' 'pride in university educated jazz' or 'economic downturn jazz'?" in *Eurojazzland*, 377.

103. Sandke, "Unforgivable Whiteness," 119.

104. Ibid.

105. Paul Gilroy, "Diaspora and the Detours of Identity," 328.

106. Sandke, "Unforgivable Whiteness," 112.

107. Ibid., 107.

108. Whyton, "Jazz as National and Transnational Practise."

109. Ibid.

110. For example, Arild Andersen, *Sagn*, and Dag Arnesen, *Rusler Rundt Grieg*; Geir Lysne Ensemble, *The Grieg Code*; and the Kjell Karlsen Big Band, *Edvard Grieg in a Jazz Mood*.

111. Eric Kjellberg, "Swedish Folk Tone in Jazz," *Jazz Facts 1998* (SMIC, Stockholm 1998), 2–3.

112. On the Legacy Edition of *Round about Midnight* (COL 519957-2), released in 2005, Stan Getz is credited with the arrangement of "Dear Old Stockholm."

113. Bjørn Kolstad, "European Jazz," *Bergens Tidende*, February 4, 1955, quoted in

James W. Dickenson, *From Grieg to Garbarek: Norwegian Jazz and National Identity* (Brumunddal: Knippa Forlag, 2011), 32.

114. Whyton, "Jazz as National and Transnational Practise."

115. E-mail exchanges with Bugge Wesseltoft and Nils Petter Molvaer, December 2012.

116. Whyton, "Europe and the New Jazz Studies," 376.

117. Campbell, Davies, and McKay, "Issues in Americanisation and Culture," 24.

118. Whyton, "Europe and the New Jazz Studies," 368.

119. Ibid., 370.

120. Gilroy, "Diaspora and the Detours of Identity," 335.

121. Andrew Solomon, "The Jazz Martyr," *New York Times Magazine*, February 9, 1997, 34.

122. Sandke, "Unforgivable Whiteness," 111.

123. Ibid.

124. Paul Gilroy, *Is Jazz Dead?* BBC Radio 4 broadcast, transmitted January 1, 2013.

125. Laura Chrisman, "Journeying to Death: A Critique of Paul Gilroy's *Black Atlantic*," *Crossings*, http://crossings.binghamton.edu/chrisman.htm.

126. Carl Woideck, *Charlie Parker: His Music and Life* (Ann Arbor: University of Michigan Press, 1996), 41, 172, 217.

127. Ginevra House, Archival Sound Recordings Engagement Officer, British Library Sound Recordings Blog, "Freeing Jazz in the Sixties," July 9, 2009, http://britishlibrary.typepad.co.uk/archival_sounds/2009/07/freeing-jazz-in-the-sixties.html.

128. Trevor Watts, *Jazz in Britain: Interviews with Modern and Contemporary Jazz Musicians, Composers and Improvisers by George McKay*, at www.academia.edu/193121/Jazz_in_Britain_interviews_with_modern_and_contemporary_jazz_musicians_composers_and_improvisers.

129. John Dankworth, "Our Jazz Is British!" *Melody Maker*, December 7, 1963, 3.

130. Mike Westbrook, *Interviews with Modern and Contemporary Jazz Musicians, Composers and Improvisers by George McKay*.

131. Ian Carr, *Music Outside: Contemporary Jazz in Britain* (London: Northway Publications, 2008), 25.

132. Michael Garrick, liner notes, *Impressed with Gilles Peterson* (Universal 064 749 2).

133. Trevor Bannister, "Introduction," in Michael Garrick with Trevor Bannister, *Dusk Fire: Jazz in English Hands* (Reading: Springdale Publishing, 2010), v.

134. Norma Winstone, interview with author, January 20, 2011.

135. Jasper van't Hof, interview with Martin Brock, *Ahlener Zeitung*, April 2011.

136. Kjellberg, "Swedish Folk Tone in Jazz," 4.

137. General Duze, quoted in Gwen Ansell, *Soweto Blues: Jazz, Popular Music & Politics in South Africa* (London: Continuum, 2004), 31.

138. Acácio de Camargo Piedade, "Brazilian Jazz and Friction of Musicalities," in *Planet Jazz*, ed. E. Taylor Atkins (Jackson: University Press of Mississippi, 2003), 52.

139. Ibid., 53.

140. Ibid., 54.

141. Ibid.

142. Mike Zwerin, "French-Vietnamese Guitarist Breaks Barriers," *New York Times*, January 17, 2001.

143. Many thanks to Risa Zincke of Intermusic, Vienna, the late Joe Zawinul's manager, for drawing my attention to this aspect of Joe Zawinul's musical personality, providing examples on DVD and the quotation from Zawinul, "Which he often said."

144. Again thanks to Risa Zincke.

145. Friedrich Gulda, liner notes, *Friedrich Gulda and Joe Zawinul: Music for Two Pianos* (Jazzline N 77 008).

146. Hugh Masekela, liner notes, *Hugh Masekela: The Lasting Impression of Ooga Booga* (Verve 531 630–2).

147. *Inspired by Tradition: Kalevala Poetry in Finnish Music* is a valuable book-length study that deals with the *Kalevala*'s influence on Finnish jazz, rock, and classical music.

148. *Friedrich Gulda—The Wanderer between Worlds*, quoted in liner notes, *Friedrich Gulda and Joe Zawinul: Music for Two Pianos* (Jazzline N 77 008).

149. Wouter Turkenburg, e-mail to author, September 2003.

150. Jef Neve, interview with author, November 9, 2006.

151. Ibid.

152. Esbjorn Svensson, interview with author, September 6, 2004.

153. Jef Neve, interview with author, November 9, 2006.

154. Michael Wollny, interview with author, September 25, 2010.

155. Christof Lauer, interview with author, October 2006.

156. Bengt-Arne Wallin, liner notes, *Old Folklore in Swedish Modern* (Dux DPL 700).

157. Nils Landgren, interview with author, October 2006.

158. Dave Stapleton, interview with author, November 2012.

159. Christof Lauer, interview with author, October 2006.

160. Danilio Perez, interview with author, August 23, 2010.

161. E. Taylor Atkins, "Toward a Global History of Jazz," in *Jazz Planet*, ed. Atkins (Jackson: University Press of Mississippi, 2003), xxiv.

162. Esbjorn Svensson, interview with author, June 1, 2006.

163. Ibid.

## 5. Jazz and Modernism

1. Jed Rasula, "Jazz and American Modernism," in *The Cambridge Companion to American Modernism*, ed. Walter Kalaidjian (Cambridge, MA: Cambridge University Press, 2005), 157.

2. The *Catholic Telegraph*, quoted on www.historylearningsite.co.uk/1920s _America.htm.

3. "Drum Taps," *Metronome*, July 1922, reproduced in *Jazz in Print (1856–1929): An Anthology of Selected Early Readings in Jazz History*, ed. Karl Koenig (Hillsdale, NY: Pendragon Press, 2002), 197.

4. "The Jazz Problem: Opinions of Prominent Public Men and Musicians," *Etude Music Magazine*, cover feature, August 1924.

5. Kenyon Cox, "Cubists and Futurists Are Making Insanity Pay," *New York Times*, March 16, 1913.

6. Joyce's *Ulysses* was first published on February 2, 1922, the author's fortieth birthday, by the Dijon-based printer Darantiere in a first edition of one thousand copies. It became legal to publish *Ulysses* in the United States only after December 6, 1933, when U.S. District Judge John M. Wollsey ruled the novel was not pornographic.

7. For example, Kevin Jackson in *Constellation of Genius 1922: Modernism Year One* (London: Hutchinson, 2012).

8. Mark S. Harvey, "Jazz and Modernism: Changing Conceptions of Innovation and Tradition," in *Jazz in Mind: Essays on the History and Meaning of Jazz*, ed. Reginald T. Buckner and Steven Weiland (Detroit: Wayne State University Press, 1991), 135.

9. Ibid., 136.

10. Alfred Appel, Jr., *Jazz Modernism: From Ellington and Armstrong to Matisse and Joyce* (New York: Alfred A. Knopf, 2002), 7.

11. Clement Greenberg, "Modern and Postmodern," William Dobell Memorial Lecture, Sydney, Australia, October 31, 1979, in *Arts* 54, no. 6 (February 1980), www.sharecom.ca/greenberg/postmodernism.html.

12. Svensk Jazz Historia Vol. 1, *Swedish Jazz 1899–1930* (Caprice CAP 22037). "Cake Walk" is track 1, CD1.

13. *San Francisco Chronicle*, "Paris Has Gone Rag Time Wild," June 10, 1900. Blesh and Janis, *They All Played Ragtime* (New York: Grove Press, 1959), 81, quoted in Nancy Perloff, *Art and the Everyday* (New York: Oxford University Press, 1993), 49.

14. Edward Berlin, *Ragtime: A Musical and Cultural History* (Berkeley: University of California Press, 1980), 13–14, 104–6.

15. Jody Blake, *Le Tumulte Noir* (University Park: Pennsylvania State University Press, 1999), 34.

16. *Los Angeles Times*, "Ben's Jazz Curve," April 12, 1912.

17. *San Francisco Bulletin*, E. T. "Scoop" Gleason: "McCall has been heralded all down the line as a 'busher,' but it now develops this dope is very much to the jazz," March 3, 1913, and "What is the 'jazz'? Why, it's a little of that 'old life,' the 'gin-i-ker,' the 'pep,' otherwise known as the enthusiasalum," March 6, 1913.

18. Ernest J. Hopkins, "In Praise of Jazz: A Futurist Word Which Has Just Joined the Language," *San Francisco Bulletin*, April 5, 1913.

19. George Gershwin, "The Composer in the Machine Age," in *The American Composer Speaks*, ed. Gilbert Chase (Baton Rouge: Louisiana State University Press, 1966), 142.

20. Waldo Frank, *In the American Jungle* (New York: Farrar and Rinehart, 1937), 123, quoted in David Meltzer, ed., *Reading Jazz* (San Francisco: Mercury House, 1993), 50.

21. Blake, *Le Tumulte Noir*, 146.

22. See Gerry Carlin and Mair Evans, *Dada and Surrealism: Texts and Extracts* by http://pers-www.wlv.ac.uk/~fa1871/surrext.html.

23. Hans Richter, *Dada: Art and Anti-Art* (New York: Oxford University Press, 1965), 20–27.

24. Jed Rasula, "Jazz as a Decal for the European Avant-Garde," in *Blackening Europe: The African American Presence*, ed. Heike Raphael-Hernandez (New York: Routledge, 2004).

25. Quoted in Hugo Ball, *La Fruite Hors du Temps, Journal 1913–1921* (*The Escape from Time, Diary 1913–1921*) (Paris: Editions du Rocher, 1946).

26. Richard M. Sudhalter, *Stardust Melody: The Life and Music of Hoagy Carmichael* (New York: Oxford University Press, 2002), 56.

27. Majorie Perloff, "The Avant-Garde Phase of American Modernism," in *The Cambridge Companion to American Modernism*, ed. Walter Kalaidjian (Cambridge, MA: Cambridge University Press, 2005), 195–221.

28. Ibid., 197.

29. Ibid., 196.

30. Sudhalter, *Stardust Melody*, 61.

31. Ibid., 57.

32. Ibid., 60.

33. Francis M. Naumann, *New York Da Da 1915–23* (New York: Abrams, 1994), 242.

34. Max Ernst, interviewed by Roland Penrose, *Monitor*, BBC TV, broadcast 1961.

35. Erik Satie, quoted in the liner notes, *Erik Satie: Francis Poulenc Plays the Piano Music of Satie and Poulenc* (El Records ACMEM 78CD).

36. The Billy Arnold Jazz Band should not be lightly dismissed. As Max Harrison has pointed out in *Jazz Retrospect* (London: David and Charles, 1977), 74, the band were cited by Darius Milhaud as having introduced him to jazz. Harrison notes that Arnold's 1923 recordings "compare favourably with almost anything then being written in America, and are superior to the 1924 Doc Cook recordings. . . . Arnold's scores are very demanding for their period, yet are executed with precision . . . and after hearing 'Carolina in the Morning' . . . few people would any longer agree that antiphonal duets between reed and brass sections were innovated a few years later by Fletcher Henderson."

37. Darius Milhaud, *Ma Vie Henreuse* (Paris: Editions Belford), 115, quoted in Chris Goddard, *Jazz away from Home* (New York: Paddington Press, 1979), 123.

38. Darius Milhaud, *Notes without Music: An Autobiography* (New York: Alfred A. Knopf, 1953), 135–37.

39. Darius Milhaud, "The Day after Tomorrow," *Modern Music*, November–December 1925, reproduced in *Jazz in Print*, 430: "During the winter of 1921–1922 in America, the journalists regarded me with scorn wherever I made out a case of jazz."

40. *Musical Observer*, March 1923, reproduced in *Jazz in Print*, 235.

41. Martin Guerpin, "Why Did Art Music Composers Pay Attention to Jazz? The Impact of 'Jazz' on the French Musical Field 1908–1924," in *Eurojazzland*, 64.

42. Darius Milhaud, from *Etudes*, 22, quoted in Andre Hodier, *Jazz: Its Evolution and Essence* (New York: Black Cat Grove Press, 1961), 248.

43. Harvey, "Jazz and Modernism," 145.

44. Petrine Archer-Shaw, *Negrophilia* (London: Thames and Hudson, 2000), 111.

45. Darius Milhaud, "The Jazz Band and Negro Music," *Living Age*, October 18, 1924, reproduced in *Jazz in Print*, 359.

46. Ibid.

47. Igor Stravinsky, *Chronicle of My Life* (London: Victor Gollancz, 1936), 130–31.

48. Hodier, *Jazz*, 258.

49. Rasula, "Jazz and American Modernism," 164.

50. Alec Harman and Wilfred Mellers, *Man and His Music* (London: Barrie and Jenkins, 1977), 1055.

51. Milhaud, "The Jazz Band and Negro Music," 359.

52. In his book *Jazz from Congo to Swing* (London: Musicians Press, 1946), 69, Robert Goffin uses the spelling "Vance Lowry," as did Milhaud. Goffin says that he followed Wiener to the Boeuf sur le Toit when it opened in 1921. Of Lowry, Andre Hodier has written: "For us of the following generation, Vance Lowrry has remained one of the legendary geniuses in which the 'prehistoric' era abounds." Hodier, *Jazz*, 250.

53. Goddard, *Jazz away from Home*, 118.

54. Darius Milhaud, from *Etudes*, 22, quoted in Hodier, *Jazz*, 250.

55. Goffin, *Jazz from Congo to Swing*, 69.

56. Léo Vauchant in Goddard, *Jazz away from Home*, 117.

57. "Léo Vauchant," in *The New Grove Dictionary of Jazz L to Z*, ed. Barry Kernfield (New York: Macmillan/Grove Dictionaries of Music, 1988), 573.

58. Nicolas Slonimsky, *Lectionary of Music* (New York: McGraw-Hill Publishing Company, 1989), 57.

59. Léo Vauchant in Goddard, *Jazz away from Home*, 131.

60. Hodier, *Jazz*, 252.

61. Ibid.

62. Franco Moretti, "The Spell of Indecision," in *Marxism and the Interpretation of Culture*, ed. Cary Nelson and Lawrence Grossberg (Chicago: University of Chicago Press, 1988), 339.

63. Greenberg, "Modern and Postmodern."

64. Paul Johnson, *Modern Times* (New York: Harper Perennial, 2001), 9.

65. Unprovenanced quotation reproduced in *Downbeat*, November 28, 1957.

66. Louis Mitchell, quoted in "The First Man to Bring Jazz to Britain," *Melody Maker*, July 14, 1956, 6.

67. Quoted in ibid.

68. Interestingly, cornet player Cricket Smith had recorded with James Europe's Society Orchestra on RCA Victor in December 1913 and February 1914, and "Castle Walk" from the latter date reveals Smith's dominant lead and Buddy Gilmore's drum breaks in the last three choruses in what is the only recorded example from the time of improvised orchestral ragtime.

69. Biographical details of Louis Mitchell from Len Guttridge, "The First Man to Bring Jazz to Britain," *Melody Maker*, July 14, 1956, 6.

70. Goffin, *Jazz from Congo to Swing*, 70.

71. Ibid.

72. Ibid., 73.

73. Robert Goffin, quotation from *Aux Frontiéres du Jazz*, in ibid., 3.

74. Ibid., 74.

75. *The Times*, January 19, 1919.

76. "Jazz 'Er Up! Broadway's Conquest of Europe," *New York Times*, December 18, 1921.

77. Johan Fornäs, "Reconstructed Identities in the Early Swedish Jazz Age," in *Jazz Planet*, ed. E. Taylor Atkins (Jackson: University Press of Mississippi, 2003), 207.

78. Francis Newton, *The Jazz Scene* (London: Jazz Book Club, 1960), 244.

79. Bernd Hoffmann, *Aspekte Zur Jazz-Rezeption in Deutschland/Afro-Amerikanische Musik im Spiegel der Musikpresse 1900–1945* (Graz, Austria: Akademische Druck— u.Verlagsanstalt, 2003).

80. Hans Janowitz, trans. Jurgen Grandt, quoted in *Jazz*, ed. Rolf Rieb (Bonn: Weidle Verlag, 1999), 112.

81. Ted Gioia, *The Imperfect Art* (New York: Oxford University Press, 1988), 25.

82. Ibid., 28.

83. Ron Welburn, "Jazz Magazines of the 1930s: An Overview of the Provocative Journalism," *American Music* 5, no. 3 (Autumn 1987): 255.

84. Eric Hobsbawm, *Uncommon People* (London: Abacus, 1999), 356.

85. Stuart Davis, *Stuart Davis*, ed. Diane Kelder (New York: Praeger, 1971), 23–24.

86. Gertrude Stein, quoted in Ann Douglas, *Terrible Honesty* (New York: Farrar, Straus and Giroux, 1995), 181.

87. Chip Rhodes, *Structures of the Jazz Age* (New York: Verso, 1998), 3.

88. *Times-Picayune*, June 20, 1918, quoted in Newton, *The Jazz Scene*, 61.

89. "The Appeal of the Primitive in Jazz," *Literary Digest* 55, August 25, 1917, 28–29, reproduced in *Riffs and Choruses: A New Jazz Anthology*, ed. Andrew Clark (London: Continuum, 2001).

90. "Jazz and Jassism," *Times-Picayune*, June 20, 1918, 4, reproduced in *Keeping Time*, ed. Robert Walser (New York: Oxford University Press, 1999).

91. Harcourt Farmer, "The Marche Funebre of Jazz," *Musical America*, June 19, 1920, reproduced in *Jazz in Print*, 144.

92. Anne Shaw Faulkner, "Does Jazz Put the Sin in Syncopation?" *Ladies Home Journal*, August 1921, reproduced in *Jazz in Print*, 152.

93. "Unspeakable Jazz Must Go!" *Ladies Home Journal*, December 1921, reproduced in *Jazz in Print*, 160.

94. Ibid., 163.

95. *New York Times*, January 30, 1922, quoted in "Talk about a Bad Press, Would Hysteria Be Closer?" *New York Times*, January 6, 2001.

96. "Primitive, Savage Animalism, Preacher's Analysis of Jazz," *New York Times* March 3, 1922 reproduced in *Jazz in Print*, 169.

97. Damon J. Phillips and David A. Owens, "Incumbents, Innovation, and Competence: The Emergence of Recorded Jazz, 1920 to 1929," *Poetics: Journal of Empirical Research on Culture, the Media and the Arts* 32 (2004): 283–84.

98. Quoted in ibid., 284.

99. *New York Times*, February 12, 1922, 1.

100. Dr. Henry van Dyke, *New York Herald Tribune*, February 28, 1921, quoted in "Talk about a Bad Press, Would Hysteria Be Closer?" *New York Times*, January 6, 2001.

101. "The Jazz Problem," *The Etude*, August 1924, quoted in Robert Walser, ed., *Keeping Time* (New York: Oxford University Press, 1999), 41.

102. See Phillips and Owens, "Incumbents, Innovation, and Competence"; Karl Koenig, ed., *Jazz in Print*; and Neil Leonard, *Jazz and the White Americans* (London: Jazz Book Club, 1964).

103. Phillips and Owens, "Incumbents, Innovation, and Competence," 284.

104. Leonard, *Jazz and the White Americans*, 45.

105. Quoted in H. O. Brunn, *The Story of the Original Dixieland Jazz Band* (London: Jazz Book Club, 1963), 174.

106. *Music Courier*, "Representatives of 2,000,000 Women, Meeting in Atlanta, Vote to Annihilate Jazz," May 1923, reproduced in *Jazz in Print*, 238.

107. "Offers New Curb on 'Disgraceful Dances,'" *New York Times*, February 23, 1921.

108. *New York Times*, October 4, 1922, 16, and July 12, 1925, Section II, 2.

109. *New York Herald*, quoted in Brunn, *The Story of the Original Dixieland Jazz Band*, 175.

110. *New York Times*, "Bluest of Blue Laws," April 17, 1921.

111. Quoted in "Jazz Played Out," *Literary Digest*, January 14, 1922, reproduced in *Jazz in Print*, 166.

112. "The Decline of Jazz," *Musician*, May 1922, reproduced in *Jazz in Print*, 187.

113. Larry Gushee, liner notes, *The Legendary Freddie Keppard: New Orleans Cornet* (Smithsonian Collection P15141), 4.

114. Ibid., 3.

115. Ibid.

116. Phillips and Owens, "Incumbents, Innovation, and Competence," 283.

117. Reid Badger, *A Life in Ragtime: A Biography of James Reese Europe* (New York: Oxford University Press, 1995), 89.

118. Quoted in ibid. See also William H. Kenney, *Recorded Music in American Life* (New York: Oxford University Press, 1999).

119. Phillips and Owens, "Incumbents, Innovation, and Competence," 285.

120. George Simon, *The Big Bands* (New York: Schirmer Books, 1981), 452.

121. Louis Armstrong, quoted in *Hear Me Talkin' To Ya*, ed. Nat Shapiro and Nat Hentoff (London: Peter Davies, 1955), 148.

122. *Talking Machine World*, October 1920.

123. Thornton Hagert, liner notes, *An Experiment on Modern Music: Paul Whiteman at Aeolian Hall* (Smithsonian Collection R028), 1.

124. Harrison, *A Jazz Retrospect*, 190.

125. Gunther Schuller, *Early Jazz* (New York: Oxford University Press, 1968), 192.

126. Ibid.

127. Don Rayno, *Paul Whiteman: Pioneer in American Music Volume 1 1890–1930* (Lanham, MD, and Oxford: Scarecrow Press, 2003), 68.

128. *The Times*, quoted in ibid.

129. Trade journal, quoted in Tim Gracyk, *Paul Whiteman 28 March 1890–29 December 1967*, www.gracyk.com/whiteman.shtml.

130. "Novelty Is Spice," *Musical America*, November 10, 1923, reproduced in *Jazz in Print*, 263.

131. Hugh C. Ernst, "The Man Who Made a Lady out of Jazz," in *Keeping Time: Readings in Jazz History*, ed. Robert Walser (New York: Oxford University Press, 1999), 40.

132. Ibid.

133. Hagert, liner notes, *An Experiment on Modern Music*, 3.

134. Ibid., 8.

135. Howard Goodall, *The Story of Music* (London: Chatto and Windus, 2013), 252.

136. As recalled by Kurt Dieterle, one of Whiteman's eight violinists at the concert, in a 1991 interview cited in Joan Peyser, *The Memory of All That: The Life of George Gershwin* (Milwaukee, WI: Hal Leonard Corporation, 2006), 82.

137. Rayno, *Paul Whiteman: Volume 1*, 86.

138. "Jazz," *Outlook*, March 5, 1924, reproduced in *Jazz in Print (1856–1929): An Anthology of Selected Early Readings in Jazz History*, ed. Karl Koenig (Hillsdale, NY: Pendragon Press, 2002), 292.

139. Lawrence Gilman, *New York Tribune*, February 13, 1924, quoted in Edward Jablonski, *Gershwin Remembered* (Boston: Faber and Faber, 1992), 30.

140. Olin Downes, *New York Times*, February 13, 1924, quoted in Jablonski, *Gershwin Remembered*, 31.

141. Leonard Bernstein, "Why Don't You Run Upstairs and Write a Nice Gershwin Tune?" *Atlantic Monthly*, April 1955, quoted in *The Gershwin Style*, ed. Wayne Schneider (New York: Oxford University Press, 1999), 95–96.

142. Larry Starr, "Musings on 'Nice Gershwin Tunes,' Form, and Harmony in the Concert Music of Gershwin," in *The Gershwin Style*, ed. Wayne Schneider (New York: Oxford University Press, 1999), 104.

143. Among countless references, see Stan Nussbaum, *American Cultural Baggage* (New York: Orbis Books, 2005), ch. 1.

144. Paul Whiteman, *New York Clipper*, February 22, 1922, quoted in Rayno, *Paul Whiteman: Volume 1*, 86.

145. Rayno, *Paul Whiteman: Volume 1*, 82.

146. Charles C. Alexander, *Here the Country Lies: Nationalism and the Arts in Twentieth Century America* (Bloomington: Indiana University Press, 1980), xii.

147. Paul Johnson, *Modern Times* (New York: Harper Perennial, 1992), 207.

148. John Andrew Johnson, "Gershwin's *Blue Monday* (1922) and the Promise of Success," in *The Gershwin Style*, ed. Wayne Schneider (New York: Oxford University Press, 1999), 128.

149. Gilbert Seldes, "Jazz Music Not Such an 'Enfant Terrible' after All," *Musical America*, July 19, 1924, reproduced in *Jazz in Print*, 324.

150. Duke Ellington, *New York Times Magazine*, January 17, 1943, 10.

151. Don Rayno, liner notes, *Paul Whiteman: Carnegie Hall Concert December 25, 1938* (Nostalgia Arts 303 3025).

152. Harrison, *A Jazz Retrospect*, 192.

153. Roy Fox, *Hollywood, Mayfair and All That Jazz: The Roy Fox Story* (London: Leslie Frewin, 1975), 167.

154. Leonard, *Jazz and the White Americans*, 89.

155. Jeffrey Magee, *The Uncrowned King of Swing: Fletcher Henderson and Big Band Jazz* (New York: Oxford University Press, 2005), 97.

156. Phillips and Owens, "Incumbents, Innovation, and Competence," 282.

157. Magee, *The Uncrowned King of Swing*, 97.

158. Hugues Panassie, *The Real Jazz* (New York: A. S. Barnes, 1960), 198.

159. Magee, *The Uncrowned King of Swing*, 38.

160. Ibid., 75.

161. Roger Pryor Dodge, *Hot Jazz and Jazz Dance: Roger Pryor Dodge Collected Writings 1929–64* (New York: Oxford University Press, 1995), 101.

162. Magee, *The Uncrowned King of Swing*, 99.

163. Ibid., 120.

164. Among others, *Cleveland Press*, May 20, 1933.

165. Not least in Stuart Nicholson, *Reminiscing in Tempo: A Portrait of Duke Ellington* (Boston: Northeastern University Press, 1999).

166. For example: "If you should ask him — Paul Whiteman is his favourite musician," in *Hot on the Air* by Jerry Wald, "Radio Reminiscing with Duke Ellington," *Evening Graphic*, Saturday, June 18, 1932.

167. Irving Mills, quoted in Nicholson, *Reminiscing in Tempo*, 119.

168. *Irving Mills Presents Duke Ellington*, quoted in ibid., 153.

169. Ibid., 156.

170. Mark Tucker, *Ellington: The Early Years* (Oxford, UK: Bayou Press, 1991), 199.

171. John Howland, "Ellington and Symphonic Jazz," *Annual Review of Jazz Studies* 14 (Lanham, MD: Scarecrow Press, 2000), 20.

172. Mercer Ellington with Stanley Dance, *Duke Ellington in Person: An Intimate Memoir* (London: Hutchinson, 1978), 34.

173. Alex Ross, *The Rest Is Noise* (London/New York: Harper Perennial, 2009), 166.

174. Klaus Stratemann, *Duke Ellington: Day by Day and Film by Film* (Copenhagen: JazzMedia ApS, 1992), 55.

175. Howland, "Ellington and Symphonic Jazz," 18.

176. Ross, *The Rest Is Noise*, 166–67.

177. From trade advertisement for Duke Ellington's "Reminiscing in Tempo," reproduced in Nicholson, *Reminiscing in Tempo*, 177.

178. Frank Tirro, *Jazz: A History* (New York: W. W. Norton, 1993), 290.

179. Harvey, "Jazz and Modernism," 135.

180. Andre Hodeir, *Towards Jazz* (New York: Da Capo Press, 1986), 26.

181. Mark Tucker, liner notes, *Duke Ellington: The Blanton Webster Band* (RCA 5659–2 RB).

182. Scott E. Brown, *James P. Johnson: A Case of Mistaken Identity* (Metuchen, NJ: Scarecrow Press and the Institute of Jazz Studies, Rutgers University, 1986), 197.

183. This has also been spelled as "Yamekraw."

184. John Howland, "Music Samples for *Ellington Uptown*," University of Michigan Press, www.press.umich.edu/mediakits/11605/howland_musicsamples.jsp.

185. *Music Trade Review*, May 12, 1929.

186. Max Harrison, Charles Fox, and Eric Thacker, *The Essential Jazz Records Volume 1: Ragtime to Swing* (New York: Mansell, 1984), 133.

187. Schuller, *Early Jazz*, 191.

188. Richard Hadlock, *Jazz Masters of the 20s* (London: Collier-Macmillan, 1966), 93.

189. Ibid.

190. Pee Wee Russell, quoted in *Hear Me Talkin' to Ya*, ed. Nat Shapiro and Nat Hentoff (London: Peter Davies, 1955), 145.

191. Richard M. Sudhalter and Philip R. Evans, *Bix: Man and Legend* (London: Quartet Books, 1974), 238.

192. Schuller, *Early Jazz*, 191.

193. Harrison, Fox, and Thacker, *The Essential Jazz Records Volume 1*, 141.

194. Digby Fairweather, liner notes, *The Jazz Modernists: 1924–1933* (Retrieval RTR79058).

195. Harrison, Fox, and Thacker, *The Essential Jazz Records Volume 1*, 140.

196. Sudhalter, *Stardust Melody*, 87.

197. Ibid., 87–88.

198. Harrison, Fox, and Thacker, *The Essential Jazz Records Volume 1*, 136.

199. A pick-up band of varying size and instrumentation, Miff Mole and his Little Molers recorded for Brunswick as the better-known Red Nichols and his Five Pennies, Mole's musical partner during this period.

200. Richard M. Sudhalter, *Lost Chords* (New York: Oxford University Press, 1999), 147.

201. Will Friedwald, *Jazz Singing* (New York: Charles Scribner's Sons, 1990), 18.

202. Appel, *Jazz Modernism*, 13.

203. Sudhalter, *Lost Chords*, 372.

204. Clyde Bernhardt, *I Remember: Eighty Years of Black Entertainment, Big Bands and the Blues* (Philadelphia: University of Pennsylvania Press, 1986), 62.

205. Jeffrey Magee, *The Uncrowned King of Swing: Fletcher Henderson and Big Band Jazz* (New York: Oxford University Press, 2005), 9.

206. Sudhalter, *Lost Chords*, 667.

207. Gunther Schuller, *The Swing Era* (New York: Oxford University Press, 1989), 516.

208. Ibid., 382.

209. Red Norvo, interviewed by Les Tomkins, "Red Norvo: My Life In and Around Jazz," www.jazzprofessional.com/interviews/Red%20Norvo_1.htm.

210. Philip Larkin, *All What Jazz* (London: Faber and Faber, 1970), 7.

211. J. R. Taylor, liner notes, *John Kirby: The Biggest Little Band 1937–1941* (Smithsonian Collection RO13).

212. Ibid.

213. Quoted in the liner notes, *The Music of Raymond Scott: Reckless Nights and Turkish Twilights* (BASTA 30-9073-2).

214. Quoted in liner notes, *The Beau Hunks Sextette: Manhattan Minuet* (BASTA 30-90562).

215. Quoted in the liner notes, *The Music of Raymond Scott: Reckless Nights and Turkish Twilights* (BASTA 30-9073-2).

216. Ibid.

217. Quoted in liner notes, *The Beau Hunks Sextette: Manhattan Minuet* (BASTA 30-90562).

218. Stephen Holden, "An Artist and Inventor Whose Medium Was Sound," *New York Times*, July 12, 2012.

219. Thomas Tolnay, "Art Blakey's Jazz Message," *Downbeat*, March 18, 1971, 15.

220. Maurice Burman, "Reggie Foresythe Created New Sounds in the '30s," *Melody Maker*, March 1, 1959.

221. Stanley Dance, *The World of Earl Hines* (New York: Charles Scribner's Sons, 1977), 74.

222. Valerie Wilmer, who unearthed many previously unknown details of Foresythe's life, in liner notes, *The New Music of Reginald Foresythe* (BVHAAST CD 0307).

223. Sudhalter, *Lost Chords*, 223.

224. Theo Uden Masman, quoted in the liner notes, *The New Music of Reginald Foresythe* (BVHASST CD 0307).

225. D. Russell Connor, *Benny Goodman: Listen to His Legacy* (Metuchen, NJ, and London: Scarecrow Press, 1988), 47.

226. George Avakian, liner notes, *Benny Goodman Plays Eddie Sauter Arrangements* (Phillips BBL7043).

227. Schuller, *The Swing Era*, 32.

228. Ibid., 35.

229. Ibid., 43.

230. Ross Firestone, *Swing, Swing, Swing: The Life and Times of Benny Goodman* (London: Hodder and Stoughton, 1993), 292.

231. The very rare aircheck of the complete performance of Artie Shaw's "Interlude in B-Flat," from the Imperial Theater, New York, in the summer of 1935 with Shaw on clarinet plus two violinists, a violist, a cellist, guitar, bass, and drums, is at www.youtube.com/watch?v=Bq1oiDOlFZo.

232. Artie Shaw in Sudhalter, *Lost Chords*, 583.

233. Liner notes, *Artie Shaw and his Orchestra: Personal Best* (BMG 743121101542).

234. Ibid.

235. Schuller, *The Swing Era*, 704.

236. Liner notes, *Artie Shaw and his Orchestra: Personal Best* (BMG 743121101542).

237. Ibid.

238. Liner notes, *The Complete Artie Shaw Volume V, 1941–1942* (RCA AXM2-5576).

239. Liner notes, *Artie Shaw and his Orchestra: Personal Best* (BMG 743121101542).

240. Schuller, *The Swing Era*, 706.

241. Liner Notes, *Artie Shaw and his Orchestra: Personal Best* (BMG 743121101542).

242. Ibid.

243. Ray McKinley and his Orchestra, *Borderline* (Savoy SV-0203).

244. On Sauter-Finegan, *Under Analysis* (RCA Victor LPM 1341).

245. Liner notes, *Sauter-Finegan* (RCA DPM 2025).

246. Simon, *The Big Bands*, 398.

247. Ibid., 399.

248. Barry Ulanov, quoted in ibid.

249. Michael Sparke, *Stan Kenton: This Is an Orchestra* (Denton: University of North Texas Press, 2010).

250. Ibid., 17.

251. Max Harrison, "The Innovations Band," *Jazz Journal International*, May 1979, 19.

252. Ibid.

253. Simon, *The Big Bands*, 435.

254. Max Harrison, "Claude Thornhill: The Real Birth of the Cool," in *The Essential Jazz Records Volume 2*, ed. Harrison (London: Mansell, 2000), 403.

255. Sudhalter, *Lost Chords*, 547.

256. Harvey, "Jazz and Modernism," 136.

257. Ibid.

258. Ibid.

259. Howland, "Ellington and Symphonic Jazz," 3.

260. Brian Priestly, "Charlie Parker and Popular Music," *Annual Review of Jazz Studies 14* (Scarecrow Press, 2000), 83.

261. Ibid., 91.

262. Andrew Ross, *No Respect: Intellectuals and Popular Culture* (New York: Routledge, 1989), 70.

263. Ralph Ellison, *Living with Music* (New York: Modern Library, 2001), xiii.

264. One group even adopted Modern Jazz in their billing. Formerly the Milt Jackson Quartet, the group changed their name to the Modern Jazz Quartet in 1953.

265. Ted Gioia, *West Coast Jazz* (New York: Oxford University Press, 1992), 259.

266. Dave Brubeck, liner notes, The Dave Brubeck Quartet, *Time Further Out: Miro Reflections* (Columbia Legacy CK64668).

267. Dave Brubeck, interview with author, November 18, 2002.

268. Dave Brubeck, liner notes, *The Dave Brubeck Octet* (OJC-101). Actually, the use of a fugue goes back at least to the modernists, such as Reginald Foresythe's use of the device in "Dodging a Divorcee," while the most popular recording of a fugue in a jazz context was Benny Goodman's arrangement of Alec Templeton's "Bach Goes to Town," recorded for RCA Victor on December 15, 1938.

269. Max Harrison, "The Dave Brubeck Octet," in *The Essential Jazz Records, Volume 2*, ed. Harrison (London: Mansell, 2000), 625.

270. Dave Brubeck, interview with author, November 18, 2002.

271. Dave Brubeck, liner notes, *Time Out*, Columbia/Legacy CK 65122, 11.

272. Liner notes, *The Real Ambassadors* (CBS BPG 62083).

273. Dave Brubeck, quoted in Gene Lees, "About This Man Brubeck," *Downbeat*, June 22, 1961, 23.

274. Dave Brubeck, quoted in Ralph J. Gleason, "Dave Brubeck: A Searching Look," *Downbeat*, September 5, 1957, 14.

275. See Art Tatum, "The Greatest Piano Solo of All Time," www.youtube.com /watch?v=aNAJlqnonO4.

276. Lee Konitz, quoted in Ira Gitler, *Jazz Masters of the Forties* (New York: Macmillan Company, 1966), 236.

277. Jack Maher, *Metronome*, May 1956.

278. Liner notes, Lennie Tristano, *The New Tristano* (Atlantic 1357).

279. Ira Gitler, *Jazz Masters of the Forties* (New York: Macmillan Company, 1966), 240.

280. Barry Ulanov, liner notes, *The New Tristano* (Atlantic 1357).

281. Lennie Tristano, in Ira Gitler, *Jazz Masters of the Forties* (New York: Macmillan Company, 1966), 240–41.

282. Ibid., 243.

283. Sonny Rollins, interview with author, September 10, 2009.

284. Robert Goffin, quotation from *Aux Frontiéres du Jazz*, in *Jazz from Congo to Swing*, 3.

285. Wynton Marsalis, quoted in Maya Jaggi, *Profile: Wynton Marsalis*, "Blowing Up a Storm," *Guardian Review*, January 25, 2003, 22.

286. Wynton Marsalis, *Swinging into the 21st Century*, Sony Jazz publicity notes, 1999.

287. Wynton Marsalis, quoted in Jaggi, *Profile: Wynton Marsalis*, 20.

288. Esa-Pekka Salonen, quoted in ibid.

# Index

Aagre, Frøy, 11

Abercrombie, John, 7

absolutism/formalism on music's meaning, 42, 43

abstract expressionism, 170

academe and jazz education: Afro-American exceptionalism, 135; and cultural relativism within jazz, 117–18; diasporic/transnational theory, 120–22, 124; and economics of jazz musicianship, 7–8; European coupling of jazz and classical, 147–49; increased interest in, 12, 14–15; and jazz as elitist art form, 18; lack of education on British jazz history in UK, 265n130; need to move from conservatism, 23–24, 257n87; relativism in, 16–18, 117–24, 129, 130; technique mastery emphasis of, 28–31. *See also* New Jazz Studies

aesthetic merit, 16, 17, 26

African Americans: first band recordings in US, 191–92; jazz as cultural contribution of, 20–21, 134–36; Louis Mitchell's band, 179; relationship to jazz as cultural form, 21–22; Still as first Afro-American composer to have symphony performed by major American symphony orchestra, 232; Still as first Afro-American to conduct major American symphony

orchestra, 232; symphonic jazz influence on arrangements, 206–8; wartime patriotism propaganda to influence, 75. *See also* racial prejudice

Akiyoshi, Toshiko, 143

Allen, Henry, 220

Allen, Howard Warren "Wad," 168

American cultural influence: as benign vs. destructive, 74–75; and Cold War outcome, 79–84; consumerism, 62–68, 86; cult of celebrity, 73–74; English language, 74; fears about and resistance to, 75, 261n31; general influence, 61–63, 86; and globalization, 94; and glocalization, 99; halo effect, 86–88; Hollywood film industry, xii, 55, 68–74, 265n129; Imaginary America, xii, 55, 58–59, 67, 68, 70, 74, 88; and imagined community, xii, 55, 58–59, 67, 68, 70, 74, 88; on Jazz Age Europe, 182, 195; rise and fall of, 1–2; role of jazz in, xiii, 75–83, 86–88, 138. *See also* soft power; United States

American Dream, 64, 67, 68

American exceptionalism, ix, 87, 88, 135–36

Ames, Margaret, 83

Anderson, Janna Quitney, 24–25

Ang, Ien, 121, 123

Antheil, George, 164